Feminist and Womanist Essays
in Reformed Dogmatics

COLUMBIA SERIES IN REFORMED THEOLOGY

The Columbia Series in Reformed Theology represents a joint commitment of Columbia Theological Seminary and Westminster John Knox Press to provide theological resources for the church today.

The Reformed tradition has always sought to discern what the living God revealed in Scripture is saying and doing in every new time and situation. Volumes in this series examine significant individuals, events, and issues in the development of this tradition and explore their implications for contemporary Christian faith and life.

This series is addressed to scholars, pastors, and laypersons. The Editorial Board hopes that these volumes will contribute to the continuing reformation of the church.

Columbia Theological Seminary wishes to express its appreciation to the following churches for supporting this joint publishing venture:

Central Presbyterian Church, Atlanta, Georgia
First Presbyterian Church, Franklin, Tennessee
First Presbyterian Church, Nashville, Tennessee
First Presbyterian Church, Quincy, Florida
First Presbyterian Church, Spartanburg, South Carolina
First Presbyterian Church, Tupelo, Mississippi
North Avenue Presbyterian Church, Atlanta, Georgia
Riverside Presbyterian Church, Jacksonville, Florida
Roswell Presbyterian Church, Roswell, Georgia
South Highland Presbyterian Church, Birmingham, Alabama
Spring Hill Presbyterian Church, Mobile, Alabama
St. Simons Island Presbyterian Church, St. Simons Island, Georgia
St. Stephen Presbyterian Church, Fort Worth, Texas
Trinity Presbyterian Church, Atlanta, Georgia
University Presbyterian Church, Chapel Hill, North Carolina

COLUMBIA SERIES IN REFORMED THEOLOGY

Feminist and Womanist Essays in Reformed Dogmatics

AMY PLANTINGA PAUW
SERENE JONES
EDITORS

 WESTMINSTER
JOHN KNOX PRESS
LOUISVILLE • KENTUCKY

© 2006 Westminster John Knox Press

Originally published in hardback in the United States by Westminster John Knox Press in 2006.

2011 paperback edition
Published by Westminster John Knox Press
Louisville, Kentucky

Scripture quotations from the New Revised Standard Version of the Bible are copyright © 1989 by the Division of Christian Education of the National Council of the Churches of Christ in the U.S.A. and are used by permission.

Book and cover design by Drew Stevens

This book is printed on acid-free paper that meets the American National Standards Institute Z39.48 standard. ♾

PRINTED IN THE UNITED STATES OF AMERICA

11 12 13 14 15 16 17 18 19 20 —10 9 8 7 6 5 4 3 2 1

Library of Congress Cataloging-in-Publication Data is on file at the Library of Congress, Washington, D.C.

ISBN: 978-0-664-23823-0 (paper edition)

CONTENTS

CONTRIBUTORS

Katie Geneva Cannon is the Annie Scales Rogers Professor of Christian Ethics at Union-PSCE in Richmond, Virginia. She is an ordained minister in the Presbyterian Church (U.S.A.).

Kristine A. Culp is Dean of the Disciples Divinity House of the University of Chicago and Senior Lecturer in Theology at the Divinity School of the University of Chicago. She is a member of the Christian Church (Disciples of Christ).

Dawn DeVries is the John Newton Thomas Professor of Systematic Theology at Union-PSCE in Richmond, Virginia. She is an elder in the Presbyterian Church (U.S.A.).

Margit Ernst-Habib has taught theology at Columbia Presbyterian Seminary. She is an ordained member of the Protestant Reformed Church in Germany.

Mary McClintock Fulkerson is Associate Professor of Theology at Duke Divinity School and also teaches in the Women's Studies Program at Duke University. She is an ordained minister in the Presbyterian Church (U.S.A.).

Martha Schull Gilliss, PhD, is an ordained minister in the Presbyterian Church (U.S.A.). She presently is serving in the Congregational Ministries Division of the denomination.

Lynn Japinga is Associate Professor of Religion at Hope College in Holland, Michigan. She is an ordained minister in the Reformed Church in America.

Serene Jones is the Titus Street Professor of Theology at Yale Divinity School, with appointments in Women, Gender, and Sexuality Studies and African American Studies at Yale University. She is jointly ordained in the Christian Church (Disciples of Christ) and the United Church of Christ.

Joan M. Martin is the William W. Rankin Associate Professor of Christian Ethics at Episcopal Divinity School. She is an ordained minister in the Presbyterian Church (U.S.A.).

Kalbryn A. McLean, PhD, is a writer and independent developmental editor. She is a member of the United Church of Christ.

Amy Plantinga Pauw is the Henry P. Mobley, Jr., Professor of Doctrinal Theology at Louisville Presbyterian Seminary. She is a member of the Presbyterian Church (U.S.A.).

Cynthia L. Rigby is the W. C. Brown Professor of Theology at Austin Presbyterian Seminary. She is an ordained minister in the Presbyterian Church (U.S.A.).

Leanne Van Dyk is Dean and Professor of Reformed Theology at Western Theological Seminary in Holland, Michigan. She is a member of the Presbyterian Church (U.S.A.).

INTRODUCTION

The authors of this book are Reformed theologians working out of feminist and womanist traditions. It could equally well be said that we are feminist and womanist theologians working out of various Reformed traditions. Reformed theology started in the French and Swiss branches of the sixteenth-century Protestant Reformation. Its particular emphases on the sovereign grace of God, resistance to idolatry, and a well-ordered life of gratitude eventually took root in diverse communities stretching from Scotland to southern France, from Hungary to South Korea, from the American colonies to South Africa. The authors of this volume all stand in this broad Reformed tradition. We are theologians of the church, with ties to the Presbyterian Church (U.S.A.), the Reformed Church in America, the Christian Reformed Church, the Christian Church (Disciples of Christ), the United Church of Christ, and the Protestant Reformed Church in Germany. The majority of us are ordained. Most of us are seminary graduates, and most are currently involved in teaching ministries at church-related colleges, seminaries, and divinity schools.

Feminist and womanist Christian theologies take special interest in the lives of women, their stories, their social roles and relations, their flourishings and failures, and their multilayered experiences of oppression. These theologies bring women's lives and experiences into the drama of the Christian message and explore how Christian faith grounds and shapes experiences of hope, justice, and grace as well as instigates and enforces women's and other people's experiences of oppression, sin, and evil. As the European American roots of feminist theology have become clear, women writing from other cultural and ethnic locations have claimed their own theological distinctiveness. Womanist theology is written by African American women and involves "a three-pronged systemic analysis of race, sex, and class."[1] As African American and European or European American women, the authors of this book also stand in womanist and feminist theological traditions. These traditions have informed our constructive theological work and helped make sense of our experience in the church and in the world. We uphold the distinctive interests of these theologies—the liberation of women and all persons—a goal that we believe cannot be disentangled from the central truth of the Christian faith as a whole. This book, then, claims a double theological heritage. When with the poet Adrienne Rich we ask "whence our strength comes" and "with whom our lot is cast," our answer reflects both our Reformed and our womanist and feminist allegiances.[2]

During our meetings at Louisville Seminary's Laws Lodge, the marquee in the lobby read, "Welcome, Reformed Feminists." A puzzled guest at the lodge asked us if being a Reformed feminist was like being a recovering alcoholic. Were we feminists who had seen the light and were trying to reform our ways? Our group joked about this interpretation of "Reformed feminism." But we are aware that this intersection of theological commitments may seem odd to many of our academic colleagues as well, because these traditions have often been defined in oppositional ways. How could a bona fide Reformed theologian embrace feminist and womanist theologies? How could a self-respecting feminist or womanist be committed to Reformed theological traditions? A source of joy and excitement in our group meetings was the realization that we were having a conversation most of us had never had anywhere else. We write these essays out of the conviction that Reformed traditions offer resources to nourish feminist and womanist concerns, and that these concerns offer a way of carrying forward Reformed traditions.

The Jewish feminist theologian Judith Plaskow asserts that when "we refuse to sever or choose between different aspects of our identity, we create a new situation. If we are Jews not despite being feminists but *as feminists*, then Judaism will have to change."[3] Analogously, if we are Reformed Christians not despite our feminist and womanist commitments, but *as* feminists and womanists, then Reformed Christianity will have to change. We would add, however, that feminist and womanist theology will also have to change. In our essays we aim for a two-way conversation in which Reformed commitments and feminist and womanist commitments shape and challenge each other. We see this mutual engagement as a contribution to the vitality of both theological traditions.

We reject two kinds of caricatures: that of a homogeneous, stable Reformed tradition and that of a feminist or womanist theology floating free of classical theological traditions. The theological writings of women and persons of color have sometimes been seen as unfortunate distractions from the proper work of Reformed dogmatics. On this view, authentic Reformed theology has been defined for all time by certain male European voices of the past. Or rather, certain contemporary *readings* of these classical voices are understood to determine the boundaries of appropriate Reformed theology today. This approach fails to acknowledge that all Reformed theologies, from the sixteenth century until today, have a social and cultural context. On the other hand, classical Reformed theologies have sometimes been dismissed as unrelievedly patriarchal[4] and of no help to the constructive efforts of feminist and womanist theologians except as a negative foil. This approach fails to acknowledge the extent to which self-consciously "contextual" theologies have been shaped by larger theological traditions; indeed, these traditions are part of their context. In this book we self-consciously seek a contextual appropriation of Reformed theological traditions, because that is the only kind there is.

As bearers of the Reformed tradition, we claim its many voices. Reformed theology has always been polyphonic—which is why it is more accurate to speak of Reformed *theologies* and *traditions*. As Eberhard Busch notes, "there is no confession that defines as a general rule what is meant by 'Reformed.'"[5] In our essays we draw from Reformed confessions written in widely varying circumstances, including the Scots Confession (Scotland, 1560), the Second Helvetic Confession (Switzerland, 1566), the Westminster Confession (England, 1647), the Barmen Declaration (Germany, 1934), the Belhar Confession (South Africa, 1982), and the Confession of 1967 (United States, 1967). We value them as communal witnesses to Reformed faith in different times and places. While no single theologian defines what counts as Reformed theology, readers will notice the special attention and appreciation given in our essays to John Calvin (1509–1564). We gladly acknowledge our debts to other central Reformed figures as well, including Jonathan Edwards (1703–1758), Friedrich Schleiermacher (1768–1834), John McLeod Campbell (1800–1872), Karl Barth (1886–1968), and the Niebuhr brothers, Reinhold (1892–1971) and H. Richard (1894–1963). Even the North African theologian Augustine (354–430), a central theological forebear of the Reformed tradition who has tended to be either derided or neglected in feminist theology, finds positive appropriation in this volume. The Reformed "canon" for us also includes senior feminist and womanist theologians such as Letty M. Russell, Beverly Wildung Harrison, and Delores S. Williams. Our constructive work as Reformed theologians is done in grateful conversation with these many voices from our past and present.

This is not a book that any one of us could have written by herself. Our ethnic and racial heritages, our geographical and denominational locations, our institutional settings and disciplinary interests all contribute the wide range of Reformed inflections displayed in this book. Our resources range from the nineteenth-century African American minister Henry Highland Garnet to the contemporary white South African theologian John de Gruchy, from the Cévennes region of France to Holland, Michigan. Our essays reflect different polities, different local heroes and heroines, different experiences of nurture and alienation in the church. Together, these essays constitute our invitation to the riches of Reformed theology.

Yet in keeping with the ethos of our broad tradition, we do not appropriate any of these sources uncritically. With John Calvin, we strive "to shape our faithfully transmitted teachings into a form which we also judge will be the best."[6] Shaping Reformed teachings "into a form we judge will be the best" requires creativity and imagination. It results in new emphases, new juxtapositions, and new challenges to established doctrinal approaches. To be faithful to a theological tradition is to discern how its truths can find new and appropriate expression in our own time. As Rowan Williams notes, "one of the deepest paradoxes of Christian faith is that our continuity with the Christian past lies not in repeating what earlier generations said, but in bringing ourselves before the same point of judgment and asking, with them, for conversion—which may mean that we do and say things they did not."[7]

As feminist and womanist theologians we acknowledge the absence of women's voices in the shaping of much of Reformed tradition. With Judith Plaskow we ask, "What in the tradition is ours? What can we claim that has not also wounded us?"[8] But we also recognize that, for better *and* for worse, our work is located in the particular ecclesiastical communities and theologies of this tradition. Acknowledging our Reformed location is an extension of the so-called third wave of Christian feminism, which has been committed to unmasking false universalisms.[9] Feminists have recognized that "women's experience" is not a generic category, and cannot be appealed to in theological constructions apart from analyses of race, class, and sexual orientation that situate and particularize the experience of real women. Likewise, "Christian experience" is another false universalism that is receiving increasing theological attention. Just as Christian feminists and womanists are now emphasizing the diversity and richness of "women's experience," so they are recognizing that their work is indebted to larger theological traditions. In her book *She Who Is*, the feminist theologian Elizabeth Johnson acknowledges that Catholics and Protestants "color the world differently in a religious sense," and insists that each "story needs to be told in its own way."[10] The authors of this volume are telling our story in a Reformed way, affirming the particular confessional context of our feminist and womanist constructions. In classical Reformed emphases on grace and law, Word and Spirit, resistance and idolatry, vocation and election, we find distinctive resources for our feminist and womanist work. We hope this book will be a challenge and invitation to other theologians, both to recognize the intersections between Reformed and feminist and womanist approaches to theology, and to drink deeply from the wells of their own ecclesial traditions.

This is not a book that could have been written even a generation ago. Only within the last twenty years has there been a critical mass of women theologians working out of Reformed traditions. We are doing what was largely impossible or at least unthinkable for our mothers. The editors are grateful for the contributions of two African American scholars, but the historical reality is that women of color are vastly underrepresented in the ranks of Reformed theologians. This unhappy circumstance reflects a cluster of intersecting factors. Reformed traditions of Protestantism in North America have not proved to be hospitable places for many people of color. Reformed communities in this country and around the world have not usually encouraged women to pursue advanced theological study. The editors see their failure to assemble a more diverse group of contributors as a call to repentance and to advocacy for structural changes that might foster better communication and collaboration among Reformed women theologians, especially in the growing Reformed churches of Asia and Africa. Theological work by women of color is work that the whole church needs.

Methodological issues have become a major preoccupation in many areas of theology. It has sometimes seemed that theologians are more interested in thinking about *how* to do theology than in actually doing it! In this volume, we neither presupposed nor achieved methodological consensus. We reflect the diverse influences of our past theological mentors and our present theological conversation partners. We harbor no illusions about a permanent alliance between Reformed faith and a particular philosophical tradition. We affirm the possibility of fruitful new interfaces between traditional doctrines and a wide variety of contemporary intellectual currents, including streams that are neutral or even antagonistic to the Christian faith. Our essays exhibit varying affinities to pragmatism, critical theory, process thought, and a Barthian suspicion of all philosophical theory. Theology always straddles a variety of other disciplines, and our essays reflect this diversity as well; some emphasize ethical themes while others take a more historical, liturgical, or psychological tack.

Our tolerance for methodological openness has its roots in both our theological commitments and our Christian practices. We share a theology of creation that affirms our human limitations, both mental and physical, and a doctrine of sin that holds that our epistemic flaws run deep. We recognize that our life in this world is marked by radical incompleteness, complexity and other-directedness, and so is our knowing. Yet we share a conviction of, and gratitude for, the Spirit's continuing presence in the church and world that encourages us to seek new understanding of theological matters, sometimes from surprising sources. We also share a commitment to the communal practices of Christian faith, which yield the kind of knowing that only comes by doing. Our theology is not abstracted from our material and cultural embeddedness, or from the way our imaginations, affections, and even our bodies have been shaped by the rhythms of life in the church. Yet this practical knowledge demands critical reflection; it cannot survive where fear or dishonesty or triumphalism reign. Moreover, our best insight into the possibilities and corruptions of the tradition we claim is subject to the critical scrutiny of others who are perched on the margins or outside the circle of our tradition. We offer these essays to the wide circle of Reformed Christians and to those far beyond it, as living voices in a tradition that claims no final theological, let alone methodological, closure.

Many of the essays in this book cover the standard doctrines of Christian theology: Scripture, Trinity, creation, humanity, providence, Christology, church and sacraments, eschatology. Some pick up theological themes that have had distinctive emphasis and articulation in Reformed traditions, such as law, grace, vocation, and election. Essays on resistance and fear reflect on aspects of the emotional and dispositional tone of Reformed life. Readers will note that there is no separate chapter on the problem of gendered God language, which has become an established locus in feminist theology. This decision was in part a recognition that gendered language for God has been a much less central topic among women theologians of color, who have had other, more pressing theological concerns. Of course, we have all been sensitized to this subject, not only by the writings of academic theologians but also by our own experiences in the church. We perceive an intimate connection between the resistance and injustices we have encountered as church leaders and theologians and the reflexive assumption that God is appropriately imaged and spoken of only in male terms. However, we recognize that there is more than one viable theological response to this problem, so we thought it best that this topic not receive its own chapter, leaving contributors free to chart their own course on this issue.

The order of the essays is both traditional and radical. Not many introductions to theology begin with a chapter on fear! But we thought Lynn Japinga's essay on fear was the right place to start, because it so well captures both the positive and negative valences of fear as a dominant sensibility in Reformed life and reflection. In the following chapter, Serene Jones shows how the doctrines of creation and law function together as support beams for Reformed and feminist constructions. Dawn DeVries's essay on Scripture and tradition retrieves the multiple senses of the "Word of God" in Reformed theology as a way of affirming the "scripture principle" without lapsing into the besetting Reformed sin of biblicism. Next, Cynthia L. Rigby ties together the doctrines of incarnation and Trinity with the theme of God's scandalous presence, a presence that refuses to abandon us and stirs us to active response, but eludes our attempts to control it. Margit Ernst-Habib's essay on election takes up the well-known Reformed emphasis on "the horrible decree" and shows how, despite its awful reputation, the doctrine of election leads us to live in the world with "good hope for all." Mary McClintock Fulkerson's chapter on bearing the image of God draws on critical theory for a theological end: she challenges our usual constructions of human identity and argues for the God-given dignity of all human beings. In her essay on providence, Kalbryn A. McLean probes the dangers and comforts of Calvin's view of providence and reflects on its implications for human agency. Martha Schull Gilliss's essay reworks traditional Reformed understandings of atonement, taking into account feminist and womanist critiques, and shows the inseparability of Christ's cross and resurrection. Katie Geneva Cannon's chapter on grace focuses on its transformative potential, especially in the lives of African Americans, to confront absurd, death-dealing disjunctions in life as well as to prompt conscious lives of thanksgiving.

The next two essays take up particularly Reformed themes. Kristine A. Culp writes on resistance against tyranny and idolatry, a theme that has also been central to feminist theology, with a special attention to Huguenot history. Joan M. Martin's essay reworks understandings of work and vocation in light of African Americans' search for dignity and meaning in their work under the conditions of slavery. In her chapter on the church, Amy Plantinga Pauw explores Reformed emphases on the "infirmity and weakness of the church" but also its enduring power as a community in which God's grace is experienced. Leanne VanDyk's essay on sacraments shows how Reformed theology contains a sacramental richness that is deeply supportive of the flourishing of women and the whole earth. Following Calvin's own reticence, our eschatological pronouncements are rather modest: our concluding chapter represents a gathering up of eschatological fragments from the preceding essays, with the aim of showing how eschatological convictions shape our lives now.

This volume was a deeply collaborative venture. Our understanding of our subject matter—Reformed feminist and womanist dogmatics—emerged only through extended conversations together. These conversations would not have been possible without the generosity of Westminster John Knox Press, the Institute for Reformed Theology at Union-PSCE, and Yale Divinity School. We are grateful for their financial support of our collaborative meetings and for the encouragement that this support represented. The interest and enthusiasm of the members of the editorial board of the Columbia Series in Reformed Theology, including the late Shirley Guthrie, helped sustain us. Our editor and friend Donald McKim deserves our thanks for his patience and wise counsel. We received much-appreciated editorial assistance from Kalbryn A. McLean and Melisa Scarlott. We thank Kathryn Reklis for her work on the indexes. We owe a special debt to Dean Dianne Reistroffer of Louisville Presbyterian Seminary, who dug into her special project fund to help host our group at the seminary's Laws Lodge and who has shown continuing enthusiasm for our project as it unfolded. Structural changes and academic opportunities for women in theological education have come in no small part from the growing number of women like Dianne in its administrative ranks.

Looking ahead, the editors dedicate this book to their daughters, Clara, Andrea, Emily, and Charis, in the hope that they too will find nurture and direction for their lives in the intersecting theological communities out of which this book was written.

1

FEAR IN THE REFORMED TRADITION

Lynn Japinga

In her memoir *A Girl Named Zippy*, Haven Kimmel describes her minimalist childhood religious beliefs: "I believed that the baby Jesus had gotten born, and that was all lovely. Christmas was also my favorite time of year, in part because of the excellent speech, 'Fear not: I bring you good tidings of great joy.'"[1] Perhaps "Fear not" is such an excellent speech because most human beings are afraid of something. Children fear bullies, the dark, and monsters under the bed. Adults fear loss, disease, danger, terrorist attacks, and the collapse of the stock market. Institutions can be fearful also. A nation, a corporation, a church, or any other group fears danger from without and within. They fear that they will die, or their identity will be compromised, or they will be taken over, or the group will self-destruct from internal conflict.

Fear can paralyze. It can make us sick. It can make us avoid activities we like. It can cause us to be cautious and closed. It can make us hide in a cocoon and try to avoid risk. Fear can be defined as an emotional response to a specific danger or the possibility of danger, such as a mugger, a tornado, or a car careening toward ours. In these cases, fear may produce the physiological responses associated with "fight or flight" mechanisms. The heart beats faster, the adrenaline starts to pump, and the body prepares to escape or engage in battle. More often, though, the object of fear is not easily identified or dealt with. We fear what *might* happen. Losing a job. Losing financial security. Losing a child. Becoming ill. We fear we will not be good enough at marriage, parenting, or our vocation. We fear that we will not be happy. We may even fear that we will live our lives bound up in fear. Consider these examples.

First Samuel 17 describes a frightening event in the life of the Israelites. Goliath the giant had terrorized the Israelite army. Forty days in a row Goliath came to jeer at the Israelites and suggest they send one of their soldiers to fight him, winner take all. And every day the Israelite army "fled from him and were very much afraid." Goliath threatened their safety, their national identity, and their faith. Fear not only made the Israelites run away; it also made them question their courage, their identity as soldiers, and their trust in God.

Contemporary North American culture also finds it difficult to cope with ongoing anxiety. We want to do something now, whether that means going to war, taking antianxiety medication, or dulling the pain with alcohol. When I wrote this chapter in 2002, the nation was debating the wisdom of a preemptive strike on Iraq, in part out of fear that Iraq possessed weapons of mass destruction. Military and political leaders were anxious because they did not know for certain and they could not control the situation. Still no weapons have been found, and it is clear that fear helped to lead the country into a very difficult war.

During one of our meetings in preparation for this book, we ate lunch with an educator who was planning a video about feminist theology and wondered if we would be featured in it. We discussed several possibilities and generated many creative ideas. Because of the controversy that has occasionally surrounded feminist theology, some members of the group wondered whether being linked with feminist theology would harm their chances of getting tenure or promotion. Others wondered whether they would be respected as theologians of the church if they were identified as feminists. Fear of disapproval or backlash can keep us from doing important but risky things. Fear can cause our lives to be constricted, narrowed, shut up.

A discussion of fear may seem an unusual way to begin a book of essays about womanist/feminist perspectives on the Reformed tradition. After all, fear is not a doctrine. But fear can be found at the root of many of the issues feminist and womanist theologians address. Scholars have noted within the Christian tradition many examples of the fear of women's bodies, women's minds, and women's power.[2] Fear has at times led the church to limit and control women's lives. Opponents of women's ordination often fear that men will stop coming to church if women are ordained, or they fear that having women in leadership roles violates the authority of Scripture. Fears about women's sexuality also appear in this debate. Similar dynamics occur in discussions about race. Predominantly white denominations fear the consequences of giving people of color genuine institutional power. Feminist and womanist theologians respond to these fears in their work. The other essays in this book will demonstrate some of the ways they do that. This essay will discuss fear itself.

The Reformed tradition has been stereotyped as particularly fearful through much of its history.[3] John Calvin is portrayed as a pinched, sour man who delighted in telling the people of Geneva what not to do. Calvin's descendants have been labeled as anxious, even a bit neurotic. Calvinism is described as a high-demand and high-achievement tradition, whose members feel guilty for the evil they have done, and even guiltier for the good they have left undone. The Reformed tradition emphasizes the fear of God and is dubious about fun-loving and joyful attitudes. One critic described the Puritans as obsessed with the idea that someone, somewhere, might be having fun. One of the most famous sermons in the Reformed tradition is Jonathan Edwards's "Sinners in the Hands of an Angry God." Edwards compared a human being to a spider God dangled over a flame, leaving students of American literature a fascinating and disturbing example of what it means to be Reformed.

It is ironic that the Reformed tradition is theoretically deeply confident about God and salvation. The Westminster Shorter Catechism asks, "What is the chief end of man?" and answers, "The chief end of man is to glorify God and enjoy him forever." The Heidelberg Catechism asks, "What is your only comfort in life and in death?" and answers, "That I belong, body and soul, in life and in death, not to myself, but to my faithful Savior, Jesus Christ." Is it possible to be comfortable in the hands of an angry God? Is it possible to enjoy a God who does not want people to have too much fun?

If it is true that Reformed churches demonstrate a high degree of fear, it poses an interesting question. Why is a church that claims to be confident about the grace of God so fearful about its future? Why is fear such a common theme in the Reformed tradition?

Some fear is rooted in theological beliefs. The Reformed tradition has emphasized the sovereignty and transcendence of God, describing God as a Judge who must be feared, respected, and obeyed. Humans should be in awe of God and never treat the relationship lightly. God is gracious and merciful but also a demanding critic with high expectations for human beings. A common image of God is a father who loves his children but strongly disapproves of disobedience or even independent thinking. God is gracious in the Reformed tradition, but God is not easily satisfied.

The doctrine of election was intended to promote confidence in the grace of God, but it does not always succeed. The Reformed tradition insists that salvation comes from God, not from human effort. Election is mysterious, and the elect are ultimately known only in the mind of God. People wonder how they can be certain they are saved. Calvin warned against such speculation, but his descendants expressed a great deal of anxiety over who would be among the elect and how they could know for certain.

The strong emphasis on sin also helps to explain the presence of fear in the Reformed tradition. The Fall damaged all human capacities. Although unredeemed human beings are capable of good, they are more likely to be selfish, arrogant, greedy, and lustful. In the political context of the sixteenth century, Calvin was legitimately fearful of the various powers and authorities around him. He believed Geneva was a fragile community, threatened by Roman Catholic powers, the forces of irreligion, and apathy. Its survival was by no means assured. Despite the stereotypes, Calvin did not rule Geneva with an iron fist, eliminate all the opposition, or always get what he wanted. Calvin felt that he was constantly battling with sin and that it often won.[4]

This chapter will attempt to map the shape of fear in the Reformed tradition, using historical examples from several denominations. What are we afraid of and why? I will argue that Reformed fears generally fall into three categories: fear of the Other, fear of being wrong, and fear of being irrelevant.

FEAR OF THE OTHER

The Reformed tradition has generally been confident that it knows God's truth and how best to live it out. Unfortunately, there have been many others who do not know God's truth or claim to know it in a different way. Reformed Christians have occasionally tried to create a pure community where they could avoid disagreement, but they were rarely able to sustain such isolation. For most of their history, Reformed denominations have had to live with pluralism despite their desire to eliminate it.

The phrase "the Other" has been used in contemporary analyses to refer to those groups who are different or who disagree.[5] One group of people might label as the Other anyone who looks, thinks, or behaves differently. When a group feels threatened or insecure, it is more likely to actively resist or critique the Other. At times the Other is frightening because it represents the powerful majority, but the Other is equally ominous when it poses a small but potent threat to a group's identity and stability. Some historical examples may illustrate the varied role of the Other.

In the hymn "A Mighty Fortress Is Our God," Martin Luther wrote, "And though this world with devils filled should threaten to undo us, we will not fear for God has willed his truth to triumph through us." Calvin expressed similar confidence in the power of God to protect the truth. But Luther and Calvin found it difficult to live out this confidence in the midst of threats from many fronts. Even more problematic than "devils" were the beliefs and actions of several groups that threatened their tenuous security during the Reformation. They may have trusted God to triumph, but they did not leave it to chance. Luther and Calvin stated their views of the truth at every opportunity, often in the form of condemnations that were sharply worded critiques of the wrong beliefs of the Other.

The Roman Catholic Church was the most obvious Other. It was powerful and influential not only in religion but also in politics. In the minds of the Reformers, the Roman Catholic Church was wrong and a danger to the true faith.[6] The early Protestants feared the Roman Catholic Church because it threatened not only their beliefs but also their lives.

It would seem logical in the face of this dangerous Other that the various Protestant groups would band together against Catholicism, but they did not. Luther and Calvin condemned Anabaptist convictions about believers' baptism and pacifism. They criticized Zwingli for his views of the sacraments and his willingness to fight physically for the faith, and they criticized social reform movements that developed out of poverty and frustration. They feared that by introducing more radical social and religious ideas, these groups might endanger whatever stability Protestants had attained. Lutherans and Calvinists also disagreed with each other, particularly about the sacraments.

The condemnations offered a way to deal with disagreement and fear of the Other. If another group was wrong, even on one point, there was no reason to engage in discussion or cooperate with them. The integrity of the gospel was at stake. Its truth and purity needed to be preserved by naming wrong beliefs. Given the circumstances of the sixteenth century, this strategy is understandable; but it left an unfortunate legacy among Protestants, who felt they could not simply disagree with another group but had to condemn them. Once schism began it was difficult to stop, and even more difficult was reuniting groups that had separated. Complete doctrinal agreement seemed essential for Christian unity.

A century later another group of Reformed Protestants had a slightly different experience of the Other. In the late sixteenth and early seventeenth centuries the Puritans were a minority group within the established Church of England. They criticized the state church for being too papist and insufficiently reformed. They vigorously protested encroachment upon their religious freedom. The Church of England had no right to tell them how to worship or what to believe. For the Puritans, the Other was the powerful state church, and it had to be opposed.

In 1630 a group of Puritans left England and settled in Boston, intending it to be a "city set on a hill" that would show the world how a truly committed Protestant community could be built. The power dynamics were reversed, and the Puritans were the dominant group. They attained their religious freedom but were not willing to grant it to others. They believed that a stable and successful community required everyone to conform to a single set of behavioral standards and beliefs. A dissenter threatened to corrupt the identity and mission of the entire community and therefore could not be tolerated. Because uniformity seemed essential to the ideal community, the Puritans frequently acted exactly as the Church of England had done. Quakers, Baptists, and advocates of religious liberty were killed, punished, or forced to leave. The Puritans insisted that the Massachusetts Bay Colony was a covenant community and those who did not share the community's values and beliefs did not have to live there. In this context, the Other, simply by being different, threatened the well-being of the community and needed to be eliminated.

One of the most infamous examples of fear in a Reformed community occurred about sixty years later in Salem, Massachusetts. The Puritan community encountered inexplicable and terrifying events. Young girls experienced fits and trances and blamed their troubles on witches. Dozens of women (often elderly and crotchety) and a few men were accused of causing pain, disease, crop failure, and the girls' fits. Historians have since identified many possible causes for the hysteria, including disease, tainted food, adolescent boredom, interpersonal conflicts, and economic distress. But the Puritans had no other means of explanation than the work of the devil. They were convinced that the devil was real and worked primarily through weak and vulnerable women. Fear of evil and the unknown thus led to the execution of nineteen women and one man. The Puritans were unable to seek out more complicated explanations for the apparent presence of the devil among them.

This event illustrates one of the most negative consequences of the fear of the Other. When people are afraid of something, but are not quite sure what, it is easy to scapegoat outsiders or problematic people as the cause of the danger. It is generally easier to blame the Other than to search for more complicated explanations of social disorder. In the 1950s, it was easier to scapegoat possible Communist sympathizers than to deal with the anxiety that Americans felt about the Soviet Union and the threat of nuclear war. Joseph McCarthy damaged many careers and reputations because he appealed to people's fears rather than to their reason.

For the Dutch immigrants in the Reformed Church in America (RCA) and the Christian Reformed Church, fear of the Other was deeply rooted in their ancestors' experience in the Netherlands. In the 1830s, some Dutch Reformed church members became involved in revival and renewal movements at the same time that the state church required more conformity. A number of them immigrated to the United States seeking greater religious freedom and economic opportunity. One group that was led to Michigan by Albertus Van Raalte eventually founded the city of Holland. Van Raalte appealed to the Dutch Reformed churches in New York and New Jersey for financial aid. The eastern churches provided the aid and invited the immigrants to join the Reformed Church, which they did.

A decade later a schism occurred. A few congregations left the RCA because they feared it was too Americanized and ecumenical. The presence of hymns along with psalms in the RCA hymnbook meant it had been infected by a nonbiblical practice. Thirty years later a larger schism occurred, this time because the RCA permitted Freemasons to be members of the church. A new denomination, the Christian Reformed Church (CRC), grew out of these schisms. The CRC fiercely resisted Americanization and ecumenism and adopted the motto "In isolation is our strength."[7]

The legacy of schism has been a crucial part of the Dutch Reformed experience. One group often left or threatened to leave whenever there was conflict. They did not like being told what to do, whether by a denominational structure or an ecumenical body. They feared being swallowed up by a larger body and losing their theological purity. In a 1967 essay in the *Reformed Review*, Jerome DeJong noted that the midwestern RCA resisted a merger with the Southern Presbyterians in part because of their ancestors' experience with the ecclesiastical octopus of the Dutch church. In DeJong's mind, merger, the anti-Christ, and the apostate church were all inextricably linked, and he insisted, "We are not anxious to be caught up in a vast, tyrannical, dictatorial system."[8] He preferred independence to entanglement. It is fascinating that 120 years after Van Raalte departed from the Netherlands, his descendants were still fighting his battles, whether real or imagined. That's a long time to carry a grudge.

The more Americanized eastern RCA churches had fears of their own. Some claimed that the RCA could not survive without becoming Presbyterian. Others argued that the only effective way to witness to the city was ecumenical cooperation. One pastor observed, "If we neglect this opportunity [to merge] what will become of us and what account of ourselves shall we give to [God]?" The co-chairperson of the RCA-PCUS (Presbyterian Church U.S.) committee asked, "How can the church witness to its Lord when by its fragmented witness it is disobedient to its Lord?"[9] The eastern clergy feared that the conservative Midwest was preventing the progress and growth of the RCA.

These examples demonstrate that fear of the Other can occur *within* a denomination. The eastern RCA thought that many of the midwestern congregations were hopelessly conservative and entrenched in a Dutch enclave with no awareness of the real world. The midwestern branch thought that the East was hopelessly liberal and had sold its theological birthright for a mess of ecumenical pottage. The fears led both groups to mistrust and stereotype each other. The ensuing conflict still shapes the RCA in significant ways. It was and is easier to scapegoat the geographical Other for problems within the denomination than to find creative ways to deal with change. Fear can be paralyzing.

The Christian Reformed Church was even more vigilant than the midwestern RCA about preserving its purity. The CRC feared worldly pursuits like alcohol, Sunday amusements, dancing, and movies because they were sinful and because the desire to be entertained threatened Christian faith and commitment. The CRC resisted contemporary theological and ecclesiological trends and was slow to embark on both foreign missions and evangelism. The doctrine of election helped to shape this rather passive response to the Other. It seemed pointless to engage in mission and evangelistic work to those God had not elected. The CRC feared conformity and contamination. If they tried to attract nonbelievers, they might dilute their doctrine to appeal to them. If they embarked on foreign mission work, they might have to cooperate with a church with different beliefs, which threatened the purity of their own. This separation and distrust may have protected the church and the faith, but it also kept the church from engagement with the world.[10]

Most of the fear of the Other in the Reformed tradition has emphasized different ideas and beliefs. The racial and ethnic Other has drawn less attention in part because some Reformed denominations and individuals have had relatively limited contact with people of other races. When they had more contact, Reformed Christians often possessed a great deal of power and were able to dominate the Other. Most have seen the racial Other as culturally and intellectually inferior. An RCA minister noted around 1630 that the Native Americans he encountered were as stupid as garden stakes. They would be difficult to convert and probably never comfortable in a church that emphasized the intellect.[11] The CRC was unwilling to begin mission work in Nigeria even though a CRC woman was already working there effectively. They said that the Africans "belong to the types of mankind from which one cannot expect the most in the kingdom of God."[12] Several centuries ago, white immigrants to South Africa (some of whom were Dutch Reformed) believed that God had given them the land as their own, but they feared the native inhabitants. Fear led them to make decisions about apartheid, land use, and educational policies that kept the native populations separate, poor, and uneducated; and the white population, wealthy, educated, and powerful. When racial policies grow out of fear and a desire for separation, power, and control, they can be deadly.

In the last half century, many Reformed denominations have demonstrated varying degrees of racism in their reluctance to integrate congregations and in the paternalistic ways they treated congregations composed of ethnic minorities. They have often assumed that this Other was different and inferior and therefore could not be a full and equal member of a church. The struggle continues in various ways in the twenty-first century. Reformed denominations are integrated, and often have a relatively influential "Black Council" or minority task force, but members of minorities still feel that they are not represented in denominational leadership and that their voices are not heard.[13] Still, the majority at times appears to resent the Other for getting disproportionate voice and representation. They fear that the Other will have too much power to determine the direction of the institution.

The negative attitudes toward women are similarly numerous. Antoinette Brown Blackwell was ordained in the Congregationalist Church in 1853, but over a century passed before most Reformed women were permitted to enter the ministry. Women have been valued as wives and mothers and unpaid church workers, but for much of its history the Reformed tradition has assumed that they are not fully capable of intellectual work or positions of authority in the church. Various reasons have been given including Scripture, tradition, custom, and comfort. Many refuse to recognize women as fully human and made in the image of God. They will grant women spiritual equality before God but not actual equality in the church.[14] Twenty years ago an RCA seminary professor spoke in a church about women in office. A man later took him aside and told him that women were not likely to be ordained there because men were afraid of losing power to women in both home and church. Since then, Reformed churches have significantly improved in their acceptance and valuing of women, but they are a long way from full equality. "The church just isn't ready" is a common excuse for unjust treatment of the female Other.

The Other is threatening because people who are different can make us question our identity and security. The more tenuous and unclear our identity, the more likely we are to see the Other as a threat. Instead of recognizing our fears and limits, we are often quick to claim that the Other is wrong and therefore a danger to us. A greater confidence in our identity and calling (without arrogance) might help us be less threatened by difference. The recurring challenge is to find creative ways to preserve group identity in a pluralist society.

THE FEAR OF BEING WRONG

For much of its history, the Reformed tradition has been fairly certain that its understanding of faith and doctrine is correct and that other traditions are wrong to some degree. During a debate about a potential merger with the Southern Presbyterians, a layperson wrote to the RCA weekly magazine: "If every member of our Church would refresh his mind on the basic doctrines explained in the Heidelberg Catechism and the Canons of Dort and would hold to these as the true understanding of Scripture, I would have no fear for our church."[15] For this author, faith was not the shared story of the Christian tradition but only the Reformed interpretation of it. In his mind, Christians who affirmed the Augsburg or Westminster Confessions lacked the true understanding of Scripture.

Lurking under this apparent arrogance is evidence of deep uncertainty. Some Reformed Christians insist that God has revealed one truth through Scripture and the Reformed creeds and confessions. These sources contain the right answers that are needed for salvation. There are no ambiguities or gray areas because God has revealed everything clearly. There are no new or different or multiple answers because the truth has been revealed once and for all. This doctrinal correctness appears to alleviate anxiety because all the answers are clear. Psychoanalyst Rollo May calls it rigid thinking and suggests that while it may protect people for a short time, it eventually fails because it does not allow new ideas or alternative ways of thinking.[16]

Rigid thinking is frequently evident in the Reformed tradition. After the Re-imagining Conference[17] ten years ago, some critics attacked the conference and its planners, and accused several speakers of heresy. There was little willingness to listen or to consider why so many women felt alienated from the church and traditional Christian doctrine.

Several years ago the RCA debated pluralism. The idea of multiple paths to salvation made some people very anxious. They insisted God would only save those who could clearly articulate faith in Jesus Christ as Lord and Savior. They said that salvation was a gracious gift of God and that God would save those whom God chose, and yet they were somewhat paradoxically convinced that right thinking (orthodoxy) was essential to salvation. Some critics were angry that the RCA's Commission on Theology wrote a paper that merely hinted at some broader ways to consider the issue.

People in the Reformed tradition have tried to ward off threats to their beliefs in hope of preserving their purity from external corruption or infection. They have succeeded in varying degrees at keeping the wrong ideas out of their community. The more insidious and difficult danger has arisen when the wrong ideas and unfaithfulness have come from within the community.

One of the most striking examples is uncertainty about grace. The belief that salvation came by grace was intended to give people a sense of confidence and eliminate the anxiety that arose when salvation depended on human works and effort. But it was not so easy. The early Puritans who had such a powerful experience of grace tried to routinize the experience by outlining the exact process of conversion. Applicants for church membership were expected to tell their conversion story according to the pattern. This rigid thinking about conversion meant that many second-generation Puritans appeared less faithful because their stories lacked the drama of their parents' faith. But rather than ask if God's grace might be evident in different ways to different generations, the Puritan parents and clergy assumed the children lacked godliness and true faith.

The Puritans also wondered how they could discern who was among the elect. It was easy to be deceived about one's spiritual life, and they feared people might claim to be among the elect when they were not. The Puritans believed that the elect would naturally demonstrate good works and good lives. Goodness did not guarantee that one was among the elect, but bad behavior—the failure to obey social norms—guaranteed that one was not. In practice if not in theory, they inverted the order of grace and good works and made works not only the evidence but also the cause of grace.

When Anne Hutchinson pointed out the flaws in the Puritan argument, the leaders accused her of antinomianism, excommunicated her from the church, and banished her from Boston. Her dissent was compounded by the fact that she exercised spiritual leadership among both men and women, and she was charged with having "stept out of her place" and claiming unlawful divine authority. The Puritans feared leadership from unauthorized sources, they feared women, and they feared Anne's claim that the Holy Spirit spoke directly to her. The Puritans wanted to eliminate her from the community lest she threaten social stability with her dangerous ideas.[18]

Paradoxically, the Reformed belief that grace did not depend on human effort seemed to create even more anxiety about whether one had actually received grace. If people were singing, "Will There Be Any Stars in My Crown?" with the Arminians, they could in theory work a little harder and get more stars. But under Calvinism, how would they know for sure that they would have a crown? It was all rooted in the mind of God. Perhaps this is why success (at least in Max Weber's analysis) became the evidence of one's election.

A related fear of being wrong concerns the role of works in the Christian life. A joke describes Luther and Calvin residing in hell while the Catholic popes live in heavenly palaces. When they question the arrangement, they are told, "Works matter." The role of works has been an underlying fear in the Reformed tradition throughout its history. What if the radical new idea of *sola gratia* was simply wrong? How could a community be motivated toward obedience and holiness if works were not conditions for salvation? How would order be maintained? These were pressing concerns for Calvin and the Puritans and others trying to build a Christian community.

The fear of being wrong resulted in part from the stress on right doctrine. Reformed theology began in controversy about beliefs. The errors of Catholics, Arminians, Anabaptists, and Lutherans needed to be pointed out and the correct Reformed doctrines made clear. The Reformed tradition has emphasized the intellectual and rational aspects of faith, and the result has been a considerable amount of fear that God will be angry if we do not get it right.

In the Presbyterian tradition, the emphasis on doing everything decently and in good order has led to a fear that the church will be wrong if its polity is not correct. The Reformed tradition has at times assumed that a majority vote reflects the will of God. The Presbyterian Church (U.S.A.) has been tied in knots during the last few years because of votes about homosexuality. The RCA argued for years about changing its polity to allow women's ordination. Whether it was the right thing or not, two-thirds of the delegates to General Synod had to agree. This style of government can preserve good order, but it does not always facilitate doing justice. The church has at times hidden behind its polity to avoid conflict and change. It has let its fear of getting the polity wrong limit its actions.

The Reformed tradition has also demonstrated a fear of divine disapproval. God is loving, and yet God will be disappointed in or angry with us if we do not act and think correctly. We claim to believe in the perseverance of the saints but seem to have a persistent fear that God will abandon us if we get it wrong.

The Reformed tradition has also struggled with the fear that others will disapprove. The PC(USA) learned the pain of such disapproval in the aftermath of the Re-imagining Conference. The CRC lost a number of congregations after debates about women's ordination and evolution. The United Church of Christ has a group of loyal opposition, which sometimes seems more opposed than loyal. Many congregations are quick to express their disagreement with the denomination by refusing to contribute or by actually leaving. This schismatic tendency promotes a high degree of fear among denominational leaders, and this fear then seems to drive the denominational agenda. The church cannot talk about an issue or take an action because certain people will disapprove. In an age of tight budgets for denominational institutions, the fear of not having enough money seems to drive many decisions. The church cannot do justice or take a risk because wealthy donors and congregations might disapprove and withhold their money.

Related to this is the fear of conflict. Conflict can be viewed positively as a disagreement between two good values where neither side is entirely right or wrong. Conflict is far more often viewed negatively, with each side demonizing the other. In the current worship wars, for example, those with a liturgical preference accuse contemporary worship of emotionalism, lack of substance, and selling out to the culture. Fans of contemporary worship accused traditionalists of being closed minded, stuffy, and boring. The dominant or majority group in an institution may charge that those who disagree are stubborn, selfish, or sinful. We lack positive ways to deal with conflict, we try to avoid it, but it does not go away.

In a 1968 overture asking that General Synod stop talking about merger with the PCUS, the Classis of Chicago argued that "the primary responsibility of the Reformed Church in America, above all other responsibilities" was to preserve "undisruptiveness" within the denominational fellowship. If a merger proposal caused conflict and unrest, then the church should not talk about merger.[19] The church has always had its disruptions, but it has become increasingly difficult to see conflict as a sign of life and healthy disagreement within an organization. Some leaders want to determine the right answer rather than allow discussion and debate. They consider conflict a sign of disunity and disloyalty rather than evidence of deeply held values and the need for more creative solutions that might honor competing values.

The fear of being wrong does not foster community. We cannot live or work with a person or group who might be wrong because they could infect us. We cannot compromise or cooperate with those who might be wrong because we fear that we could disintegrate. We become so concerned with getting it right that we cannot take the risks that the gospel requires.

THE FEAR OF IRRELEVANCE

Some elements of the fear of the Other and the fear of being wrong may seem quaint and even passé in the contemporary Reformed tradition. We are more inclusive now and less concerned about correct doctrine. But there is a third fear that haunts the Reformed churches, and most churches to some degree. It is the fear of irrelevance or loss of influence. Sociologists call it secularization. The church is not as popular or as valued as it once was. This is reflected in a precipitous loss of members during the last three decades in most Reformed denominations. Congregational giving has not kept pace with denominational expenses, and denominational staff members do more work with fewer resources. Churches have experienced bitter conflicts over homosexuality, women's ordination, and the Re-imagining Conference, and the disagreements make some people wonder if there is a future for the church. Some analysts observe that the only glue currently holding many denominations together is the ministers' pension plan.

The fear of irrelevance is shared to some degree by a number of religious traditions, especially in mainline Protestantism. The Reformed tradition is not unique in fearing the loss of its identity and influence. American mainline Protestantism is now often called "sideline Protestantism" because of the perception that its religious pronouncements have little effect on the country's major cultural, political, and economic decisions.

These fears are not new. In 1905 an RCA minister lamented what he called "the lost sense of God."[20] Instead of religion influencing all of life, it was limited to only a small sphere of Sunday activity. It no longer had the power to shape business or economics or intellectual pursuits or ethical choices. This theme of declining influence shaped most religious commentary in the RCA during the twentieth century. Only in the 1950s did religion appear to be thriving, and even then the editor of the RCA denominational magazine questioned the quality and depth of the religious faith espoused by many of the people who were attending church.

The relationship between the church and the world has been a source of anxiety and disagreement throughout the history of the church. At times the church was powerful, and at other times it was subservient to the state and relatively voiceless in the world.[21] When the church is strong, it is accused of meddling and moralism, and then it sometimes retreats into silence and passivity. When the church is criticized for quietism, it has sometimes adopted a militant effort to impose Christian values upon the world. The relationship with the world has created anxiety because it is so difficult for the church to discern an adequate response to social issues. During the Vietnam War, young adults sharply criticized and often left churches that refused to speak out against the war. Other people criticized churches that opposed the war for meddling in political issues about which they knew nothing, as well as for idealism and Communist sympathizing.

At times the church's fears of irrelevance are masked by other concerns. The presidential election in 1928 made Protestants anxious about what would happen if the Roman Catholic Al Smith were elected. The rhetoric in the midwestern RCA periodical suggested that the pope would control the president and eliminate religious freedom in America.[22] These fears were certainly real to them at the time, yet the larger but unspoken issue was the loss of Protestant hegemony in America. RCA clergy and laypeople realized Protestants had lost most of their power to shape public opinion. They were becoming irrelevant, and they did not like being out of control. Attacking a Catholic candidate was one way to deal with their fear that if a Roman Catholic became president, Protestants would completely lose their influence.

The debate over alcohol during this period illustrates similar dynamics. RCA rhetoric criticized drunkenness and related vices such as poverty and the lack of self-control. RCA clergy were most concerned that American society paid little attention to the church. The RCA repeatedly insisted on the need to obey Prohibition laws while Americans continued to defy them. Clergy complained that the whole fabric of the moral order was unraveling. How could America be a decent, moral, law-abiding society if people continued to drink? One particularly poignant statement complained that there were stills in the backyards of the RCA's own members![23] The ultimate sign that the church was becoming irrelevant was when even its own members refused to obey its teachings.

Similar rhetoric insisted on the need to preserve Sunday as a day for rest and worship rather than amusement. RCA clergy were angry that the fourth commandment was taken so lightly by American society, and they occasionally supported legalist strategies to limit Sunday recreation. More significantly, however, they feared that the teachings of the church simply did not matter. One author pointed out that the church had tried to keep the Sabbath holy by discouraging Sunday drives, but with little success. During World War I, the government asked people not to drive on a particular Sunday to save gasoline, and they willingly complied. The fact that people respected the request of the government more than the church signaled the increasing irrelevance of the church.[24]

On occasion the church contributed to its own loss of voice because it failed to address the source of a social problem. During the first several decades of the twentieth century, there was a large gap between rich and poor and considerable unrest among laborers. Many Reformed clergy instructed the poor to be content, thrifty, and hard working and never to go on strike. It was difficult for many Reformed churches to move beyond the morality of the workers and address the causes of their unrest: capitalism, low wages, and lack of power. Middle-class Reformed Christians tried to deal with workers by converting and controlling them. They were reluctant to critique the economic issues that caused the conflicts.

At times the church has tried to avoid dealing with social issues. In the nineteenth century, southern Presbyterians developed the doctrine of the spirituality of the church. The church was called to deal with spiritual issues, not matters of government, politics, or economics. This notion allowed the PCUS members to hold slaves and yet be good Christians. They accused abolitionists and northern Presbyterians of straying from the true gospel with their emphasis on social reform. In the twentieth century, the PCUS remained silent about the civil rights movement for the same reason. Some Christians respected the PCUS for emphasizing spiritual matters and not getting distracted by contemporary social issues, but others thought the PCUS had abdicated its voice for justice.

Contemporary attendance patterns and membership statistics make it clear that religion is considered irrelevant to much of life in this century. Some people who do attend church find that it provides personal meaning and a sense of community but does not influence social or personal decision making. Others simply do not attend because there are so many other ways to spend their time and because church is no longer the social expectation that it was, for example, in the 1950s. Church is not essential to salvation or success.

Numerous explanations have been offered for this shift. Some analysts blame the church for being too strict, too lax, too boring, or too concerned about its own members and neglecting outsiders. Others blame the people who do not attend for being sinful, worldly, preoccupied, or simply unconcerned. Other analysts attribute the changing patterns to a broader cultural pattern of secularization that the church can do little to change.

These questions of why people neither attend nor listen to the church consume much of the church's energy at this point in its life. Church leaders seem almost desperate to reverse the decline and start to grow again, and they are looking for strategies to make the church more strict or more appealing or more mission minded. In 2001 the General Synod of the RCA voted to establish a goal to become one of the fastest-growing churches in America by 2011. The goal is presented in language of mission to a lost and broken world, but at times it is not clear whether the RCA is genuinely concerned about the world or is primarily interested in its own survival.

ANTIDOTES TO FEAR

This chapter has offered a rather sobering analysis of some of the fears and limitations of the Reformed tradition. Subsequent chapters will discuss some resources in the Reformed tradition and in feminist theology that offer ways the church might become less fearful.

Perhaps one of the best antidotes to fear is to search within the Reformed tradition for its distinctive strengths. When David volunteered to fight Goliath, King Saul offered David the use of his armor. David tried it on, but it was much too large, so he went without it, choosing instead the legendary five smooth stones. How often does the church choose the wrong armor to deal with its fear? We choose to fight fear with things that don't fit us. Arminian theology. An appeal to guilt. Simplistic church growth strategies. We get desperate, and we are willing to try anything, without considering whether it is the right thing. We think the future of God's church is up to us. We think that the survival of the gospel depends on our doing the right thing and finding the right strategy. But it is the wrong armor.[25]

How can the church be honest about its fears and find constructive ways to deal with them? Fear is not necessarily wrong or sinful but can be a realistic and appropriate response to threats of violence and loss of life and identity. The more important issue is how individuals and congregations deal with fear. Do they ignore it? Do they project their uncertainty onto another group and blame them for causing anxiety? Do they use inappropriate means to eliminate feelings of fear and anxiety without understanding the real causes?

Fear is often portrayed positively in the Reformed tradition: "The fear of the Lord is the beginning of wisdom" (Prov. 9:10). Fear of the Lord means awe and respect for the power of God. This fear shapes ethical decisions by reminding us that God's ways are different from the world's ways. The midwives in Exodus 1, for example, refused the Pharaoh's command to kill the Israelites' male children because they feared God and God's commands took precedence over those from a human ruler. Fear of God should not make us terrified or paralyzed but respectful. God is not to be approached casually or viewed as a personal valet.

The corollary to the fear of the Lord is an appropriate sense of human limitation and finitude. We should not think more highly of ourselves than we ought to think, but we should not think less of ourselves, either.[26] The doctrine of total depravity has occasionally led to a kind of passivity. Reformed Christians have excused their half-hearted work for justice by saying that the social order cannot be transformed because of the presence of sin. Human beings can never get it right, so they should not bother to try. Calvin would have criticized such reluctance. Sin is pervasive in the good that humans do, but they are still capable of good because of God's gracious and redemptive work in the world. Self-criticism and humility are essential virtues particularly for relationships with the Other, but Calvinists have often seen the glass of human abilities as more empty than full. What would it mean to see ourselves as God's people called to seek and embody God's grace and justice in the world?

The Reformed tradition has always emphasized grace as the heart of its faith, but do we really believe it? We claim that God loves creation and humanity in spite of its brokenness and that God has the best interests of the world at heart. We claim that God seeks our good and our happiness. But we sometimes act as if God wants us to pay for our sin by suffering and living stoically obedient, joyless lives. We are afraid, and we have forgotten that the Reformed tradition speaks more of grace than of sin and more of God's delight in humankind than of God's displeasure. If we really believed that God was gracious would we fear that we are not doing enough to please God? Would we be anxious about our numbers? Would we be so concerned with being right?

The Reformed tradition has often been driven by a strong sense of self-righteousness. We alone are left. God chose us. God preserves us, and we need to preserve our identity. We are God's elect and ought to remain pure and isolated. The world is sinful; we are saved. We seem to have a sense of entitlement to God's grace that we deny to the Other. But what if we substituted gratitude for entitlement? What if we could be grateful for God's goodness and grace to us, without assuming that God is not good to the rest of the world? We might then see election as an avenue God uses to be gracious to the rest of the world (as Abraham was called to be a blessing to the nations in Gen. 12). South African theologian John de Gruchy remarks that "thankfulness or gratitude is the springboard for Christian ethics."[27] Gratitude might help us avoid some of the paternalism that has shaped much of the Reformed tradition. We have at times displayed a pharisaical thankfulness that we are not like these others. What if instead we demonstrated a publican sense of humble gratitude for God's gracious forgiveness and empowerment? Then perhaps we could recognize that God has been gracious to many. To Lutherans. To the indigenous people of South Africa. To Native Americans. To the recipients of our missionary efforts. To women. To all of us in various ways. Perhaps if we saw the myriad ways God's grace is at work in the world and stopped being so afraid that there is a limited quantity of that grace, we could be more thankful for the signs of God's grace that appear throughout the world.

Since fear has often led to dominance and avoidance of those who are different, another useful antidote might be a positive relationship with the Other that seeks to establish justice and build community. John de Gruchy argues that the third use of the law might be a way to restore an emphasis on justice to the Reformed tradition. Calvin advocated the third use of the law not as a way to impose anxiety and bondage, but to emphasize the free choice of obedience as a gift of the Spirit and an expression of gratitude and love for one's neighbor. Obedience is not something Christians do because they must appease or pay a debt to God but because they want to live in a way that shows gratitude for God and care for the neighbor. De Gruchy believes that if the Reformed tradition could recover Calvin's conviction, it might find both relevance and relationship as it seeks to do justice for the poor and oppressed.[28]

The Reformed tradition has frequently demonstrated an arrogance that says we are right because God chose us. These "chosen" people have often been fearful of those who are not chosen. An antidote to this fear might be a more appropriate and humble sense of confidence rooted in God's grace. We may not have all the answers about the doctrine of election, but we trust God's intentions for the church and for the world. Perhaps if we recognized that the church is God's church, we would not always need to shore it up. We would have less need to preserve, protect, and defend the Reformed faith if we trusted that God will protect God's church.

Using the right armor to deal with fear means knowing and valuing our identity and history as Reformed Christians. We should not give up our Reformed emphases to win popular approval or find a quick fix for anxiety. But we also need to hold the past and even our identity somewhat loosely. When something new is created, we lose something from the past so that the new has room to take root and grow. Perhaps the loss of Protestant hegemony is something like that. Reformed churches have lost a dominant voice in American culture, but instead of perpetually grieving this loss of influence, they might try to discern what new opportunities await the church in the twenty-first century.

The current fear of terrorism demonstrates that even a superpower nation cannot always be in control, cannot always fix and manage, and cannot protect its citizens from every danger. Perhaps one gift the church might offer the world is a model for tolerating anxiety and fear in more productive ways. What if the congregations of the Reformed tradition could demonstrate compassion for and community with the Other? A commitment to justice. Less of a need to defend ourselves and our ideas. Openness to the fact that others might be right, even if they are different from us. A recognition that all people belong to God. We will never abolish fear completely because it is part of the human condition, but perhaps if we were less controlled by fear we could be motivated and shaped instead by the "good tidings of great joy" that are the center of the Christian faith.

2

GLORIOUS CREATION, BEAUTIFUL LAW

Serene Jones

God has so wonderfully adorned heaven and earth
with as unlimited abundance, variety, and beauty of all things
as could possibly be, quite like a spacious and splendid house,
provided and filled with the most exquisite
and at the same time most abundant furnishings.

Nothing could have been more perfect in beauty than
the government which God had exercised over the Israelites . . .
the order of things was so arranged that nothing better could be
    imagined.

—John Calvin

On the first day of class each spring, I ask students in my seminar on "Calvin and Reformed Theology" to list one or two themes that they believe mark Calvinist thought. Quickly, they realize how diverse this "reformed" heritage is, and how passionately people feel about it, in ways that are both negative and positive. Students blink, grin, or just shake their heads, as they hear classmates expound on brands of Calvinism that they didn't even realize exist, much less still claim lively adherents. Wearing everything from nose rings and torn-up jeans to paisley ties and spiked-heeled shoes, my students speak in an impressive variety of voices: women, men, North Americans, South Africans, Koreans, conservatives, liberals, third-generation Presbyterians, recent converts to the Vineyard, gays, straights, ordained ministers, resolutely antiordination laity, pious biblical literalists, equally pious biblical illiterates—all of them ready to learn something about this eclectic tradition they claim as their own.

Despite their personal diversity, however, their list of Calvinist topics is usually quite predictable. Early in the discussion, the theological issues of *sola scriptura* and the *sovereignty of God* are raised up. These are quickly followed by topics of *original sin* and *total depravity*, subjects that typically elicit either jokes or a quick tale about why someone left the church. With these terms on the table, the list then turns to that ever-famous doctrine *double-predestination,* a topic that, like sin, immediately provokes either nods of approval or shivers of disgust, sometimes both in a single person. At this point in the discussion, almost like clockwork, someone brings up the execution of Servetus in Geneva and Calvin's supposed attempt to build a Swiss theocracy. There is usually a silence after these comments, but if we are lucky, the discussion continues. If one of the last students is well versed in Calvin's theology, we are treated to a summary of *justification* and *sanctification* or even better, a recital of God's almighty *providential rule*, that sturdy bulwark of Calvinist piety.

It is always striking, however, that this predictable list of themes almost invariably fails to include two doctrines that Reformed Christians have long considered foundational: *creation*, the vast, living world that God has created and continues to sustain; and *law*, God's intentions for the right-ordering of that world. That these are important themes can hardly be disputed. In his major life's work, *The Institutes of the Christian Religion*, Calvin starts off the whole theological enterprise with an extended treatment of "knowledge of God the Creator," a discussion whose length and depth far surpass that of either double-predestination or total depravity.[1] Similarly, at the center of Calvin's reflections on "knowledge of God the Redeemer," we find over a hundred pages of material devoted to the law, a topic that receives more attention than gospel and provides the theological core of the doctrines of sanctification and justification. In Calvin's thought, the two doctrines are also importantly linked. In short, creation describes God's gift of life in all its complex fullness and beauty, and the law refers to God's perfect guide to how that life might be lived most fully and wonderfully. When paired in this way, they stand together like support beams that hold up and give framing shape to the larger, more elaborate structure of his theological house.[2]

In this chapter, I look at both themes and describe why I believe they are so important to feminist remappings of our Reformed traditions. I argue that they are not only doctrines we cannot live without, they are doctrines that offer amazingly fresh resources for today's churches. To see this, consider the core issues at stake in each. When we theologically engage *creation*, we are wrestling with our fundamental beliefs about the broad created world we inhabit and the nature of our humanity. We ask theological questions like, Who and what are we as creatures of God? How should we understand the complex life system in which we find ourselves? For feminist theologians, no questions have prompted more discussion than those about human nature and its relation to our worldly existence. Most often, our queries have taken the following forms: What does it mean to say someone is a "woman" or a "man"? Do these identities point to irrevocable differences in our fundamental nature, or are they a product of nurture? How do we think about our bodies and our relation to the biosphere, to human history, and to all that comprises the social and natural world in which we dwell?

Consider, too, the topic of *law*. Theologically, it concerns our deepest convictions about how we should arrange our collective and private lives so that they reflect God's will for the flourishing of creation.[3] This leads us to think about the legal rules that regulate our communities as well as all those law-like cultural practices that determine how we go about our daily affairs. What sort of political, economic, and cultural structures should we adopt as a society, a church, a neighborhood, a family, and as individual persons? What laws should we live by, both internally and externally? Feminist theologians ask, in particular, How should we organize our social worlds so that women (and all people) are not oppressed but flourish? What economic, political, and social structures and laws need to be in place to ensure human and global well-being? What sort of rules might ensure fullness of life for all, including in that "all" the nonhuman world as well as the human?

These rather general comments on creation, law, and feminism may seem pretty abstract. But in fact we deal with them all the time, in very commonplace, obvious ways. As just one example, consider our heated cultural discussions of "the family." When the writers of this book first gathered to figure out the direction of our work together, we shared, at a personal and political level, an overwhelming sense that "home life" was becoming increasingly difficult to maintain and that our bodies and spirits were breaking down under the pressures we face. Even in the most feminist of households, we agreed that women who work full-time jobs (like us) still do the lion's share of domestic work, a fact confirmed by numerous studies of contemporary household labor patterns.[4] In addition, women tend to put a lot more energy into managing the emotional complexities of home life than our male companions and friends. As we wrestled with this, the themes of creation and law surfaced constantly. Are there "created" (natural) differences between men and women that make redistributing the work of "care"[5] difficult, if not impossible? Or do women do more of this kind of work not because of nature but because the social formation of gender, race, and class expectations around domestic labor begin at such an early age and are so persistent that it is hard to escape them? Is a single person a family? Is a group of friends? Why don't workplaces offer better policies and programs around child care and parental leave? Why aren't men rewarded more for domestic labor? Why is paid domestic work done disproportionately by women of color?[6] Why aren't nontraditional families afforded the same benefits as traditional ones? In all these ways questions about creation and law abound.

Many other practical examples of creation and law surfaced in our collective conversations as well. We discuss big topics like the challenges of globalization and the character of postcolonialism; the declining significance of nationhood and the future of capitalism; the nature of human sexuality and the ongoing struggle to think about race, ethnicity, and migration in critical and emancipatory ways. We also noted smaller, more personal places where these doctrines emerged, conversations about things like the loss of a beloved pet, the unexpected brain tricks of menopause, the joys of cooking eggplant, the devastation of breast cancer, the local politics of recycling. In all these contexts, assumptions about the relation between "nature" and "social rules" abound.

Creation and law concern the basic character of the world/humanity and the correct ordering of our social life together. It is hard to imagine two more salient topics for Reformed church people and feminists alike to discuss and debate. In the pages ahead, I bring these two conversations together in a manner that reflects their confluence in my own life and in the lives of many people who claim to be both feminist and Reformed. As far as my "Reformed sensitivities" are concerned, they are in many ways quite traditional. As a theologian, I have long valued the work of John Calvin, and I use him as a jumping-off point for rethinking creation and law.

As far as my definition of feminism is concerned, I agree strongly with Amy Pauw's claim that our understanding of what it means "to be a feminist" varies widely (and wonderfully so). At the heart of it, however, stand four convictions that are central to me as a theologian. First, I believe that God wants women to flourish as creatures equal in beauty, stature, and power to men. Second, only a faith that actively encourages this flourishing is worthy of the God who gifts us with life, love, and hope. Third, Reformed doctrines need to be both critiqued and treasured when it comes to the flourishing of women. As we all know, Christianity (including Calvinist traditions) has a long, ambivalent history in this regard, particularly when it comes to doctrines of creation and law. Fourth, it is clear to me that understanding both the oppression and flourishing of women involves not just looking at gender but also at the more intricate weave of dynamics, identities, and histories that makes all of us (men and women, together) who we are. As such, learning to think in theologically critical and creative ways about race, class, sexuality, ethnicity, geography, labor, education, health, and so on, is crucially important to the endeavor of faithful living.[7]

A BEAUTIFUL FAITH

As the diverse essays in this volume illustrate, there are many ways to explore a doctrine. In this chapter, I follow a course that might seem to many students rather unusual. I turn to creation and law and explore the *aesthetic* character of each doctrine. What do I mean by "aesthetic"? The short answer is this. To do aesthetic analysis is to engage in an examination of a topic's quality as beautiful or as appealing and tasteful. This exploration typically takes two distinctive forms. First, it explores at a philosophical or conceptual level the qualities that make something beautiful. Implicit is an analysis of the concept of beauty itself. What is Beauty? it asks. Second, aesthetic analysis also dissects at a more minute, detailed level what particular features of something—an idea, an object, a person—make it appealing (or not) to us. This second level of analysis focuses on the qualities of a given topic or object—its form, shape, texture, proportions, feel, sound, color, and so forth. In the case of something like "law" or "creation," for example, aesthetic analysis asks at the first, conceptual level, Is the law beautiful and if so, why? This analysis also involves asking, second, at the more detailed, particular level, What does creation look like when we see it in our mind's eye: what does it taste like; what colors appear when we hear the term; what memories do we associate with it; what kind of music does it play?

Doing this second level of analysis requires attending to the kind of affective responses—or better, the kind of desires—a given topic elicits in us. It asks, for instance, about our passion for law or creation. Do we find it attractive, desirable, and compelling? Or does it make us fearful or leave us indifferent? Asking about the desirability of a doctrine like law forces us to be aware of dense emotional reactions that the topic evokes in us, including reactions that are unconscious and nonideational. This awareness includes taking our bodies into account, for our feelings and our physical actions and reactions often tell us more about what we believe than do our openly expressed convictions. It also makes us aware that our affective desires are not one-dimensional but thickly layered and complex. We, as such, are prompted to reflect on the sources of these multilayered aesthetic judgments and reactions, those both conscious and not. Although it is quite possible that some of these reactions are hardwired into us, most of our feelings about "beauty" are formed by our culture. We learn them at home, in the media, at school, and on the street. We imbibe them in the language we are taught and in the bodily habits we are trained in from childhood on. As such, they are open to discussion and negotiation.

In my work as a theologian, I increasingly find aesthetic analysis a fruitful avenue of approach because it allows me to explore at a more complex level how Christian beliefs are formed; what they look like; how they feel; what they lead us to do; how they shape our bodies, our relationships, our sense of self, and our most fundamental grasp of God and the world. I first became interested in these things—the body, desire, relationality, the unconscious, form and materiality, feeling and emotion—through my work in feminist theory, an area of reflection that has long been interested in such topics. This interest is partly because these topics have traditionally been labeled "feminine concerns" (as opposed to supposedly "masculine concerns" such as "reason"), and partly because the oppressions that women suffer often take place in these realms; the harms we experience are often emotional and unconscious and involve twisted desires as much as obvious prejudices and conscious choices. It is through the work of feminist theory, for example, that I became aware of the degree to which my understanding of gender, race, class, sexuality, and so many other things was shaped by the verbal and written language I had been taught to speak since childhood as well as media images and music I had learned to enjoy since I was young. Feminist theory also helped me to see that if we were to begin shifting our views of things like gender, it would have to be here, at a broad cultural level where our unconscious and conscious desires are formed, as much as at the level of rational arguments and policy discussions. Thus, as a feminist with a pragmatic interest in social change, I found the aesthetic avenue of approach helpful because it required taking seriously the concrete practices, cultural patterns, and communal actions—and not just the reasoned ideas—that make us who we are.

Combining all these interests, I find the approach of *feminist theological aesthetics* useful because it insists that what we *do* is profoundly affected by what we *desire*, and that what we desire is deeply determined by our perceptions of what is *beautiful*. When I apply these insights to my study of doctrines like creation and law, my bedrock theological questions are, How do our beliefs about these two topics shape our imaginations and our desires? What kinds of people do these doctrines make us? In asking these questions, I find it helpful to think of "doctrines" as a core component of the cultural training that Christians undergo in the church. Through doctrines, we learn habits of thought and body that shape not only what we rationally think about God but also what we desire and find beautiful with respect to the Divine. Faith is complex and includes multiple desires, loves, dispositions, feelings, and affects: its aesthetic texture is thickly layered. Doctrines play an important role in this layering insofar as different doctrines nurture different dispositions and plays of mind. It is only in their mix that one gets a full picture of the faith-formed self and community. This is particularly true, I will show, with respect to creation and law and their aesthetic interplay with gender, race, class, and so on.

Calvin and the Beauty of God

It is not an accident, given these feminist and theological sensibilities about aesthetics, that I find the theology of John Calvin so appealing.[8] Calvin understood the task of theology to be not just rational reflection but also aesthetic formation: it shapes our desires and imaginations as much as convincing our minds. Although he never directly uses the term *aesthetics*, it is what he refers to when he states that good theology moves "our heart."[9] Accordingly, when Calvin writes about creation and law, he uses richly poetic language designed to make us see and feel certain things—he wants us to be moved and shaped by these realities. Moreover, as he writes about them, he frequently tells his reader exactly what kind of effect they should be having on us: they should make us confident, uncertain, angry, embarrassed, secure, accepting, open, and judgmental, to name only a few of the dispositions he describes. He also describes the plays of mind they should invoke and the forms of life they might encourage, and he insists that not all doctrines will cultivate the same dispositions. It is only through the complex interweaving of theology's many doctrines that we get a picture of full-formed Christian life.

At a more profound level, Calvin believed that God is beautiful. The word he uses to capture this divine beauty is *glory*. Throughout the *Institutes* he asks us again and again to ponder the glory of God, an image with vast and sensual evocations. God's beauty captivates us; its aesthetic power is completely enthralling. We are called, as believers, to desire God with all that we are.

As Calvin further unpacks this image of God's glory, however, his account is not quite what one might expect. What about God is so glorious? It is not primarily God's majesty or the infinite scope of God's knowledge or power—the things we normally associate with divinity.[10] According to Calvin, what we discover at the epicenter of this radiating glory is a God who deigns to be *for us* (*pro nobis*). God's glory thus resides in God's decision to create us, to remain interested in our lives, to seek our good, and to offer us what we need to flourish. What is most remarkable about this Divine decision to create, Calvin insists, is that God does not do it out of any necessity or sense of compulsion; it is a free, completely gratuitous act. God does it simply because God desires to do so. Calvin further tells us that this generous, beneficent glory is made known to us primarily in God's *work* on our behalf; we behold it when we see what God's hands and feet are doing for us in the world and in our lives.[11]

The Glory of Creation and Law

What more powerful instances of this work are there than creation and law, God's dual acts of creating us and of giving us guides by which to live and flourish? Moreover, these beneficial acts are not just *good* for us—according to Calvin, they are stunningly *beautiful* to behold. The acts of creating and law giving are works of art, crafted by God, the master Artist, to persuade and please us. In contemporary parlance, they are like award-winning video dramas that illustrate God's love in a manner that moves and persuades us. Note that in this description creation and law are not static, finished objects; they are acts, or better, motion pictures. Moreover, unlike most movies that we see, these acts tell the story of our own lives, stories of God with us in ways both personal and cosmic.

Calvin uses different words to describe what we experience when beholding God in these acts—terms like *reverence, trust, thanksgiving,* and *praise*—all of which he collectively labels "true piety" or "faith."[12] Here again, aesthetic language surfaces. To have faith is to be passionately drawn to a Divine reality that you are persuaded is beautiful and that you desire to be near and even to dwell within. Faith is more of an embodied, affective form of knowledge than a calculated knowledge resulting from careful, rational assessments of God. The fear it evokes is one of wonder and joyful awe, not servile cringing. Calvin further describes how the dispositions this beautiful God creates in us cause us not just to feel but to *act* in particular ways. Again, this beautiful faith is inescapably a practiced, lived faith.

In sum creation and law are "the theater of God's glory," one of Calvin's favored images.[13] They are compellingly beautiful performances of Divine mercy and goodness that nurture feelings of gratitude, praise, and exuberant hope. Beholding them thus causes us to have faith, to love God, to see the world (creation) as a gift, and to engage our neighbors and environs as delightful and pleasurable places in which God's rules (law) should reign. From a feminist perspective, viewing them from this angle is exciting and promising, because it places part of the weight of the doctrines' meaning in the uses to which they are put and the forms of life they encourage.[14] In this regard, the doctrines of creation and law are imaginative dramas that not only shape the way we view the world but also the kind of people we become. Caught in the grasp of their aesthetic power, we are formed by their beauty.

CAPACIOUS CREATION

As I just mentioned, Calvin's description of creation is "the theater of God's glory." In this theater, God "acts" by continually making, sustaining, and ordering the teeming world as a whole.[15] God is also acting through the activities of human thought, which include the insights of science, the wisdom of human government, the miracle of language, the complexities of history, and even more ephemeral realities like our dreams.[16] The entire expanse of time unfolds on this stage—all our comings and goings are fashioned and displayed here, not only those events that we celebrate and remember but also those tragedies and harms that haunt us and sometimes escape our memory. This theater is, in fact, so enormous that every dimension of our lives exists within its walls.[17]

Creation is not only a theater but *the dwelling place* of our lives: it is the vast and open but also contained space in which we exist, the home in which our lives unfold, the world in which we move.[18] It is also the space in which God dwells with us and we, with God. These images resonate well with Calvin's own. Throughout the *Institutes*, he repeatedly describes God's creation as a realm or a provenance or a kingdom, emphasizing the territorial character of God's relation to the world. Existence is figured as a land—large and complex terrain—completely surrounded and inspired by the Divine who, as the sovereign Lord, not only owns and rules it but also made it and continues to live within it.

As a feminist theologian, I find it helpful to add to Calvin's geographic, spatial images some images of God holding or embracing or even better, enveloping the world, images that capture a sense of fecund containment and fluid co/indwelling. In the Christian tradition, theologians have often used the images of the mother's body—womb and breasts and arms—to capture this, the feminine corpus representing materiality, origination, body, fluid containment, and sustenance.[19] Creation is pictured as not only woven together in God but also continually nurtured and fed in the space of the maternal Divine.[20] Calvin uses similar imagery in his comment on Isaiah 49:15: God "did not satisfy himself with proposing the example of a father . . . but in order to express his very strong affection, he chose to liken himself to a mother, and calls [the people of Israel] not merely 'children,' but the fruit of the womb, towards which there is usually a warmer affection."[21] Interestingly, Calvin also uses womblike language to depict God's dwelling within us; for him, our knowledge of God is a Divine seed that God implants in our viscera or more literally, our innards or wombs.[22] God envelops us and we, in turn, envelop God.

These metaphors are intriguing from a feminist perspective not just because they refer to women's bodies (in sometimes highly problematic ways) but because they allow us to think in more complicated and richer ways about the creative character of God's relation to the world as its creator. On the one hand, these images allow us to maintain some of the tradition's more important claims about creation. In the context of these images, we can affirm that the world is a treasured *gift* of God, and as such, an *extrinsically dependent reality*. It would not exist apart from God's constant will to make it so. Further, these images insist that we view creation not as an extension of God or a part of God's body but as a reality that is truly *different* from the Divine and yet loved and held in its distinction.[23] These features of the doctrine of creation—the giftedness of life, the dependent relational character of our existence, and the affirmation of radical difference—are crucial from a feminist perspective.

In the Reformed tradition, however, there has also been a tendency to emphasize these features of God's work as creator by portraying the relation between God and the world in legal, contractual terms—as a covenant between two wholly distinct parties. While this image rightly helps us see that the creator and the creation are not identical, it risks stating the difference in such stark terms that the intimacy of God's relation to world is obscured. God is figured primarily as an overlord or owner whose relation to his serfs or workers is mediated by a set of rules that are to be obeyed.

In the maternal metaphor, this relation looks very different. Like the contract metaphor, difference is maintained—but between the two, there is a constant exchange of fluid and blood across the boundaries dividing them. In this regard, there is indwelling in the midst of distinction, albeit one in which the life inside the womb and at the breast is clearly extrinsically dependent on the stronger creative will of the mother.

Moreover, in this feminist image, the fluid movement between the two is conceived of as a material exchange; bodies indwell; their borders are porous. In contrast, contractual images tend to depict Divine-human exchanges as nonembodied and not touching, making it appear as if the world and God primarily relate to each other as two distanced, speaking subjects. In the image of the world in God's womb or at her breast, difference is both established and engaged through substantial, enfleshed interactions. Here, embodiment is not eschewed as just an accidental side effect of being a creature, as it has sometimes been imagined in more legalistic versions of Reformed thought. Instead, the body becomes the place of the Divine-human co-dwelling. Here, of course, one cannot help but reflect on the nature of Christ's incarnation and what that tells us about the character of Divine indwelling.

Creation as the Space of the Imaginary

Although Calvin does not linger long on images of the maternal body, its usefulness as a metaphor for God's creative work is clear. I have been helped to see this by the work of feminist theorists who, using language more poetic than biological, ask us to explore the imagistic richness of the mother-child relation, both in the womb and in early childhood development. In this idealized space, the child experiences a sense of open but snug containment, held as she is within the space of the mother's encompassing existence. Here, the line between the two bodies exists but is never clear; its borders are permeable. The task of attaining definition and distinction takes second place to the more primordial task of discovering the security of connection and embodied relationality. The self swims in the stability of belonging to a whole that precedes even the distinctions of selfhood. This open, containing space provides and nurtures the baseline pulse of the creature who will become self; it is the foundation upon which the self will grow. In the language of feminist theory, this place is sometimes poetically referred to as the space of the *imaginary*—the world of the unconscious where all experience resides in unspoken fullness, where distinction exists but in constantly shifting form, and where identity remains as indeterminate as it is inexhaustible.[24] To craft imaginations that can experience this space of fluid belonging as *belonging to God*—could that be what this doctrine of creation is designed to do?

Viewed from this perspective, the work of this doctrine is not primarily to teach us right and wrong, up and down, good and bad. It is, instead, to nurture our primal sense of life in God and its totalizing, all-encompassing scope. Just as the mother's body provides the metaphoric space of our most primitive instincts about existence, so too, God's performed acts of creation teach us to feel the pulsating rhythms of God-given life. These rhythms don't reverberate just through the good, beautiful things that happen in our lives. They reverberate as well through the work of convention and culture and through our traumas, our nastiest of desires, and our most unsatisfied of wants.

The Beauty and Horror of Creation

When Calvin is delineating the scope of creation, he shows no evaluative preference for what is "natural" over what is "cultural."[25] The ingenuity of human invention is as much a theater of glory as a tranquil lake or snow-covered mountaintop. Similarly, he insists that creation includes not only God's originating work but also God's ongoing, providential work. God is as active in our day-to-day life as God is at our birth and our death. Likewise, with respect to history and our broader planetary life, there is no privileged arena of Divine activity. God is there in all of it. In this broad view of creation, many of the classic dualisms we typically use to order our thoughts about the world are dismantled. Calvin's theology does not valorize, as privileged dwelling places of God the Creator, the organic over the inorganic, the complex over the simple, the well-ordered over the seemingly chaotic, the young over the old, the masculine over the feminine, or the material over the ideal, to name only a few of the distinctions it challenges. Creation, for him, simply refers to all that is. It is all being performed on the same glorious stage.

Calvin's broad description of creation includes not only what we typically think of as the glorious performances of human life at its best. Scenes of our suffering and sinning, the dramatic losses of our lives, and the horrible realities of our history are performed here, too. To make this point, Calvin offers his readers a painfully memorable description of God's providential work that includes a child starving because the mother's milk has dried up in her breasts.[26] As an image lifted up in the context of his doctrine of creation, Calvin uses it to show us that God is present everywhere, even in places we prefer not to see. In the vast dwelling space of planetary life, there is no nook or cranny from which God is separated, no realm of living that is not actively held in God's embrace. Even the barren womb and the empty breast—the abused woman's blackened eye, the AIDS-stricken teenager's red-spotted throat—are sites of Divine presence.[27] According to Calvin, God is there, performing the work of creation.

Over the centuries, interpreters of Calvin have balked time and again at his fierce insistence that God is actively (not passively or permissively) present in the horrifyingly ugly as well as the compellingly beautiful moments of our lives. From a feminist perspective, this insistence would seem to imply that God has somehow historically orchestrated the oppression of women, among many other things. If this is so, then the problems we confront with Calvin's theology are enormous. Is there any room for human agency in Calvin's doctrine of creation, or are we just puppets whose strings are pulled by a grand puppeteer who controls everything that transpires in this grotesquely glorious theater? Given these questions, it would seem that with respect to both human agency and Divine identity, feminist theology should reject this part of Calvin's doctrine and, in doing so, join countless others who have found this portion of the *Institutes* untenable.[28]

I have begun, however, to read Calvin's doctrine of creation differently by paying attention to two "aesthetic" aspects of the doctrine I previously overlooked. First, I have attended more carefully to Calvin's own account of the dispositions or character traits he wants this doctrine to cultivate, the kind of person he hopes will be shaped and compelled by the aesthetic power of his account. Second, I have tried harder to understand the aesthetic pull of the doctrine as a whole and in doing so have found the images of the maternal body and of dwelling place quite helpful. When viewed from these two angles, things began to look different.

Consider the dispositions he associates with the doctrine. When Calvin describes the horrors in which God participates as creator, he does not seem primarily interested in doing so in order to convince his readers that God's power is arbitrary or absolute. Quite to the contrary, he adumbrates the virtues of confidence and sturdy faith, not fear, when he tells us we should be comforted by the knowledge that God is present even when bad things happen. This knowledge should increase our "trust" in God's beneficence. Calvin seems to say that we rightly feel like helpless children because when one considers the sufferings of our world, we are in fact vulnerable, helpless creatures who nonetheless, and remarkably, belong to a vibrant, active, engaged God. When read this way, I discovered in Calvin a refreshing realism about the trepidations, harms, and tragedies of our daily and historical lives. The doctrine of creation was designed not as a context for making points about human agency and divine morality but rather as an imaginative context designed to fashion selves and communities who are capable of being faithful in the midst of painful, incomprehensible reality. Helplessness, vulnerability, belonging, trust, inclusion, wonder, and an empowering sense of acceptance—these are the feelings Calvin reaches for in his audience.

In contrast to this view, the doctrine of creation is usually conceived as a place where Christians go to learn the art of making solid, discerning judgments about the true nature of things. It delineates who we are as women and men; young and old; rich and poor; white, red, brown, and black; and so on.[29] Viewed from this perspective, the task of the doctrine is to provide a clearly readable map of the world and the place of our lives in it. I want to suggest, however, that from a feminist theological perspective there is wisdom in resisting the temptation to turn the doctrine of creation into a template for righteous living.

As most people who have lived in Reformed communities would agree, there has been a strong tendency in the tradition towards a kind of moral and aesthetic repulsion at the specter of unregulated or misdirected desires and the messy lives they create. This is as true in progressive churches as it is in conservative ones. We teach our children to make rigorously discerning judgments about forms of life that are correct and those that are not. Similarly, we repress or despise feelings or desires that are not "nice" and experiences that do not "fit" the supposed map of life we have learned to champion. One way to describe this restrictive dynamic aesthetically and spatially (territorially) is to think of it as our constant Reformed tendency to "exile" the undesirable. The good unfolds in space of God's action, and the bad exists beyond it, a position that dramatically calls into the question the sovereign reach of the Divine presence and love.

This dynamic becomes existentially problematic in individual and communal lives when horrific harms befall us or when we ourselves act on destructive "exiled" desires. When our lives slide off the hill of "righteousness" and tumble into the realm of the "unholy," whether by fault of our own or not, it is easy to envision its collapse as occurring outside the territory of God's creative presence. The power of Calvin's capacious doctrine of creation is that it will not allow us to see it this way; the realm of unholy is as much God's as is the holy, and the beauty of both realms resides not in their calculable order but in the sheer fact of their inclusive existence. His doctrine of creation crafts imaginations that can experience our *belonging to God* in all its complexities.

TURNING TO LAW

This reading of creation as "the imaginary" may seem discomforting because many of our best theological instincts are driven by our high-minded desire to map our worlds so that we can navigate their improvement. Feminist theologians want to create new structures for human flourishing. Does viewing creation in this capacious, nonjudgmental manner mean ironically that we should now exile this tendency towards righteous map making and world constructing?

I think not, and here, again, the insights of feminist theory suggest a provocative alternative. When the space of the maternal imaginary is explored in feminist theory, it is often positioned next to a series of poetic musings on the Father. Like the maternal, this space has its own aesthetic logic, one that is related to and relies on the feminine but nonetheless remains distinct. Here, the focus is not on the Father's enveloping body but on his language, his speaking, his rule-giving ordering function. In contrast to the child's fluid identification with the mother, the Father is encountered as decisively "other." He symbolizes difference and determination. His is the realm of the *symbolic*, the world of delineated thought and organized perception.[30] It is in relation to him that we learn to use words to create and manage our worlds, mastering the art of crafting forms and drawing borders. In all these ways, we become creatures who have experiences by virtue of our capacity to learn and apply rules. These rules make reality something we can possess and control. As such, the aesthetic space of the Father is the realm of signification, the arena in which we take on identities, become social agents, and are sent out to engage the world as morally responsibly actors.

While there are some features of this aesthetic of order that resonate with Calvin's doctrine of creation, the language of order appears more frequently in his discussion of the Torah, covenant, and law. This suggests to me that perhaps one way of interpreting the relation of creation and law in Reformed theology is to see them as spaces within which two very different but complementary dimensions of Christian identity are being fashioned. In the space of the first, the self experiences being held in the flow of an existence enveloped by God; in the second, the self become a God-following line drawer, a speaker, an actor, a contractual partner, a judged and judging participant in the social order. Both types of formation are needed in a full-formed faith; neither one necessarily precedes or displaces the other just as neither is inherently more natural or cultural. Both depend on learned habits of mind and practice, and both draw on cultivated, imagistic economies of meaning.

When we come to the topic of law, the language of sin abounds, insisting its presence into the theological imagination with a persistence not found in Calvin's doctrine of creation. According to Calvin, sin is an insidious and all-pervasive disease that robs humanity of the vision we need to see the glory of God displayed in creation. Falling upon us with vicious force, it blinds us to the beauty of the world and distorts our capacity to appreciate the splendor of the Divine's capacious indwelling. Caught in its grip, we blindly thrash about, destroying everything around us, disordering our world, our relationships, and most importantly, our love of God. Because of this, Calvin argues, God graciously finds other routes by which to communicate with us, avenues of connection that not only permit us to see the glory of God but also allow healing balm to flow toward this dread disease that plagues us. God does this by providing Holy Scripture to serve as "spectacles" or as the "lens of faith" that corrects our vision so that we can enjoy, once again, the theatrical display of creation. A central component of this scriptural witness is the law, a vehicle that God uses to correct our ways, return us to the path of righteousness, and point us towards the promised gift of human flourishing. In this regard, law is both the way back and the way forward into the doctrine of creation.

Defining Law

Calvin defines *law* in the following way:

> I understand by the word "Law," not only the Ten Commandments, which set forth a godly and righteous rule of living, but also the form of religion handed down by God through Moses . . . to remind them of the covenant made with their fathers, to which they are heirs.[31]

There are several features of this short definition (which Calvin spends many pages developing) that I find intriguing. First, consider how he describes the Ten Commandments. They "set forth a godly and righteous rule of living." Building on his earlier images of God's act being displayed before us in creation, Calvin here depicts the law in similar aesthetic terms—it "sets forth" God's rule-making performances. Stated this way, the law does not look primarily like a set of abstractly asserted standards for measuring right behavior but more like an exquisite, acclaimed portrait that presents to us a vision of the godly life. The law is an aesthetic space— a portrait of a life.

Second, note that Calvin does not limit the law to the Ten Commandments but broadens it to include "the form of religion handed down by God through Moses." What this suggests to me is that this portrait of Godly living is not just a picture of people who are precisely following the ten rules God has set out for us. Although it surely includes this, his picture of law is bigger, more all-encompassing. It portrays a whole way of life—a religion, as he calls it—which includes not just our expressed actions but our beliefs, attitudes, desires, and feelings as well. It refers to everything we would include under the rubrics of "the life of faith," albeit this time viewed from the perspective of the orders that structure us and not just our profound interconnection to all that exists in God. From a feminist perspective, this broadening is exciting because it beckons us to think ever more widely, creatively, and critically about the theological value of the social structures and cultural rules that shape our lives, an endeavor that feminist theologians have long applauded.

Third, note that Calvin's definition makes it clear that the law is not just given to individuals; it is given to a group of people, a community of folks Calvin calls (in the patriarchal language of his day) "our fathers." By this he meant the ancient people of Israel as well as the communities of his own day who gathered to discuss and enact their covenant with God. From a feminist perspective, I appreciate this communal emphasis because it stops us from focusing solely on individual moral actions as the site of Divine directive (although it surely includes these) and turns our attention instead to the broader social order. It asks us to imagine a village, a realm, a nation, a world, going through the paces of a life ordered towards God. When the focus shifts in this way, it becomes important for contemporary people of faith to think with as much theological seriousness about such things as racism, poverty, and the structural challenges of sexism as about whether or not one's neighbor told a lie or one's daughter stole a bike. The law trains us to trace communal plays of mind and corporate patterns of actions as easily as we track the ins and outs of individual moral behavior—a task that feminists have wrestled with for years.

A fourth intriguing feature of Calvin's definition is his description of how we receive the law. He first insists that it is a gift of God—one of God's glorious acts of beneficent love—but he immediately adds that it is "handed down" to us through Moses as "heirs" of the covenant. Here, Calvin makes it clear that the law does not come to us like a rock thrown directly from God's heaven toward our heads. Rather, it is a mediated process. It comes to us through "Moses," the man Calvin believed wrote the Torah and whom Calvin describes as a crude speaker but a good story-teller and an artful accommodator.[32] I appreciate this emphasis in Calvin because it makes clear that rules of faith that regulate our lives always come in concrete human forms that are mediated socially and formed in the space of our everyday human interactions. They are, no doubt, gifts from God, but the specific shape they take in our lives depends on the form they are given in the culture where they rule. Again, from a feminist perspective, Calvin offers us permission to take seriously the culturally mediated dimensions of law's formation.

Law's Enticing Beauty

Beyond this definition of law, Calvin also offers a number of insights into the mechanism by which Torah works in our lives. The most striking of these is his insistence that law has the power to shape community not simply because someone in authority gives it that power—God or the religious authorities or even the weight of tradition—but because the people who accept it find that it is so beautiful they cannot help but adore it and seek to live within it. In other words, for Calvin, we should follow the law because it entices and compels us! As he puts it, the law "invites and attracts" through its "sweetness and delight."[33] It "kindles our desire" and "holds our minds." The sheer glory of the law makes us want it. Just as

Calvin portrays the created order as witnessing to the aesthetic, powerful attraction of God, so too, the law witnesses to God's will for the world via its power to entice and excite. As with creation, it shines forth the wonder of God's beneficent goodwill towards us.

As to what this beautiful form actually looks like, Calvin once again turns our attention to the works of God in the world. To see what law looks like, we must observe the kind of community it forms. Interestingly, when he describes that community, he highlights the affective desires that motivate it, not the strict patterns of morality that structure it. In other words, he gives us an aesthetic account of the law's communal order. He insists that its principal marks will be practices of praise and love of God and neighbor. As he states it, "to fulfill the law would be to attain to that goal of love so as to love God 'with all one's heart, all one's mind, all one's soul and all one's might.'"[34] He elaborates this further when he describes the state of conforming to the law as "blessedness," "happiness," "righteous living," "perfect joy," and "the perfect pattern of holiness." What the law strives for is the establishment of a particular kind of desiring community: one bound by covenant obligations that strives to embody the will of God as it is manifest in the passions of our hearts and the communal shapes of our love.

This attention to love as the defining desire of the law fits well with recent feminist attempts to expand our understanding of law beyond its usual association with the strict concept of justice. For many people who live in today's liberal democracies, the assumption is that justice—or the triumph of law—will be achieved when we establish social equilibrium or balance. This usually means ensuring an equal or fair distribution of goods in a community and a shared respect for universally acknowledged human rights.[35] Justice is achieved when people get what they deserve according to accepted social conventions. Mercy, on the other hand, is depicted as a gift that falls upon us undeserved, an act that exists precisely in its difference from distributive equality. Mercy thus occurs when justice is bypassed or overruled by an unjustified act of forgiveness.

Although Calvin is not opposed to expounding on a distributive view of Divine justice and its important relation to our human forms of distributive justice (a task he takes very seriously later in the *Institutes*), in book 2 the actual concept of "justice" plays little to no role in defining the content of law as it forms our lives. When it comes to fleshing out what communal life under the law actually looks like, he offers us broad and suggestive statements about the dispositions which form the life of faith. He doesn't delineate a set of prescriptions or commandments—a strict collection of "thou shoulds" and "thou should nots." Rather, he unfolds a set of guiding insights that are more affective than they are moralistic. As to what these guiding insights consist of, Calvin tells us that the content of the law is "grace." What does he mean by this? Here again, Calvin offers us rich resources for feminist reflection.

Justice and Mercy

In many forms of contemporary Protestant piety, there is an unexamined assumption that the relation between law and gospel is one of supplantation. According to this view, the law represents the set rules commanded by the God of the Old Testament, a God whose standards for human flourishing are so high that no one can meet them and whose subsequent wrath for our failure is eternally damning. In this view, the gospel is imaged, then, as the gentle mercy that is revealed to us in Jesus Christ who, despite our failure to live up to the law, offers us everlasting forgiveness and in doing so, trumps (or better, supersedes) the power of law to condemn. While this scenario may be popular among many folks who claim the Reformed heritage, nothing could be further from the position we find in the *Institutes*. For Calvin, the law is itself an act of Divine love, a benefit poured out *pro nobis* that we might know and embody the path of true flourishing; as such, law is itself a form of Divine grace. Furthermore, within the law we find God accomplishing both forgiveness of sin and the power for new life, both mercy and a form of just living. Thus, for Calvin, Christ does not replace, supplant, or override the law. Instead, Christ fully enacts it by becoming, in our midst, both a complete and full sacrifice and a perfect model of regenerate existence. In this existence Christ performs—in the purest and clearest form possible —the double grace that inspires and constitutes law.[36]

The Three Uses of the Law

Having offered a general definition of the law and its purpose, form, and goal, Calvin then gives his readers an account of three different ways in which the law can be used. To understand why Calvin finds it important to outline the "uses" of the law, recall that, according to his theology, the purpose of doctrine is not just to convey abstracted propositions about the divine but, more importantly, to build up the community of faith and to inspire and strengthen its life of worship and praise. The proper function of doctrine is to build piety; therefore, doctrine's truth is, for Calvin, measured in large part by its ability to achieve this practical goal towards which it aspires. When it comes to the law, it is not surprising that he makes the same claim. As a way of strengthening piety, the goal of the law is building just and merciful forms of social life, forms as beautiful as they are good and true.

In order that the law not be put to such bad or unfaithful uses—a fear that Calvin often had about the law—he describes three distinct ways in which the law should be properly deployed in community. The fact that each of these uses is so distinct suggests that Calvin appreciated the ability of theological doctrines to accomplish different things at different times in the Christian life. It also demonstrates Calvin's belief that one and the same doctrine might serve multiple functions at the *same time* and in the *same space* of a single community or an individual life. As to what piety actually consists of, however, these "three uses" suggest that Calvin believed a more complex answer is needed, one that takes into account the fact that we are complicated creatures, and that diverse dispositions of heart, attitudes of mind, and plays of imagination need to be invoked and woven together to form a self or a community capable of loving God truly. It is in the context of Calvin's discussion of the law's use that we see, at its best, his ability to craft aesthetically such a complex play of mind and affect.

The first use of the law is, for Calvin, its convicting or, better, its negative use. When we look at the moral codes that have been handed down through the law of Moses, we see how miserably we have failed to live up to them. In the shining light of the abundance promised to us in the law, we see by contrast how utterly devoid our own lives are of its glow because of our failure to enact its requirements. As Calvin states it,

> Because observance of the law is found in none of us, we are excluded from the promises of life, and fall back into the mere curse. . . . For since the teaching of the law is far above human capacity, a man may indeed view from afar the proffered promises, yet he cannot derive any benefit from them. . . . [F]rom the goodness of the promises he should better judge his own misery . . . so that we discern in the law only the most immediate death.[37]

When we witness the glory that could be ours if we fully embraced the law, we see by negative contrast how broken and distorted our reality actually is.

To depict this brokeness, Calvin returns again and again to metaphors related to vanity—the sin of not being able to see things for what they are because one is so invested in a distorted, vain depiction of what a beautiful human being is. A distorted aesthetic sensibility is thus one of the central features of our lawlessness. Building on this idea, he delineates the power of law's mirror to expose sin we do not want to see, sin hidden under the guise of propriety or buried deep in our hearts. In particular, he discusses covetousness—the sin of jealously desiring what others have, a form of competitive acquisitiveness—as sin that needs to be "dragged from its lair, else it destroy wretched man so secretly that he does not even feel its fatal stab."[38] With this example and others, he sets before his readers a whole host of sins which, in contemporary language, we might call "unconscious" sin—sin that dwells in the noncognitive corner of our unconscious and in our bodies. He also includes in this category sins that become so socially normalized and habitual that they cease to be visible as sin.

What is the effect of exposing these sins? As Calvin puts it, the law causes the faithful to see that they are "upheld by God's hand alone; that, naked and empty-handed, they flee to his mercy and repose entirely in it, hiding deep within it, and seizing upon it alone for righteousness and merit."[39] In short, the law in its first negative use causes sinners to see that they are "justified by grace alone through faith alone." The only truly pious response is thus gratitude and delight. Thus the law in its first use functions properly for Christians only when it becomes cause for celebration, not condemnation.

Having laid out the first use of law, Calvin then lays right next to it another use—what he calls its "public use." In this account of law, Calvin tells his reader that, for believers and unbelievers alike, the law can serve the broad social function of providing human communities with a general set of rules for the proper regulation of social order. These laws may not be understood as specifically religious, at least to a person who does not believe in God, but they still serve to ensure social stability. They do so partly by virtue of the threat of punishment that attends them. If they are not followed, our society tells us, there will be a price to pay. As Calvin states it, the law in this second use serves, "by fear of punishment to restrain certain men who are untouched by any care for what is just and right unless compelled by hearing the dire threats in the law."[40] In this way, the second use of law operates as a "halter to check the raging and otherwise limitlessly ranging lusts of flesh."[41]

Next to this civic account of the law Calvin then lays out his most famous account of law's proper function—a function often referred to simply as "the third use." Calling it the "principal use of the law," he describes it as follows: "The third and principal use, which pertains most closely to the proper purpose of the law, finds its place among believers in whose hearts the Spirit of God already lives and reigns."

The law is sweet. It gives us instruction on how to live righteously and well. In his now famous turn of phrase, Calvin also states that "[t]he Law is to the flesh like a whip is to an idle and balky ass, to arouse it to work."[42] The law "exhorts us to perfection." It serves as "a lamp to our feet, a light to our path." It points us towards our goal of "sweetness and delight." It teaches and directs us in the ways of God. It "forms us and prepares us for every good work."[43] The law provides the physical and mental structure within which we become who we are in Christ. In this third use the law is, in short, the form-giving mold out of which Christian existence emerges. By it, we are crafted into selves who "live in God."

CONCLUSION: DOUBLE-VISIONS

As these last words from Calvin let us see, however, the aesthetic power of his prose and his vision of a beautiful God are not without their costs, particularly from a feminist perspective. Under the auspices of attracting us to the law, he gives us images of whips and servitude, of goads against laziness and exhortations to obedience, of demanding masters and entice-ments to the sweetness of enslavement. For survivors of domestic violence, for women who still bear the wounds of chattel slavery on their backs, for the children whose lives are being worked away on the floors of distant factories, these words might not sound so wonderful or enticing. There is no hint of comfort in them, no promises of human flourishing. The prose feels harsh and demeaning. And it is. There is no way around it.

So what do we do with passages like this one . . . and all the many oth-ers in Calvin that I have rushed past in this exercise in feminist re-framing? At the end of this chapter, I have no easy, conclusive answer to offer. In a way, this whole book—in its collective wisdom and its fierce wrestling—is an attempt to answer this question. It is a question that each year, when I teach the Reformed tradition, my students and I are left with. I always hope that somehow, in the course of the semester, they have gained insight into Calvin, into the rhythms of their heritage, the paces of their faith, and com-plicated fullness of being a Christian in today's world. But if they are only left feeling happy and content with what they found here, then the class seems profoundly incomplete. If they have become a bit disoriented and restless, however, I feel our study was a worthy endeavor. I take this as a sign that by plunging into Calvin's texts and its theology, their views of God have shifted, their vision changed, their hearts' own beating slightly altered. But altered how?

When we gaze across the treasures and terrors of our tradition, looking for its core truth, what we behold is not a collection of theological "con-cepts" that magically resolve our quandaries or a fail-proof "principle" that fixes everything. Instead, I hope that we see the time-weathered spaces of thought and the deeply carved patterns of life to which we are heirs. A life? Its carved patterns? Its weathered spaces? Where does this get us?

Perhaps it should look like this: When we see visions of our sisters and brothers sleeping in overcrowded shelters, trembling in chattel pens, doz-ing off on assembly-line floors, and yes, even mindlessly riveted before TV car commercials after a double-duty workday—when these visions cross our mind's eye, our faith should cause us to focus on them in a certain way. Our understanding of the fluid capaciousness of creation should compel us not to turn away but to stand and witness it all, fully, to feel its embod-ied, blood-filled connection to our own lives and not be afraid. As we breathe in that reality, our bodily sense of the law should kindle in us a fiery desire to make it better, to free the captives, to pursue the path of human flourishing, and in all this, to revel in our ever-more-beautiful knowledge of God.

3

"EVER TO BE REFORMED ACCORDING TO THE WORD OF GOD"

Can the Scripture Principle Be Redeemed for Feminist Theology?

Dawn DeVries

If modern and postmodern theology in general are highly attentive to questions about theological method, then feminist and womanist theologies among them are no exception to the rule. How does a theological argument get off the ground, and by what criteria are we able to decide whether a particular theological account is more or less adequate? Feminist theologians have reflected deeply on these sorts of questions, and their proposals have challenged longstanding biases in androcentric theology. If one were to look at four elements included in almost any discussion of theological method—Scripture, tradition, reason, and experience—then one would discover that feminist theologians have made important contributions toward revising the conception of each of them.

Among the earliest writings of feminist theologians, one finds the effort to retrieve and reincorporate women's experience into accounts of all the major doctrines of the Christian faith. The conscious or unconscious omission of women's experience, they claimed, led to distorted and fundamentally inadequate theological expressions that did not represent at least half of the human race. As feminist theology continued to develop, however, the category of "women's experience" itself became problematic, since it implied a singularity, based on biology or a static notion of "women's nature," that could not be substantiated from the actual lived experience of women. While feminist theologians have not given up their concern to recover women's experience, they have arrived at far more nuanced accounts of what is meant by "women's experience."

Feminist theologians have also turned a critical eye on the concept of reason employed in classical theology. For androcentric theologians, "reason" often functions to subsume the concrete under the abstract, to divide the world into bifurcated schemes (male/female; culture/nature, etc.), and to propose so-called universal categories that actually serve to subjugate women and other oppressed groups. Feminist theologians found a natural affinity between their suspicion of classical theological appeals to reason and the critiques of modernist notions of rationality advanced by postmodernist theorists. Language, logic, and the process of thinking itself have all been scrutinized for their implicitly patriarchal or andocentric biases.

Scripture and tradition, too, have been the focus of an enormous amount of writing by feminist theologians, historians, and biblical scholars. Some of their work is devoted to recovering the history of women that has been suppressed both in the primary source material and in subsequent studies of it. Feminist biblical scholars have attempted to retrieve strands of the biblical traditions that are more helpful for women, and to expose the patriarchal values threaded throughout the biblical texts. Feminist biblical scholars have often engaged in an ideological critique of the canonical Christian Scriptures. Neither Scripture nor tradition can be trusted, they argue, as reliable disclosures of God or God's will for the world. As cultural goods produced almost exclusively by men, Scripture, creeds, dogmatic canons, and confessions are all saturated with the assumptions and the values of patriarchy, and thus only a critical reinterpretation of them can contribute to the struggle for women's full humanity.

Reformed theology from its earliest days has also been concerned about theological method. Like the other evangelicals of the sixteenth century, Reformed theologians attempted to purify the church from what they took to be its corrupt theology and practices by appealing to the gospel or Scripture as a critical norm, often against well-established traditions of the Roman Church. Further, Reformed theologians such as Calvin construed the most fundamental theological problem to be how one comes to a true knowledge of God.[1] For this reason, it was incumbent upon any good Reformed theologian or confession to give an account of the method by which one might come to have such a true and saving knowledge of God. While Reformed theologians acknowledged that reason and experience could be sources of insight about God and the self, they argued that, because of the corrupting influence of sin, these were always to be subordinated to the only sure source of knowledge—God's self-revelation in the Word.[2] Just where this Word is to be found, however, as we shall see, is not a simple matter to answer for the Reformed tradition as a whole. Nonetheless, Reformed theologians quite typically order the sources and norms mentioned above in a hierarchy in which "the Word" comes first, tradition second, and reason and experience third and fourth. Insofar as "the Word" comes to be closely associated with canonical Scripture, Reformed theology can reasonably be said to subscribe to the so-called formal principle of Protestantism—that correct doctrine and rules of conduct are to be determined *sola scriptura*, by Scripture alone.

If these brief introductory paragraphs set out a fair summary of the respective positions of feminist and Reformed theology regarding the sources and norms of theological discourse, there seems to emerge an immediate conflict between them. Feminist theologians tend to avoid hierarchies—even methodological ones. Thus the Reformed practice of ordering the various sources hierarchically under the Word is immediately suspect. In addition, feminist theologians insist that only a hermeneutics of suspicion is adequate to determining the meaning and use of Scripture and tradition for the contemporary church. Neither Scripture nor tradition is wholly trustworthy: both must be read critically in order to expose the patriarchal and androcentric elements in them, and to render fresh interpretations that are no longer harmful to women. But Reformed theology has traditionally looked to Scripture as precisely the one source and norm that does not need to be critically dismantled: *sola scriptura*! While Reformed and feminist theologians might be able to agree about the corruptibility of tradition and its need to be reformed, then, they appear to be opposed to each other on the question of Scripture's reliability as a norm by which tradition can be critiqued and reinterpreted. This poses a particularly difficult problem for the theologian who wishes to contribute to the handing on of Reformed tradition while at the same time embracing feminist commitments. Can the "Scripture principle" be saved for a Reformed feminist theologian? Or must we, on this point at least, force a choice between Reformed and feminist theology? That is the question that I would like to explore in this chapter.

My argument, in short, is that Reformed theology, with its historical and dynamic understanding of tradition, is well able to contribute something to the work of contemporary feminist theology; however, this is only true insofar as the "Scripture principle" is carefully defined so as to avoid one of the besetting sins of Reformed theology: namely, biblicism. In order to demonstrate this thesis, we must first consider how tradition has been defined by Reformed theologians and confessions, and how this concept of tradition relates to the so-called Scripture principle. Next, we must explore carefully how Reformed theologians understood the use of Scripture as a critical tool. Finally, we can then offer a Reformed/feminist reconstruction of the Scripture principle. If my argument is sound, then it is possible to be both Reformed and feminist in regard to questions of theological method.

ECCLESIA REFORMATA SEMPER REFORMANDA EST: THE REFORMED CONCEPT OF TRADITION

The Reformed among the evangelicals of the sixteenth century oversaw radical changes in the faith and practice of Christian churches in their territories. In Calvin's Geneva, for example, a carefully crafted set of ecclesiastical ordinances ordered the replacement of hierarchical episcopacy with a fourfold ordained ministry of pastors, doctors, elders, and deacons. The ordinances also called for a thoroughgoing reform of church life and the practices of piety among the laity. Attendance at sermons, frequent celebration of the Lord's Supper, and mandatory catechetical training of the city's children were prescribed, and deviation from these requirements could lead to censure from the consistory. In addition, a number of practices having to do with social welfare were explicitly demanded of the community, such as visitation of the sick or imprisoned, and provision of medical care and other support to the city's poor.[3] Conspicuously missing in the plan for evangelical life in Geneva were references to invocation and veneration of the saints, observance of regular fast days, penitential disciplines, and the like. These remnants of Roman piety were left behind with the adoption of the Reformed agenda for Geneva. The changes so achieved were radical and thoroughgoing—almost nothing remained as it was before.

What enabled such a revolutionary agenda to be adopted and executed in Geneva? While the probable causes are complex, surely one of the significant factors was the revised concept of tradition that was taken up in Reformed confessions and theology from the very beginning. Already in the Berne Theses (1528), for example, God's Word is set against human traditions, and traditions are said to be binding on believers only insofar as they are grounded in and commanded by God's Word.[4] Similarly, the Scots Confession (1560) states that "if the interpretation, determination, or sentence of any doctor, Kirk, or council, is contrary to the plain Word of God written in any other passage of the Scripture, it is a thing most certain that this is not the true understanding and meaning of the Holy Ghost, even if councils, realms, and nations have approved and received it."[5] In the Second Helvetic Confession (1561), Bullinger writes, "We reject human traditions, even if they be adorned with high-sounding titles, as though they were divine and apostolic, handed on to the Church by the living voice of the apostles, and, as it were, through the hands of apostolic men to succeeding bishops which, when compared with the Scriptures, disagree with them; and by their disagreement show that they are not apostolic at all."[6] The Westminster Confession of Faith (1647) sums up the Reformed confessional view of the authority of tradition succinctly: "All Synods or Councils since the Apostles' Times, whether general or particular, may err, and many have erred; Therefore they are not to be made the Rule of Faith or Practice, but to be used as a Help in both."[7] Dogmas, creeds, and long-standing church practices all must prove themselves by the Word, or else, found wanting, be reformed according to the Word.

In the 1559 edition of Calvin's *Institutes of the Christian Religion*, he, too, deals with the question of the relationship between Scripture and tradition in four chapters that have to do with the church's authority in defining articles of faith and practice (4.8–11). His argument, in short, is that the church's authority in these matters is always subordinated to the Word of

God—indeed, it could be said that the church's power to define doctrine finds its boundaries precisely in the authority of the Word.[8] What this means is that human traditions, even longstanding and revered traditions that have been sanctioned by churchly authority, are always subject to revision. No doctrine, no church practice is beyond criticism. As Jan Rohls has argued, the Reformed position on the relationship between Scripture and tradition amounts to a "fundamental relativization of tradition, and thus of creeds and dogma."[9]

Freed from constraint by binding traditions, radical reforms of church doctrine and life were possible in a way that they had not been before, and hence a saying came to be used as a shorthand description of Reformed churches: *ecclesia reformata semper reformanda est* (the Reformed church is always to be reformed). This view of tradition as open and subject to constant reform and revision, then, is a hallmark of Reformed theology from its earliest days. The measuring stick by which the church is to be reformed, however, is equally clear: only according to the Word of God does it discover its proper beliefs and practices. But what is meant by the expression "Word of God," and where is it to be sought? That is the next question we must examine closely.

SOLA SCRIPTURA: THE FORMAL PRINCIPLE OF PROTESTANTISM AND THE REFORM OF TRADITION

The actual expression *sola scriptura* cannot be found as such either in Calvin's writings or in the earliest Reformed confessions.[10] It seems to be a slogan coined later in order to sum up the Reformers' teaching on Scripture and tradition. Similarly, the idea that the *sola scriptura* is the "formal principle" of Protestantism, standing alongside the "material principle" *sola fide*, and that the Lutherans emphasized the latter while the Reformed placed more importance on the former, was an invention of nineteenth-century theology.[11] This did not prevent many theologians, including Karl Barth, from making grand claims about the importance of the so-called Scripture principle for the Reformed tradition. Barth goes so far as to call it "the article on which the church stands or falls"—a role reserved in the Lutheran tradition for the doctrine of justification by faith.[12] How did a phrase unknown to the first generation of Reformed theologians come to occupy such an important place in the Reformed imagination? That is a story that can be traced through the Reformed confessions themselves.

The earliest Reformed confession, Zwingli's Sixty-Seven Articles (1523), makes all of its criticisms of Roman Catholic doctrine and practice through reference to the gospel, whose sum is taken to be Jesus Christ. The criterion of reform is evangelical and christological, and Scripture is hardly mentioned.[13] But only a little over a decade later, the First Helvetic Confession explicitly identifies the Word of God with the "holy, divine, biblical Scripture."[14] Subsequent confessions tended to reinforce this identification of the Word with Scripture, and thus many of the later Reformed confessions take a particular interest in defining precisely which books are included in Scripture.[15] The question inevitably arose, On what grounds can one consider Scripture to be God's own Word? In answer to this question, the confessions proposed theories of inspiration, which increasingly come to be explicitly focused on the actual biblical words themselves. The Westminster Confession claims that the original Hebrew and Greek texts are the actual words of God. Later, the Helvetic Consensus Formula (1675) takes this one step further: even the vowel points of the Hebrew in the Masoretic text are understood to be divinely inspired.[16]

The earliest Reformed confessions, such as the Berne Theses, argued that the Christian church was "born of the Word of God."[17] For this reason, they rejected the idea that the church established the boundaries of the canon. The later confessions, therefore, developed theories as to how particular books came to be recognized as belonging to Holy Scripture. The biblical books, they argued, are self-authenticating—that is to say, the Scripture proves its own authority. This claim is always paired with the insistence that the Holy Spirit drives home the conviction that Scripture is God's Word through his "internal testimony."[18] If, however, the Scripture is to interpret itself, then it must be sufficiently clear, and hence the confessions go on to develop the doctrine of Scripture's clarity or perspicuity.[19] Finally, strong claims are made for the necessity of Scripture so understood: it is *infallible* (i.e., it will lead to no error when correctly interpreted), and it is *sufficient* (i.e., it contains all necessary truths for human salvation).

Calvin's 1559 *Institutes* presents much the same doctrine of Scripture, albeit without some of the technical vocabulary developed in the later confessions. Already in book 1, Calvin argues for the necessity of Scripture. Although God clearly manifests Godself in the created order and in human beings themselves, sin blinds them to this revelation. Only as the "spectacles" of Scripture are put on can humans rightly interpret God's self-revelation in the world and in human nature.[20] Humans will accept the corrective lenses of Scripture, however, only insofar as the Holy Spirit testifies to its truth and authority in their hearts.[21] Word and Spirit always go together. The correct interpretation of Scripture, however, is a matter that can present some difficulties, and in a later chapter of the *Institutes* Calvin outlines a process by which the church can best arrive at it. Individual interpretation, he argues, can never have the same authority as a collective hearing of the Word by the ministers of the church gathered together and invoking the assistance of the Holy Spirit. Indeed, it is this collective hearing of the Word that constitutes the true usefulness of councils or synods for the church.[22] While Calvin can speak of Scripture as the "oracles of God," which spring, as it were, from God's own mouth, he also repeatedly emphasizes the fact that Scripture has a *target* (*scopus*): namely, Jesus Christ who is the substance of the gospel and the mediator of salvation.[23] Scripture, then, is to be seen not so much as a sourcebook of information about many different subjects, but rather as the road map to Jesus Christ and all the benefits he confers on those whom God has chosen to save. In this sense, for Calvin, it is possible to distinguish between the Word of God and the words of Scripture.[24] One other point is worth mentioning about Calvin's doctrine of the Word: insofar as the Word points to or presents Jesus Christ, preaching is also the Word of God.[25] This assertion, too, tends to break the strict identification of the Word of God with Scripture alone.

Clearly Scripture holds a place of incomparable esteem in Reformed theology. No other text can be trusted to contain the measuring stick for reform according to the Word of God. But it is also clear that the Reformed understanding of the Word of God itself cannot always be said simply to equate the Word with the words of Scripture. In the earliest confessions, the doctrine of Scripture is not yet significantly developed, and the criterion of reform is seen as the Gospel. Insofar as they recognize that Scripture has a center or target, Reformed theologians make a relative distinction between the Scripture and the Word of God. In addition, the Reformed view of preaching as a sacrament of Christ's presence tends to expand the concept "Word of God" to embrace the present teaching of the church. At the same time, one can trace in Reformed theology the development of an increasingly narrow focus on the words of canonical Scripture—even down to the jots and tittles. In the twentieth century, Karl Barth and Emil Brunner both sought to free the tradition from such a narrow biblicism, and for this reason both of them were rejected as heterodox by the strictest advocates of Reformed orthodoxy.[26]

There seems to be a tension in the Reformed tradition, then, between an extended understanding of a "Word of God" that comes in several forms—preeminently in the person of Jesus Christ—and a restricted usage in which this "Word" is normally taken to denote the words of the Bible. While it may initially appear to be helpful to specify precisely the location of God's Word, in fact, historically speaking, just the opposite often proved to be true. Closer identification of the Word of God and the words of Scripture invited the temptation to use the Bible in precisely the way in which earlier theologians said it should not be used—as a general rulebook for Christian views on almost anything. To take but one example, the debate about the institution of slavery in the United States was carried out largely through a battle about the correct interpretation of Scripture. Both abolitionists and defenders of slavery claimed to have the Bible on their side. However, as historians look back on the debates today, it is clear to many that the defenders of slavery had the best of the exegetical arguments. Abolitionists were driven to argue not from the plain sense of the words of Scripture but rather from the "spirit" of Christ or the gospel, and such appeals were unconvincing to those who took the biblical words themselves as the Word of God.[27] Interpretation of the Bible, finally, was unable to decide the fate of chattel slavery in the United States, and a common consensus about what God's Word on this issue might be was arrived at not with hermeneutics but with cannons. What would have happened had there been a different understanding of what constituted God's "Word"? The ambivalence between the extended and the more restrictive usage of the descriptor "Word of God," then, may well lead us to question, Should the proper slogan for summarizing the criterion of reform have been *verbum divinum* and not *sola scriptura*?

NACH GOTTES WORT REFORMIERTE KIRCHE: A FEMINIST READING OF THE CRITERION OF REFORM

Feminist theologians, like Reformed theologians in the sixteenth century, have called for reform of church and society. There is fundamental agreement between these two theological movements on the status of tradition. Both see tradition as a human cultural product that is, accordingly, liable to error and corruption and thus in need of regular correction and reformulation.[28] While feminist theologians most often locate the root cause of this tendency to corruption in a patriarchal system that values male humans inordinately, Reformed theologians more typically speak of error and corruption as arising from human sinfulness that extends throughout the human race and in each person throughout all of one's faculties. The Reformed feminist theologian could certainly affirm that patriarchy and androcentrism are particular forms of human sinfulness that have given birth to bitter consequences for our life together. At the same time, insofar as she took seriously Reformed theology's conviction that humanity is totally incapable of overcoming its sinful alienation from God (often misleadingly called the doctrine of "total depravity"), a Reformed feminist theologian would never be tempted to argue that a world beyond patriarchy is possible without God's gracious action on our behalf. Further, she would be unlikely to believe that the eradication of patriarchy and androcentrism alone would be sufficient to reconcile humanity with God; human sinfulness breaks out in ever new forms whenever one form has been cut off.

Differences between feminist and Reformed theology also emerge on the question of the criterion of reform. Feminist theologians do not present a single answer to this question. Some appeal to a "canon within the canon" that authorizes doctrinal reforms, such as Rosemary Radford

Ruether's appeal to the "prophetic-liberating strand" within the Bible. Others appeal to originating events or precanonical traditions as evidence of a nonpatriarchal kind of Christianity. Elisabeth Schüssler Fiorenza's work can be read, at least in part, in this way.[29] Other feminist theologians take the present experience of women in church and society as the critical norm: whether a particular doctrinal construction contributes to women's release from the oppression of patriarchy and their reception of the possibilities of a fully human existence is the only significant question that, for them, needs to be asked. Still other sorts of feminist theologians broaden the criterion of present experience to include all humans, so that what contributes to "human flourishing" is taken to be correct doctrine. Another group of "eco-feminist" theologians might broaden the category even further and ask whether a doctrine contributes to the health of the planet. All of these appeals to experience require attention not just to individual, personal experiences, but also to empirical data that could corroborate claims about women's status in church and culture, the relative health and prosperity of the human race around the world, or the state of the terrestrial environment and its many inhabitants. Among those feminist theologians who have been most influenced by postmodernism, the matter of norms becomes even more difficult. Insofar as neither the human subject and its experiences, nor language (as used by Scripture and tradition), nor even reason itself are universal or stable entities, appeals to any of them as an authorizing norm would seem to be pointless or self-deluded. Yet insofar as they do not want to give in to a kind of nihilistic relativism, feminist theologians of this variety still try to define ad hoc and pragmatic norms, often derived from a postmodern "pastiche" of different theories appropriated in the service of particular political goals.

Reformed theology, on the contrary, from its inception and through the end of the twentieth century, continued to appeal to the "Word of God" as its primary authorizing norm. As we have seen, the definition of this term was not always one that was shared by all; but interestingly, both the "liberal" and the "conservative" poles of the spectrum of Reformed theologies wanted to appeal to it. Tradition can be a useful source and norm—indeed, we owe it our deference because of the deliberative collective process by which it was formed. But it is fallible. So, too, reason and experience: their value as critical norms is limited because they are human and therefore liable to the vitiating influence of sin. What makes the "Word of God" such a powerful norm for Reformed theology—indeed, a norm beyond human questioning—is precisely that it is understood to be something not human but divine.

Undoubtedly there will be critics of such a claim. Can humans not only receive but also apply a "Word" from God—a "Word" taken to come from beyond the natural passage of nature and history—as a critical norm? I certainly cannot anticipate all the possible objections to such a notion within the limits of this chapter. Many contemporary theologians would have difficulty with this idea because of what it implies both about God and about the humans who receive the "Word." Insofar as God is not conceived as a personal being but as the "ground of being" or "being itself" or "ultimate reality," to name but a few alternative conceptions, it is difficult to imagine how God could have a "Word" at all. Since humans only employ words within complex systems of usage or "language games," that "Word," even if it were to come to them, could have no objective otherness to the human "hearers" of it—no meaning that transcends the use to which it is put in one context or another. I will not be able to offer a comprehensive response to such criticisms in the following paragraphs. My goal is more modest. Specifically, I will attempt to lay out a way of understanding the classical Reformed appeal to the "Word of God" as the primary source and norm that could be embraced by a Christian feminist theologian.

The phrase "Word of God" is a metaphor; it points to the way in which God's activity comes into human consciousness.

The phrases "Hear the Word of the Lord" or "This is the Word of the Lord" are familiar ones, both from their use by the prophets in the Old Testament and by their regular liturgical use in Christian worship. In each case, words that have been spoken or read are said to be, contrary to immediate appearance, not human (or not *just* human) but divine words. But can God literally speak or formulate words? Even in classical theology, the metaphorical character of this claim is recognized. God is spirit, "without body, parts, or passions," and hence does not have the requisite physical equipment to produce speech.[30] God's "voice" is like God's "hands" or "mighty arm"—it is a way of describing a being in language we can understand, even though we know that the terms are strictly improper. Calvin called this kind of language "accommodated." It is language whose purpose is to communicate divine truth to finite minds. Scripture itself, Calvin argues, is an example of such an accommodation to human weakness. In it God "speaks" just as parents speak to their infants, in a kind of "baby-talk."[31]

If the metaphorical character of God's "Word" is not yet convincing, however, consider the claim of John 1:14: God's "Word" has taken on flesh and come to dwell among human beings. Jesus is the incarnation of God's Word. John Hick has argued that this claim can only be understood metaphorically, although the earliest expressions of it were intended to be literal. That is because there is no logically valid and religiously satisfying way of understanding the claim that someone is simultaneously both fully God and fully human. If, on the other hand, one considers the possibility that incarnation talk is metaphorical—that is, speech of the type that speaks of one thing in terms of another—it is rather easy to make sense of how the metaphor applies to Jesus. Hick writes,

> In the case of the metaphor of divine incarnation, what was lived out, made flesh, incarnated in the life of Jesus can be indicated in at least three ways. . . . (1) In so far as Jesus was doing God's will, God was acting through him on earth and was in this respect "incarnate" in Jesus' life; (2) In so far as Jesus was doing God's will he "incarnated" the ideal of human life lived in openness and response to God; (3) In so far as Jesus lived a life of self-giving love, or *agape*, he "incarnated" a love that is a finite reflection of the infinite divine love. The truth or the appropriateness of the metaphor depends upon its being literally true that Jesus lived in obedient response to the divine presence, and that he lived a life of unselfish love.[32]

In other words, Jesus' person was a revelation of the divine activity in the world, the divine will for human life, and the divine being whose nature is love. To speak of Jesus as the "Word of God" is to claim that in all that he says and does, he is an expression or self-manifestation of God.

The "Word of God," then, is a metaphorical way of speaking of revelation.[33] In revelation, human minds receive an impression of who God is and what God is doing—an impression evoked by God's own activity in presenting or manifesting Godself. Since God is being-in-act or pure activity, God is always and everywhere manifesting Godself. The world, in fact, is saturated with God's presence. Calvin spoke of the world as the "theater of God's glory" while Friedrich Schleiermacher preferred to see it as the "theater of redemption."[34] Both expressions nonetheless imply that throughout the created order God is revealing God's identity as creator and redeemer. This leads directly to the next proposition: God's "Word" comes in multiple forms.

God's "Word" comes in multiple forms.

Karl Barth contributed a great deal to revitalizing Reformed theology in the first half of the twentieth century with his doctrine of the "threefold form" of the Word of God: revealed in Jesus Christ, written in Scripture, and proclaimed in the church. Specifically, he attempted to break loose the strict equation between the Word of God and the words of Scripture that had come to dominate Reformed theology since the end of the seventeenth century.[35] Only Jesus Christ, God's revelation, can be truly identified or equated with God's Word. The Bible and church proclamation instead bear witness to God's past revelation and anticipate God's future revelation. Barth understands the Word of God as an event that occurs when and where God wills to speak. In fact, the Latin phrase *Deus dixit* becomes the shorthand in Barth's theology for the freedom and objectivity of God's self-revelation. The event of the Word always takes place as a result of divine initiative and activity.[36]

The three forms of the Word are those that the church is commissioned to use and to proclaim. This does not mean, however, that God does not speak elsewhere. In an oft-quoted passage, Barth claims, "God may speak to us through Russian Communism, a flute concerto, a blossoming shrub, or a dead dog."[37] In sovereign freedom, God can speak in many different forms. The church, however, is specifically commissioned to bear witness to the revelation it has received in Jesus Christ as attested in Scripture and made present again through God's power in the church's proclamation. For Barth, then, the Word of God can and does come in many forms.

There is, perhaps, a difficulty with this conceptual scheme. Even while it attempts to break the identification between God's Word and the words of the Bible, insofar as the only access that the church has to the revelation in Jesus Christ is the words of Scripture, the relationship between the various forms is circular. Both revelation and proclamation in a sense rest on the written testimony of the prophets and the apostles. Barth clearly does not wish to suggest that God is somehow bound by the human words of Scripture—indeed, he explicitly denies this. But with respect to humanity, a submission to Scripture is certainly required.[38] This has consequences for how the "Word of God" functions as a dogmatic norm or criterion: the church and its theologians are finally driven back to the Bible as the primary norm insofar as it is only through canonical Scripture that the event of God's Word can take place for Christians. It would take a substantial book to analyze the way Barth himself actually makes use of Scripture normatively in *Church Dogmatics*. I will risk saying here, however, that at least in some places, it is difficult to see, finally, how Barth's actual appeal to Scripture as a norm differs from the Reformed Orthodox theologians from whom he wished to distinguish himself.[39]

While I finally agree with Barth that we need a criterion by which to discern the event of God's Word, I want to suggest that theologians who appeal to the Word of God as a primary norm need to pay attention even to forms of the Word beyond the three that he privileges. If the entire created order is in some sense a manifestation of the being and activity of God, then God's Word "speaks," as it were, even in the language of the natural and social sciences or the arts. Insofar as the theologian attempts to make the language of faith comprehensible within the intellectual milieu of a particular culture, she will need to attend to the broadest range of forms of God's Word. For this reason, the Reformed feminist theologian need have no scruples about freely making use of insights gained from outside the words of the Bible as further indications of God's self-manifestation, and these extrabiblical forms of the Word may even lead to revised understandings and applications of the biblical words.

> **Canonical Scripture is not so much a form of God's Word,
> as rather the means of grace through which God's Word
> is ever and anew received in the Christian community.**

It was a mistake of Reformed theology in the past to identify too quickly and too thoroughly the Word of God and the Bible. The Word comes in many, many forms. But even Karl Barth, who did so much to break the easy association of the Word and the words of the Bible, did not go far enough. To speak of the canon as the "Word of God written" is to leave the door open to the alien whom one has driven out of the house.[40]

We can gain a clearer picture of how Scripture is related to "God's Word" if we consider the way it is actually used in Christian communities. Perhaps the most important—if for no other reason than for its frequency—is the regular use of canonical Scripture as the basis of Christian preaching. What happens in the "Word event" of preaching?[41] In Reformed churches, the process could be described as follows. After a prayer for the illumination of the Holy Spirit, a passage of Scripture is read aloud within the congregation. Then a person appointed to the task and presumably well prepared offers an interpretation and application of this text to the present context of the congregation. During the sermon, those present will hear or pick up on many different things, as anyone who has ever preached can testify. But among the many possible responses that one looks for in a Reformed church are surely the following: a powerful sense of the identity and presence of Christ; gratitude for God's abundant blessings; increased confidence in God's loving providence; intense awareness of one's moral failures; reassurance in the face of doubt or difficult circumstances; and challenge to act or to refrain from acting in certain ways. In all of these responses (and in the many other sorts of responses that are possible), the hearer has a sense of receiving the Word of God.

Presumably, the same experience could not be had sitting in an armchair at home all alone. The gathered congregation, the invocation of the Spirit, the public reading of Scripture, and the living voice of interpretation all go together in an act that resembles a sacrament. In sacraments, human elements consecrated to a special use by the power of the Holy Spirit are the means through which God's grace is communicated to the recipients. Similarly, in preaching, human elements (Bible, lector, preacher) consecrated to a special use by the power of the Holy Spirit (not only in the prayer of illumination, but also in the Spirit's inspiration of the authors of the biblical texts and the communities who gathered these texts together as the Christian canon) are the means through which the hearers receive the Word of God.[42]

Scripture, of course, is used in many other ways in Christian communities.[43] But it is in its liturgical use in preaching that the following claim is made: "This is the Word of the Lord." The uses of Scripture in education and formation presumably contribute a great deal to what is actually experienced in the preaching event. The richer and deeper one's understanding of biblical texts is, the fuller the range of responses one can have to new interpretations of it. More problematic for feminist theologians has been Scripture's use as a dogmatic criterion or norm. Single texts may be quoted as the justification for particular theological opinions that are offensive or harmful to women. And when these texts are questioned, the answer given is, "This is the Word of the Lord." Insofar as the Bible itself is not understood as the Word of God but as the primary *means of grace* through which the Christian community expects to receive the Word of God, a link in the chain of such facile theological arguments is broken.[44]

For the Christian theologian, God's self-revelation
in the person of Jesus is the primary form of the Word;
other forms will be recognized and received in relation to it.

This proposition is not intended to rule out the possibility that God's Word comes to some people quite apart from Jesus Christ. It claims, more specifically, that *Christians* are, by their own self-description, people who have found grace and truth in Jesus Christ—that is to say, they have been reconciled to God through their relationship to him. When Christians try to discover what God is "saying," therefore, they will always expect it to be consistent with what has already been "said" in Jesus Christ. For Reformed theology in its earliest days, this hermeneutical principle—the *scopus scripturae*—functioned as an important lens through which to understand the claim that Scripture "interprets itself." The whole Bible, both Old Testament and New Testament, was taken to have a central meaning that could be summed up as the gospel of Jesus Christ. If that was the central meaning of the book, then everything else contributed to that meaning. This led the older theologians to make some interpretative moves that most of us would be uncomfortable with today, such as discovering a Christology of the Old Testament. Nonetheless, the fundamental insight is a sound one, and it is relatively easier to apply consistently when one understands the Scripture sacramentally. If Jesus is the embodiment of God's Word, then one must look first to that revelation in order to read rightly whatever else can be found in the Bible. This is not to argue for a "canon within the canon." Presumably all the texts that the church has discovered to be effective means of grace can be trusted so to function in the future. Rather, the christological center simply orients the church as it expects a fresh disclosure of the Word.

A proposition such as this one may come as a critique of certain forms of feminist theology. Contemporary women's experience is simply *not* the equivalent to God's self-manifestation in Jesus Christ. Insofar as a feminist theologian wishes to remain a Christian, all other forms of the Word—even women's experience, which can also be a form of the Word!—must be oriented in relation to Christ. Pragmatic deliberations as to what "works" best for the flourishing of women, or humans, or the created order may well be entailed by a fresh hearing of the Word of God. But they are not in themselves sufficient criteria for establishing correct doctrine. At the same time, the *scopus scripturae* comes as a critique to Reformed theologians who wish to appeal to every word and sentence of the Bible as divine words, even when they appear to be directly contradictory to the Word in Christ. For the Christian, only Christ as he is known through the power of the Spirit can function as the criterion by which to discern God's Word in its many forms—even in its form as disclosed through Scripture.

Because the Bible functions primarily as a means of grace, Christian theology must treat the canon as open with regard to its normative significance for doctrine.

This proposition does not intend to suggest that new books would be added to the canon commonly recognized by Reformed churches. The point, rather, has to do with how the existing canon is used in formulating theological arguments. Among Reformed theologians who accept the doctrine of plenary inspiration, the temptation is always to use biblical texts as relatively separable units of information that can be appealed to in order to document or strengthen a particular theological argument.[45] But even theologians who account for Scripture's authority in a different way often treat the various texts within the canon as essentially similar texts to be interpreted and applied in similar ways. If, instead, we were to treat Scripture as a *means of grace*, then we can take seriously the way in which God's self-disclosure through it is sometimes used against its own words. Such an event does not occur in the privacy of a theologian's study. On the contrary, it is in the church's collective hearing of God's Word under the power of the Spirit that these often surprising reversals occur.

Perhaps an example will help to clarify. For hundreds of years, women were excluded from ordained ministry in all Reformed churches. The basis for this exclusion was the church's belief that it heard God's Word in such passages as 1 Corinthians 11:3–16; 1 Corinthians 14: 33–34; Ephesians 5:22–24; Colossians 3:18; 1 Timothy 2:11–15, among others. The General Assembly of the Presbyterian Church in the United States, for example, in 1832 sent a pastoral letter to the churches that said, "To teach and exhort, or to lead in prayer, in public and promiscuous assemblies, is clearly forbidden to women in the Holy Oracles."[46] But for many Reformed churches, including the Presbyterian Church, something new was heard in the twentieth century: namely, the radical claim of Galatians 3:28, that "in Christ" there is "neither male nor female." As churches collectively received this Word under the power of the Spirit, it caused them to look with new eyes at other parts of the Bible and to "hear" them differently. The gradual transformations that occurred as a result ultimately led many Reformed churches to do away with the ban on women's ordination. The canon itself never changed as to its contents, but the way in which it was interpreted and the relative authority given to various passages did change. Some passages, such as Galatians 3:28, were taken to have farther-reaching significance than previously recognized, and thus to have greater right to norm church doctrine than other passages, such as 1 Timothy 2:11–15. It seems to be a simple matter of historical fact, then, that what was once understood to have authorized a particular doctrine of the ministry no longer counted in the same way: the boundaries of the canon as a critical norm, in other words, had shifted. The canon was in fact treated as an open one.

For some theologians such shifts in the interpretation and theological use of Scripture would be seen as highly problematic. For the Reformed theologian, however, they should not be. The Word of God cannot be fully contained within a limited collection of books any more than it could be fully contained within the human flesh of Jesus of Nazareth.[47] Here it is appropriate to quote another slogan attributed to the Reformed: *finitum non capax infiniti*—the finite is not capable of the infinite (the point might have been better expressed, the finite cannot *contain,* or impose limits on, the infinite). The Word of God will always be bigger than the Bible, and bigger still than agreed-on interpretations of the Bible. That is why Reformed churches have put the regular preaching of the Word at the center of their common life. There is always the expectation that God will speak anew and that God's Word could come unexpectedly—as a surprise.

At this point we must also argue against attempts to fix forever a "canon within the canon." There are many ways in which this can be attempted. For an earlier generation of Lutheran theologians, it was through the application of the dialectic of law and gospel. For many theologians in the nineteenth century the appeal was to the historical Jesus. For some more recent liberal theologians who privilege a historical-critical approach to Scripture, it is through an appeal to the "earliest apostolic witness." And for some contemporary feminist theologians, the appeal may be to the original, non-patriarchal Jesus movement, or to the "prophetic-liberating strand" within the Bible.[48] The problem with all such moves is precisely that they close the canon. If God is the one who freely "speaks" through the human words of Scripture, then none of those human words can be ruled out *a priori* as a means of grace. And insofar as any of the biblical texts could so function to enable a fresh hearing of God's Word, it could also be taken up and used in a new way as a dogmatic criterion.

One might ask, then, why we should limit ourselves to the sixty-six books commonly recognized by Protestants as canonical Scripture. The canon-forming process took centuries, and many books hovered on the margins of the canon for all those years. Why not include some that were finally left out, or exclude some that were finally included? A complete answer to this question would take far more space than I have remaining in this chapter. A short answer, however, consistent with a Reformed view of tradition, might be as follows. The process of forming the canon in essence involved groups of Christians identifying those writings through which they reliably encountered a Word of God. Since the time in which the canon was officially determined, groups of Christians have continued regularly to encounter a Word of God in these texts. Presupposing that the Spirit of God is at work throughout the Christian community construed in its broadest sense, contemporary Christians—including those who are Reformed and feminist—have every reason to trust that precisely these texts will continue to work as means of grace, or as vehicles for conveying the Word of God.[49] Were they to substitute a different set of writings, however, the collective experience of the Christian community would no longer justify their confidence in the texts; that would have to be established in some other way. And the Reformed theologian, convinced of the ever present and powerful reality of sin, would be obliged to question the motives and justifications a small group of people could have for establishing a new sacred canon. The collective experience of the many, for Reformed theology, is always more reliable than the select experience of the few. Having said all this, however, we must acknowledge that not even all Christians share the same canon. And there is undoubtedly great usefulness in reading canonical texts in close connection with other texts contemporary to them. But in seeking for the "regular and ordinary" means of grace, Reformed feminist theologians need not go outside the accepted canon.

In German-speaking territories, the Reformed church was identified as the *nach Gottes Wort reformierte Kirche*—the church reformed according to the Word of God. As we have seen, by appealing to the Word of God as an authority above all human cultures and traditions, the Reformed were able to accommodate what amounted to revolutionary changes in their societies. This was not, however, because they were by nature antiauthoritarian and eager for revolution. On the contrary, their comfort with radical change sprang from radical trust in the power of God's Word.

In the same way, feminist theologians have been calling for radical transformations of culture and society for nearly fifty years. While great strides have been taken towards the goal of women's full equality in church and society, much yet remains to be done. Not all Christian feminists, and probably no post-Christian feminists, will find the understanding of Scripture and tradition sketched in this chapter to be helpful or persuasive. But for those who wish to remain in conversation with the Reformed confessional tradition, perhaps some of the obstacles are now removed. Feminist and Reformed theologians share a conviction that tradition is not a fixed and unchangeable body of truths received from our predecessors to be handed on intact, but rather a human cultural product that is always being reshaped through its transmission in new circumstances. Further, they agree that as a product of sinful or patriarchal humans, tradition demands critical correction.

I hope I have shown sufficiently, within the limits of this chapter, that the Reformed theologian's appeal to the Word of God as the criterion for reform in no way entails uncritical acceptance of the words of the Bible as the Word of God. On this point, too, feminist and Reformed theologians can agree: sometimes the words of the Bible themselves need to be criticized or even rejected. The doctrine of Scripture outlined above attempts to take account of the fact that Scripture as such has both oppressive and liberating power. When consecrated to a special use through the power of the Spirit, the Bible can be the regular and ordinary means through which God is revealed. But the Word is never enclosed within the words in such a way that it could be a human possession. Quoting Bible passages as "proofs" in theological arguments may not, and often does not, have anything at all to do with the Word of God.

In spite of the ever-present temptation to biblicism, then, the Reformed feminist theologian will not want to let go of the Word of God as the primary theological norm. Reliance on the power of the Word as the criterion of truth has enabled the most radical sorts of theological revisions in the past, and it can continue to do so in the future. Longstanding customs, widely accepted decisions, and even the words of commonly recognized holy books must bow to the authority of the one Word that is ever disclosing the meaning of ultimate reality for us.

4

SCANDALOUS PRESENCE

Incarnation and Trinity[1]

Cynthia L. Rigby

THE SCANDAL OF PARTICULARITY

Christian theologians are fond of speaking of "the scandal of particularity." By it, they mean God's radical entry into existence with us, known especially through the incarnation of God in the person of Jesus Christ. What makes the incarnation so scandalous is, first and foremost, that the last thing we expect from the omnipotent Creator is to be born as a baby, in a particular moment and place in time, to a particular woman named Mary. To lie in a manger wrapped in swaddling clothes certainly seems outrageous behavior for the One who measures the waters of the earth in the hollow of her hand.[2] And if we are scandalized by how the incarnation challenges our conceptions of *God*, our shock might only be deepened by what it says about *us*. For to take seriously the fundamental Christian conviction that "God is with us" also tells us something about ourselves that we might be reticent to acknowledge: namely, that all of us—with our creaturely limitations—are loved, claimed, and valued by God.

The "scandal of particularity" is sometimes misunderstood as highlighting the uniqueness of Jesus Christ over and against other would-be messiahs. But the phrase does not mean that Jesus is the "only way" to God. In some sense, in fact, it accomplishes quite the opposite of setting Christ apart from others. To be scandalized by the event of Jesus Christ is to recognize that the One who is *totaliter aliter* ("totally other") has entered fully into ordinary existence with us. God, in the person of Jesus Christ, is not then set apart in his humanity any more than any human being is set apart from any other. As Daphne Hampson well notes, a central tenet of the Christian faith is that Jesus is representative of, rather than the single exemplar of, an entire species. To think of Jesus as "one of a kind," in contrast to this, would be "equivalent to the claim that there was a single beetle."[3] If Jesus is not truly one of us, it makes no sense to claim that God is with us in and through him.

The scandal of particularity, then, has its finger on the pulse of the doctrine of the incarnation, pushing us to consider its implications for our lives in relationship to God. It also offers insight into the doctrine of the Trinity—into why it makes a difference that Christians know God not as a generic deity but in the relational particularity of God's being and acts. Just as it is scandalous that the One without whom nothing was made that was made lay crying in a manger, it is astounding that we are at liberty to address the infinite God as "Father."[4] And in the person of the Holy Spirit we learn that this God who is with us, who has invited us to intimate terms of address, has even *indwelled* us for the purpose of comforting,[5] interceding,[6] and guiding.[7]

Attention to the scandal of particularity as a way of understanding that "God is with us" inspires an approach to the doctrines of the incarnation and the Trinity that is at once both feminist and Reformed. It accomplishes this, in part, both by supporting and by drawing attention to concerns of both feminist and Reformed thinkers. Feminist theologians, committed to honoring the value of finite, creaturely existence and—correlatively—critical of docetic approaches[8] to Christology, may look through the lens of the scandal and honor the full humanity of the one who is fully divine. They may, similarly, appreciate the trinitarian teaching that God's acts reveal that God is "for us."[9] But these same theologians may rightly be concerned about the ways in which the particularities of Jesus Christ as well as the particularized, male references to the persons of the Trinity, have been used to establish hierarchies among human beings. Those with particularities thought to coincide more closely with Jesus have regrettably been seen as more human than those who bear fewer resemblances. Reference to the first person of the Trinity as "Father" has been used to preclude female imagery for God. Feminist theologians might, then, ask, How do we honor the particularities of Jesus, as well as the triune God's particular acts of self-revelation, in ways that honor all creatureliness in its differentiation and diversity? How does our confession that "God is with us" lead to the affirmation of all life, rather than the privileging of some at the expense of others?

Reformed theologians look to the scandal of particularity as a way of naming how the unknowable God is known to us. God is whomever and only whom God has determined Godself to be, and this God has revealed Godself in the person of Jesus Christ, known to us in the historical figure of Jesus of Nazareth. Reformed theologians might be concerned, however, that misappropriations of the scandal of particularity might lead to compromise on the matter of the divine aseity—the idea that God is self-derived, self-determined, and self-sufficient. To say that "God is with us" is not to say that God needs us in order to be God. While the full humanity of Jesus Christ reveals the humanity of God, this implies neither that God is only human nor that humanity is divine. While the acts of the triune God truly reveal God's being, this does not mean that the content of God's being is reduced to God's redemptive acts. Reformed theologians are attentive to how we speak about God's humanity and the concrete, historical character of God's acts without compromising on the divine sovereignty. For Reformed theologians, to embrace the reality that God has acted within the historical limits of space and time apart from recognizing that this same God is eternal—that is, is *not* confined by these limits—is to miss the scandal altogether. What is scandalous is not simply that God is human. Rather, what is scandalous is that the God who is human is at the same time the God who is beyond anything we can ask or think.

The remainder of this chapter is devoted to exploring, from a Reformed and feminist perspective, the implications of the scandalous message of the doctrines of incarnation and Trinity. In short, these doctrines teach us that God's presence with us not only reassures but also challenges, provoking transformation. To embrace God's scandalous presence is, then, to acknowledge that all our positions and efforts are at once both provisional and integral to the work of God. I make this argument, first, by recognizing the scandalous character of God's presence as it is made known to us in God's incarnate and triune self-disclosure. I then explain why and how we have resisted this scandal. Finally, I explore how reclaiming the scandalous presence of God opens us to new ways of seeing, thereby inviting us to change, inclusion, and justice.

RECOGNIZING THE SCANDAL

"God is with us." No Christian conviction is more fundamental than this. We celebrate it at Christmas, marveling that this particular baby, born of a peasant woman named Mary, is Immanuel. We remember it at Easter, testifying that nothing can compromise God's presence with us—not even death. We wrestle with the biblical texts and the stories of our lives, seeking to discern where and how, exactly, our ever-present God *is* present.

But the Christian conviction that God is with us has far from a spotless track record. Too often, convictions about God's presence have been used to endorse sinful human actions. In recent history, for example, German Christian soldiers killed the chosen people of God with the logo "*Gott mit uns*"—"God with us"—inscribed on their standard-issue belt buckles.[10] In recent years, Christian leaders in the United States continue to debate whether President Bush is remiss in claiming that "God is on our side" in relation to the declared war on Iraq.[11]

Certainly, the Reformed tradition is clear that God never abandons us, even in our sin. "In life and in death we belong to God," we confess.[12] The radical message of the gospel is that we are *not* left behind, despite appearances to the contrary. But, as feminist theologians consistently point out, we too often misapply God's persistent presence as endorsement of our own views and agendas. To say that God is with us does not mean we are, therefore, automatically in the right. God's job is neither to notarize our actions nor to serve as a trusted caddy who walks by our side, offering suggestions for how we can best make the shot. Rather, God is with us to challenge, question, shape, and transform us.

The idea that God's presence continues to create us is one that is shared by both Reformed and feminist thinkers. Reformed theologians have been fond of saying that the church is "Reformed and always being reformed, according to the Word of God." Eager to discern ever anew the dynamic work of the Word, they have wrestled again and again to articulate the relevance of the doctrines of the church, including the church's teachings about the incarnation and the Trinity.[13] Reformed theologians of the sixteenth century, far less apt than their twenty-first-century counterparts to embrace novel understandings of Christian doctrines, nevertheless believed that a return to classical understandings of the incarnation and the Trinity would lead to spiritual renewal. Feminist theologians are among those who are, as a whole, skeptical that a simple return to classical understandings will reawaken our sensitivity to theological themes such as the scandal of particularity. Still, feminist thinkers such as Rosemary Radford Ruether, Catherine Mowry LaCugna, Elizabeth A. Johnson, and Kathryn Tanner devote ample time and energy to exploring the classic Christian tradition in the hope of retrieving and reconstruing forgotten relics that might have a transformative impact. It is with a Reformed and feminist agenda in play, then, that I turn now to considering the doctrines of the incarnation and the Trinity with an eye toward discerning their relevance to our lives of faith today.

INCARNATION

I wear a sweatshirt around Christmastime that provokes reflection on the scandalous character of God's self-revelation. It pictures the nativity with the star of Bethlehem hanging above it. A single thought bubble extending from the site of the birth reads, "It's a GIRL!" People studying my sweatshirt don't know what to make of this. First they laugh. Then they look quizzical, concerned that I might be suggesting Jesus actually was a girl. Sometimes they comment on why it is funny to imagine Jesus as a girl. "If he had been female," one astute person remarked, "no one would have noticed when he gave up his life for the sake of others." Whatever the ruminations, the beauty of this sweatshirt image is that it provokes reflection on the particular details of the event: the census-frenzied town, the moment of exclamation, the sex of the child.

To many theologians of the early church, the idea that the omnipotent God would enter into the limits of creaturely existence was both untenable and offensive. Arius, for example, was deeply concerned that to see the knowable Jesus as "of the same substance" (*homoousios*) as the Father would be to compromise on the divine unknowability, and therefore on the very character of God. How would our understanding of God be affected by the claim that the one who is *homoousios* with the Father was formed through the gestational processes of a woman's body,[14] studied the trade of a carpenter, befriended unsuccessful fishermen and widows, and was executed as a criminal? If the historical figure of Jesus of Nazareth was thought to be fully divine, would not our understanding of God's immutable ("unchanging") character be severely compromised? How could we continue to say that God is impassible ("unaffected"), for example, while at the same time insisting that the one who is as much God as God the Father struggled in the Garden of Gethsemane and suffered on the cross?

Despite the sticky problems associated with claiming Jesus as fully divine, the *homoousios* was affirmed at the Council of Nicea (325) and the Council of Chalcedon (451). Lest the radical implications of this affirmation be buffered by downplaying Jesus' full participation in the human condition, Chalcedon also emphasized that Jesus Christ is *homoousios* with *us*. While those who drafted the Chalcedonian Statement could not articulate *how* the divinity and humanity existed as "two natures in [the] one person" of Jesus Christ, they did join in declaring that the two natures were united "without confusion and without change, without separation and without division."[15]

Why did these early theologians uphold that which they could not explain? A great deal was at stake, they believed, soteriologically. A unifying point in the debate over the *homoousios* was a common commitment to the truth of Gregory of Nazianzus's insight: "That which [is] not assumed [is] not healed, but that which is united to [the] Godhead is also saved."[16] Nazianzus's statement affirms both the crucial importance of God's entry into existence with us and our participation, as beloved creatures, in the divine life. It articulates why the union of the human and divine natures in the person of Jesus Christ matters to creaturely existence. Salvation is possible precisely because the Word was made flesh.[17] Jesus Christ is neither "God in disguise" nor merely the most exceptional human being who ever lived. He is, these early believers insisted, the fully divine one who is fully human and the fully human one who is fully divine. Because this is true, we may look to Jesus Christ and gain confidence both that God is with us and that we are with God.[18]

In more recent times, theologians such as Friedrich Schleiermacher and Daphne Hampson have questioned the brandishing of the Chalcedonian Statement as a means of promoting Jesus Christ's uniqueness.[19] Certainly, to evoke "fully human and fully divine" as a means of setting Jesus apart from all other human beings is to neglect the soteriological concerns that propelled the discussions of the early church, for it is not then our existence into which Jesus Christ entered. When Nazianzus's insight is used as an interpretive lens, however, the statement provokes a sense of wonderment that this very one who is fully divine is exactly like us as a fully human person. What is so incomprehensible about God's self-revelation is that God is known by us, even as we are known by God. What is so shocking about God's acts is that we are included in them. What is scandalous about God's presence is that it is known in real, everyday life—in all its frailty and glory.

TRINITY

A friend and pastor who serves a Unitarian church once asked me what difference it makes to confess that God is triune. After all, she explained, unitarians believe that God loves us and relates to us without making such a confession. I shared with her my conviction that to confess God as triune is simultaneously to make the audacious claim that we know the unknowable God truly because this God has made Godself known to us. Trinitarian faith does not first posit God's existence and then assert that this God loves. Rather, it recognizes that God loves and relates because God is loving and related. God's loving and relating are not only something God *does* but also who God really *is*. As Daniel Migliore puts it,

> The power of the triune God is not coercive but creative, sacrificial, and empowering love; and the glory of the triune God consists not in dominating others but in sharing life with others. In this sense, confession of the triune God is the only understanding of God that is appropriate to and consistent with the New Testament declaration that God is love (I John 4:8).[20]

The triune God's attempts to enter into relationship with us are not only for our benefit, then, but also (by God's own self-determination[21]) for the benefit of God, whose very existence is marked by mutuality rather than by control.

To confess God as "Father, Son, and Holy Spirit" is to bear witness to the fact that God has met us in particular moments, in particular ways. God the Father/Mother/Creator knew every day of our lives before we were ever born.[22] God the Son/Jesus Christ/Redeemer entered into existence with us and continues to represent us.[23] God the Holy Spirit/Sophia/Sanctifier guides us and sustains us, interceding on our behalf when we have no words of our own.[24]

To call upon the triune God, then, is itself an act of faith. It reveals our conviction that God has acted, and does act, in concrete moments of history. It bears witness to the utter freedom of God; the perfect correspondence between God in God's acts (economic Trinity) and God in God's being (immanent Trinity).[25] It boldly claims not only that God does things for us, but that God *is* for us. It immerses us, knee-deep, in the scandal of God's presence. It is the basis on which we recognize ourselves to be not only recipients of the divine benefits but also participants in the divine life.[26]

As in the case of the christological controversies, the trinitarian controversies were marked by debate about how to honor both God's unsearchable character and God's self-revelation in discrete moments and events of history. Concerns about revering the divine while recognizing the full entry of God into creaturely existence were operative at Nicea and Chalcedon. Similarly, concerns about compromising on neither the unity of the Godhead nor the equality of the trinitarian persons (*hypostases*) were raised in the East/West discussions at the Synod of Alexandria (362). The Cappadocians[27] were convinced that emphasis should be placed first on the distinct agency of the members of the Trinity, and then on the oneness, or the substance, of God. After all, they argued, we do not know God apart from God's concrete acts in history, so it makes sense to begin our God-talk from where God has met us. The Western position, later developed by Augustine, held that to begin with the discussion of the distinct acts of the Godhead was to risk compromising on the simplicity (or oneness) of God.

Catherine Mowry LaCugna, a feminist historical theologian, has argued persuasively that the Western tradition would do well to reappropriate an emphasis on divine personhood. Understanding God first as "one" and then as "three" presents God as a self-sufficient entity ("1") who only then does things for us ("3"), LaCugna explains. Beginning with the threeness—the personhood—of God, on the other hand, establishes community and relationality as primary. "All of existence," then, "is seen to derive from an absolutely personal principle," LaCugna argues.[28] "The shared life of all persons, whether human or divine, consists in the communion that arises out of genuine diversity among equals."[29]

While LaCugna has been rightly criticized for neglecting the nuances of Augustine's understanding,[30] her attention to the primacy of community and relationality in the life of the Godhead has been helpful in challenging us to rethink what impact God's scandalous presence should have on the way we live. To confess that God is triune is to know that God is *for* us in God's very being. To reflect God's triune image in relationship to one another, then, is not to lord over one another. To be God-like, when God is understood to be a community, is not to be self-sufficient but to live in relation.

To embrace the reality of who the triune God is, then, would mean everything would change. It would mean that societal structures committed to self-sufficiency and the accruing of power as a commodity would give way to life patterns characterized by mutuality and the sharing of power.[31] It would mean that we who confess "God with us" would be less focused on defending our "rightness," conscious that our identity does not rest in God's endorsement of our doctrine or actions but in God's claim on our lives. It is at this point of potential transformation that our resistance to the scandalous nature of God's presence is often most evident. But why is this the case?

RESISTING THE SCANDAL

The story of Moses and the burning bush (Exod. 3:1–15) offers a rich example of God's scandalous presence and our resistance to it. Moses hardly knows what to do with the fact that the God of Israel has chosen to speak with him out of a particular bush, giving him a particular mission. It seems almost as though he is looking beyond that bush, beyond that moment, beyond the particular details of the work he is being called on to engage. He is looking for some kind of universal answer, for something to ensure his safety and security, for a better handle on who God is. "Who shall I say sent me?" Moses asks. Relaying the name of God would certainly be more persuasive, he seems to think, than telling the story of the burning bush. Being able to perform a few signs, and having Aaron there to compensate for his stuttering, would again help direct attention away from the particularities of the situation and toward Moses' authority and "rightness."

"I am who I am," God says, "and I will be who I will be." With this response, it is clear that God is not satisfying Moses' desire by handing him a divine calling card. No "master key" to the divine reality is offered. Rather, God seems to be discouraging Moses from looking for answers beyond the particulars of the revelation itself. "I am who I am," God says. "I am speaking to you in this particular moment, from this particular burning bush, about a situation I want you to address in a particular way. Why look beyond what is right before your eyes in an attempt to gain more comprehensive insight into who I am? I will be who I will be."[32]

This reading of Exodus 3 hints that God scandalizes us in God's acts for at least three related reasons: first, because God really shows us who God is; second, because God is different than we expect God to be; and third, because we are different, in relationship to this God who is different, than we expect ourselves to be. The fact that God reveals Godself truly, as incarnate and triune, does not mean that what we see is *all* of who God is. But it does mean that the acts of God as Creator, Redeemer, and Sustainer are more than clues behind which stands the "true God," in all God's fullness. Unlike the wizard in *The Wizard of Oz*, there is no God "behind the curtain" who is other than the God revealed.[33] As Barth puts it, there is no "God behind God." God's acts reveal God's being.[34] The economic Trinity *is* the immanent Trinity.[35] To put energy into unmasking a "God behind God" is to miss out on knowing the God who is right before our eyes.

As the early shapers of the doctrines of the incarnation and the Trinity recognized, this God who is self-revealed is not always who we expect this God to be. Theologians have long argued that this frustrates us because it means a loss of our own power and control. With Peter, we expect our "right" confession that Jesus is "the Christ, the Son of the Living God" to mean that we will have the upper hand, not that we will enter with him into the way of the cross.[36] We reject the scandal, according to this logic, both because we are too prideful to be suffering servants and because we are offended by the idea that God would suffer in this way.[37]

Some theologians suggest an additional, and possibly a more fundamental, reason we resist the scandal of particularity. We resist, they argue, because we cannot bear grace. Paul Tillich reflects on the character of our resistance in a provocative sermon on Psalm 139. While most of us read this psalm and are reassured that God will never abandon us, Tillich reads it and is horrified that we can never escape God.[38] "Where can I go from your Spirit? Or where can I flee from your presence? If I ascend to heaven, you are there. If I make my bed in Sheol, you are there. If I take the wings of the morning and settle at the farthest limits of the sea, even there your hand will lead me, and your right hand shall hold me fast."[39] Tillich implies that the constant presence of the infinite God is unbearable to us because it challenges us to recognize our relative finitude. While living with this recognition no doubt entails checking our pride, Tillich suggests a far greater challenge is before us: to acknowledge this presence not as something that negates us as finite beings but as one who embraces us for who we are. Knowing we are accepted, as Tillich later wrote, means standing up to and living into God's uncompromising presence, God's unfathomable grace.[40]

But why, again, is it so difficult for us, in the words of Tillich, to "accept the fact that we are accepted"? Reflecting on the absurdity of the incarnation, Søren Kierkegaard addresses this question by exploring the category of "offense." He explains that, while we commonly imagine ourselves to be "offended" by God's scandalous presence because it seems to compromise on the divine majesty, our offense on behalf of God is actually only a cover for where our true resistance lies. What really offends us is not what the incarnation says about *God*, but what it says about *us*. To recognize the radical character of God's presence with us can only mean that we are valued, precious, and loved by God. Such an idea is offensive because we do not think of ourselves as loveable. Grace, when you come right up against it, is very difficult to bear.[41] With Moses, we wonder how it is that *we* could be chosen; that God has entered into existence with us and drawn us into the life and work of God.

In recent years, feminist and womanist theologians have gone even further in developing the idea that we resist the scandal because we cannot fathom our own value and loveability.[42] Valerie Saiving, Judith Plaskow,

Jacqueline Grant, Delores Williams, and Serene Jones are among those who have pointed out that women resist God's claim on their lives, not because they are too prideful to resign control. In contrast to men, women are less likely to deny their finitude than they are to acknowledge it so readily and completely that they will, in a sense, disintegrate in the face of the infinite God. Addressing this problem, feminist and womanist theologians insist that an authentic experience of grace is not something that furthers or perpetuates self-denigration. As Jones explains, feminist theologians emphasize the "transformative power" of grace, believing that "human beings can be converted, changed, redeemed, reborn, remade."[43] Encountering the God who meets them in particular moments and in particular ways affirms women's value and propels them to become active agents in relationship to the events of their lives.[44] Williams offers a compelling example of this phenomenon in her description of the transformation that has occurred for African American women when they have "encounter[ed] the sacred . . . in their visions." Recognizing God's particular claim on their lives, Williams explains, has historically led African American women to be "liberat[ed] from 'unworthiness' . . . to a state of 'somebodiness.'"[45]

THE SHAPE OF OUR RESISTANCE

Our resistance to the scandal takes many forms. Let me briefly discuss three that are of particular concern to Reformed and feminist theologians. First, we universalize the particularities of Jesus Christ, using them to establish that those with certain particularities should be privileged over those with others. Second, we marvel at the *acts* of God without really believing they reveal God's self to us. And third, we reduce God's eternal being to God's redemptive acts, as if what we see is all of who God is.

It is an unfortunate historical reality that people have always tried to capitalize on Jesus Christ's particularities *by using them to privilege certain particularities over others.* It has even been true, at times, that groups of people with certain particularities have projected these onto Christ, simply for the purpose of pointing to Jesus' particularities as justification for lording over others. This was the case, for example, in Nazi Germany, when Jesus was portrayed with blond hair and blue eyes—an exemplary specimen of the Aryan race. Tragically, it was those whose eyes, hair, and skin more closely resembled those of the historical Jesus who were murdered in the name of God's presence.

Jesus' sex is the particularity most often used to justify privileging some over others. When Rosemary Radford Ruether asked, "Can a Male Savior Save Women?"[46] she was responding to the formation and teaching she received in the church. Every Sunday she would go to mass and see a priest before her, celebrating the Eucharist. The priest was always male. The explanation given to her, which is also the official position of the Roman Catholic Church today, is that women cannot be priests because they do not "bear physical resemblance to Christ."[47] Christ's maleness functions clearly, in the logic of this statement, as a universal. It is considered to be more true to who God is than femaleness is. As Francis Martin explains, male and female occupy "different *modes* of humanity." Female humanity is disclosed "through the mediation and activity of Mary and the church"; male humanity "is disclosed in the sacrificial love of Christ."[48]

Insofar as the church teaches that God assumed male and not female humanity, it is no wonder Ruether and other feminist theologians have questioned whether Jesus is the Savior of women. Remembering Gregory's insight ("that which he has not assumed, he has not healed") and stating the problem in terms of popular American culture—"If Jesus is from Mars and I am from Venus, then I am in big trouble!" Clearly, because Jesus is the Savior of women as well as of men, we must acknowledge that Jesus Christ's humanity is *homoousios* with Jill's, just as it is *homoousios* with Jack's.[49]

Thinking of male humanity as normative, or Jesus' male humanity as "generic,"[50] is tough to avoid. At the time John wrote "the Word became flesh," and in the days when the Chalcedonian believers insisted that Jesus Christ was "fully human," it was probably the case that they were thinking of "flesh" and "humanity" as male. As many feminist theologians have pointed out, with Aristotelian biology in play for centuries, male human beings were thought to represent normative humanity. Female human beings were considered to be human, but less human than males. Literally, women were considered to be "damaged" human beings.

The impact that centuries of this kind of thinking has had on our perceptions of the value and roles of men and women cannot be overestimated. Unquestionably, patriarchal structures have capitalized on Jesus' maleness as a means to ensure that men are in control and that women are there to serve them. In order to avoid responding to the scandalous reality that God has entered into the limits of creaturely existence to be with us, we have refused to understand Jesus' maleness as an indication of God's entry into creaturely limitation. Instead, we have thought of Jesus as encompassing normative (male) humanity rather than entering into humanity with us by incarnating a particular instance of it. If God is male, then hierarchical structures that privilege men over women can be justified. As Mary Daly puts it, "if God is male, then the male is God."[51] Power, and control, and "rightness" can be preserved. The scandal can be avoided.

A second approach to resisting God's scandalous presence is *to minimize the relationship between God's acts and God's being*. When this is done, one can speak eloquently about God's particular actions in history without altering one's prior assumptions about God's impassibility or omnipotence. This approach is evident, at times, in the theological reflections of Calvin. Convinced that God, the perfect being, is unaffected by anyone or anything, Calvin explains biblical references to God's changing God's mind or being influenced by us as "figurative."[52] For example, when the biblical text speaks of God's "repenting" of having created humanity (Gen. 6:6) or of being "hostile toward us" (e.g., Rom. 5:10), Calvin insists that God did not actually repent or become wrathful, but rather that these descriptions are anthropomorphisms used for our benefit, to compensate for our limited capacity for understanding.[53] In Calvin's view, an unchanging God cannot really repent; an unaffected God cannot actually become angry. "The mode of accommodation is for [God] to represent himself to us not as he is in himself, but as he seems to us," Calvin argues.[54]

Certainly, we who are incapable of reaching God on our own must rely on God's accommodation. But to identify the divine accommodation as other than true to Godself is to come perilously close to saying it is not *God* we know in God's acts. Such logic can be employed to avoid the scandal by minimizing the reality of God's presence.[55]

One problem with such an approach is that it stands in the way of our seeing who God really is—particularly those aspects of God that do not "fit" our preconceived notions of what God is like. Along these lines, our avoidance of God's scandalous presence is reflected in our tendency, when reading the gospel stories, to think of the two natures of Christ as though they can be separated. He wept at Lazarus's tomb? Struggled in the Garden? Cried out on the cross? Well—that was the "human" side of Jesus. He walked on the water? Healed the blind? Rose from the dead?—that, clearly, was the "divine" side. By escaping the dialectical tension affirmed at Chalcedon, we can readily avoid wrestling with scandalous questions such as, What do Christ's weeping, struggling, and cry of desolation tell us about who God is? What do Christ's miracles and resurrection tell us about who we are as Christ's brothers and sisters?

A third approach to resisting the scandal is *to reduce God's being to God's acts.* Ironically, this tack is taken by those of opposing theological perspectives. Some feminist theologians, weary of centuries of theology in which particularities have been ignored and God portrayed as a self-sufficient, distant patriarch, have given up on considering God's being as distinct from God's acts. To do so, they hold, inevitably leads to a kind of "trumping" of particularity and creatureliness by divinity and transcendence. Rita Nakashima Brock and Sharon Welch have gone so far as to argue that all traces of belief in a transcendent God must be renounced if we are ever to recognize the value of our finite, relational existence.[56] They want to take the scandal out of God's presence, believing that God is in no way "other" than the ordinary beauty and fragility of life.

At the other end of the theological spectrum are those who manage God's acts so meticulously that they seem to forget there is more to who God is than what we (with our limited perspectives) know of what God has done. I am thinking, here, of some of the contributors to the volume edited by Alvin Kimel entitled *Speaking the Christian God*.[57] At several points in the book the content of God's self-disclosure is treated as though it is self-evident and not open to interpretation, giving singular insight into what God is like. The title of Kimel's own essay points to the problem. It is simply, "The God Who Likes His Name."[58] Kimel presumes that God, who is actually known by many names in Scripture and in the Christian tradition, is wedded to God's name the way some of us are attached to our names. But it is a far different thing to say *what God likes* than it is to say *what God is like* on the basis of the divine self-disclosure. Certainly, to say God is like a father, an angry mother bear, or a woman who sweeps her house to find the lost coin is not the same thing as to say God "likes" certain names over others. The former respects God's scandalous self-disclosure in particular ways and at particular times. The latter projects our sentiments and preferences onto the very being of God. To say what God is like, based on God's self-revelation, is not necessarily to claim mastery of all that God is like. To say what God likes, as though one has had a private audience with God, and further with the purpose of setting perimeters around what God is like, is to presume that one's interpretation of God's self-disclosure is exhaustive. Again, the scandal is lost—the point becomes wielding the all-encompassing name of God rather than celebrating the conversation with the burning bush.

RECLAIMING THE SCANDAL

The scandalous presence of God is not something that is easy to reclaim, regardless of the fact that, as I have here argued, it is central to our Christian convictions. Returning to the debates of the early church in order to get a feel for what was at stake is helpful. But in our very different contexts today, it is not enough simply to "repeat" the statements of earlier theologians. Instead, it is necessary to "reinterpret" classical ideas in ways that both take theological and philosophical developments into account and make sense to our contemporary faith journeys.[59] As Kathryn Tanner puts it, "every Christian has to figure out what Christianity is all about . . . what Christianity stands for in the world."[60]

Annie Dillard agrees with me that human creatures are called to recognize and participate in God's scandalous presence. But she does not think this is such a difficult task. Gently mocking the calisthenics theologians go through in contemplating concepts such as the "scandal of particularity,"

Dillard gives us what she thinks is an obvious way "in" to the reclamation of God's presence:

> That Christ's incarnation occurred improbably, ridiculously, at such-and-such a time, into such-and-such a place is referred to—with great sincerity even among believers—as "the scandal of particularity." Well, the "scandal of particularity" is the only world that I, in particular, know. . . . We're all up to our necks in this particular scandal.[61]

Dillard herself seems free of the pervasive sin of avoiding the revelation that is right before our eyes by trying to get behind it. She reminds us that we already have a pretty good set of tools for receiving this God who meets us as a baby/carpenter/rebel rouser in first-century Palestine. After all, are not all of us particular human beings, surrounded by other particular beings, bound by our respective limits? Resonating with Dillard's observation that "we're all up to our necks in this particular scandal," I am in certain ways impressed by humanity's tenacious (but sinful) insistence on being other than the frail and limited creatures that we are. Dillard's challenge to us, however, is to resist our resistance to our creaturely condition and instead to reflect on the character of existence itself. Looking at ourselves and the particular creatures that surround us will help us gain insight into what it means to claim that God has entered into this existence with us.

Dillard would approve of the way Calvin handles this matter. While he firmly believes the elect know God only by virtue of special revelation, Calvin also thinks the elect can then go out and see God by way of general revelation. He draws frequently from nature and from personal observation of human nature in reflecting on the character of God's presence with us. At one point, he draws an analogy to the relationship between a caretaker and a child in order to explain the character of God's revelation. "God is wont . . . to 'lisp' to us," he says, the way a nurse lovingly speaks to an infant in arms.[62]

Calvin also reflects a great deal on the character of Jesus Christ's ongoing existence in light of what he surmises is indispensably human. To be human, Calvin posits, is in some sense to be *physically located*. He objects to the "papist" idea that "the glorious body of Christ [is] not only spirit-like but also infinite and not confined to any one place."[63] Jesus' body could not be physically located in the eucharistic elements, Calvin thinks, because Jesus' body is in heaven, and human bodies cannot be ubiquitous. If someone had asked him whether Jesus is really "sitting at the right hand of the Father," Calvin may well have replied, "Of course not! That image is certainly a metaphor. Sometimes he gets up and walks around!" In his commentary on John, at the point where the text says that the resurrected Jesus "came and stood in the midst" of the disciples, Calvin adamantly argues that Jesus must have come through a door.[64] Embodied human beings simply cannot walk through doors, he implies, and the resurrected Jesus was embodied.

Based on his observation of the love of human mothers, his reading of Scripture, and his conviction that God's acts never exhaust God's being, Calvin also argues that it is beneficial to refer to God as "Mother" as well as "Father." Responding to objections that the title "Father" is "more appropriate to God," Calvin reminds us that "no figures of speech can describe God's extraordinary affection toward us, for it is infinite and various." He further explains that "God has manifested himself to be both . . . Father and Mother" so that we might be more aware of God's constant presence and willingness to assist us."[65]

Calvin and Dillard model how the use of contemplation, imagination, and simple observance can assist us in reclaiming the scandalous presence of God. When we neglect reflection on the sacramental quality of God's presence—that God is known in a human being; that God acts in space and time—we run the risk of using "God with us" merely as a comforting slogan or a validation sticker for our own opinions and actions. Apart from communion with the ordinary, evoking God's presence becomes a means for escaping or surviving the world rather than living in it as those who are not of it. On the other hand, when we revel in the beauty and banality of creaturely existence with the growing recognition that the extraordinary is known precisely in and through the ordinary, we are continuously astounded by the magnitude of God's grace. Met in each moment by the God whose relentless presence is known even in the details of our everyday lives, we are ever-in-process of being reformed, transformed, and made into new creatures.

IMPLICATIONS

A popular song from a few years back expressed a deep desire that God enter deeply into existence with us. "What if God were one of us?" the singer asks. As matters currently stand, the lyricist believes, God is at a distance, unreachable by everyone except, perhaps, the "pope . . . in Rome."[66]

To rephrase the question slightly, What would life be like if we lived with the awareness that the triune God is with us and for us, knowing that God *is* "one of us" in Jesus Christ? Let me close by making three suggestions.

First, if we were really to recognize that God is "one of us" in Jesus Christ, *we would equally value all people, with their varying particularities*. How could we do otherwise, once we realized that God entered into our human condition not to be the greatest CEO who ever lived, not to provide criteria for establishing appropriate hierarchies, but to lift us up to fellowship with God? Ruether, drawing from the *kenotic* imagery of Philippians 2, describes the incarnation of God as the emptying of the patriarchal throne.[67] Mary, in the Magnificat, recognizes that the entry of God into human history by way of her womb causes profound reversals of *kyriarchal* systems.[68] "God has filled the hungry with good things," she says, "and sent the rich away empty."[69] Barth, also drawing from Philippians 2, writes that God entered into the human condition in order to exalt all of us. "The Christmas message speaks of what is objectively real for all human beings, and therefore for each of us, in this One," he writes.[70] In short, God's scandalous presence with us has an "equalizing impact," condemning our attempts to lord over others and inviting us to live in solidarity with one another, even as God lives in solidarity with us.

There is no place where the equalizing impact of God's scandalous presence is more evident than when we come to the Table. We taste and see the elements: the particular loaf of bread, the particular cup of wine, the body and blood of Christ. And we are both comforted and discomforted; knowing God is with us and terrified by the prospect; speaking with conviction even as we marvel, humbly, that we are included. Around the Table, filled with the Spirit who unites us to this particular one, we glimpse what it might mean to join with others with their particular particularities. It would mean that all people called to ministry would be ordained. It would mean seeking to broaden our God-language not on the basis of "rights" but because we desire to participate ever more deeply in the reality of the triune God who continues to meet us in each particular moment.[71] It would mean a lot of things that we simply cannot yet fathom.

Second, to live into God's scandalous presence is *to recognize that we are essential to the work of God.* Such realization fills us with "fear and trembling."[72] The one who has entered into existence with us and exalted us to the very life of the triune God "no longer calls us servants, but calls us friends."[73] Through our union with Christ, "God is at work in us, enabling us to will and to work for God's good pleasure."[74] Living into the scandalous presence of God has nothing to do, then, with spending our lives trying to "pay God back" for what God has done for us. Or with "being right." The incarnation and Trinity both reveal that we do not have the luxury of standing back from God and negotiating terms of exchange. It means, rather, that we are subjected daily to the question, "Do you love me?" followed by the charge, "Feed my sheep."[75] As God is with and for us, so we are called to be with and for one another.

To know God's presence is to be constantly disturbed by God's seeming absence. Believing that God is with us, we are agonizingly aware of God's yet-unfulfilled promise to "bring the kingdom to earth as it is in heaven." We yearn for this kingdom, grieving deeply when we cannot see it in evidence, seeking to expedite its coming by doing God's will.

Finally, to live into the scandal is *to recognize that our role in all this is simultaneously both invaluable and provisional.* As Jacqueline Grant suggests, to call Jesus Christ "God" reminds us that the rest of us are not.[76] Thus, the scandal of particularity, far from validating unjust hierarchies, levels our assumptions about what constitutes and who has access to the "right answers."

This does not mean that we speak without conviction about the presence of God. On the contrary, living into the scandal empowers us to say even more confidently that "God is with us." But "God with us" is no longer code for proclaiming that we are in the right. Rather, it is a reminder that we are subjects of the God who has scandalized us by laying claim to us, the God whose Spirit is opening us to ever-new ways of knowing God and ourselves.

5

"CHOSEN BY GRACE"

Reconsidering the Doctrine of Predestination

Margit Ernst-Habib

You seem to be expecting to go to some parlor *away up* somewhere, and when the wicked have been burnt, you are coming back to walk in triumph over their ashes—this is to be your New Jerusalem!! Now I can't see anything so very *nice* in that, coming back to such a *muss* as that will be, a world covered with the ashes of the wicked! Besides, if the Lord comes and burns—as you say he will—I am not going away; *I* am going to stay here and *stand the fire,* like Shadrach, Meshach, and Abednego! And Jesus will walk with me through the fire, and keep me from harm. Nothing belonging to God can burn, any more than God himself; such shall have no need to go away to escape the fire! No, *I* shall remain. Do you tell me that God's children *can't stand fire*?

—Sojourner Truth

Sojourner Truth (1797–1883), the abolitionist, preacher, and former slave, reacts with these strong words, barely disguising her disgust, to a sermon she heard at a meeting of the Second Advent movement. This movement, a Protestant group founded in 1863, proclaimed the imminence of the second coming of Christ, at which Christ will divide the human race into those "elect" who will be saved and those "wicked" who will burn. Though it certainly has its own characteristic emphases, this preaching in some ways reflects a broader understanding during Truth's time of what will happen to the "elect" and the "damned" when Christ returns; Truth might as well have spoken to numerous other Christian communities, including churches of the Reformed tradition. Indeed, with these drastic words, she summarizes a common understanding of her time, but not of her time only. This idea seems to be actually gaining immense popularity today, if the success of books such as the Left Behind Series is any indication. Even today, a good many people here in the United States might assume that Christian churches are teaching a similar interpretation of what happens "at the end of time" and react in a likewise disgusted way, joining Sojourner Truth's exclamation, "I can't see anything so very *nice* in that!"

In churches of the Reformed tradition (and beyond) this discussion is usually linked with the term predestination or the term election. But what exactly is it that the doctrine of predestination/election teaches? Is there just one doctrine of predestination, or are there differing teachings sub-sumed under this name? And do these teachings warrant those disgusted reactions? Before discussing the topic of predestination and its varying interpretations, it might be helpful to provide one working definition of a traditional understanding of predestination and election—keeping in mind that there are actually as many different definitions and under-standings of predestination as theologians who have worked with this doctrine. One way to briefly summarize predestination is the following:

> Some Christian theologians, particularly in the Reformed tradition, have seen [predestination] as indicating God's eternal decree by which all creatures are foreordained to eternal life or death. It may also be used synonymously with "election" and indicates God's gracious initiation of salvation for those who believe in Jesus Christ.[1]

Accordingly, double predestination may be defined as "the term for the view that God both predestines or elects some to salvation and condemns others to damnation, both by eternal decrees."[2] In other words, according to this definition, God has decided from the beginning who will be saved, not based on the works of the believer, but out of God's grace. Emphasiz-ing God's grace, one could also define election as God's gracious and irre-versible gift and promise of salvation: "You shall be my people and I shall be your God" (Ezek. 36:28).

Theologians did not come up with this teaching "out of the blue" but found the roots for it in Scripture. A major root for predestination and elec-tion is to be found in the First Testament in the central event of Sinai: God chooses Israel to be God's people. There are also Second Testament pas-sages that have been of great importance to theologians: "God chose us in Christ before the foundation of the world" (Eph. 1:4), and "those whom he [God] predestined he also called; and those whom he called he also justi-fied; and those whom he justified he also glorified" (Rom. 8:30), to name but two of the central passages for any discussion of predestination.

It is of great importance to note what the term "predestination," both in classical and contemporary theology, does *not* mean: Predestination is "not to be confused with providence, that is, God's governance of all things, nor with fate or philosophical determinism."[3] Predestination does not mean predetermination, that everything in life, good as well as bad, is pro-grammed, and human beings must simply accept their "fate" in passive obedience. Misunderstanding predestination is, of course, not a recent phenomenon; in 1940 Pierre Maury remarked, "Outside the church, there are many more in number who protest violently against predestination and heap up arguments against it; for they see in it only a sort of fatalism, or some other kind of philosophical position."[4] And yet, even with this misunderstanding removed, the doctrine of predestination still seems to carry with it the undertone of human passivity and an arbitrary and (for some) cruel divine decision. This undertone seems to influence strongly the reactions of many, if not most, contemporary Christians. Therefore, the next part of this chapter will present a brief discussion of major arguments against the doctrine of predestination. Following this discussion, I will suggest a rereading of three classical understandings of predestination/election, namely, those of Augustine, Calvin, and Barth, in search of insights that might be helpful for feminist and womanist theologies within (and maybe beyond) the Reformed tradition. The final part of this chapter will summarize these insights and findings and relate them to some key issues in feminist and womanist theology.

THE TROUBLE WITH PREDESTINATION

In many churches in the United States, the doctrine of predestination, or rather various interpretations and misinterpretations of it, leaves people decidedly uncomfortable, if not outright repelled. This seems to be a peculiarly North American problem; predestination/election is not as much of an issue in many other churches of the Reformed tradition. For example, contemporary confessional statements from around the world rarely discuss the doctrine of predestination. Instead, for the most part, these confessions place the doctrine of election in the context of the church, following the tradition set by the Heidelberg Catechism.[5]

Predestination is usually under attack from different directions, and feminist theologians have shared these concerns and added their own questions. Main arguments against traditional understandings and misunderstandings of predestination often center around one or more of the following issues: (1) the focus on individuals and their "private" salvation; (2) the tendency to concentrate on the "afterlife" while omitting our life here and now, (3) the limited character of human agency with respect to salvation; and, finally, (4) the implicit or explicit danger of an exclusive and hierarchical understanding of the chosen ones.

The first set of main arguments against the doctrine of predestination/election deals with the issue of individualism. Though the biblical understanding of predestination has to do with the "chosen people," it is often understood in an individualistic manner: Am *I* saved? Do *I* belong to the number of the elect? How do *I* know that I am going to heaven? The good news of God's promise to God's people ("You shall be my people and I shall be your God") has been reduced to something private, something I have to achieve for and by myself. This individualistic attitude can produce people who don't care much about community, not even the Christian community, since all they worry about is their own individual salvation. Thus it may produce proud people, who are sure they are saved, but it may also produce anxious, fearful persons who look at themselves for a confirmation of their chosenness—and may not find it. One could ask, what role do Christ and Christ's church play when each believer is alone responsible for her or his own salvation? Sojourner Truth responds to the preaching of the Second Advent movement with her faith in Jesus, who "will walk with me through the fire and keep me from harm"; but traditional (mis)understandings of predestination have often neglected the central role of Christ and Christ's community.

Second, common understandings of predestination tend to deal with a notion of salvation that focuses primarily on the afterlife—the question "Do I belong to the chosen ones?" is equated with "Will I go to heaven after I die?" Here God's gift and promise of salvation (which is, as I have indicated above, one way to understand predestination) is not discussed as something important for the Christian life here and now, as a transformative act of God's grace, but as a kind of "afterlife insurance" to be claimed when we die. Feminist and womanist theologies, on the other hand, emphasize the life-transforming power of God's unmerited grace, and are in general not very much interested in speculation about eternal life and immortality.[6] Rosemary Radford Ruether, for example, once asked pointedly, "Does feminism have a stake in immortality? . . . Is the idea of immortality the expression of a male individualism and abstraction from real-life processes that feminist consciousness should reject?"[7] Therefore, eschatology, or the study of the "last things" (the second coming of Christ and the last judgment), is not discussed in feminist discourse in terms of "last" things as if they had no relation to the "present" things. On the contrary, Christian hope is rediscovered as a community-building and radicalizing impulse,[8] and a reformulated understanding of predestination would have to take this critique into consideration.

A third general concern with respect to the traditional teaching of predestination contends that it limits human agency since the final decision of who is "in" and who is "out" is solely God's sovereign decision, with human beings contributing nothing to it. Humans appear to become mere puppets with respect to their salvation. This argument seems to hit a nerve especially among many North American Christians for whom free will appears to be a cornerstone of human nature and identity. I have rarely met a student or church member belonging to the Reformed tradition who does not wholeheartedly believe in the free will of all human beings and who is not taken aback when learning that the Reformed tradition indeed teaches that the human will is *not* free—at least with respect to the ability not to sin. There is almost no other issue that seems to me (as a native German) to be so telling of the particular contextual character of piety in the United

States as the understanding of freedom in general and free will in particular. The traditional teaching of predestination seems to work against all those deep-rooted convictions and beliefs.

Feminist and womanist theologians add their own particular concerns with respect to the issue of "agency." Being in control of one's own life, body, and mind is a general concern of our contemporary society, but it is of particular importance for women who have been denied this control over much of history and are, in fact, still denied this control in many places both outside and inside the rich Northern Hemisphere. Feminist and womanist ethics thus claim the importance of understanding women as both autonomous and relational subjects; and in this context, "agency" has become something like a keyword of feminist theology.[9] "Agency" is understood as a personal and political reality at the same time: "a capacity for the transformation of selves in, through, and for the transformation of communities."[10] Traditional teachings of predestination explain that God is the only one to decide about our salvation and that nothing we do will make any difference—is God not portrayed here like an arbitrarily deciding Heavenly King, denying us any form of agency? Does this doctrine teach what women have been told for centuries, namely, that they do not have the power to change anything important in their lives and in the life of their communities?

Kathryn Tanner, arguing that Christian beliefs have a direct influence on attitudes and actions of the believer, lists possible negative reactions that might emerge from a belief in predestination with its limited human agency:

> Terror over the inefficacy of the works one had counted on to secure one's righteousness before God; . . . rage against an arbitrary and potentially cruel fate; . . . anxiety over whether one has really been saved in Christ; . . . quietistic resignation in the face of a destiny one cannot influence; . . . prideful disdain for the "ungodly" lives of people whom God has not chosen; . . . rigid behavioral requirements for church membership as indications of election, and moral scrupulosity, therefore, about any failure to abide by such norms.[11]

How are feminist and womanist theologians supposed to react when confronted with what seems to be the exact opposite of agency concerning their salvation? One important question is therefore whether the doctrine of election can have liberating character at all, or whether it is more likely that this teaching leads to passivity and desperation.

Finally, some people argue, not unlike Sojourner Truth, that any interpretation of predestination is per se exclusive, limiting God's grace in Jesus Christ to a number of elect while the rest of humanity is "damned," forever barred from salvation. In effect, this position argues that the Good

News of the gospel is turned into bad news for some; this doctrine is said to represent "pathetic inhumanity."[12] This has been a major argument against predestination throughout the whole history of the church, but it gains a special momentum in a time challenged (and sometimes frightened) by pluralism, in which the issue of inclusiveness has emerged as one of the central concerns.

Even though they have not yet developed a comprehensive analysis or reformulation of the doctrine of predestination, some feminist theologians following this line of thought clearly want to question those understandings of predestination that represent a "hierarchical model of privilege that sets some persons outside of God's hospitality."[13] Letty Russell, for example, identifies a close relationship of patriarchy and an (idolatrous) understanding of election, which leads to a deformation of election that "combines the idea that election is a free gift of God's grace with the idea that election is a form of privilege that justifies the exclusion and domination of others."[14] The Jewish feminist theologian Judith Plaskow has critiqued the concept of election and chosenness with particular respect to its understanding of difference in a similar way:

> It is the notion of chosenness that is the chief expression of hierarchical separation and therefore the most important focus for discussion. . . . If Jewish feminism is to articulate a model of community in which difference is acknowledged without being hierarchalized, it will have to engage the traditional Jewish understanding of difference by rejecting the idea of chosenness without at the same time denying the distinctiveness of Israel as a religious community.[15]

According to Plaskow, one of the possible immediate and destructive consequences of the (misinterpreted) idea of chosenness, translated into the realm of politics, can be seen in the wide-ranging discrimination against Palestinians in the Occupied Territories of the West Bank and the Gaza Strip and in the State of Israel (i.e., the "non-chosen non-Jewish"): "The recent history of the religious right in Israel would seem to suggest that belief in chosenness can go hand in hand with the worst idolatry of the state and the willingness to justify any sort of abuse of the non-Jewish Other."[16]

With all these questions, warnings, objections, and potentially harmful understandings, why should a feminist theologian be interested in this subject? Why should a feminist theologian, even one within the Reformed tradition or in dialogue with it, spend time and energy re-discovering this doctrine, which seems to work against some of her core concerns? Why not deposit it on the dumping ground of those theological doctrines that have proved to be destructive not only for women but for all people who do not fit into the definition of the "chosen race" because of their gender, race, class, or sexual orientation? Why not abandon the subject of predestination altogether, when it includes the discussion of God's "horrible decree,"[17] as even Calvin himself put it? Why not simply turn to the life-affirming and transforming good news of God's grace in Christ?

One obvious reason would be that the doctrine of predestination has been of such great importance to the Reformed tradition; it has even been called "a special mark of Reformed theology."[18] Yet there is more. Over the past few years, I have come to see that a new look at the doctrine of election can help us to get to the core of the good news (though we will have to clear away a load of obstacles on the road!). It can lead us away from misunderstanding election as the neutral predecision of an omnipotent but basically uncaring and arbitrary God to understanding anew "the divine Yes spoken in advance."[19] The doctrine of election can illustrate to us the gift of God's extensive grace, as Letty Russell observes:

> In the history of the church, the doctrine of election points to the need for identity as human beings in the world. Those who are nobody affirm their own self-worth as children of God by claiming that God has chosen them and enabled them to live faithfully. In this sense, to be chosen of God is to be granted full human identity and worth as a gift of God's love. No wonder not only the tribes of Israel, and the nobodies of the early church, but also those in every culture who have been considered less than human, or outcasts, have found reassurance that God has chosen them as covenant partners. In this aspect the idea of election enables communities to resist racism and other forms of oppression.[20]

It is exactly this double aspect of reassurance and empowerment for the marginalized that causes me to take a fresh look at the doctrine of election, hoping to find good news for today's church and world.

FROM AUGUSTINE TO BARTH: REREADING TRADITIONAL UNDERSTANDINGS OF PREDESTINATION

As Letty Russell has pointed out, the doctrine of predestination needs to be read in its context. Even though this teaching might sound "horrible" to us when we first encounter it, we shall not get to a deeper understanding of it as long as we fail to see it in relation to the author's context and work. That is why I would like to propose a rereading of the classical tradition of the doctrine of predestination, beginning with Augustine. Contrary to popular opinion, neither Calvin nor Calvinism in general is to be "blamed" for inventing the doctrine of predestination. Instead, Calvin is only one in a long line of theologians who offer interpretations of God's election. As many other theologians had done before him, Calvin based his doctrine primarily on Augustine's interpretation of Paul.

Augustine

Though Augustine (354–430) was not the first one to deal with predestinarian thoughts,[21] his understanding proved to be especially influential in the Western discussion of predestination. Although his radical understanding of predestination and irresistible grace was not widely taken up in the church, and was even rejected at the Council of Orange in 529, its importance commands us to take a closer look at his teaching and context. Seeing Augustine's teaching in context means first of all recognizing that his doctrine of predestination can be rightly understood only as a continuation of his already-developed doctrine of grace, which he articulated in contradistinction to the British monk Pelagius. Pelagius argued that since God holds us responsible for our sins, we must have the power to stop sinning, to do good works, and to obey the law. Otherwise God would be making a highly unfair demand on us: God would not command what we cannot do! He agreed that human beings need God's help in leading a sinless life, up to a certain degree. But he also believed that humans have to make the first step if they want to receive it. What Pelagius proclaimed was basically his version of "God helps those who help themselves," and his message resembles closely a popular contemporary preaching style especially favored by a certain kind of evangelical TV preacher. (To a non-American hearer, this message often sounds very much like a religious version of the "American Dream," where everything is possible for those who only work hard enough.)

Augustine was profoundly disconcerted by Pelagius's view, not because he thought that this was simply a heresy, but because of the effects this teaching would have on Christians. His motivation for rejecting Pelagius was a deep pastoral concern. Based on his own experience, he asks how sinful human beings are able to turn away from their sin and turn to God, when sin so binds the human will that they are not able to take even the first step—here, the doctrine of original sin was born. For Augustine, Pelagius's teaching was not good news. Quite the opposite, he was convinced that *everybody* would be damned if Pelagius were right. No, he argued, God does not help those who help themselves, precisely because human beings are *not* able to help themselves. God helps those who can*not* help themselves, who are desperate and discouraged:

> First we had to be persuaded how much God loved us, in case out of sheer despair we lacked the courage to reach up to him. Also we had to be shown what sort of people we are that he loves, in case we should take pride in our own worth, and so bounce even further away from him and sink even more under our own strength.[22]

Only after God reaches out to us and lovingly persuades and encourages us to trust in God's grace can we turn away from sin and be encouraged to reach up to God. This is God's gracious love at work in human beings, that in knowing our sin we already know that we are forgiven.

Though in our day Augustine has been made responsible for almost everything that went wrong in theology, especially in relation to his understanding of original sin, the time has come to explore how Augustine might actually be helpful for a liberating theology. Especially for women who suffer from a paralysis of guilt and feelings of unworthiness,[23] Augustine's emphasis on God's prevenient grace might actually be a healing experience, a "route to liberation":

> Having identified . . . his sins, [Augustine's] strategy was to place all reliance on the grace of God, whose mercy he believed is greater than our own self-judgment. Augustine, in his rejection of the doctrines of Pelagianism, refused to accept the pessimistic and uncompassionate idealism, which held each individual personally responsible for all their moral failures. His own teaching about Original Sin, whatever its imperfections, was far less individualistic for it portrayed our sinful nature as something corporate and inherited, thus making it in some sense a collective human responsibility rather than the cause of despair for the solitary individual sinner.[24] . . . Paradoxically, it is the realization that we are not God, that we are subject to sin and cannot be the final judge of ourselves that has the power to liberate us from the paralysis of guilt and to regenerate hope.[25]

This is one of Augustine's core concerns (though I admit that he often makes it quite hard for us to see): uplifting sinners and assuring them of God's unfailing grace. And this grace is not a mere declaration of pardon, a purely forensic forgiveness of sins; it is the gift of God's grace that transforms the recipient: "This grace not only makes us know what we should do, but also makes us do what we know; it not only makes us believe what we should love, but makes us love what we believe. . . . In that way [God] not merely reveals the truth, but also imparts love."[26]

Out of this emphasis on God's unmerited grace that transforms the minds and hearts of those who cannot help themselves emerges Augustine's interpretation of predestination. God saves in Jesus Christ, who suffered and died for us. Nothing we can do can revoke this salvation because it is based exclusively on God's eternal decision. Sojourner Truth said, "Nothing belonging to God can burn, any more than God himself," and, interestingly, Augustine uses a very similar image: "If any of these [the elect] should perish, God is mistaken; but none of them perishes, because God is not mistaken. If any of these should perish, God is overcome by human sin; but none of them perishes, because God is overcome by nothing."[27]

For Augustine this constituted the good news, yet he asked himself, Does not Scripture also talk about those who will be rejected; about a limit to God's grace? Augustine thought so, and he solved the problem by developing the concept of predestination: All human beings are sinful and deserve damnation; everyone belongs to the *massa damnata* ("the damned mass"); yet God has in eternity decided to elect some (though not on the basis of their merits) and to save them from damnation. Augustine was convinced that this was not unfair since all deserve damnation, and some get only what they deserve. Though he acknowledged that this arbitrariness of God seems to contradict God's love, he did not try to reconcile these contradictions; for him they were part of the mystery of God. However, Augustine did not claim to know who the elect and who the reprobate were; quite the opposite, "for as we know not who belongs to the number of the predestinated, we ought in such wise to be influenced by the affection of love as to will all men to be saved."[28]

This last quote might help to soften the image of Augustine a little bit; though he firmly believed in predestination, he advised his readers not to claim what is only God's: the knowledge of who is elected. No one can claim to know who is "in" and who is "out." But even with this warning, Augustine's teaching of predestination has been misread and misused to divide human beings into the ones God has chosen for salvation ("the chosen race," "God's own people") and those who will be lost for all eternity. As Russell and Plaskow have reminded us, this idea has proved to be harmful and oppressive not only in the history of the church but also in society.

With all this in mind, is there anything feminist and womanist theology can or should learn from Augustine? As I have already noted, I think there is indeed something valuable to be found here, namely, his insistence on God's irresistible grace. Augustine, who has been called "the doctor of grace," can remind us of the good news that we do not have to take the first step to remake ourselves, to be right with God. We do not need to be righteous to be loved by God; we receive God's grace despite our not being righteous. This grace of God is a transformative grace, a grace that creates new identities. This Yes, which will not be reversed, contains liberating power especially for women who are plagued by feelings that they never will measure up, that they are not good enough, that they are not worthy. With this Yes we receive a new role as God's beloved daughters and sons, called and enabled to live in right relationships, not only with God but also with ourselves and others.

John Calvin

Turning now to Calvin (1509–1564) and his understanding of predestination, we find that he follows Augustine's teaching very closely, so that he could actually be called a "reimpristinator of Augustinian theology."[29] At some points, Calvin even seems to rely more heavily on Augustine than on Scripture—something he usually does not do. Like Augustine, Calvin points out first of all God's sovereign grace and the inability of humans to save themselves. He, again like Augustine, does not begin with God's eternal decree but rather develops his understanding of predestination as a consequence of his "emphasis on God's free and sovereign grace in salvation: the problems of human inability and man's reliance for salvation upon the sovereign grace of God as mediated by Christ are the two grounds of Calvin's predestinarian conceptuality."[30] And contrary to yet another common misunderstanding, predestination is not the central dogma on which Calvin's theology is built.[31] It is true, however, that for Calvin it certainly was the "crown of soteriology,"[32] a keystone for his doctrinal arch.

Calvin's placement of this doctrine within his doctrinal framework varies quite a bit across his writings. But, differing from Augustine and the Scholastic tradition, Calvin always treats predestination in the sphere of Christology or soteriology. This placement is not unimportant, for it indicates that Calvin does not view predestination as something to be discussed in a speculative fashion (as part of the doctrine of God or special category of providence, for example) but as something established in the salvific Christ event. For example, in book 3 of the last edition of his *Institutes*, Calvin discusses predestination under the title "The Way in Which We Receive the Grace of Christ: What Benefits Come to Us from It, and What Effects Follow." It is only in Christ that the believer can find comfort in this doctrine:

> But I do not merely send men off to the secret election of God to await with gaping mouth salvation there. I bid them make their way directly to Christ in whom salvation is offered us, which otherwise would have lain hid in God. For whoever does not walk in the plain path of faith can make nothing of the election of God but a labyrinth of destruction. . . . Christ therefore is for us the bright mirror of the eternal and hidden election of God, and also the earnest and pledge.[33]

Again, this placement is more than just a doctrinal game; like Augustine, Calvin is motivated by a deep pastoral concern: how can we know whether we are elected? He saw that by looking at oneself, one ends only in despair. It is not in who we are and what we do that we find any confirmation of our chosenness. It is not even our faith that secures our salvation since for Calvin "election . . . is the mother of faith."[34] It is only in Christ that the believer can find comfort.

> Rare indeed is the mind that is not repeatedly struck with this thought: whence comes your salvation but from God's election? Now, what

revelation do you have of your election? This thought, if it has impressed itself upon him, either continually strikes him in his misery with harsh torments or utterly overwhelms him. . . . But if we have been chosen in [Christ], we shall not find assurance of our election in ourselves; and not even in God the Father, if we conceive him as severed from his Son.[35]

Interestingly, Calvin bases his discussion of predestination here not only on Scripture (and Augustine) but also on experience: "We teach nothing not borne out by experience,"[36] the experience of those tormented by the question of whether they are chosen or not. Calvin wants to give comfort to these distraught believers: It is not yourself but God's grace in Christ in which you can trust with your whole heart. Alongside his theological experience, Calvin's experiences in his historical context provide us with another key for understanding his teaching of predestination: Protestant Christians of his time were facing dreadful difficulties, persecution, and even death all over Europe, and thus Calvin stressed predestination "as an assurance of God's grace sufficient to sustain faith even to martyrdom."[37]

As much as Calvin tried to avoid any kind of speculation about election, he did not elude it completely.[38] Calvin took Scripture very seriously, and he came to the conclusion that Scripture does not talk only about election but also about reprobation (some people are left in their sinful state and will not receive salvation but eternal punishment). Though he called this a "horrible decree," he was still convinced that this is what Scripture teaches, for example, in Romans 9. This led Calvin to the conclusion that he had to talk about God not only choosing some for salvation but also passing over others. In his teaching of double predestination, election and reprobation are set side by side as opposing equivalents, as one can see in his well-known definition of predestination: "We call predestination God's eternal decree by which he compacted with himself what he willed to become of each man. For all are not created in equal condition; rather, eternal life is foreordained for some, eternal damnation for others."[39] Following this line of thought, the salvation event in Christ, which was so highly emphasized in Calvin's teaching, could be seen as having only "instrumental but not fundamental significance";[40] in other words, Christ only carries out God's eternal decree.

Helpful as Calvin might be with his insistence on God's sovereign grace in Jesus Christ, motivated by the pastoral concern of comfort to troubled believers, ultimately his teaching of double predestination may lead us on a dangerous path, as did Augustine's. Again, against Calvin's intention, we may be tempted to divide humanity into the chosen and the reprobate, into those who are "in" (which usually means "us") and those who are "out" ("the others"), with all the dire consequences that follow.

Karl Barth

The approach of Karl Barth (1886–1968) to election represents a fundamental change in theological discourse.[41] Like Augustine and Calvin, Barth also emphasizes God's grace in Christ as the source of salvation and basis of election, but his arguments differ considerably from Calvin (whom he criticizes extensively) and might prove helpful for a feminist reformulation of the doctrine.

In freedom and love as defined in and through Christ, God has chosen to be the God of human beings—this is for Barth the foundation of all of theology. Against the mystery of the traditional teaching of predestination, in which God's decision includes a Yes and a No, Barth claims that the doctrine of election contains only good news; it is "the sum of the gospel . . . the gospel *in nuce*"[42] since it speaks of God's freedom in which God is "the One who eternally loves."[43] God, as the relational triune God,[44] has decided from the beginning to be in relationship with human beings as their God and has created human beings to be in relationship with God, so that they may be God's people:

> The fact that God makes this movement, the institution of the covenant, the primal decision "in Jesus Christ," which is the basis and goal of all His works—that is grace. Speaking generally, it is the demonstration, the overflowing of the love which is the being of God, that He who is entirely self-sufficient, who even within Himself cannot know isolation, willed even in all His divine glory to share his life with another. . . . It occurs even where there is no question of claim or merit on the part of the other. It is love which is overflowing, free, unconstrained, unconditioned. . . . It is love which is patient, not consuming this other, but giving it place, willing its existence for its own sake and for the sake of the goal appointed to it.[45]

This covenant of God with God's people Israel has been fulfilled in time, a covenant with sinners who do not deserve to be partners.[46] Barth redefines the object (and subject) of election and argues that it is *not* the individual believer first of all who is elected but the human being Jesus Christ who is *the* elect: "In its simplest and most comprehensive form the dogma of predestination consists . . . in the assertion that the divine predestination is the election of Jesus Christ."[47] But, following the logic of Chalcedon (Christ being truly divine and truly human), Barth adds that Christ is at the same time not only the elect but also, together with the Father and the Holy Spirit, the one who elects. It is in Christ's double role that Barth finds assurance for believers. Barth was convinced that "only a consistent Christocentricity can secure and guarantee a thoroughly nonspeculative character for our theocentric theology."[48] There can be no more questioning whether

I am elected, since Christ is the elect, and I am elected in him: "We have to see our own election in that of the man Jesus because His election includes ours within itself and because ours is grounded in His. We are elected together with Him in so far as we are elected 'in Him.'"[49] In this sense, "double" predestination has a new meaning. It does not describe God's twofold decision to save some and to pass over others, but it encompasses rather "first, a predestination of God to be gracious and, second, a predestination of humanity to be chosen and redeemed. Election means grace."[50]

Barth stops short of explicitly teaching universalism (that all will be saved) since he does not want to assume God's final judgment, but it is hard to see how this does not follow from his arguments. Since Christ is *the* elected as well as *the* rejected, because he has taken upon himself the rejection of humankind, there can be no more fundamental difference between the two groups of "elected" and "rejected"; they stand alongside each other, mutually attached to one another,[51] united in the one hope in Christ: "It would be to ignore Jesus Christ if we were to attempt to deny to others the hope upon which the elect themselves are also exclusively dependent—and even more, if we were not prepared to regard them wholly in the light of this hope."[52]

As a feminist theologian, this line of thought offers me a helpful perspective: like other liberation theologies, feminist theologies claim God's preferential option for those who are marginalized and oppressed, rejected by society and church, rejected by those who have the power to define who belongs to "the chosen" and "the rejected." Barth's argument provides a profound critique of the very ground of any definition of chosen and rejected. Seen from a christological perspective, there can be no valid argument for any kind of arrogant exclusiveness. On the contrary, all human beings stand in solidarity with each other because Christ stands in solidarity with them.

Barth also offers yet another useful insight in his discussion of what it actually means to be elected, to be called by God. As I noted in the beginning of this chapter, predestination has often been misunderstood as a kind of "afterlife insurance" for the elect. Barth vehemently criticizes this attitude. For him the divine gift includes a task; being elected means being elected for service to God and others. Being a Christian means first of all being a witness to God in word and deed, sharing in partnership Christ's prophetic work.[53] The freedom Christians can live is indeed a "freedom from," but primarily it is a joyful "freedom for,"[54] freedom for serving God and for serving fellow human beings:

> The liberation of the Christian takes place . . . as he is drawn out of soli-
> tariness into fellowship. The glories and miseries of isolation, of self-
> dependence, of loneliness, are now over for the Christian. As a witness

of Jesus Christ he has nothing more to seek or find in this dark cavern. With every step which he takes as such he moves . . . over and into fellowship with Jesus Christ, which at once opens up in two dimensions as fellowship with God, . . . and as fellowship with men.[55]

Barth explicates numerous biblical stories of calling and concludes that the assurance of personal salvation and the mission and sending of the called ones as one community always go together.[56] In that sense, God's election is only complete when it becomes actual on our side, when we make our own election to be for God in the world.[57] Personal salvation, for Barth, is not the central focus of Christian life and piety, but participating actively in God's mission is.

Of the three authors we have considered, Barth seems to provide the most helpful insights for a feminist exploration of election. His emphases on God's grace in Jesus Christ, Jesus Christ as *the* elected and rejected, and on election for service seem to correspond with some concerns of feminist and womanist theologies as previously discussed. On the basis of the discussion of these three authors, what issues might we want to explore further?

ELECTION FROM A FEMINIST PERSPECTIVE

As I have indicated throughout this chapter, I am convinced that the doctrine of election can indeed be liberating. Following the four issues and concerns I have identified in the section "The Trouble with Predestination," I will explore some insights we have gained on our way through classical theology and employ their contribution for feminist and womanist theologies.

First, as we have learned from Karl Barth, the graceful election by God in Christ is not first and foremost a "private" election. Christ is the only elected person, and in him, we are elected as the community of Christ's disciples, not as a group of individually elected persons. This line of thought is, of course, not new. Part of the Reformed tradition has consistently dealt with the issue of election not in the context of the individual's salvation but in the context of the Christian community. The Heidelberg Catechism, for example, does not speak about predestination at all but only discusses the church as the chosen people of God (question 54). And already here we find that being chosen implies assurance as well as a task:

Q. 55: What do you understand by "the communion of saints"? First, that believers one and all, as partakers of the Lord Christ, and all his treasures and gifts, shall share in one fellowship. Second, that each one ought to know that he is obliged to use his gifts freely and with joy for the benefit and welfare of others.

Being chosen for a task means that *all* members of the community have received gifts of grace (though differing ones) and that they are "obliged" to use them "freely and with joy"—a call to self-critique for a church where not only women but also other marginalized groups are excluded from using their gifts to the "benefit and welfare of others." Excluding those who are different from us (with respect to gender, race, age, class, sexual orientation) from this task keeps them from being faithful disciples of Christ.

There is another issue at stake here: God's graceful election does not focus on the individual only, and, even more, being chosen does not set a limit to what we see as our community. God's election is not a "private" election, but it is also no "Christian" election. As Barth has reminded us, "in view of [Christ's] election, there is no other rejected but Himself. It is just for the sake of the election of *all* the rejected that He stands in solitude over against them all."[58] Election in Christ, therefore, means the election of the community of all human beings, and the church is called to be, in words and deeds, a witness to this gracious election. (I will discuss this aspect subsequently under the fourth point.) It would be well to follow this line of thought and develop this argument even further than Barth did: how would we understand election, if we do not limit God's gracious act to human beings but extend it to all of God's creation?

Second, the doctrine of election does not primarily promise us an "afterlife insurance"; it has immediate consequences right here and now. If we as Christ's disciples are elected for a task, then election cannot deal with eternal life only. Understood this way, election does not lead to "quietistic resignation in the face of a destiny one cannot influence,"[59] but rather to the opposite: active engagement in and for the world. As partners in God's mission, though, we are not taking over God's mission from God, but participating in it as those who are set free for service. Being elected by God does not make us into the "privileged ones" over against those who are "rejected"; instead, God's gracious election sends us out not only to serve God but to serve our fellow human beings and God's good creation as well.

In this context, it is important to note that feminist and womanist theologians have spent some time redefining the terms "service" and "servant" in light of Christ, the Lord and Servant.[60] A redefined understanding of service "implies autonomy and power used in behalf of others."[61] Yet even after being redefined, it remains a term only to be used with great caution, especially in the United States, with its history of slavery, segregation, and racial discrimination, as Jacquelyn Grant has reminded us.[62] With her warning in mind, I suggest adopting Grant's term in describing the task of election: becoming disciples of Christ.

To return, then, to election: its purpose is to follow Christ on his messianic journey. This discipleship includes friendship, friendship with Christ as well as friendship with those who have no friends. As friends of

God, we act not like children nor like servants but as adults, called out by God. In this sense, we indeed become agents, which leads us to the third aspect, the understanding of human agency.

Within the traditional Reformed understanding of *human agency*, we may be passive before God with respect to our salvation, but, following Kathryn Tanner, the noncompetitive relation between God and human beings means that human agency does not have to decrease so that God may increase: "The creature's receiving from God does not then require its passivity in the world: God's activity as the giver of ourselves need not come at the expense of our own activity. Instead, the creature receives from God its very activity as a good."[63] This agency, though, is distinguished from God's agency in a decisive way; our acts do not have saving powers since the "saving power of Christ is already complete and does not need repeating or reenactment by any of us."[64] This is not a call to mere humbleness (a call women have heard only too often!) but a liberating, life-giving message: Even as agents and partners in God's mission, it is not up to us to "save" the world or ourselves. As still sinful yet freed and free agents we engage in an active discipleship and friendship with the triune God by reflecting God's gracious goodness.[65]

This gracious goodness is not only a declaration by God that we are no longer held accountable for our sins; rather it is, as Calvin has called it, a double grace, for it transforms us into new people and gives us a new identity. As Augustine said, God's grace makes us not only know what we should do but also do what we know. It is Christ's righteousness that makes us into new people. Yet this alien righteousness does not remain "alien," for it transforms us: "Conversion to faith is when one is forgiven because of God's imputation of an alien righteousness, a performative conversion in which we receive a new role, one that calls us to live as those who are loved by God."[66]

This new role, the role of God's beloved, includes covenant partnership. We indeed become agents, agents for the sake of God's mission in and for the world. We are elected for a task.[67] To ward off any hints of works righteousness, it is essential to stress again that our fulfillment of (or our failure to fulfill) this task does not decide whether we receive God's grace; yet this grace is aimed at enabling us to strive for fulfillment. That is why a feminist interpretation of election—even with a new emphasis on human agency—should continue to put God's loving grace in Christ into the center of the discussion. Teaching election in today's competitive world needs to stress the fact that we do not have to help ourselves first in order that God might help us. The divine Yes is indeed God's first and last word, though it includes God's No to our sins. But even God's No can be liberating, because we know that we are not the final judges of ourselves, and that the final judge is the Judged One, Jesus Christ. As Angela West has written, knowing God as the final judge can have "the power to liberate us from the paralysis of guilt and to regenerate hope."[68] In emphasizing God's grace first, God does not become an arbitrary God, resembling a blind and cruel fate. Emphasizing God's grace in Christ, the elected and elector, opens us up from self-doubts and worries about our "being saved" since we are as God's beloved creatures elected with and in Christ. It also frees us to focus on the question of what "salvation/liberation/redemption" actually means for "women in their different contexts"[69]—in short, how women experience the grace of God in their lives.

Fourth, how do we live this grace of God, and what does this friendship with God mean for our relation to others? It does not lead to a hierarchical separation (Plaskow) from any other human being or group of human beings. It does not lead us to prideful disdain (Tanner) of others. Instead, it leads us into the most profound solidarity, especially with those who are rejected, who are marginalized in church and world. Those who see themselves elected with Christ through faith are called to take up his lifestyle of compassion and hospitality to our neighbors in need.[70]

The life of the elected is not a life of domination or privilege but a life of solidarity. Election rightly understood cannot, as Berkouwer has observed, "be more seriously misinterpreted than when it is seized as a basis for self-exaltation and pretentiousness."[71] Again, the grace of God is not a gift to be stored and looked at occasionally, but an enabling and empowering gift. In receiving God's gift of grace, we are called to become God's gift for others. We are reconciled to God, but we are also ambassadors of God's reconciliation; and this reconciliation will have to be spelled out in concrete details in every time and place. Being elected can mean, very concretely, to resist racism and other forms of oppression, to work against any kind of dehumanizing and unjust structure and power, to work for the flourishing of all created life. Through God's gracious election in Christ, boundaries are broken up, definitions of who is "in" and who is "out" are fundamentally challenged; the "chosen race" can only mean the "human race."

But we are not living in paradise yet. Even though we know that in Christ we all are already elected to be God's reconciled community, reality seems to prove the opposite. Everywhere we look we find people exploiting one another and nature and abusing political, economical, or social power in brutal and selfish ways, thus violating the image of God in others and in themselves. How do we, as God's ambassadors of reconciliation, react to those who so flagrantly abuse their powers? Can we remain an "inclusive" community by providing hospitality even to those who work and live against all we believe in? Are there not situations where we have to follow those passages in Scripture that also speak about God's inhospitality; are there not times, "when we must resist offering hospitality to certain persons because of their destructive powers, when we are called instead to pray that

God will show them hospitality, while delivering us from them"?[72] There definitely are times and situations where we are called to be "exclusive," but it is difficult for a Christian community to discern when and where excluding people is grounded in our faithfulness to God's reconciliation and *not* in our own agendas, dislikes, and prejudices. Exclusion needs to be the last step in a long process of inviting into community those who act in destructive ways. Because of Christ's election and the chosenness of all humans in Christ, any form of exclusion can only be provisional, aimed at ultimate reconciliation and reunion—though we may not live to see it. The Belhar Confession of the Dutch Reformed Mission Church (DRMC) in South Africa (1982) provides an informative and enlightening example of the provisionality of exclusion. Fighting against the theological foundation and practical consequences of apartheid in church and society, they confessed that those who adhere to a theology of apartheid are heretics and have already left the Christian community. Excluding apartheid supporters from all forms of community, then, merely names the fact that apartheid supporters have already turned away from the Christian gospel and Christian community. This exclusion was a most serious act and not taken lightly by the DRMC; and it was always was seen as a provisional act only, as the accompanying letter to the confession states: "Our prayer is that this act of confession will not place false stumbling blocks in the way thereby to cause and foster false divisions, but rather that it will be *reconciling and uniting*. We know that such an act of confession and process of reconciliation will necessarily involve much pain and sadness. It demands the pain of repentance, remorse, and confession; the pain of individual and collective renewal and a changed way of life. . . . We pray that our brothers and sisters throughout the Dutch Reformed church family, but also outside it, will want to make this new beginning with us, so that we can be free together and together may walk the road of reconciliation and justice. . . . We believe that this is possible in the power of our Lord and by his Spirit."[73]

The Confession of Belhar reminds us that the "exclusiveness" of Christ as the elected and elector can only be understood in a fundamentally inclusive sense: In Christ, God has elected humanity in all its diversity.[74] This does not mean that the Christian religion or church now possesses the divine truth—God's truth always remains God's truth since God is not bound to the church. We may even learn something about what it means to be elected from those outside of the Christian church who reflect the work of the Holy Spirit in their lives. This has a double consequence for interreligious dialogue: we can no longer see others as "others," as those whose souls we have to save from damnation; we can only see them as fellow elected and witness to them our understanding of what election means. At the same time, we remain radically open to what God may be teaching us through them:

> We remember that God has not left himself without witness in any nation at any time. When we approach the man of faith other than our own, it will be in a spirit of expectancy to find how God has been speaking to him and what new understanding of the grace and love of God we may ourselves discover in this encounter. Our first task in approaching another people, another culture, another religion, is to take off our shoes, for the place we are approaching is holy. Else we may find ourselves treading on men's dreams. More seriously still, we may forget that God was here before our arrival.[75]

In the section "The Trouble with Predestination," I quoted Tanner's list of possible negative reactions that might emerge from a belief in predestination/election. With these steps towards a reformulated doctrine of election, we may be able to come closer to the more liberating and life-giving aspects of this teaching, which Tanner describes:

> Comfort in the assurance that one's failings may be remedied by God; . . . thankfulness and love for God's free mercy; . . . trust that God's offer in Christ is reliable; . . . concern for good works as the appropriate consequence of one's election; . . . forgiving tolerance of the failings displayed by oneself and others, in recognition of the fact that moral achievements are not what distinguishes persons in the eyes of God; . . . courage to persevere as Christian workers in the struggle to overcome sin and evil.[76]

My hope is that seeing the doctrine of election from this perspective may indeed bring us closer to the good news in Christ.

THE *IMAGO DEI* AND A REFORMED LOGIC FOR FEMINIST/WOMANIST CRITIQUE

Mary McClintock Fulkerson

The topic of the *imago Dei*[1] is in many respects at the heart of feminist theology. It refers to the claim that however different and alienated from God we are, human beings bear some likeness to the divine. Indeed, to say we are created in the image of God is to identify the human capacity to be in relationship with God, or, better, to claim that relationship with God is the human vocation. Thus, the image is a symbolic condensation of what in the Christian tradition it means to be fully human. Its significance increases further upon recognition that the *imago Dei* has the double function of referring both to human beings and to God. It thereby directs us to ask not only about the way in which God is imaged and what that communicates, but about how such imaging contributes to the valuing and devaluing of human beings as well. In important respects the *imago Dei* can serve as an index of *whom* the tradition has seen as fully human.

Given such complex potential, it is not surprising that feminist theology has contributed much to theological conversations about the way human beings image God, most particularly by foregrounding issues of representation in relation to the question of whom the tradition sees as fully human. Mary Daly's famous comment that "if God in 'his' heaven is a father ruling 'his' people, then it is in the 'nature' of things and according to divine plan and the order of the universe that society be male-dominated" is, in this sense, an example of theological reflection upon the *imago Dei*.[2]

The resources of Reformed traditions also provide insights into what it means to be fully human, insights that can be productive for feminist theology. Conversely, Reformed theological commitments are capable of further development in light of feminist theological explorations. For mutual enrichment both conversations will have to expand.

THE COMPLIMENT OF THE *IMAGO DEI*

Scripture is a prime source for thinking about the image of God. The opening chapters of Genesis tell of God's gracious creation—from light, the

earth, vegetation, and animals to the human being—attesting to God's pro-
nouncement that this plurivocity of being is good. The creature called '*adam*
gets special notice when God says, "Let us make humankind in our image,
according to our likeness" (Gen. 1:26). From Scripture the theme of the
imago Dei enters the theological tradition of the church, where for centuries
it had no particular doctrinal locus. The variety of claims about anthropology—human being as created, as distorted by sin, and as redeemed—are
all within the purview of the *imago Dei*, wherever they appear. Thus, for a
classical theologian relevant discussions of the image can occur anywhere,
from discussion of the knowledge of God to the doctrine of the church.
Indeed, before the modern turn to the subject, anthropology was not a separate doctrinal locus or topic of theological consideration. Its various
dimensions typically appeared in sections on God as creator, in the form of
reference to the nature of creatureliness; in doctrines of salvation, in discussions about the nature of sin and its transformation; and in Christolo-
gies, as accounts of the implications of the iconic character of this ideal form
of humanity.[3]

John Calvin, for example, could discuss the *imago Dei* in relation to
knowledge of God, the end of human being, the distorting effect of sin, or
the restoration of the image through Jesus Christ.[4] Indeed, for Calvin and
many other Reformed theologians, Jesus Christ is the paradigmatic image
of God. Most important, the image functioned historically as a way to signal the finite goodness of human being. Even though in need of restoration
through Jesus Christ, the human creature is thereby marked for a relation
to God. This marking of the image has been identified with different features
of human being over the ages. In addition to an implied physical resemblance (Gen. 3:8ff.) and stewardship over creation, premodern accounts
have typically identified the image with rationality or the rational soul
(Thomas Aquinas), a reflecting mirror of God's reality (Calvin), and the
conformity of the human will with the divine (Calvin and other Reformed
thinkers).

Given the profound compliment paid to human being by this notion of
creation in the image of God, the important question is whether it has been
a compliment paid in equal measure to all. From a feminist perspective,
historically this has not been the case. While not refused the fruits of
the *imago Dei*, namely, salvation, women have been viewed by much of the
Christian tradition, Reformed and otherwise, as lesser bearers of the
image. Indeed, the first topics of concern for feminist and womanist theologians have been those associated with representations of women and
the human in the tradition.[5] For example, accounts of creation that draw
from Genesis have produced quite a number of problematic views of
women's nature in the history of Christian biblical interpretation. Stories
of Eve's so-called secondary creation after Adam have served to warrant

women's subordination, just as her encounter with the serpent and the expulsion from the garden have grounded arguments for her less rational nature and her suffering in reproduction. The Bible is then read to portray woman as a dimmer creature than man, divinely ordained to be his submissive helpmeet.[6] A further exacerbation of that kind of insult occurs in another topic where women come off badly—associations of women with sin. The exploitation of Eve's encounter with the serpent for theories of female carnality and weak, temptation-susceptible nature has a long history. These are easily developed in the direction of the sexualization of women's bodies and the association of female flesh with danger and evil, as well as the racialization of this flesh.[7]

While a full account of the Reformed tradition's participation in such denigrations is too long to give here, suffice it to say that the general belief of the church fathers from Calvin through the formative period of American Presbyterianism was that women's nature and place excluded her from positions of authority. Heavily shaped by surrounding cultural assumptions, this view was thought to be clearly authorized by Scripture. While asserting women's spiritual equality with men, male church leaders were fond of quoting 1 Timothy 2:12: "I permit no woman to teach or to have authority over a man; she is to keep silent" as justification for the exclusion of women from ordained leadership. In the face of the explosion of women's participation in voluntary societies and missions in American Presbyterianism in the early nineteenth century, this exclusion was codified into a constitutional prohibition against women's ordained leadership.[8] Given this contradictory history of affirmation and denigration of women, the challenge is to take this rich tradition of the image of God and extend it most fully to all human beings. How might the resources of the Reformed tradition be appropriated by feminist thinking to pay all human beings the compliment of the *imago Dei*?

DEVELOPING A REFORMED THEOLOGICAL LOGIC

As already suggested, the resources of Reformed theology for the task of extending the *imago Dei* are not to be found by attending to what is said explicitly about women. Indeed, formative events of the Reformed tradition—the policies of Geneva, the tirades of John Knox, Calvinist scholasticism, the North American modernist controversies at the turn of the century, and the long-standing refusal to ordain women—render women invisible when they are not offering denigrating images of them. The resources of Reformed theology most useful for the challenge raised by feminist and womanist thinking have little to do with what has been said explicitly by the classic Reformers about "femaleness" or "race," except as reminders of the fallibility of even the best of the fathers. Rather, it is the resources of a theocentric tradition about idolatry that are most promising in relation to freeing the doctrine of *imago Dei* from its entanglement with various kinds of practical injustice. Particularly by attending to contemporary Reformed thinkers who have developed understandings of the social cost of idolatry, we find theological clues for attending to the problematic accounts of subjects identified by feminists and womanists. Let us look at these themes and then consider them in relation to the critical issues raised by feminist and womanist thought.

A most obvious Reformed resource for the dilemmas of feminist and womanist thinking about the *imago Dei* comes from the Reformed commitment to the redemption of a good creation distorted by sin. This, indeed, is the larger theological framework within which feminist theology has and will continue to work. The Reformed tradition's commitment to the goodness of creation in its finitude is a bedrock theological conviction that funds joy in and celebration of the creation as God's good work. The Second Helvetic Confession of 1566 reminds us, "As the Scripture says, everything that God had made was very good, and was made for the profit and use of man."[9] The tradition has always identified humanity *as such* as at least theoretically created in God's image and thereby potentially in relation to God; it thus grounds women's existence in God's gracious economy and allows us to expand what counts as good creation in the public consciousness. It also, crucially, fuels resistance to the deformation of this good work and provides the theological rationale for insisting that redemption is not the complete reinvention of human being—a denial of finitely good bodies and desire and will.

However, some adjustments are needed if this logic of redemption is to be made good for the groups that have been only "theoretically" included. For starters, the Reformed notion of sin centered most clearly on idolatry, which John Calvin took to be the basic sin of the medieval church. Indeed, the primary way to define idolatry for Calvin was pride, the desire to be like God. As we know from feminist responses to one of the modern expositors of a doctrine of sin, Reinhold Niebuhr, this continued focus on human pridefulness is most likely to capture the experience of white males rather than that of women of any race or class. Sin looks different for populations that lack the social space and power to indulge in self-promotion.[10] The crucial connection of idolatry to social sin needs expansion as well. There are indications that the sin of idolatry was understood as something that entailed the oppression of marginalized communities; for example, Calvin and other sixteenth-century Reformers connected the Catholic Church's idolatries to the oppression of minority religious communities such as their own.[11]

However, contemporary understandings of identities as socially constructed, that is, as defined by social conventions, will require much more complicated ways to connect idolatry to social brokenness, raising issues of gender, race, and sexual orientation that were foreign to Calvin's frame of reference.[12] Thus, a first adjustment to this expansion requires attention to the forms of human sin that are not adequately represented in such notions as pride.[13]

A second adjustment, about which I will say more later, requires that we think about more than simply adding marginalized groups to what counts as good creation. Simply to add new subjects to that honored status would ignore insight yielded by feminist attention to representation, namely, that reigning frameworks are not neutral; they are liable to be marked by interests that screen out marginalized populations. It will be better, as I will show, to speak of destabilizing accounts of subjects than of additive ones. Three elements of the notion of the *imago Dei* as good creation will help us think about extending that destabilizing.

First is the affirmation of the *theocentric* or God-centered nature of human beings. Human beings are incomplete, are unfulfilled, except in relation to the true God. As Calvinists insist, human life is to be lived to the glory of God alone, *soli Deo Gloria*.[14] This is to say that no worldly entity can finally satisfy human longing; it is a longing for the eternal—for God. Importantly, this view of a theocentric creature does not draw us away from the world. Rather, to describe human being as theocentric or theonomous is to describe the creature's distinctive posture of *engagement with* the creation.

Indeed, the second crucial point in this theological anthropology is that our relation to God is inextricably connected to our relation to the neighbor, a unique manifestation of the creation. A God-centered posture toward the world is one that honors the worldly entity in its finitude and particularity, a finitude not hierarchically valued (maleness over femaleness, whiteness over blackness, hetero-desire over homosociality), but valued in its magnificent plurality.

Third, Calvin understood the *imago Dei* as a task—the display of gratitude for God's gifts—and not simply a feature of the human soul. The relation to the neighbor is the place for just such a display, and it is that relation to the neighbor that signals whether the finite creation is honored in all its plurality.[15] As Calvin puts it in the *Institutes*,

> we are not to consider that men merit of themselves but to look upon the image of God in all men, to which we owe all honor and love . . . therefore, whatever man you meet who needs your aid, you have no reason to refuse to help him. Say, "He is a stranger"; but the Lord has given him a mark that ought to be familiar to you, by virtue of the fact that he forbids you to despise your own flesh. Say, "He is contemptible and worthless"; but the Lord shows him to be one to whom he has deigned to give the beauty of his image. Say that you owe nothing for any service of his; but God, as it were, has put him in his own place in order that you may

recognize toward him the many and great benefits with which God has bound you to himself. Say that he does not deserve even your least effort for his sake; but the image of God, which recommends him to you, is worthy of your giving yourself and all your possessions.[16]

As a Calvinist theologian attempting to develop Reformed thinking in a liberationist direction, John de Gruchy is quite instructive as we attempt to develop these themes. Arguing that the *imago Dei* is fundamental to Calvin's ethics, he points out that damage to the image is inevitably damage to the relation to the neighbor.[17] De Gruchy takes this mutual connection with utmost seriousness: When the glorification of God comes "at the expense of humanity," even an account of God is "an idol that needs to be smashed in the service of human and social liberation."[18] The Reformed conviction that God is at work reforming all reality sets up a logic that requires us to ask new questions about previously accepted social arrangements, always alert to human deformations of the *imago Dei*. This Reformed logic does not simply add outsiders to our institutions, but moves to destabilize existing arrangements that have been falsely secured with idols. In that destabilizing, the logic thereby expands gracious, God-sustained neighbor relations.

USING A REFORMED LOGIC: STARTING OUT

How might this Reformed theological logic help in addressing feminist and womanist concerns? Let us take up these concerns by noting several developments in their very definition. By doing so, we begin to see a variety of forms of what we will later understand theologically as "damage to the image," as de Gruchy puts it. A first level of concern typical of Second Wave feminism—the period of emerging U.S. feminist consciousness in the early 1960s—deals with explicit exclusion of women from the opportunities afforded men. In the wider society these concerns included political representation, equal treatment under the law, and access to education and career; in the church, concerns focused on access to leadership, ordained and otherwise, and the full power to speak and to represent Christ. This level of concern and its typical response can be generally identified as the concern with inclusion. It is about adding women to the current structures of church or society.

This first problematic of the exclusion of women is typically focused on the harm of images that denigrate and subordinate women. Thus it requires generation of counter images that confirm and celebrate the goodness of woman as finite creation. Such work has been done by feminists and womanists for some time now in the form of creative imaging of the goodness of female bodies, the honoring of female agents, and the refusal of stereotypical attributions of maleness and femaleness and their racializations. Insofar as the Reformed tradition's understanding of the goodness of finite creation can be galvanized to celebrate the fuller texture of finite creatureliness, it is an important resource that, not incidentally, continues the project of modern Reformed theology. Calvin's idea that the *imago Dei* is a *task* characterized by the display of gratitude is quite useful in this regard, for it aids in disengaging the human "likeness" to God from narrow identification with such historically male-associated features as reason. To enact the *imago Dei* is not to have a particular (gendered, racialized, etc.) identity, but to live in a mode of thankfulness and dependence on God.

Similarly for the early feminist criticism of categories of sin marked by male experience, we can appeal to the crucial Reformed linkage of sin against God with sin against the neighbor. This can move us away from the need to think of idolatry only as the assertive ego with its male associations. De Gruchy's warning that an account of God can function as an idol when it comes "at the expense of humanity" is a Reformed version of feminist and womanist concerns about use of the historical tradition to denigrate human identities. As de Gruchy insists, such idols must be smashed "in the service of human and social liberation."[19]

As we think of application of this logic to broader examples of instances of exclusion/inclusion, we might begin with the public visibility of a group, which includes recognition of the group by those who draft laws, write theology, create culture, and attend to all forms of producing public reality. According to this criterion, illustrated by such issues as including women in leadership, we would say that at various points women as a group have historically been prevented from access to full citizenship, property rights, economic resources, forms of education, and political and cultural leadership—including ordination, among other things. For such an account of representation (or lack thereof), the Reformed theological logic is useful to fund arguments for the *inclusion* of women as a group historically rendered invisible. By showing that harm results from such exclusions and their associated confinements (to the domestic sphere or to worse depredations for those not historically put on domestic pedestals), the Reformed logic sets in motion the "always being reformed" imperative. The proper (just) relation to the other—women—is more important than any reading of Christian tradition that supports asymmetrical relations.

In this use of the Reformed logic, iconoclasm is directed toward any tradition, biblical or otherwise, that contributes to these exclusions, because human traditions are finite and created and not eternal or absolute. With such a challenge, the sin is identified as the placing of false qualifications on full participation in the church and God's good creation. The church is judged to diminish the *imago Dei* of women by its assimilation of various cultural constructions about what women can properly do. Gender conventions cannot

be made into idols; or, more subtly put, hierarchical anthropologies con-
travene the Reformed belief that God alone, not maleness (or any gendered
or racial identity), is the grounding source of well-being for human creatures. The claim would be, then, that women as well as men are created in
the image of God, and denigration of their bodies, sexuality, or female
natures is a sinful denial of the goodness of a finite creation.[20]

USING A REFORMED LOGIC: RADICALIZATION

The concern with inclusion clearly involves questions of representation.
Damage to the image of God occurs when images of women and things
pertaining to women are problematic or absent. Thus far these questions have largely focused on representations that have directly to do with
"women's issues." However, it is not simply demeaning gendered and
racialized symbols in the tradition that constitute the problem; nor is it only
the exclusion of female subjects from leadership roles, public speaking, or
positions of power to represent Christ, to name a few instances of religious
disempowerment. A form of analysis crucial to the broader exploration of
this issue is illustrated by an early article by Valerie Saiving, "The Human
Situation: A Feminine View."[21]

Although it contains a quite dated account of women's experience and
sexual differentiation, Saiving's work went beyond the complaint about the
explicit historic disempowerment of women. By focusing on the occlusion
of female experience in Reinhold Niebuhr's and Anders Nygren's accounts
of sin and redemption, Saiving initiated the crucial task of identifying the
gendered character of *all* theological discourse. The crucial implication of
her work is that denials of the full humanity of women are not confined to
explicit accounts of women's inferiority. Issues of gender are operative in
theology *whether the subject matter is historical women or not.*[22] A theology of
sin and redemption can disempower or diminish women by presenting a
purportedly universal view of human nature that fails to take their experience into account.

This logic must be taken to a more complicated level still as we attend to
representational analysis which recognizes that gender issues are no more
restricted to naturalized women subjects than they are to specific symbols
or teachings about women. Criticism that has yet to be adequately explored
includes the destabilizing of race and binary gender by theologians as well
as feminist theorists. To help think of this more radical understanding of
potential damage to the image of God, I move to the sense of representation
that concerns the power of discourse, or signifying, to create reality.

As feminist thinking moved beyond specific topics associated with
inclusion of women in the world of men, making "representation" the cen-

tral issue for a theology of the *imago Dei*, feminists and womanists came to recognize that discourses, or the sign systems that produce meaning, embody power relations. And while theories about these productions of meaning developed elsewhere, such work as Saiving's and Grant's has the important implication that language is not simply transparent to reality. Instead, language produces that reality and does so in ways that can both transform as well as obscure and diminish it. The early version of this development occurred in discussions of God language, suggesting that language does not simply provide access to the reality that is God, but produces human experience of God for good or ill. Inquiry was most focused in such discussions on the effects of representations of the human in relation to images of God and the savior.[23]

Outside of theological circles, attention in feminist and race theory to the productive force of representation has led into new theoretical territory.[24] This is prompting feminist and womanist theologians to shift attention from two stalwarts of these theologies—"women's experience" and the notion of women as (naturally) anatomically sexed subjects—to the *production* of subjects who are interpellated, or come to have an identity, as "women."[25] While it would be impossible to give up completely the model of women's experience, the shift to the study of discourse has resulted from an awareness of the limits of confining feminist thinking to women's experience. Sheila Briggs rightly observes about earlier feminist theology, "*Women's experience* becomes synonymous with *women's lives* and with *women's reality.*"[26] By treating gender as relevant only when subjects identified as women are under consideration, or as only about what these subjects understand about their lives, feminist thinking bypasses the gendered and racialized dimensions of all theological discourse. For example, human identities are racialized even when the woman experiencer may not think of herself as "having race." Thus theological confinement to "women's experience" as it is articulated in women's self-understanding can sideline important issues such as race, sexuality, and class.

As Joan Scott points out, feminist focus on women's experience "operates within an ideological construction that not only makes individuals the starting point of knowledge, but that also naturalizes categories such as man, woman, black, white, heterosexual, or homosexual by treating them as given characteristics of individuals."[27] While counterintuitive at first glance, the feminist point here is the need to scrutinize any a priori or taken-for-granted feature that defines a kind of human being rather than simply depending on what a person claims as her/his *experience*. The danger of taking a priori or naturalized identities for granted is well illustrated by the claim of the nineteenth-century American Presbyterian F. A. Ross that Africans are "the most degraded in form and intellect . . . of all the races of mankind."[28] Naturalized identities do not necessarily represent the "real," authentic subject, but rather the dominant group's construction of that subject's reality. Instead of accepting the naturalized identity of "women" subjects, we must study discourse, or the way processes of meaning create identities for such subjects and the power dimensions of these processes. This requires feminist and womanist theologians to attend to processes of meaning that are, in a sense, over and above the consciousness of particular women subjects, because it is such processes that signal the even more complex ways that damage is done to the image of God.

Let us take up some examples. These examples constitute considerable challenges for theology, for they interrogate what have often been thought of as indisputable in the defining of human being. They invite us to take seriously De Gruchy's claim that even an account of God can be "an idol that needs to be smashed in the service of human and social liberation." A first example is the view that some people have race and others do not; the second is that seemingly unquestionable concept, binary gender, or the notion that there are two kinds of people, males and females.

In the example of race, one particularly astute book title reminds us of how some appeals to "women" function to exclude: *All the Women Are White, All the Blacks Are Men, But Some of Us Are Brave.*[29] The important point is that the *frame itself* must be inspected for what it renders invisible. The example of race is helpful here to think about the power of discourse to frame reality in such a way that "women" means "white" and "blacks" means "men," as the title puts it. Womanist theologies have long pointed out that the possibility of making "gender" one's most important identifying characteristic is available primarily to those who do not have to see their race because of its advantaging effects. Most recently feminists have begun to acknowledge that its "woman" is white woman; the subject "woman," then, is a false universal.[30] It falsely claims to embrace all women. The primary opposition or "difference" for women of color may not be men, but whites, both men and women.

To begin to think this way is to define gender and race not as natural "givens" but as complex processes of subject production. Critical attention to the history of race shows its malleability and association with power. Key in that history was the production of a number of "scientific" theories of the inferiority of nonwhite races that dominated European and North American thinking in past centuries and produced the notion of race as a category of significant biological human difference.[31] As a socially constructed ordering of subjects rather than a natural trait, race is an unstable category for identity, and one (frequently) employed to the advantage of those with the power to assign it.

Feminists now must think of race and gender as simultaneous productive processes for all subjects, not just for so-called women of color. They must analyze the racialized character of the category "women" (usually white).

This is to say that being "white" can no longer serve its hidden function to identify this group as neutral, that is, exemplar of the female human being. Becoming white is a social accomplishment in relation to and won at the expense of the other. As such it defines a boundary between privilege and its opposite and cannot be treated simply as a natural feature of humanness.

A second example, binary gender, also extends the notion that power is connected to the frames that define and produce subjects. By challenging assumptions that there are two kinds of people, men and women, recent feminist theory has pushed beyond its own use of the model that held sway in the 1980s, the view that social conventions rather than biology determine the features of "real femininity" or "real masculinity," a view known as the social constructionist paradigm. Disputing this paradigm in which only *character traits* and *roles* were understood to be constructed, noted feminist theorist Judith Butler now argues that the idea of "naturally" sexed bodies of men and women should be questioned, thereby broadening the previous focus on sexual stereotyping and its results to investigations of how binary sex is actually a social construction that continues to advantage heterosexuals.[32]

In a binary paradigm, *woman* is a term that only has meaning in relation to *man*.[33] Moreover, this frame of meaning produces and reproduces the connections between binary, sexed identity and the normative linking of desire with the opposite sex. The use of the term "woman" within this binary frame reproduces the heterosexual division, because a "woman" is defined as a certain kind of anatomical subject who naturally desires her gender opposite (man). To be "homosexual" in this regime is to be deficient, even if the people using this framework promote the inclusion of gays. For without challenging binary notions of gender, the call to include the "lesbian" is simply to reinforce the subject-world that renders her deviant. Having gender is having an identity that "causes" desire for the other gender. Anything outside of this regime is disordered or falls off the map.[34]

These understandings of the power of representation with regard to race and sexual desire challenge theologians to think of the production of subjectivities as human discursive processes, not as pregiven or God-given identities. Otherwise we, feminists and womanists included, continue to be caught in additive notions whereby a woman "has" race or sexual preference or class, but only as a secondary attribute to what is most important, that is, not being a man. Quite simply, other definitional markers (such as race or class) may have more salience in the formation of subjects' lives, with all their constraints and possibilities, and these other markers alter the meaning of gender. Their effects cannot be simply added to the already-known effects of being female.

With this challenge to think radically about human individuals, the real genius of Reformed thinking comes into play. New forms of "damage to the *imago Dei*" come into view with this thinking about race and gender—the damage inflicted by systems of meaning that are part of the cultural and political processes of the social world, systems that are typically reproduced unconsciously. To resist these systems, Reformed deconstruction of the effects of idolatry must go beyond de Gruchy's work and beyond feminist and womanist attempts to include women—that is, to allow women access to the political, cultural, economic, and churchly realms of the social order. The logic of inclusion assumes and leaves in place certain structures of meaning, such as dividing up human subjects by conventions about their identities based on race, sexuality, or other markers. Most importantly, it renders these identities as "natural," and therefore not subject to question.

While we cannot avoid defining people—there is no other way to be determinate, finite creatures—these definitions and the power regimes that support them must always be subject to criticism. Reformed logic that is able to criticize the function of hierarchical notions of masculinity and femininity to keep women "down" is important, but it cannot be the only way to employ the logic of continual reformation. That logic of God's redeeming of a good creation must extend to the ways that systems of language and meaning are deployed. Thus this logic must include a destabilization that does not come to a halt with the identification of sin with current deformations around race, gender, and sexuality. That destabilization must be propelled by a posture of worship, and as such it can never be allowed to freeze. Reformed feminism can continue to honor God by exposing new idolatries. And it can take up the task of the *imago Dei* by displaying gratefulness to God that (literally) in Christ, there is neither male nor female.

If I am right in saying that to be created in the image of God is a symbolic condensation of what in the Christian tradition it *means* to be fully human and *who* the tradition has seen as fully human, then these seemingly radical explorations of our language and frames of meaning are theologically justified. Calling for such a reform of feminist and womanist theological reflections can be taken as a healthy sign of our Reformed status. Occlusion is always operative in our theologizing, and feminist thinking is as likely to be guilty as any other form. Fortunately our symbols and narratives and traditions sometimes outrun our consciousness and reflective understanding. The United States Constitution, for example, could state that "all men are created equal" when it in fact only meant white propertied men. And the excluded communities could (sometimes) hear themselves in the discourse and then go on to use it against its authors to expand the community of the legally enfranchised. In some analogous fashion, the reality of the God that we glorify, as well as the function of our traditions about Her, may well be trusted to continue to outrun our limited theological sense, calling us on to God's future.

CALVIN AND THE PERSONAL POLITICS OF PROVIDENCE

Kalbryn A. McLean

I have my suspicions about John Calvin, that great *pater familias* of the Reformed traditions. I suspect that he was really quite neurotic in his need for control. I suspect, in fact, that he was a man who thirsted for order in a time when chaos was the only true king. The more he lived with the social unrest of his era, the greater became his yen for order and the more elusive his ability to create it. But like any good Christian with an ounce of sanity and self-awareness, he suspected the same of himself and recognized the beginnings of a certain idolatry, a certain grasping after something that could properly belong only to God. So what else was he to do but hand the reins back to God—what else, but defer to the Perfect Father in perfect control? And so he relinquished his own deep longings for control, in what may well have been a supreme gesture of self-humbling, by articulating a doctrine of absolute providence in which God causes and directs every little thing that happens under the sun. On the other hand, perhaps Calvin was not simply deferring to a male parental figure; perhaps he was transferring his own neurosis onto God, thereby placing himself at a safe remove from it without giving it up entirely. Or, perhaps it was both—an act of sacrifice and neurotic projection—that gave rise to Calvin's doctrine of providence, in which God Himself seems to govern the world as an overly directive parent. This, of course, is psychological speculation.[1]

As I wrestle with the legacy of Calvin's doctrine of providence in the Reformed traditions, I find it difficult to move beyond such caricature and suspicion. I have the sense that what holds sway in the minds of fellow believers is a doctrine of providence that corresponds to this caricature rather than Calvin's fuller, pastorally motivated doctrine; and I sometimes find myself stuck in this flattened view as well. Yet not without reason: even when I return to the source, to Calvin's *Institutes*, I am jarred by his insistent rhetoric about God's absolute control and can see how the image of an overbearing deity has come to the fore. Other readings in Calvin may balance this forceful text, but I think his exposition of providence is ambiguous nonetheless. This ambiguity, the attending need to address the popular vision of providence it allows, and a sensitivity to Calvin's original writings and intentions make for a challenging engagement of his theology—particularly with respect to a doctrine that has suffered political co-optation for unjust causes. Writing the reflections that follow has thus felt like something of a juggling act, and other theologians will no doubt signal where balls have gracelessly left the air. But I want to state clearly from the outset that I am responding more to what I perceive as the translation of Calvin into contemporary popular belief than to Calvin's original doctrine in all its nuances. I nevertheless hope to honor enough of Calvin's original intent of strengthening his community to construct a meaningful understanding of providence for a modern audience.

My specific interest in this essay lies in presenting a doctrine of particular providence that navigates a course somewhere between a God who does everything and a God who does nothing—and this primarily with an eye toward empowering women. With Calvin's doctrine of absolute providence as my starting point, I begin a conversation among several theologians, as well as a host of implied cultural, psychological, and literary theorists, about the character of God's involvement in our world. Among the factors that give rise to my approach to this doctrine lurks my concern with the psychological states that produce and are produced by theology—hence my opening portrait of Calvin. Likewise, I am interested in how various psychological postures resulting from the intersection of personal and social circumstance determine how we receive the doctrines articulated in the academy and church. In order to explore how our own psychic workings may shape our understandings of God, for better and for worse, I rely on contemporary therapeutic discourse, now as readily available to a lay audience as to trained professionals in the field (although with widely varying consequences). The nineteenth-century philosopher Ludwig Feuerbach recognized this dynamic and made a similar point, though from a different perspective: what we call "God" is actually humankind's vision of idealized humanity projected onto a contemplated divine other.[2] However we construe the nature of our projections, whether as conscious ideal or unconscious psychic process, our visions of God inevitably embody some projected content; and this content has both individual and collective origins. Indeed, as feminists and womanists have amply demonstrated, the personal itself is also political—and in this case theological. Providence, that most politically charged of doctrines, often receives the burden of our hopes and fears because we typically look to providence for the possibility of change in our individual lives as well as the righting of political wrongs. (Biblically, providence often falls under prophetic jurisdiction.) So we should expect our dread and longing to be writ large into our visions of God, especially here. In this context, the insights of psychotherapy and cultural criticism won't safeguard us from projecting our needs, wants, and political agendas onto God; but they can help us understand how our projections inform both the creation and reception of theology and thereby allow us a greater sensitivity to how doctrine functions in the human community. Let us begin, then, by considering Calvin's original doctrine of providence and its legacy in modern Christian belief.

CALVIN'S SOVEREIGN FATHER

Calvin maintains the traditional doctrinal link between creation and providence and thus portrays God as both Creator and Sovereign: by divine prerogative, our heavenly Father brings the world into existence and presides over it as Governor and Sustainer. In his emphasis on God's sovereignty, Calvin is concerned to preserve God's utter freedom of action, God's agency. Thus, God's providence is absolute, and by this Calvin means that both general and particular providence are all-encompassing. Providence continually upholds creation in existence and imparts to particular created beings as much effectiveness as divinely willed—nothing and no one exercise their own power except insofar as God wills them to do so, and God may bend their movements according to the divine purpose. God's omnipotence here is not simply a general impulse that once initiated the order of nature but a ceaseless activity that regulates everything that happens in absolute specificity. Therefore, particular providence is thoroughgoing, that is, not restricted to occasional divine acts. Rather, everything is foreseen and foreordained by God the Father according to God's immutable secret plan. With respect to humankind, this means that God directs our every step so that we, too, are God's instruments.[3]

At first glance, this view of providence seems to assert that our lives are entirely scripted and we the mere performers of the unfolding drama, which makes it hard for some interpreters, this writer included, to conceive of our acting here as truly free. God, as author of all things, even plans evil in its specificity and uses it to serve the divine purpose. When confronted with existential malice and tragedy, we humans may find this a baffling portrait of the God whom we worship and from whom we seek comfort. There are, indeed, some important subtleties in Calvin's thought that temper this view. But popular belief tends not to reflect these subtleties, and so we are left with a distorted and perplexing vision of God. In the spirit of fairness, however, let me pursue one point of subtlety in Calvin's thought.

In his treatise against the Libertines, Calvin insists that God's providential direction of all things never violates the integrity of the free creature. He writes of general providence that "this universal operation of God's does not prevent each creature, heavenly or earthly, from having and retaining its own quality and nature and from following its own inclination."[4] More specifically, Calvin argues that God's causality in all acts—particular providence—neither determines the moral character of human activity nor taints God's own righteousness. He writes, "For we must not suppose that God works in an iniquitous man as if he were a stone or piece of wood, but He uses him as a thinking creature, according to the quality of the nature which he has given him."[5] And this iniquity our Father uses to providential ends, which always advance the good of creation. Here we can detect Calvin's anatomy of the human act, wherein divine and human motives may function simultaneously but nevertheless stand completely at odds. While God always moves out of justice and love (even if this love includes wrath or discipline), humans may act out of purely selfish motives. God's plan "absorbs" the resulting human behavior into the divine goodness without nullifying creaturely impetus. Stated another way, God's intention for a certain act seems to supersede human motivation as the ultimate "meaning" of that act, though we may not have access to that meaning. Nevertheless, according to Calvin, God is, in fact, acting in and through evil behavior.

What, then, does this imply about our free will and accountability? Calvin argues that despite God's foreordination of evil, we willfully and knowingly commit sinful acts and are therefore fully accountable for them. Adam had free will as part of his natural gifts, says Calvin, but chose to be unfaithful to God, thereby losing his freedom, as well as ours. God did, in fact, ordain that Adam would have this freedom and then lose it; but as far as we're concerned, we should focus on the reality of Adam's (and our) unfaithfulness and not try to take our reasoning back prior to Adam's fall—not try to penetrate the Father's inscrutable wisdom. The result is that our will now lies in bondage to sin and we regularly commit sinful acts, which are nonetheless part of God's overall plan. This compatibilist notion of human freedom, wherein God's direction of our agency is believed not to conflict with or annul our free will, rests on Calvin's dissection of the sinful act: again, the actions of those who sin are in line with God's purpose, but their intentions are not. Sinners strive against God; they do not will to do God's will. This double level of divine and human intention and causality allows humans to act by their own design. And in this separation between human motive and divinely directed action lies human guilt. Thus, God's fatherly providence remains both absolute and unimpeachable as it actively seeks our good.

Further, Brian Gerrish points out that Calvin's predominant association with the paternal image lies not in power or authority but in "devoted, affectionate care."[6] Hence, as God's beloved children, we stand first and foremost in the care of a profoundly loving providence and need not fully understand God's ways to trust them. In theory, then, the faithful who read Calvin's doctrine of providence will see both in his words and in the very God they seek a benevolent parent rather than a controlling and scrutinizing despot.

In theory, anyway. But no text, no matter how great a rhetorician its author, has within it the means to dictate precisely how it is read. The above qualifications notwithstanding, Calvin's doctrine of providence remains ambiguous, and this ambiguity has given rise to multiple readings of his theology. Moreover, quite apart from the textual ambiguity looms the indeterminacy of the reading or hearing subjects, who bring to any given doctrine their own interpretive filter through which they assimilate theological meaning—another twist on the projection dynamic. Calvin's doctrine of providence has migrated and mutated into popular culture, and I believe we now have within the Reformed traditions a deeply entrenched image of God as controlling Father—an heir is an heir, no matter whether we consider it legitimate—and this culturally loaded image merits our attention.

Assuming, as suggested above, that social situation shapes our interpretation of doctrine, let us consider our current cultural climate. In recent years, we've been hearing concern from the religious right about the moral decay of our social fabric. In particular, they have been the most vociferous group in denouncing the decline of "family values" and the ultimate ruin this will bring to our nation. But members of the more conservative Christian denominations aren't the only ones who perceive our own time as frightening and chaotic, especially following the events of 9/11. While some fear the challenges of homosexuality or the dangers of international terrorism, others perceive the threats to our nation's well-being in terms of the religious right's entrenchment against homosexuality, the foreign policies of our own government, or the increasing predominance of fear itself. Moreover, as our technology stretches its long, gangly legs past our moral traditions, as diversity resists cultural hegemony in unprecedented fashion (a positive if challenging development), we find the familiar giving way to the scary, exciting unknown of history, and we're looking for our sea legs. When we intuit dangers ahead, some of us jump ship and head back to dry land, swimming as we might against the tide of inevitable change. Those of us still on board are looking for some other form of security, but looking nonetheless. Having mostly jettisoned our Grand Narrative cargo, those master stories that purport to explain reality, we still find ourselves wondering, Is there yet some provisional (contextual, rhetorical) but nevertheless functionally absolute truth, some ethical North Star by which we can guide our vessels?[7] And what could this possibly look like?

In the context of this quandary, I find myself oddly enticed by Calvin's doctrine of providence. How reasonable, how comforting to think that in a world of rapid material and moral change, God is still completely in control; for here we have a vision of God and the world in which every detail of created existence is directed and attended by an omnipotent, omniscient, gracious God, with nothing whatsoever left to chance. All we need do is trust that this is so, that God is our North Star—and the wind in our sails—and draw comfort from that. Indeed, this message played a central role in Calvin's effort to nurture the faith and rouse the spirits of his own beleaguered community, persecuted as it was by the French Catholic monarchy. So why wouldn't such a word of reassurance be relevant for our own time?

Before trying to answer that question, let us further consider our social context, now from the perspective of gender. To all the challenges described above, women must add their continuing struggle against various forms of discrimination. True, feminism has made dramatic advances in promoting women's causes, not the least of which has been the recognition of its own internal racism, classism, and homophobia and the attending need to embrace diversity. But many sexist attitudes and structures still exist, just as the legacy of belonging to a historically disenfranchised group lingers. Women's increasing presence in executive positions in the business world, for example, has abated but not purged from our culture the belittling of women's competence, while much of society continues to elevate men's abilities. Further, girls and women are still highly vulnerable to emotional abuse and to physical and sexualized violence, often, though not always, precisely because they are female, and often, though not exclusively, at the hands of men. The historical exclusion of women from social, economic, and political power; ideological disdain for our abilities; and the abuse of our personal bodies and psyches has led to multilayered experiences of trauma over generations; and this trauma, however pointed for any one woman, makes its way into our spiritual beliefs, particularly with respect to how we think about God's involvement in our lives.

My point here is not to entrench women's identity in a victim role—quite the contrary. But I do wish to suggest that a general, if now more subtle, questioning of women's competence as decision makers too frequently intersects with concrete incidents of emotional and physical violence. Either one of these cultural phenomena by itself can undermine women's sense of agency; their intersection, however, indisputably lowers women's self-esteem, dislodges their instincts and judgment about the world around them, and thus hinders their ability to act. Although these dynamics do not affect all women equally, theology must speak to such experiential trends, both as it articulates new doctrines and as it seeks to understand how doctrines new and old might be received.

From this perspective, I find Calvin's doctrine of providence and its various incarnations much less comforting. The image of a (fatherly) God planning all our actions in detail, yet holding us accountable for our failures, strikes me as counterproductive to empowering women. Because images of directive male power abound in our culture, it is too easy to read Calvin's fatherly God through these images; indeed, I think appropriations of such images for God are as often intentional as they are unconscious and automatic, however disloyal to Calvin they may be. In turn, this overlay of patriarchal power onto God tends to reify male power in our culture, to shore up the status quo, while threatening to undermine women's agency—or, at the very least, it tends not to strengthen it. Given the complexities and pitfalls of this doctrine, it is understandably tempting to look elsewhere for a vision of providence, or even to do away with the doctrine of particular providence altogether. But before moving too hastily in either direction, let us take one last view of Calvin's thought by considering in more detail its benefits and drawbacks.

With his emphasis on God's perfect, gracious sovereignty, Calvin invites us into an assurance of order and a surrender to God's will and wisdom without the need to wrap our minds around all the specifics of why. "Trust," he urges. And as suggested above, some sense of order, however mysterious or inscrutable, is no small comfort these days; it is (or can be) a good thing for our belief in the prevailing goodness of life. At a doctrinal level, Calvin also guards God's perfect freedom over against the limited moral scrutiny of mere mortals and their tendency to appropriate God's providence self-righteously. Hence, for example, neither the religious right nor religious liberals have license to say, "God is on *our* side." Further, Calvin accounts for the origination of evil as well as its existence in terms of God's loving purpose, which God will indisputably bring to fulfillment. The pastoral import of Calvin's absolute providence thus lies in its assurance that even when bad things happen, we haven't fallen outside of God's fatherly care and eternal plan. It seems to me that this doctrine is a detailed riff on Romans 8:38–39: "For I am convinced that neither death, nor life, nor angels, nor rulers, nor things present, nor things to come, nor powers, nor height, nor depth, nor anything else in all creation, will be able to separate us from the love of God in Christ Jesus our Lord." And therein lies part of its appeal for me—an undaunted conviction of God's love for us originally proclaimed in a time of persecution.

Further, at a sociocultural level, affirmation of God's utter control may provide other spiritual rewards. Our culture, not unlike my quasifictionalized Reformer, prizes supreme individual control, an illusion that can be maintained only at great psychological cost given the vicissitudes of life. So insistence on God's absolute providence renders a much-needed corrective to what has moved beyond a cultural idol to become a communal pathology. God, not mortals, is in control of everything: the good, the bad, and the ugly; and we do well not to try to usurp God's position.

However, I still find Calvinist portrayals of providence troubling, just as I find many compatibilist notions of human freedom unconvincing.[8] God in this portrait appears to be a micromanager and we the bewildered, struggling administrators of a plan we can't even begin to comprehend. We don't have enough information to rely on getting it right. But if we do get it right, the glory goes to God; if not, the blame falls to us. That seems to me a trap if there ever was one, a gilded invitation to constant self-indictment with no message of self-love to balance it. From a psychotherapeutic perspective, Calvin's image of an all-governing Father may evoke the developmental hazards of micromanagement more than the solace of a vigilant deity.

Here, feminist theology and theory pose their challenge. While Calvin's view of providence may well communicate some truth about the incommensurability of divine and human agency, it has a tendency to depict the latter as infantile and ineffectual. If we work with the model of sin as human pride, as Reinhold Niebuhr suggested, the humiliation of human agency—of hubris—seems inoffensive, even appropriate.[9] But Judith Plaskow and those feminists who have followed her lead have amply shown that this interpretation of sin is heavily skewed toward masculine patterns of socialization and behavior.[10] Women's patterns, in contrast, tend toward self-effacement and subordination and a correlative diminishment of our agency and responsibility, both in society's view and our own. Consequently, we are less enabled to assume responsibility for ourselves as equal members of the human community. What we need is a doctrine of providence that calls us more fully into our agency, not less so. In this context, the Calvinist legacy—that is, the popular if distorted understanding of God as sovereign Father—risks undermining the development of agency, particularly of women, but also of all marginalized persons. For those individuals who have no sense of personal empowerment, who feel that they can't accomplish anything, or "make a difference," or "get it right," how does the pervasive image of a controlling father lift them out of this whirlpool of incapacity? My worry is that it functions more to paralyze and discourage, both individually and communally.

Accordingly, feminist theologians, among others, have also been concerned that this construal of providence supports the status quo more often than the prophetic office, despite Calvin's intentions to strengthen his community for survival and defiance against oppressive powers. Herein lies a deep tension in Calvin's thought. Instead of encouraging resistance to social injustice, it may be interpreted as calling both the oppressed and oppressors alike to accept their place in the world as God's will, whether as punishment or reward, predestined curse or blessing, obedience test or life lesson; and it advocates the potentially complacent attitude that what is not resolved fairly in this lifetime will nevertheless meet with perfect resolution eschatologically. Yes, this view of providence can bring a sense of peace in the face of otherwise hopeless situations; indeed, a woefully large number of communities live under such dire circumstances. Their situations may be an appropriate context in which they themselves can preach absolute providence, not as a call to resignation but as a defiant source of hope. However, at a political level, this doctrine seems to me a potential recipe for quietism and political docility, especially when preached by those persons and groups in power, as it often has been.

Again, Calvin's well-conceived rhetorical intentions hardly guaranteed a univocal reading of his theology in his own time, much less in ours. This interpretation of providence is now heavily fraught with its historical misuse to justify oppressive ideologies and practices. With this in mind, it's tempting to throw out the idea of particular providence altogether. Nevertheless, I think Calvin's pastoral intentions, the spirit of his doctrine, are worth preserving; indeed, there is something theologically sound and empowering about holding fast to the idea that God is directly involved in our lives. And historical misuse notwithstanding, real believers, including marginalized and persecuted folks like Calvin's community, take real comfort here. So my goal in the rest of this essay will be to articulate one (though hardly exhaustive) way of thinking about this doctrine that balances particular providence with the need to enhance women's agency. But before I begin my constructive proposals, let me digress to consider the work of one theologian who does think we should throw out particular providence so that we can better understand how much we would lose by doing so.

THE OTHER EXTREME: MAURICE WILES

Weighing in for the Anglican tradition, Maurice Wiles offers relief from Calvinist visions of an overly controlling God.[11] Indeed, Wiles's views and attitudes about providence seem to be quite the opposite of Calvin's. On my first reading of Wiles years ago, I thought that his largely nonintervening version of providence was too dilute to inspire hope and inadequate to scriptural accounts of God's action in the world. However, I revisited Wiles just as I did Calvin and also found his ideas oddly appealing on the second read. First, Wiles's articulation of providence doesn't present a God whose action in the world can be seen to conflict with human agency. Second, his theology thwarts any glib efforts to make God our Dr. Feelgood or the great protector who takes sides (ours) and comes to (our) timely rescue. Though he doesn't focus on them, Wiles is clearly cognizant of the abuses of the doctrine of providence whereby God's person, along with select historical events, is co-opted into justifying one's own or one's community's position at the expense of others. Because Wiles rejects the notion of particular providence, his interpretation cannot easily be enlisted to support the status quo of unjust social arrangements. It thus responds, at least implicitly, to feminists' main concerns about the doctrine. Perhaps, then, we should consider his argument as promising ground on which to rearticulate a doctrine of providence.

Wiles advances as his working premise the idea that "God's act" is the single act of creation, unified in its purpose and ongoing in its execution. Building on a description of "act" or "action" as a set of occurrences unified under an overarching intention, Wiles proposes that we conceive of God's action "in relation to the world as a whole rather than to particular occurrences within it."[12] He recognizes the centrality of human freedom to any discussion of these issues and resolves to uphold the radical and genuine nature of that freedom, to the extent that he advocates a thoroughgoing incompatibilist notion of free will. According to Wiles, human freedom forms part of the kind of world God originally created and still creates with the intention that personal and collective choices authentically influence the movement of this world to a poorer or richer existence. Toward that end, Wiles argues, God freely limits God's own omnipotence and omniscience. God undertakes to create this world (for all we know, this is the only world God considered creating) with a certain intention in mind—something like perfect relationship to God and others, we may assume—and will surely bring that intention to fulfillment as part of the unified divine act. This description of God's creative act leads Wiles to locate God's providence at the macrohistorical rather than the microhistorical level, contrary to Calvin. He thus effectively forestalls any arguments that depict God as manipulator or absolute controller and maintains the radical nature of human freedom.

Wiles wants to foil misguided understandings of what God does in the world and any attending unrealistic expectations. It is, indeed, spiritually discomfiting to think that God saves one (presumably) good person or community but not another. It is much more theologically palatable to argue that God simply doesn't intervene in that way. Yes, God actively cares for us, but not in an intrusive, arbitrary fashion. We must hope soberly, knowing that although God will bring good to bear in the end, God will not lead random rescue missions or even actively take sides. Temporal justice and the day-to-day care of others in need thus remains part of our human vocation. At the same time, Wiles's argument addresses the primary sociopolitical concerns about the doctrine of providence noted above. His refusal of particular providence debunks the notion that God preserves the status quo of those in power: if God does not intervene (or predestine) in specific ways, providence cannot be recruited for particular ideological causes. Moreover, this same refusal safeguards creaturely freedom in such a way that responsible human action remains possible, and we can all take our social praise and punishment on the chin. Here we find both ownership and accountability, and we generally prize those in the West—although, as previously suggested, our conceptual culture has often deprived women of both.

So why not accept this solution? Throw out particular providence altogether, and then we can trust in the ultimate fulfillment of God's gracious purposes while remaining free agents in the universe. It seems simple enough. This solution, however, doesn't strike me as spiritually satisfying—not that spiritual satisfaction can be the primary criterion, but it needs to be included. Whereas on some readings Calvin makes a lot of room for God and very little for humans in terms of freedom, Wiles makes a lot of room for humans but not so much for God.[13] To put it in personal terms that build on Calvin's paternal imagery, an overbearing parent may serve us no worse or better than one who is completely laissez-faire or uninvolved. Further, the fact that rejection of particular providence disallows God's appropriation for specific causes cuts both ways: those wielding oppressive power cannot reify their position by co-opting God for their own purposes, nor can the oppressed hope that God will aid them to resist injustice. And because I believe that God's active participation in our lives does enable us to withstand hardships both personal and political, I find myself unwilling to reject the doctrine of particular providence altogether.

Surely, there must be a happy medium between Calvin and Wiles, something that makes room for both divine and human freedom. For help reaching this happy medium, I turn now to the work of womanist theologian Delores Williams.

MAKING ROOM FOR BOTH

In her *Sisters in the Wilderness*, Williams offers us a coat of many colors, a mix of history, exegesis, story, theology, and analysis that aims at creating a new language and perspective for modern theologies, particularly those concerned with evil as embodied in structures of oppression.[14] Because her approach is less doctrinal than Calvin's and Wiles's and does not address providence systematically, I will rely on extrapolation and paraphrase to convey her implicit ideas on providence.

Williams begins her book by giving us a brief autobiography and describing for us her social location, so that we may glean from this information whatever we deem helpful for understanding her theology and its personal-historical origins. In so doing, she makes her story available as a critical tool and even weaves that story into the very public/published fabric of her theology. Williams then moves on to a larger narrative, one that focuses on the history of the entire African American community and, particularly, of African American women. She further links this history to the biblical stories of Hagar and thus roots the Christian history of her community in a long-standing religious history and tradition. At the same time, her reading of the biblical accounts stands within the Judeo-Christian tradition as much to challenge as to embrace it.

Williams takes the Hagar stories, Genesis 16:1–16 and 21:9–21, as paradigmatic of black women's experience. Working from an already well-established tradition among African American women, she draws parallels between the challenges Hagar faces and the imposed suffering, broadly conceived as economic and sexual oppression, that has historically shaped the lives of women of color. Williams's empathic focus on Hagar counters the dominant tendency of Judeo-Christian exegesis to identify more strongly with Abraham (primarily) and with Sarah (secondarily) as the progenitors of the chosen people. Nevertheless, with help from both the text itself and historical-critical analysis, Williams acknowledges the real and potential victim status of the characters in relation to each other and to the broader culture. For example, Hagar, as the slave of a Hebrew woman, is the victim not of an unfettered woman of power but of a person who is herself bound by the wider structures of patriarchal bias in her native culture. Williams thus refuses any simplistic rendering of the dynamics of power inscribed by the layers of text. While the details of Williams's explication present a rereading of the stories that is both creative and insightful, for my purposes I shall concentrate on their portrayal of providence as illustrated in Williams's analysis.

The Hagar stories, like much of the Hebrew Scriptures, are punctuated by God's direct intervention—particular providence, to speak doctrinally—in the lives of the characters. We are already familiar with God's action on behalf of Abraham and Sarah through the assurance of Isaac's birth and inheritance, an intercession that has both personal and communal implications. But prior to this event (in Gen. 16), we meet the childless Sarah who gives Abraham her Egyptian slave Hagar so that they might have children by her. Hagar conceives, contempt erupts between Sarah and her servant, and the former treats Hagar so harshly that she flees, pregnant and with no means of survival, into the wilderness. Here, Williams draws our attention to God's action on behalf of Hagar in this decidedly desperate situation. The movements of providence function at two levels (as they do later for the Hebrew couple): God consistently cares for Hagar's person while simultaneously working to fulfill the divine plan for Israel through Abraham and Sarah. In the wilderness, God greets Hagar and advises her to return to her mistress and her husband—a directive that, though not ideal, Williams interprets as necessary for Hagar's survival. Adonai also promises Hagar numerous descendants and thereby reassures Hagar of survival while offering her the hope of future freedom for her progeny. Hence, God does not act by fiat, altering historical realities, but rather works through unfavorable circumstances to ensure both personal and communal well-being. In fact, the biblical stories portray divine action for Hagar as oriented toward enhancing her own ability to act and survive; toward this apparent end, providence operates through guidance, promise, ministry, and empowerment, as we shall continue to see in Genesis 21.

After returning from the wilderness, submitting herself to Sarah and Abraham, and bearing Ishmael, Hagar must again confront the animosity of her mistress. God's promise of Isaac has been fulfilled, and Sarah is now unwilling to let Ishmael share the promised inheritance with her son; so she asks Abraham to cast Hagar out with the boy. Abraham proves reluctant, but God commands him to follow the wishes of Sarah so that the full inheritance will indeed fall to Isaac. Abraham obeys, and Hagar once more finds herself destitute in the wilderness. As before, God comes to Hagar, this time as her son is on the brink of death and her own near future holds the same. God intercedes by offering more life-saving guidance while also providing Hagar with the vision to see for herself new resources for survival. Ultimately, Genesis 21 indicates that Hagar and Ishmael not only survive but build an autonomous existence for themselves in the desert, where "God was with the boy" (Gen. 21:20). Hagar, with the clear and unfaltering assistance of God, has triumphed over her many and varied instances of oppression (under Abraham, Sarah, and Jewish law) and manages to raise her only offspring in the wilderness. She thus symbolizes for Williams both black women's faithful perseverance and victory and their status as cherished recipients of God's providential care.

Again, Williams offers no systematic commentary on providence. But her account of the Hagar stories does underscore the all-encompassing character of providence: God cares for the so-called oppressors, who are often victims themselves, and the oppressed alike; and God acts for the welfare of both particular individuals and the community as a whole. She thus eschews any exclusive ideological appropriation of providence on behalf of a certain group. Although she herself speaks from a group whose historical oppression has been justified by appeals to particular providence, Williams apparently deems this doctrine important enough to preserve in spite of its risks.

Williams's exploration of slave narratives and black women's contemporary experience corroborates the significance of particular providence within her community. She tells how women such as Sojourner Truth and Harriet Tubman all believed that God assisted them in their efforts to become free and to liberate others—efforts that were largely successful. Further, building on Hagar's stories in the wilderness and their appropriation by black women, Williams explains, "For many black Christian women today, 'wilderness' or 'wilderness-experience' is a symbolic term used to represent a near-destruction situation in which God gives personal direction to the believer and thereby helps her make a way out of what she thought was no way."[15] She then tells of some of her peers sharing their wilderness stories in such a way to illustrate, implicitly, that particular providence still plays a primary role in the faith and perseverance of contemporary black women.

Here, divine providence is multifaceted and complex, working toward the fulfillment of God's will at both the personal and collective levels; and it does so while also addressing the competing needs and desires of several individuals whom God seems to love equally. Stated otherwise, providence is directly involved but does not take sides. Yet if we are willing to surrender the biblical author's insight into God's specific actions (and inactions) and step into the characters' perspectives, we might concede that God's providence here is at best inscrutable, at worst seemingly capricious. Why does God lead Hagar back to Abraham and Sarah, only to command Abraham to cast her out yet again? From within the story, it might well seem that God is taking sides—and what a cruel game for Hagar. There is resonance with Job here: God temporarily subordinates the well-being of the individual to an inscrutable divine plan, only to restore or improve that individual's fortune later on. But we have the benefit of the big picture at our fingertips; Hagar did not (nor did Job). What can we reasonably expect Hagar to believe about God's action on her behalf? Perhaps from her perspective, Calvin would have been on the mark.

Williams's interpretation of this scriptural freeze-frame of providence favors Calvin over Wiles inasmuch as it preserves a notion of God's specific activity in the world. Williams writes, "All of our talk about God must translate into action that can help our people live."[16] How could belief in a God who doesn't take particular actions on behalf of creation found such a language? Given Calvin's own rhetorical concern to nurture piety and faith, this is a question he might well have asked himself. On the other hand, Williams, like Wiles, also attempts to honor the integrity of human freedom in a way that Calvin does not (again, assuming rejection of compatibilist notions of human freedom). God does, indeed, step onto the scene, but the characters act in accordance with God's overt guidance, not as actors constrained by a script. Williams thus maintains a view of humanity's agential autonomy while also preserving the notion of God's freedom to be actively engaged in our lives in and through particular circumstances.

A DEVELOPMENTAL PERSPECTIVE

Whichever theological perspective we favor thus far, we may still seek an understanding of particular providence that synthesizes the concerns of all three theologians. Marilyn McCord Adams (another Anglican), in her response to Wiles, introduces a distinction between two possible modes of providential care.[17] Working from a premise of disproportionate agencies, where one agent is incommensurably more "qualified" than the other, she describes the potential effects of the "bigger" agent on the "smaller": these effects may be either agency obstructing or manipulating, or agency enabling or developing, the latter including such effects as may be necessary for the "smaller" agent to function at all. She illustrates this distinction with an analogy to mother and infant, where the former's love and nurturing of the child establish a safe environment in which the child can take the increasing risks of personal development. The mother's care must include both presence and particular acts through which the child grows and learns. And these acts, Adams asserts, cannot count as manipulative until the child's agency reaches a certain level of autonomy. Adams then connects this to the divine-human relationship: she argues that the ontological gap between God and creatures is so great that, in comparison to God, human persons never move beyond agential infancy. Thus, God, as Holy Spirit for example, may throughout our lives serve as an enabling agency for us without yet violating our freedom.

I find the distinction Adams makes to be a compelling response to Wiles's desire to preserve human freedom vis-à-vis God, one that does not discard particular providence altogether. Further, it corresponds to Williams's portrayal of providence from the Hagar stories as well as to the reliance of African American women on an active, empowering providence in their daily lives. While God has not liberated these women from their oppression by radically altering the hard facts of history, God has supplied them with the inner strength, faith, and vision to find and use ever new resources in their struggle for freedom and abundant life.

At the same time, given feminist concerns about views of providence that render women's agency infantile, we have cause for caution here. Therefore, I would like to add to Adams's idea the possibility that God, or particular providence, works through persons who invite God to do so. This suggestion assumes a certain level of awareness of both God and self and may thus require that we extend human agency beyond Adams's metaphor of infancy—perhaps to something like a fumbling adolescence, or young adulthood. But I believe it surmounts the problems concerning human freedom equally well while acknowledging our need and burgeoning capacity, given God's support, to make difficult decisions and act on them, sometimes for good, sometimes for ill. Furthermore, if, through God's self-limitation, we are as radically free as Wiles argues, then we must also have the choice to open ourselves and our field of action to God and others. God allows us to act freely; correlatively, can we not also invite God to act freely through us, assured that God's agency is perfect? Surely we can extend such hospitality to God's will only through God's ever available grace; and while doing so may represent a conscious choice, it may through God's grace also become a spiritual disposition that need not be rechosen at every moment. This hospitality toward God redefines us as vessels of God's providence rather than mere instruments, and it enhances our God-given freedom as well as our ability to enjoy that freedom for the benefit of ourselves and others.

BEYOND GOD THE FATHER

As noted previously, Brian Gerrish reminds us that Calvin depicts God not so much as a stern disciplinarian but as a loving, attentive father, one whose constant care seeks to raise up his children from the sin that binds them. As we consider God's providence, we can benefit from recuperating this image both from Calvin's work and from our own culture, where, alongside negative stereotypes, we also have real models of loving, affectionate fathers. In fact, we have a responsibility to seek out and advocate such models. Nonetheless, simply to switch from a stern to affectionate paternal image does not solve the problem. A doting parent—whether father or mother—who gives well-meaning, "devoted, affectionate care," might also be controlling and invasive in the very effort to care for a child, thus undermining the child's developing agency. Cultural attitudes about male competence may mitigate this effect for boys as they grow; but dismissive attitudes toward female competence may exacerbate this same effect in girls as they become women. Calvin did not intend to make God's fatherly power and human freedom a zero-sum game, wherein the more power God exercises, the less freedom we have. However, as Calvin's doctrine intersects with our culture's familial patterns and its gender prejudice, his original intent may be lost on modern believers. A zero-sum game may be exactly what we experience—particularly if sin distorts our perceptions as thoroughly as Calvin argues.

So we need to use our imagery carefully, and we benefit from having multiple images at our disposal. Thus far, I've been speaking of God the Father, using parental images for God just as Calvin does. But we also have ready access to other divine persons and their images in the Trinity. God is both a faithful son to the Father and a loving sibling to humans. While this is fertile ground for other images of providence, I will not treat them here. Rather, I turn now to the third person of the Trinity, God as the noncorporeal, nongendered Holy Spirit.

THE WILD CHILD

I began this essay with the operating assumption that the personal is political and that the personal/political inevitably, by way of projection or filtering, makes its way into our theology. In our culture at this point in history, the personal is unavoidably gendered, so our projections onto God will likely be coded for gender as well. Let me revisit Calvin, then. He was a powerful male theologian, albeit in a persecuted community, who attributed absolute control to a male-figured Godhead, wherein God the Father and God the Son play the primary roles. We might see in this picture a man deferring to other men. There could be some valuable masculine humility here, especially assuming a partial validity of Reinhold Niebuhr's interpretation of sin as (male) pride. But the power in Calvin's vision basically stays in the male line, and what we believe to happen in the Godhead is often used to prescribe and justify what happens in society. We are accustomed to male power in our culture, especially protective paternal power, so this imagery may work for many people, including many women. However, no single image works for everyone, and this one poses a hindrance to some believers. Not only does the power here seem to belong exclusively to a masculine province, but the nature of that power may undermine any human agency that is not secure in itself.

In a climate of still precarious gender negotiations, I thus find it difficult to conceive of providence in terms of God the Father, precisely because I butt heads with the image of God that the Calvinist legacy presents. God here is too controlling, too invasive, and it seems that one's role is to be passive and helpless, without any power to influence the world. I also sense here an impulse to feel, alternately, punished or rewarded, leaving the believer trying desperately to figure out what one did wrong or right to deserve one's fate. If only we could get a copy of that script . . . If we look to God the Son and sibling, perhaps we will find that he offers a good example of how to live our lives in this world—maybe *he* is the script. But then, sinlessness is a tough act to follow, and we may get into trouble here too.

So it makes sense to turn to that wild child of the divine family, the Holy Spirit, the much-neglected person in the West, except in the charismatic traditions. And perhaps because the Spirit has been so neglected, it has largely escaped the gendering tendencies of our culture. I, at least, tend not to think of the Holy Spirit as gendered; but the fact that it has sometimes been conceived of as feminine does not hurt the feminist cause. Perhaps here we have an image of an agency-empowering providence—one who does not stand over us in a controlling position but instead swirls around us, ever present and shape shifting, ready to infuse us with energy when our bodies grow weary, ready to sharpen our vision when our eyes become heavy, ready to give us tongues of fire when we need to denounce injustice and still sing God's praise. Any of these acts of empowerment constitutes a moment of direct but nonintrusive divine activity in this world. If our developmental stage as humans falls somewhere around a very young adulthood, then we are less in need of a constantly intervening parent and more in need of an empowering parent who gives us leave to explore life with a wise, trustworthy friend. Without forgetting that the persons of the Trinity are one, we may think metaphorically of God the Father and Son as having sent the Holy Spirit for precisely this role—the role of a supportive particular providence. The Spirit is that mentor who loves us no matter what, who encourages us to take risks, to make mistakes, even to fail—even to succeed—and yet helps us feel the joy of God's love, resist injustice, and celebrate the gift of life. As we receive the Spirit, who has always received us first, perhaps the Spirit also teaches us the pleasure and freedom of hospitality, emboldening us to fling wide our doors to an active, empowered love for God, neighbor, and self. Although Calvin said it differently, I think his intention was to convey this same liberating power of God on our behalf.

There is no one "correct" image of God or of providence. Calvin insists that God accommodates the divine message to our human capacities of understanding and of being moved. I believe this happens at both collective and individual levels. Surely, Scripture offers some parameters for what we should and should not say about God. But if God speaks to us where we are, should we not also show sensitivity to a diverse audience in our theology? Moreover, if God is truly sovereign and truly free, then the Holy Spirit is not bound even by Scripture. It remains to us, as a community, to articulate ever new and faithful images of God for the community, with the assistance of that unpredictable, grace-giving Wild Child in our midst. I have attempted here to present some images of providence that will be helpful to many readers, but particularly to women and, by extension, persons in the margin. The result is incomplete and provisional; and, as Calvin knew so clearly, only inasmuch as it inspires faith and piety will it hold value for the community of believers.

8

RESURRECTING THE ATONEMENT

Martha Schull Gilliss

"Great is the mystery of faith . . ." pronounces the minister right before the distribution of the communion elements. We the congregation respond with conviction, "Christ has died, Christ is risen, Christ will come again." Thus concludes the prayer in which we remember with grateful hearts God's supreme love active among us and extending into the future. I really love this part. Since I was a very young child, I have witnessed communion in Presbyterian churches. In those days, children could not participate in communion until they were confirmed; yet on the sidelines, as it were, I vividly remember absorbing words about blood, sacrifice, suffering, and death, mysterious words about rising and destroying death, words about eternal life.

"Christ has died, Christ has risen, Christ will come again." Much later in seminary, graduate school, and now in "middle age," these are the words that come to mind when I think of the doctrine of the atonement. This simple but profound proclamation of faithful hope is the culmination of the mystery of faith. In light of these words, I find it difficult to separate the suffering and death of the cross from the hope of the resurrection. As the apostle Paul insists, "If we have been united with him in a death like his, we will certainly be united with him in a resurrection like his" (Rom. 6:5). The doctrine of the atonement embraces both. John Calvin states,

> So then, let us remember that whenever mention is made of [Christ's] death alone, we are to understand at the same time what belongs to his resurrection. Also the same synecdoche applies to the word 'resurrection': whenever it is mentioned separately from death, we are to understand it as including what has to do especially with his death. . . . By rising again he obtained the victor's prize—that there might be resurrection and life.[1]

Indeed, the atonement also embraces the new heaven and earth promised in "Christ's coming again." Atonement is literally "at-one-ment"; it refers to the full spectrum of gracious divine actions that make creation "at one" again with God. As the nineteenth-century Reformed theologian John McLeod Campbell states, "the atonement is to be regarded as that by which

125

God has bridged over the gulf which separated between what sin had made us, and what it was the desire of the divine love that we should become."[2] The doctrine of the atonement is about the initiative and aims of God's love.

We rehearse this doctrine and participate in its profound mystery every time we celebrate baptism and the Lord's Supper. We also find in the atonement an ethical mandate for human existence and a guide for our future hope. But it is especially here that atonement doctrine has encountered harsh theological dissent. As a Reformed feminist, I want to weigh carefully my tradition's controversial "celebration" of sacrificial and substitutionary models of the atonement—specifically their focus on wrath and punishment—against the womanist and feminist critique that neither ethical existence nor salvation can possibly be founded upon these models. I agree that truncated forms of atonement doctrine indeed have felt more like bad news than footholds into the joy of the resurrection. But I wish to reinterpret Reformed emphases on satisfaction and substitution rather than abandon them. The atonement is about God's unmerited love for us shown in Jesus Christ, which makes us at one with God and empowers us to overcome forces of sin and death. Properly understood, the doctrine of the atonement encourages the faithful to risk daily practices of love, resist evil, and approach the future with confidence and trust. "Dying you destroyed our death, rising you restored our life, Lord Jesus, come in glory!"

REFORMED APPROACHES TO ATONEMENT

From the start, New Testament writers and theologians employed a variety of images to express the salvation given in Christ. As the Confession of 1967 states,

> God's reconciling act in Jesus Christ is a mystery which the Scriptures describe in various ways. It is called the sacrifice of a lamb, a shepherd's life given for the sheep, atonement by a priest; again it is ransom of a slave, payment of a debt, vicarious satisfaction of a legal penalty, and victory over the powers of evil. These are expressions of a truth which remains beyond the reach of all theory in the depths of God's love for all people. They reveal the gravity, cost, and sure achievement of God's reconciling work.[3]

Deceiving the devil and transforming us through a supreme demonstration of love are additional word pictures later Christians used to express how Christ met human lack and restored us to the joy of communion with God. But in the Reformed tradition atonement doctrine has often been fixed around a small group of images and expressed in limiting ways. Reformed theologians have typically followed the late medieval theologian Anselm in his emphasis on the substitutionary sacrifice of the incarnate Son on the cross as the satisfaction owed to God because of the offense of human sin; but Reformed atonement doctrine has often added special emphasis on wrath and punishment. We are made "at-one" with God because on the cross Christ satisfies the Father's wrath and suffers punishment in our stead. This approach to the atonement has shortcomings. First, on this view the death of Christ overshadows the redemptive significance of his birth, life, resurrection, and return. Second, the Trinitarian character of atonement is eclipsed. Third and most importantly, viewing the atonement as an external means of propitiation for sin or assuagement of God's wrath tends to obscure the central message of grace freely given.

For example, the Heidelberg Catechism, written in 1563 as a teaching tool in question-and-answer format, frames its account "Of Man's Redemption" with the insistence that "sin committed against the supreme majesty of God be punished with extreme, that is, with eternal punishment of body and soul." The only way humanity is able to "escape this punishment, come again to grace, and be reconciled to God" is through a "payment in full" to God's righteousness. This happens especially on the cross, where Christ "bore in body and soul the wrath of God against the sin of the whole human race, so that by his suffering, as the only expiatory sacrifice, he might redeem our body and soul from everlasting damnation, and might obtain for us God's grace, righteousness, and eternal life." According to the Catechism, "the righteousness and truth of God are such that nothing else could make reparation for our sins except the death of the Son of God."[4] In this Reformed account of the atonement, every other dimension of Christ's presence with us becomes a satellite of his death. Christ's incarnation is a necessary prerequisite to the efficacy of his atoning death; his life is suffering that anticipates his death; his resurrection allows us to "share in the righteousness which he obtained through his death";[5] and our comfort in his coming again turns on the fact that his death has already removed God's curse from us. As the central act of human redemption, the cross is depicted as the sacrifice of a merciful Son to win over a wrathful Father, with no role given to the Holy Spirit. The Trinity's oneness in purpose, love, and will is obscured. Finally, themes of divine punishment and human suffering predominate all the way to the end, when the returning Christ "will cast all his enemies and mine into everlasting condemnation."[6]

John Calvin clearly employed this satisfaction-and-substitution model of the atonement in his writings.[7] Yet he recognized that images of Christ's redemption are grounded in perceptions of our dire human need. As he states in his commentary on Galatians, "if the death of Christ be our redemption, then we are captives; if it be satisfaction, we were debtors; if it be atonement, we were guilty; if it be cleansing, we were unclean." Multiple images of the atonement do not dilute the power of love that the doctrine conveys. However we explain it, Christ has done something for us that we cannot totally account for using images available to us. Simply put, the atonement reveals divine love as grace meeting human lack, or sin. The spiritual and pastoral dimensions of atonement doctrine render it inappropriate to adhere rigidly to only one or two images.

Calvin also expanded the traditional Reformed emphasis on the cross with attention to the centrality of the resurrection:

> For since only weakness appears in the cross, death, and burial of Christ, faith must leap over these things to attain its full strength. We have in his death the complete fulfillment of salvation, for through it we are reconciled to God, his righteous judgment is satisfied, the curse is removed, and the penalty paid in full. Nevertheless, we are said to "have been born anew to a living hope" not through his death but "through his resurrection" [1 Peter 1:3]. For as he, in rising again, came forth victor over death, so the victory of our faith over death lies in his resurrection alone.[8]

The atoning work of Christ is not only about weakness and suffering. It is also about victory over the forces of death. As the apostle Paul asserts, "if we have died with Christ, we believe that we will also live with him. We know that Christ, being raised from the dead, will never die again; death no longer has dominion over him. The death he died, he died to sin, once for all; but the life he lives, he lives to God. So you must also consider yourselves dead to sin and alive to God in Christ Jesus" (Rom. 6:8–11). Jesus Christ has humbled himself to save us from suffering inflicted by ourselves and others, "not to engrave that lowliness into the world as its final good," as Kathryn Tanner puts it.[9] Reflections on Christ's atoning work cannot therefore rest in the suffering of the cross alone. Calvin states that our salvation involves both Christ's death and resurrection because "through his death, sin was wiped out and death extinguished; through his resurrection, righteousness was restored and life raised up."[10] The resurrection ensures that the gracious, atoning power of Christ lives among believers to this day and into eternity. Emphasis on the resurrection underscores that Christ's atoning work is not only for us as individuals, but for us corporately. The "living hope" we receive brings us so close together that we become Christ's body, the church. The resurrection also points forward to the dynamic eschatological mystery of the world's reconciliation with God and leads believers into an unknown and ever-changing future with the full strength of faith.

Calvin upheld the recognition of divine justice in doctrines of the atonement, but he grounded God's demand for justice clearly in love. He constantly fell back on the parental image of God who yearns for a relationship of love and respectful obedience with us. "God established in Christ the means of reconciliation, so that nothing should get in the way of God's love for us."[11] There is no law of repayment or punishment distinct from God that constrains God's freedom to love. God sent Christ into the world to reveal this love by saving humanity from sin and its suffering. While God condemned the sin that is in us, God did not condemn humanity.

Satisfaction, the notion that Christ's atoning work implies some kind of change in God by meeting God's demands for righteousness, remains a theme in Calvin's and many other Reformed accounts of the atonement. Yet it does not have to be understood in terms of the appeasement of God's wrath by the punishment of Christ. Leanne Van Dyk clearly shows how John McLeod Campbell retained a notion of satisfaction while refuting penal accounts of it. Campbell posited that Christ's act on the cross, far from a passive acceptance of punishment, was the perfect confession of both "the outrage of sin" and the righteousness of God's condemnation of it, through which Christ "absorbed the wrath of God."[12] Christ's suffering on the cross was, moreover, a sacrifice of love for our sin. It was a sacrifice in that he loved despite rejection. But his sufferings were not penal in character nor should they be viewed as valorizing suffering. Rather, Christ's sufferings on the cross revealed the love of Christ for God and Christ's sympathy for God's condemnation of sin. They disclose what "our sins are to the Father's heart."[13] They reveal the cost of the gift to God, the sorrow and pain of rejection.

Likewise, substitution, as it has been classically used, has suggested to many a kind of passivity in which Christ "allowed" himself to be put to death in a horrible way to stand in for our deserved punishment. By contrast, Van Dyk stresses that Christ's sufferings are "the form that holiness and love of God takes in the glaring reality of sin."[14] In this scenario of reconciling love, the role of the cross is to substitute for our own denial and even ignorance of our sin a perfect confession that both claims and condemns it. In the cross of Christ, the gift of divine love undoes the deception and violence of sin and evil, stripping them of their power over us. The gift of divine love is resurrection life, a mode of life that is not passively determined by sin and violence but actively by love.

On McLeod Campbell's account, the gift of Christ's confession is tied to the cross; hence, once for all. But it has ongoing effects in our lives. The risen Christ abolishes the power of sin to bind us for eternity. The ascended Christ's intercession to God for our sake continues this confessional movement through history as the work of the Holy Spirit. Christ's sacrifice of confession works an internal transformation in our hearts, so that we are able to confess in like manner with the assurance that we are pardoned rather than condemned. What remains for us is life in the Spirit, life lived as participation in the great gift of reconciliation to God and others.

Some Reformed theologians have criticized McLeod Campbell for placing too much weight on what happens in human existence as a result of Christ's work (the "subjective" side of the atonement) and not enough on what Christ accomplishes on our behalf (the "objective" side of the atonement). His approach has been likened to that of the eleventh-century theologian Peter Abelard, who understood the atonement in terms of the transforming example of divine love. This criticism misses the element of Christ's satisfaction in McLeod Campbell's approach. Because Christ has already satisfied God's righteousness, Christ's perfect response as an act of compassion on our behalf lets us "be irresistibly drawn by its sheer moral and spiritual power to repentance and a full realization of our status as adopted children of God."[15] Whether McLeod Campbell's emphasis on the confession of Christ is finally persuasive, he is helpful in providing a Reformed approach to the atonement that decenters punishment, traces the full drama of Christ's presence with us, and recognizes the Trinitarian character of our salvation.

All Reformed accounts of the atonement acknowledge that salvation is divine gift, not reward for moral striving. We are not redeemed because we are perfect imitators of Christ. The atonement accomplishes more than persuading humanity to lead better lives. The radicality of human evil and Christ's suffering must not be denied nor their legacies rendered invisible. It is God who makes the way for the restoration of right relationship with us. Undeserving of this relationship because of sin and unable to free ourselves from demonic forces by ourselves, we are dependent for our salvation on God's gracious initiative. The emphases on substitution and satisfaction in Reformed understandings of the atonement come out of the recognition that Christ does for us what we cannot do for ourselves and that somehow what he does clears a path for our apprehension of and participation in God's love.

But I would also insist on making the atonement comprehensible as primarily the act of love that it is. Jesus did not give himself to death to win the love of God for us but rather to reveal God's power in the face of terrible human evil. In this way Jesus' death is consonant with his life. The violent death of Jesus on the cross represents the holy tragedy of God's suffering the effects of sin and death precisely by revealing a greater power, a new reality of reconciled communion. Abelard's insight into the transforming power of God's love as continuous through Christ's life, death, and resurrection has to be retained in my Reformed feminist account. His account is valuable because it pays attention to how the doctrine of the atonement ought to function in Christian life.

Furthermore, I emphasize that the atonement is the work of the whole Trinity, a truth that is obscured by models that focus narrowly on the punishment of the cross. The triune model of otherness in love and the freedom inherent in the nature of its gift giving sets the pattern of right relation. The doctrine of the immanent Trinity asserts that this model of freedom in self-giving characterizes the internal life of the Godhead. But it is also characteristic of God's relations with creation, referred to as the economic Trinity. In the freedom of love God became human in order to assume our otherness with its sin; in this same freedom Christ chose to obey God's will. Through this assumption of human life, Christ transformed our human wills so that we might be made open to God's grace and become one with God. In the power of the Holy Spirit, bestowed upon believers through the risen Christ, we actively take part in this grace, freed from the bondage and burden of sin. The doctrine of the atonement revolves around that unique power inherent in Christ's life, death, resurrection, and coming again—the indomitable power of love, in which the triune God is supremely free to be for us and for all creation.

CHALLENGES TO ATONEMENT DOCTRINE

Christian feminist and womanist theologians are rethinking the way atonement doctrine functions in human lives, in alignment with the totality of Christ's life, death, resurrection, and return. How does the doctrine of the atonement encourage Christian believers to live? They recognize that all images of the atonement employ the language and sociopolitical thought of a particular time. Voices from the margins—the edges of traditional ecclesial and theological authority—have been speaking for quite some time into the central halls of power, naming different modes of sin, such as hiding from one's gifts and calling, and claiming grace as the promise of liberation from this and other kinds of bondage. These voices are enlarging the tradition to conform more fully to the wideness of God's reconciling grace. For instance, many women do not feel grace *initially* as a call to sacrifice themselves but rather as a summons to discover and claim their gifts as real and viable assets both for their communities of faith and for their societies. Some feminists have asserted that real power, both divine and human, is experienced not as power *over* others but rather as power *with and for* others. Power over others establishes a hierarchy of individuals competing to attain the best fruits attainable from a limited totality of good. On this model, the power of God and human creatures is a zero-sum game—the more power God has, the less creatures have. By contrast, power with and for others creates community, and this is the kind of divine power at work in the atonement.

A central problem with making a punitive substitutionary image of the cross the norm is that it can encourage the passivity of systematically oppressed persons. For example, the Reformed womanist theologian

Delores Williams has challenged the notion that Christ suffered as a substitute for human sinfulness. She charges that this image of substitution is not salvific for black women, whose forebears experienced sexual and domestic surrogacy during their enslavement in the United States. To counter this image, Williams posits self-love, regardless of what flies in its face, as the sine qua non of salvation. Much in the lineage of Abelard, she lifts up Jesus' life of resistance, the survival strategies that he taught, and the ways he became himself the salvific heart of the atonement.[16] The stress on agency implied in this interpretation, she believes, is more helpful for persons who have lost their identity because of an unexpected, *unchosen* experience of being thrust into an alien, dehumanizing experience of surrogacy.

Williams claims that violence and suffering can have no positive role in liberation from sin, and that to glorify anyone's suffering allows the glorification of all suffering. Moreover, if Christ's suffering was in fact willed by God, the temptation arises to construe Christ's unquestioning obedience as a moral virtue. Williams wants black women to recognize and expose the violence against them for what it is, not to elevate it to a salvific mode of being or a power with saving potential. Williams's radicality culminates in her assertion that the cross represents "the image of human sin in its most desecrated form. . . . Jesus does not conquer sin through death on the cross. Rather, Jesus conquers the sin of temptation in the wilderness (Matt. 4:1–11) by resistance. . . . Jesus conquered sin in life, not in death."[17] Williams understands the crucifixion exclusively as a symbol of violence and wrongful suffering. Christ's earthly life, rather than his death and resurrection, is the heart of the atonement. Jesus' life presents us with the challenge to accept the responsibility of loving God, self, and neighbor, and to resist violence. This includes claiming self-worth, an act that embodies resistance against evil and injustice.

I agree that the cross as Williams understands it is not at all salvific. When the saving work of Christ is identified solely with the cross, the phenomenon of suffering is removed from its context and risks being falsely valorized. This approach to the atonement can imply that to be fully human is to suffer for the welfare of others, without regard to one's own, and that such suffering epitomizes the value of a moral life. Yet, Williams's treatment risks rendering the cross irrelevant in the transformation of human existence from the state of alienation to reconciliation. A Reformed feminist approach does not have to identify the cross only with the evil it destroys. The power of Christ's life, divine love offered as free grace, is not a different power than that revealed on the cross. When linked to Christ's life and resurrection, the cross provides the capacity both to question the fallible systems that have instituted unjust laws and created inequitable situations and to scrutinize options for resisting evil. Ultimately the cross is a site of perfect reversal of evil and sin by the strength of divine love.

Closer to my own view of atonement and the role of the cross and suffering in human salvation is that of another womanist theologian, Jacquelyn Grant. Grant claims that God neither inflicts nor desires suffering and finds warrant for this in Scripture, which she reads through the lens of Jesus Christ as the beginning and the end of the revelation of God's Word.[18] God suffers with those who suffer; and as they turn to the Holy Spirit for instruction, they affirm God's goodness and sovereignty over the source of their pain. In this view, Jesus is present as co-sufferer who empowers in times of oppression. Just as black women have identified with Jesus' suffering, through the power of the Holy Spirit they have believed that Jesus has also identified with them. From this sense of unity, black women have been able to comprehend that oppressive existence is not their God-given destiny but rather their particular context in which to experience hope.[19] Grant points out that the phenomenon of suffering itself is amoral; what is problematic is the linkage of suffering with punishment of sin. Grant and many others receive strength by regarding Christ's suffering in a different kind of light—as compassion. In this sense, Christians who suffer achieve a kind of unitive, resurrective power that helps them to carry on with their lives.

I want to stand with Grant but develop her thoughts about how the doctrine of atonement functions from my own perspective as a Reformed—and white—feminist. The crucifixion draws from the power of the resurrection. The cross is vital to the Christian faith. I agree with Grant that suffering is amoral in itself, although it is all too often experienced as evil, as an involuntary violation of good. The suffering on the cross, however, was freely chosen, and in this sense it was an ultimate act of compassion. While we should never valorize suffering as key to moral behavior, we should not trivialize the power of freely choosing to take on the suffering of others. In like manner, sacrifice is amoral. It can be an act of destructive violence (Jepthah's sacrifice of his daughter's life), or it can be an act with redemptive power (as in Ruth's sacrifice of her individual freedom to stay with Naomi rather than abandon her). It can also be a gesture toward reconciliation that reestablishes a bond between alienated parties. The cross must remain at the center of our theology as the act in which God compassionately takes our brokenness and violence and mysteriously absorbs them into God's own self in order to transform them in the power of reconciling love.

This transformation makes possible a new way of life. The power God reveals on the cross does not languish before evil but has the strength to absorb it and to replace it with something new. God offers this strength and this love back to us as a gift of resurrection grace. We experience this grace already in the present time and in fullness in the promised reign of God. It is not a matter of enduring suffering and sacrifice now because we are promised that things will get better in the future, but precisely the truth that things are better now because Christ has risen, and Christ's ongoing transformation of the world calls us to active participation.

A "RESURRECTION" OF THE ATONEMENT

Like everyone alive today, the apostle Paul, formerly Saul of Tarsus, was not a follower of Jesus while Jesus lived on earth. His experience of salvation, in which he was overwhelmed and blinded by a bright light, morphed into a life of grateful response to Christ's acceptance of him. In his postresurrection encounter with the risen Christ, Paul was called by name and claimed as apostle, his terrorist acts of violence against Christ's followers revealed for what they were. In that searingly bright revelation, however, Paul felt not condemnation but acceptance and call. He knew that Christ whom he had been persecuting was not condemning him but interceding on his behalf before God, and that his terrible sin was no longer a barrier that would separate him from God. Paul's experience of the risen Christ was an unexpected gift, a gift given in compassion and filled with hope for a new way of life. This gift changed Paul forever so that he no longer lived for himself. His life became shaped in and through a community by a power that blew from the future and not from the past.

With Paul, we too know Jesus as the *risen* Christ. Therefore, a reconstruction of how atonement doctrine shapes Christian life must be given in light of the resurrection. Like Paul, we may be blinded temporarily by the glory of God's grace, but this same grace helps us in our weakness to make this gift our own. The resurrection reveals the creative power of the triune God to restore life to broken creation. The one God is both Creator and Redeemer, the creative source of all goodness and the giver of all good gifts. The ongoing presence of the Holy Spirit assures us that God is with us and for us until the end of time. This claim is sustained by the unity of the cross and the resurrection, which together reveal the at-one-ment of God and the world because the risen Christ has ascended into heaven and intercedes with God in our behalf. United with Christ in his life, death, and resurrection, we daily live into our salvation. I like Cynthia Rigby's reading of this mystery: "Through the work of the One who is with us and for us as the Word made flesh, our salvation is our being drawn *into* the depths of the divine being."[20] The doctrine of the atonement functions to draw us into the depths of God's triune life.

I will develop these ideas of "resurrected atonement" using two images. The first image is gift, the gift of freely given love. The second image is healing. By focusing on the power of the Holy Spirit as the agent who relates us to the saving power of Christ, each image combines the traditional "objective" and "subjective" poles of the atonement theory. Substitution, suffering, and satisfaction are all components of this mystery, although they are grounded in divine love rather than wrath and punishment. Taken together, these images of gift and healing will help reinterpret and reclaim these traditional aspects of Reformed atonement theory.

THE GIFT OF LOVE

God desires the well-being of the whole world. But the violence of human sin frustrates this desire, destroying our relationships with other creatures, and isolating us behind walls of guilt, fear, and resentment. Some images of the atonement depict God as countering human violence by passing it on and inflicting it on the innocent victim Jesus. But in my Reformed feminist approach, God is not a mirror of human violence. The cross and the suffering it incurs reveal the pain of human violence and God's fitting response of judgment whenever violence assaults life. The cross is a reminder of the violent consequences of human evil and sin. But resurrection power reclaims again and again the freedom of God to redeem the world despite ongoing violence. In the atonement, God steps into our "warring madness." In Christ God absorbs our violence, refusing to pass it on. In its place, God gives us the gift of forgiveness and reconciliation. This divine invitation to enjoy reconciliation is efficacious precisely because it derives from something other than—and infinitely greater than—us. Christ intercedes, or mediates, between humanity and God and clears the way to forgiveness by enduring and overcoming the violence of human sin. Forgiveness is God's gift of love that binds us back together, thus satisfying God's desire for creation's shalom.

The gift of love is the clear message of the atonement: "God so loved the world that he gave his only Son, so that everyone who believes in him may not perish but may have eternal life. . . . Indeed, God did not send the Son into the world to condemn the world, but in order that the world might be saved through him" (John 3:16–17). The root of God's gift of love is the sheer freedom of the triune giving and receiving. The Spirit binds us to Christ, who unites us with our Creator and assures us of God's eternal love. This grace is not only revealed (as an objective truth) but also given to free us to participate in this grace in the power of the Spirit (as a subjective reality). This gift of freely given love undoes the dehumanizing effects of violence and helps us claim our responsibility as agents of God's love in a broken world.

The suffering caused by violence can dehumanize us. However, Christ's suffering lacks the common connotations of subjugation and victimization, and his agency dislodges the associations we habitually connect with our own suffering. The example of the cross does not encourage our passivity before undeserved suffering but instead urges active resistance to it in the power of the Spirit. Christ's resurrection condemns all those systems that seek and effect subjugation. The love shown in the atonement challenges all that stands in the way of God's gracious purposes for creation. The atonement invites us into an embodied spirituality, a sense of the resurrected and reconciling Christ living with us, guiding our feet. Our salvation in Christ empowers us to name violence for what it is and to resist it by forming alliances of faithful people who are able to risk hopeful peacemaking. When through the Holy Spirit we choose life-enhancing acts, we participate in the overcoming of violence, sin, and death that the resurrection promises.

God's gift of love in the atonement is an empowering grace, the source and image of the possibility of *joyous* self-giving. Instead of being consumed by resentment and desire for revenge, we are given the freedom of being able to forgive precisely because we have already been forgiven. Individually and corporately we are empowered to respond according to the practical meaning of love revealed in the atonement. The gift of the Spirit is with us always, continually renewing us through the power of this great love. This is the renewal of life, in which we receive the power to relate to others and to ourselves in nonviolent, life-giving ways, assured that God loves us. The meaning of the atonement is that we become one with God. We are scooped up in nonhierarchical, noncoercive divine love and given a new way to live. We die with Christ to the old life and rise with Christ to a new life filled with possibilities that we do not yet fathom.

HEALING

The image of healing captures something of the sense of the reversing, resurrecting power of divine compassion operative in the atonement. Humanity is diseased and ailing and cannot heal itself. God's grace is prevenient, preceding any steps we may take away from the dead ends of our broken, unreconciled life. The power of Jesus' resurrection was previewed in the miracles of healing he performed almost everywhere he went. In Christ God enters our human predicament, bearing our pain and binding up our wounds, in order to satisfy God's desire for a new and right reality—God's reign of wholeness and reconciliation. In my Reformed feminist model of the cross, Christ's sufferings neither pay off an egregious debt nor found a violent order. Rather, freely chosen from the fullness of divine being, these sufferings reveal God's nature and will for the world. The strength of God's compassion is paradoxically its vulnerability to creation's need. The atonement announces that God is present even in the midst of the deepest suffering and that healing and new life are possible in such situations. But it also reveals that God opposes all forms of broken-ness and ill-being. The Holy Spirit creates in us the desire us to follow in the risen Christ's steps in such a way that we are healed, not destroyed.

The healing power God offers us in Christ counters the logic of martyr-dom that has been associated with the notion that Christ's blood was spilled in place of our own. No longer are we led to think that such a kind of sacrifice reflects the height of moral goodness, which we are now to emulate. The victorious image of the risen Christ offering healing of all that ails humanity beckons women—and all people—to work on behalf of God's reign. The experience of being healed posits a kind of unity with Jesus Christ through the Spirit in which we receive the benefits of a full human agency. We are called to stand in firm but compassionate opposi-tion to all that would wound or break the creation, trusting in God's promise of a new heaven and a new earth.

Because Christ has risen and given us the Holy Spirit, Christ's healing compassion gives us hope for the future. To the powerless and the broken, to those excluded from participation in the fullness of life, Christ's com-passion is grounded not in what has been but rather in a sense of what is possible; it is in its fullest sense creative power. Divine healing compassion re-creates and renders whole that which was formerly wounded and bro-ken. It transposes our suffering into a new context by bearing this possi-bility for renewal and growth. We are called to manifest the hope of this compassion by refusing to accept unjust suffering and by taking risks for the sake of God's reign.

Having received the gift of forgiveness, we find ourselves part of a new community, Christ's community, that is on a journey to holiness and heal-ing. As we repent and receive the gift of forgiveness, Christ lifts us from the cavernous void of lostness in which we inevitably find ourselves to live as whole persons. The love revealed on the cross is different from a roman-ticized, unrealistic love of others. Rather, it is characterized by humble conviction of the rightness of just action and a passion for forming and sus-taining right relations.[21] The pattern of discipleship based on Christ's com-passion is characterized by the give-and-take of mutual acceptance of one another as healed members of Christ's community. We welcome others into solidarity, into the enjoyment of life as forgiven community.

Christ Jesus has promised the actuality of true peace: the well-being of creation where all are fully satisfied because everyone has enough. The true meaning of the atonement is not death or judgment, but abundant life.[22] "I am the bread of life," Christ promises. "Whoever comes to me will never be hungry, and whoever believes in me will never be thirsty" (John 6:35). By confronting and undoing the power of sin, the triune God brings actual hope and real transformation to the human condition, giving us a foretaste of our everlasting life in God. In the midst of our suffering and discouragement, the power of God's love, which does not bend to injustice or other forms of evil, dispels our fears of final defeat. The truth of grace, established once and for all in the cross and resurrection and continuing powerfully in the present, enables us to trust God's promise of a new heaven and a new earth. This eschatological image nurtures our hopes for the full glory that awaits Christ's "coming again" and gives us courage to do all that we can "to disciple" its reality into being. *Christ has died, Christ has risen, Christ will come again!*

9

TRANSFORMATIVE GRACE

Katie Geneva Cannon

My family have been members of the Presbyterian Church since we arrived in America from Africa in the late 1700s (that is as far back as we can trace our lineage). As enslaved persons in North Carolina, my forebears were required to sit in balconies and partake of the communion elements only after all whites had been served. They are buried in church cemeteries in Huntersville, North Carolina, their graves indicated by first names only. There is no written history of their Christian lives. After Emancipation in 1867, a missionary from Scotland, Luke Dorland, came to Mecklenburg and Cabarrus counties in North Carolina and started schools and churches for freed women and men. My family members were active in all-black Presbyterian congregations in the all-black Catawba Presbytery, which was part of an all-black synod that was also named Catawba (consisting of the Presbyteries of Catawba, Yadkin, Cape Fear, and Southern Virginia). Our overarching sociocultural reality as Presbyterian Christians was a world of blackness crammed inside one of dominating whiteness.[1]

As black Presbyterians, grace was the basic motif of our lives. I have long known that grace is an unmerited gift from God. However, not until recently did I understand grace as a sacred, life-transforming power for those of us whose identities are shaped by multiple forces at odds with the dominant culture, primarily those of race, sex, and class. God's freely given gift of grace enables us to resist the forces of death and degradation arrayed against us and to affirm our dignity as beloved persons created in the image of God.[2]

Frank T. Wilson's elemental story *A Continuing Pilgrimage: Black Presbyterians and Black Presbyterianism* describes black people's socioreligious incipiency in the Presbyterian household of faith.

From the establishment of the first Presbyterian Church in North America at Southold, Long Island, in 1640 to the date of the first General Assembly in 1789 there was, undoubtedly, a trickle of black traffic in and out of this communion under a variety of conditions. By the time of the founding of the First African Presbyterian Church in Philadelphia in

139

1807, there were at least two generations of black persons with some kind of Presbyterian contact and identification.[3]

Knowing that the black Presbyterian heritage is always threatened by invisibility in an overwhelmingly white tradition, Wilson presents stories of the extraordinary ministerial work and imagination by those twice over—black and Presbyterian.[4]

Henry Highland Garnet (1815–1881), Edward Wilmot Blyden (1832–1912), and James Herman Robinson (1907–1972) are hardly household names in American Presbyterianism, much less in the Reformed theological tradition as a whole. The contributions of African American Christians to Reformed faith and doctrine have been largely ignored. This essay seeks to remedy this situation, because expanding the canon of Reformed voices also expands our understanding of grace. Mainstream American Presbyterianism has often promoted abstract, disembodied notions of grace that do nothing to address the structures of domination against which African American Presbyterians struggle. African American Presbyterians like Garnet, Blyden, and Robinson rejected stereotypical rhetoric about African peoples, both on the continent and throughout the Diaspora, and articulated understandings of grace that respond to the existential realities of black people. As Priscilla Massie declares, "a renewal of faith can occur only to the extent that false and oppressive ideas about people and their situations are exposed and confronted by the insights of those whose sense of justice is illuminated by experience. While the black experience is indeed a particular experience, its revelations on the meaning of truth and justice are valid for all."[5] This essay will explore the revelations of black Presbyterian experience on the meaning of grace.

I am a lifelong black Presbyterian. The earliest proponents of womanism—myself included—entered theological education in the 1970s acknowledging the fact that we had been blessed and inspired by the black church community throughout our existence. One or two women even professed that they were called to the ministry in their mothers' womb. Most of us served on the junior usher board, sang in the gospel choir, and won prizes as members of Bible drill teams in our local judicatories. All of us had long histories of memorizing multiverse speeches, poetic prayers, and prosaic poems for pageantries and recitation programs throughout the church's calendar year. Much of our nurture in the black church came from women. In examining the history of Christian education among African American Presbyterians, Gayraud Wilmore calls attention to "the extraordinary role that the Black church women have played . . . in the survival and conservation of the culture of African American people."[6]

To describe the determining influences of race, sex, and class in my life as a black Presbyterian, I borrow a parable created by our sister theologian, Musa Dube of Botswana in Southern Africa. Dr. Sister Dube describes our faith journey as "a long walk in a hall of mirrors."[7] My personal, amplified version of *a long walk in a hall of mirrors* goes like this: There was once a hall full of mirrors, magnificent mirrors, mirrors that extended the full-length of walls, registering the reality of women and men of significance. These mirrors ran from the baseboard on the floor to the very top of the ceiling, illusive and exclusive representations, categorizing data of importance, as well as what religious traditions will be revered, and what national holidays must be celebrated. And yet, as a person of African descent, I struggle to see my image, my reality, in this hall of mirrors. From time to time, on rare occasions, these mirrors of hegemonic structures of race, gender, and class ideologies reflect a fragment, a fraction, a piece of an image that should be the face of a person of African descent, but the image in this hall of mirrors always appears as something undesirable.

The starting point for me began as a kindergartner at age three. As I learned to read, it became clear that whenever I looked into the mirror I always saw the face of someone else, a man by the name of Jim Crow and a woman by the name of Jane. Pauli Murray coined the term *Jane Crow*, equating the evil of antifeminism (Jane Crow) with the evil of racism (Jim Crow).[8] However, I am using *Jane Crow* to name the specific manifestations of white supremacist practices acted out by white women against people of color. These images of Jim Crow, Jane Crow, and the Crow children served as guardians of the fanatically powerful campaign of white supremacy, scrupulously ruling out all contacts of equality between the races.

Each and every morning I stood tall, crossed my heart, and pledged allegiance to the flag of the United States of America. I recited the Lord's Prayer, quoted the Beatitudes, and answered questions from the Missouri Synod Lutheran catechism. Yet at the same time I lived in a world that demanded and commanded that I go to the back of the bus even though I paid the same fare. Before the age of five, the unbending social codes of conduct between blacks and whites required that I go through back doors and drink out of "colored" water fountains. This racial etiquette was traumatic, and it was violent. So complete was the circle of segregationist laws, the rigidly enforced codes of white supremacy,[9] that it was against the law for me to play in tax-supported public parks, to skate in tax-supported public rinks, to swim in tax-supported public pools. Even though my classmates and I sang all the verses to the song "My country 'tis of thee, sweet land of liberty," we had to remain self-consciously aware that it was against the law for us to go to the public library; nor could we borrow a book from the white side (versus the "Negro" side) of the teeny-tiny bookmobile that traveled monthly to the rural areas of Cabarrus County. It was even a transgression for us to sign up for the Kannapolis citywide spelling contest.

Traveling back and forth to Atlantic Beach, the only public oceanfront property in the Carolinas designated for black people, we knew, as Martin

Luther King Jr. stated so well in his now-famous 1963 "I Have a Dream" sermon, "no matter how heavy our bodies were with fatigue, we could not obtain lodging in the motels along the highways nor in the hotels in the cities." Like detectives, we had to discern the minute as well as the gigantic extensions of this social framework of white supremacy, even to the point of deciding at which gas station we could refuel, making sure that we never risked acting in any way that might be detrimental to our health and safety.

The larger society in which I grew up mirrored the all-white police force, which worked with no search warrants and had absolute power. Police officers committed unspeakable horrors of brutality against black people in general, and vindictive assaults against black men in particular, arresting my sisters and brothers on trumped-up charges. The powerbrokers' collusion with white lawless vigilante groups such as the Ku Klux Klan and the White Citizen Councils was a grim reality. The religious leaders; the university professors; the local, state, and federal politicians; the moguls of the media world—those who make up 39.2 percent of the population yet hold 95 percent of top jobs in all sectors of society[10]—vanished into the shadow of alleyways and side streets while lynch mobs, using the rawest violence, boldly paraded through the main arteries downtown.[11]

This is not to imply that in the hall of exclusionary mirrors there is a lack of constructed black images. There are plenty of pictures of African American women, men, and children portrayed with thick lips and grimacing teeth. These unforgettable caricatures of black women, men, and children depict us as ugly, smelly, hideous masses of loosely connected arms, legs, eyes, and hands. There are multitudes of caricatures throughout popular culture and all over mass media of African American people laughing when nothing is funny and scratching where nothing is itching, simply uttering, muttering, humming, and hawing incomprehensible ebonic sounds. These distorted images, reflections, and representations of my kinfolk and my skinfolk have become more compounded as I walk into one mirrored room after another, moving from segregation to desegregation to re-segregation. Image after inescapable image strips us of our selfhood and robs African Americans of our dignity, because everywhere we turn, there are signs, less explicit, more implicit, that still read "FOR WHITES ONLY."

In turn, these same mirrors in this long hall resist reflecting positive images of our ancestors' contributions throughout civilization. Contemporary African American theologians have offered a significant critique of the history of slavery, domination, and imperialistic colonization in Africa and throughout the African Diaspora.[12] They have noted the ongoing effects of systemic intentions and official paradigms of biological, geographical, and theological determinism generated by European expansionists and their descendants, who posited supposedly reliable signifiers of measurable dimensions that exist among the human species in order to position themselves at center stage, as the most highly evolved subjects in all areas of life.[13]

Let it be remembered that down through the years, powerbrokers, "with all the certainty and correctness granted by Enlightenment epistemology,"[14] used such lies to justify slavery, colonial conquests, apartheid, and frequently genocide, invoking always a divine sanction declaring that God has ordained the natural order this way. Such erasure is the essence of cultural hegemony. As Cornel West notes, "White supremacist ideology is based first and foremost on the degradation of black bodies in order to control them. One of the best ways to instill fear in people is to terrorize them. Yet this fear is best sustained by convincing them that their bodies are ugly, their intellect is inherently underdeveloped, their culture is less civilized and their future warrants less concern than that of other peoples."[15] Each and every time the hall of mirrors presents our foremothers and our forefathers as liabilities to civilization, the groundwork is laid for effective sociopolitical policies that isolate, alienate, and exterminate a whole race of people.

This walk in the hall of mirrors brings me back to the centrality of grace. Grace has to sustain those of us whose identities are shaped by multiple forces at odds with the dominant culture, primarily race, sex, and class. Rosetta E. Ross's plural approach to grace in *The Dictionary of Feminist Theologies* is pivotal to my understanding. Ross juxtaposes the inherited, traditional definitions of the term with a number of different meanings that feminists and womanists associate with grace. In particular, she juxtaposes the divine mercy and power "whereby God recovers individual persons from sin while granting forgiveness and new life" with ethical definitions of grace in feminist theologies that point to "communal action with sociopolitical consequences."[16] Through this juxtaposition, I have come to understand that grace has particular relevance not only for investigating the transformative, life-giving power experienced by those who share in the complex religious heritage of black Presbyterianism, but also for articulating Presbyterian interpretations of emancipatory strategies in the black experience. Divine grace that comes to us, exposing us as individuals directly to God's loving-kindness, must also be discussed from a critical perspective that is informed by our experiences in sociopolitical history.

For about two hundred years, since the founding of the first African Presbyterian Church in 1807, black Presbyterian clergy and laypersons who have touched on the subject of grace have focused on two themes that demand our attention.[17] First and foremost, grace is a divine gift of redeeming love that empowers African Americans to confront shocking, absurd, death-dealing disjunctions in life, so that when we look at our outer struggles and inner strength we see interpretive possibilities for creative change. Second, grace is the indwelling of God's spirit that enables

Christians of African descent to live conscious lives of thanksgiving, by deepening our knowledge of forgiveness given in Christ, so that even in situations of oppression we celebrate our status as beloved creatures made in God's image. This double definition indicates the complex role that the doctrine of grace plays in the lives of black church folk. Black Presbyterian clergy and laypersons, invested as they are in the story of salvation, seek to understand and pass on "a body of religious knowledge that has served to ensure survival, elevation, and liberation of African and African American people through the centuries."[18] In the remainder of this essay I explore the ways in which black Presbyterian history and sacred rhetoric bring these two aspects of transformative grace into sharp focus for those of us who are black and part of the family of Reformed churches.

DEFINITION ONE

Grace is a divine gift of redeeming love that empowers African Americans to confront shocking, absurd, death-dealing disjunctions in life, so that when we look at our outer struggles and inner strength we see interpretive possibilities for creative change.

Toni Morrison's novel *Beloved* tells us that enslaved African Americans transcended their victimization as subjects in the world by embracing grace as God-given survivalist intentions against "the nastiness of life."[19]

> She did not tell them to clean up their lives or to go and sin no more. She did not tell them they were the blessed of the earth, its inheriting meek or its glory bound pure. She told them that the only grace they could have was the grace they could imagine. That if they could not see it, they could not have it.[20]

Morrison says that slaveholders were stealing and selling African American children at such young ages that oftentimes mothers had not formed a lot of memories. Imagine the trauma of giving birth to children and not being able to recognize your children's hands in a pile of hands; no idea of what their permanent teeth looked like; no knowledge as to how their jawbones changed. Yet Morrison contends that desperation for transformation was so deep, "if we had had more water, we would have made more tears." Grace kindles the imagination, so that out of "the nastiness of life," new possibilities for creative change emerge.

Charles H. Long reminds us that, above all, religious consciousness among enslaved African Americans meant coming to terms with the opaqueness of their condition and at the same time opposing it. As our first definition of grace emphasizes, "they had to experience the truth of their negativity, and at the same time transform and create another reality."[21] In other words, Long contends that African Americans needed to know that they were not simply pawns of the American government and its machinations, but real people. Enslaved Africans had to take stock of who they were and who else was in the world. By God's grace they had to come to their own independent judgment about the nature of the world and their place in it. As Long claims,

> Enslaved people who were thrust into the Atlantic world had to find a new power of being. They had to find a power that would sustain their being because the powers-that-be would not sustain them. There had to be some other vision than the vision of Europeans from maritime Christian countries who were running slave ships. There had to be some other kind of condition of being a human being than the one put forth by the practitioners of democracy who lied, cheated, stole, lynched and raped anytime they wanted with impunity. So African people created a new orientation in the world.[22]

Transformative grace gave African people the power to look at the death-dealing disjunctions of their lives and see interpretive possibilities for creative change.

Gayraud S. Wilmore connects the outer struggles and inner strength of African American Presbyterians to a *Reformed double-consciousness*.[23] He draws on W. E. B. DuBois's critique of white supremacist normativity in the classic book *The Souls of Black Folk*:

> It is a peculiar sensation, this double-consciousness, this sense of always looking at one's self through the eyes of others, of measuring one's soul by the tape of the world that looks on in amused contempt and pity. One ever feels his twoness—an American, a Negro; two souls, two thoughts, two unreconciled strivings; two warring ideals in one dark body, whose dogged strength alone keeps it from being torn asunder.[24]

Wilmore takes a further step by particularizing this tenuous dilemma in the experience of being black and Presbyterian.[25] This may sound a surprising or far-fetched assertion, but Wilmore stresses a very obvious point. The large majority of black Presbyterians develop "second-sight" within the Reformed faith by filtering Eurocentric Christian doctrines through African American folk traditions and images of Africa as a place of origin. True, there may be some rare and recent exceptions, but by and large the majority of us whose families have been African American Presbyterians since the 1800s, and who continue to be haunted by the long legacies of white supremacy and patriarchy, possess Reformed double-consciousness.

Wilmore points out that Presbyterians of African descent live in the constant danger of being thrust back into the status of a disregarded and subjugated minority within a predominantly white denomination that has not been able to overcome its racism.

> We give special significance to a fundamental tenet of the Reformed faith: the freedom of the Christian person. . . . We believe that God alone is the Lord of conscience. The only sovereignty we acknowledge is God's. As Black and Reformed Christians we refuse to submit, as we did in slavery, to the control of any majority that arrogates to itself power that belongs only to God, especially power based on the assumption of racial superiority.[26]

Wilmore goes on to say that provisional autonomy in Black Presbyterianism, a theoethic of in-between-ness, is "informed by a consciousness of the significance of Africa as the Mother Continent of humanity—the place where God's presence was first made known to human beings":

> It is not our intention to exaggerate the connections between Africa and contemporary Black Presbyterians, but the historic valorization of Africa as the place of origin by Black Presbyterian theologians of the nineteenth century, like Henry Highland Garnet and Edward Wilmot Blyden, encourages us to continue searching for the roots of our spirituality in that continent. God first met us in Africa. God would not permit African culture to be totally expunged from the Christian faith that our slave ancestors developed on this soil.[27]

In a world where, as Wilmore notes, "Blackness has been cynically disvalued and the Christian faith sinfully distorted to serve the interests of European and American slaveholders and segregationists,"[28] this Reformed double-consciousness is a way of opening up interpretive possibilities for creative change within the Reformed tradition.

Both of the nineteenth-century African American Presbyterian ministers cited by Wilmore, Henry Highland Garnet and Edward Wilmot Blyden, are religious minds of great magnitude, probing the relation of divine grace to dramatic conditions emerging from geopolitical realities.[29] In 1864, Presbyterian minister Garnet became the first African American to address the United States Congress on the anniversary of the ratification of the Thirteenth Amendment to the Constitution abolishing slavery. As an abolitionist, he was one of the most controversial African American leaders of the nineteenth century. He called for a black uprising to eradicate slavery in order to free millions who were suffering under the weight of slavocracy's interlocking oppressions.[30] In celebrating black (Presbyterian)ness with the peoples of West Africa, Blyden declared the goal as "Africa for Africans."[31] In essence, Blyden encouraged people of African descent around the world to take inventory of their socioreligious contexts and return to Africa. As a Presbyterian minister, Blyden brought attention to the way that literary representations reduced African peoples to beasts of burden within Eurocentric theocultural norms. He published numerous pamphlets, essays, and books rebutting theories of black inferiority. In their different ways, these early articulators of a Reformed double-consciousness linked the power of divine grace to "communal action with sociopolitical consequences."

Powerfully and compellingly, Presbyterian scholar Delores S. Williams makes a connection between recent feminist and womanist attempts at re-imaging divine grace and the ongoing efforts of black Christians to reinterpret the faith: "Reflecting upon my heritage, which was passed on by Black preachers, parents, and grandparents who worked and prayed in the segregated South where conservative, White Christians lynched innocent Black Christians, I realized that Black Christians in the United States have always been forced to re-image the Christian religion." Noting the backlash against the women, including herself, "who dared share their re-visioning" at the Re-imagining Conference,[32] Williams wonders where conservative Christian voices were at Ku Klux Klan cross burnings, "when the cross was being re-imaged, not to symbolize redemption or salvation, but to signal hate, death, and destruction of Black people." As an African American Christian, she recognizes the necessity of re-imaging of Christianity

> in order to redeem it from the desecrated imagery of White Christians who snatched Black Africans from Africa in slave ships named Jesus, Mary, Liberty, John the Baptist, and Justice. Almost two million Blacks died in the middle passages of those ships due to cruel, inhumane treatment they received from White, male Christians. As a result, we Blacks (who became Christians with historical memory) re-image Jesus, Mary, John the Baptist, justice and liberty. From this centuries-long re-imaging of Jesus emerged a beautiful, redemptive, Black liberation theology.

As the contributors to *Black Witness to the Apostolic Faith* contend, many African American Christians interpret the historic creeds, confessions, and doctrines in distinctive and nontraditional ways, in favor of what they consider remaining more "faithful to the essential meaning of the Gospel."[33] Likewise, Delores Williams calls upon "feminist-womanists and other freedom-seeking women" to keep on discerning the "mysterious ways" of God's grace.[34]

DEFINITION TWO

Grace is the indwelling of God's spirit that enables Christians of African descent to live conscious lives of thanksgiving, by deepening our knowledge of forgiveness given in Christ, so that even in situations of oppression we celebrate the status of imago Dei.

Whereas the first definition of grace emphasizes the power grace gives to confront the profound disjunctions of life and creatively reinterpret both our situation and the symbols of faith, the second definition lifts up our dignity as creatures made in the image of God, and our calling to be Christ's active disciples. Grace transforms both our understanding of divine and creaturely realities and our joyful, responsible agency in the world.

When Presbyterian minister James H. Robinson[35] accepted the invitation as the first African American to deliver the Lyman Beecher Lectures at Yale Divinity School[36] in 1955, a lectureship that is considered to be one of the most prestigious speaking invitations on Christian ministry in the United States, he spoke out about preaching as a divine activity that discloses the grace of God to the human soul. To be sure, as a pastor in New York City Robinson knew about the dangerous complacency among God-fearing women and men in a nation that is flushed with a succession of victories and satiated with economic prosperity, at the height of vaunted achievements and technological ascendancy in the arts and sciences. He too knew experientially, as a person who grew up in abject poverty, what happens when Christians do not make time to develop an awareness of God's free gift of forgiveness in one's inner life. Robinson's warnings against our spiritual spring running dry, leaving us helpless in life's parched, barren wilderness, come together with stories of living water in both testaments of the Bible.

In order to stand in the healing presence of God, Robinson says that we must wrestle with urgently pressing theological questions, such as "What must I do with my life—with the power, the knowledge, the wealth, and the leisure which modern advance puts at my disposal? And when life tumbles in, how do I keep my equilibrium and reinstate my life without going to pieces?"[37] Robinson insists that, as we plunge into ever greater inexorable dimensions of complex knowledge systems and professional expertise, at the heart of God's demands is the Christian responsibility to live the radicality of the gospel.

In his lectures, Robinson is especially concerned with the function of grace in the lives of ministers. He identifies grace as the conveyor of God's call. Like a pipe for water and wire for electricity, Robinson says that grace is the theophanic conduit between the divine call to the holy service of ministry and the compelling, personal relationship between the minister as a redeemed sinner and a forgiving God. The distance between Christian ministry and other professions in a secularized society is as great as that between the fall of Adam and the resurrection of Christ. "The work we do is holy," Robinson declares, "and the place from which we preach is a holy place—as holy as the spot where Moses stood when God called him.[38] This is why Robinson characterizes those who accept the divine gift of grace as *stewards of the mysteries of God*. He does not believe that Christians should be parrots; to the contrary, God-fearing women and men are called to be prophets. To elaborate this, Robinson writes that purity of heart is more important than intellectual capacity. The willingness to wait and listen is a much more valuable asset than facility of speech. Humility of spirit is worth more than renown or pulpits of great fame.[39] Grace offers ministers possibilities to speak boldly to the spiritual deficiency and religious needs of congregations so that the people of God possess the moral discipline to resist making God a captive of their own racist and sexist imaginations.

As the anthology *Black Preaching: Select Sermons in the Presbyterian Tradition*[40] admirably shows, the preachers keep themselves and their congregations rooted in the message that every person is a reflection of the divinity. Their exposition of the sacredness and inherent worth of every human being is uncompromising; the status of *imago Dei* has no superior. God's grace comes to humanity, touching each of us directly, so that, assured of our intrinsic dignity, we can each live into our highest and most noble self.

William G. Gillespie draws on his ministerial work as a pastor and community activist to link grace with situations of oppression in black life. His text *When You Think You Have Had Enough* provides a classic formulation of the absurdity of the sociocultural reality of African American Christians:

> We represent causes that are good, but no good comes from our work. We support people who give themselves relentlessly to a good cause and they are killed, imprisoned, or silenced by the forces of evil. We knock on doors that are closed to black people until our knuckles are raw, but the doors remain closed. We prepare ourselves for jobs we never get, for housing we cannot buy, for clubs we cannot enter, for churches where we are unwanted, for dreams that never come true.[41]

White Christians have appealed to grace as an unearned gift from God to keep themselves from depending too much on their material and moral accomplishments. In Gillespie's hands, it becomes clear that God's grace, bestowed voluntarily and without compensation, calls Christians to challenge the assumed norms and oppressive privileges of others. The great power of this sermon and the others in this volume is that they clearly connect grace and the status of *imago Dei* in a most immediate way.

In his sermon "Top Value Stamp," William S. Mercer invites black Presbyterians to deconstruct race and sex privileges—no matter the cost and against all odds—without substituting new isms, such as ableism, ageism, lookism, or heterosexism, that would merely have the effect of crafting additional tiers in the ecclesiapolitical hierarchy. Jesus regarded every person as an immortal soul. This fact forbids sex discrimination as well as racial discrimination. All artificial barriers are removed before God.[42] This, then, is precisely the essence of God's grace in action, wherein the coming of Jesus Christ offers love and positive restoration to our authentic status of *imago Dei*. Therefore, grace is liberation from dominant theologies and hegemonic myths that posit that African Americans are destined by God to fill a subservient place in society, as "hewers of wood and drawers of water, now, henceforth and forevermore."[43] As individuals redeemed in Christ, we relinquish internalized oppression and become trustworthy moral agents. Marked by conscious lives of thanksgiving and increasing knowledge of forgiveness, graceful Christians are open to manifestations of the glory of God in the daily work of justice.

"Beyond Ourselves" by Barbara Campbell offers cogent insights into the celebration of the status of *imago Dei*, wherein she invites the audience to "look at ourselves as God looks at us." She correctly asserts that when we accept forgiveness for our sins, our hearts overflow with thanksgiving, so much so that we can no more keep silent than a flower can withhold its fragrance or the sun keep back its light. "Christ comes into human life to change natures and dispositions, to change moods and temperaments, to banish fears and worry. Also, he can remove shame and guilt, provide a new dynamism, new purpose in life, new joy, and a peace that nothing could destroy."[44] As James H. Costen puts it, grace is at work "when Jesus invites us down from our hang-ups, from our positions of insecurity." "Like Zacchaeus," Costen says, "Jesus offers us the possibility of addressing our needs at their very source—at home where we live."[45]

Leland S. Cozart also sees forgiveness and grace as two distinct but simultaneously connected aspects of the sacred, life-giving power that calls Christians back to our divine purpose. Like Campbell, Cozart accentuates the acceptance of God's grace rather than human initiative in his understanding of embodied faithfulness. As he states in "The Missing Ingredient," "we are saved not by our goodness but by grace through faith. That which we truly need is offered by God in Christ."[46] Cozart writes that the clue to faithfulness is not in the question we put to life, but in our response to the question life puts to us.

Lloyd Green also argues that we must maintain a delicate balance between awareness of the pure divine favor of grace and recognition of our accountability to the entire created order. Green writes that to expose injustices may cause division and pain; but to ignore injustices will result in the destruction of the church as an instrument of God's will.[47] The concerns of justice and grace belong together. Thelma Davidson Adair's sermon, "Jesus Christ, the Same Yesterday, Today—Forever," also ties together grace and Christian responsibility. In a clear and prophetic manner Adair spells out the central meaning of Christian living: "Members of the Christian community cannot take their commitment to Christ seriously, while complacently hearing the report that ten thousand hunger deaths occur in the world each day in the year. We cannot dismiss casually the triage theory, the 'sorting out' principle, in which the belief is advanced that half of the world's hungry should be left to perish in order that another half may be fed and kept alive."[48] Adair calls the church to take seriously the divine mandate to grow together into the body of Christ by her insistence on our role in transmitting the gift of grace to others in concrete action.

In "A New Birth of Freedom," Clinton M. Marsh echoes this same theme for the black church community: "The broad message of Scripture does not support the idea of Christianity as a mere spiritual Cape Canaveral, concerned solely to be a launching pad for heaven. God, to whom time and eternity are indivisible, affirms not 'I did make' nor 'I will make,' but 'I *make* all things new.' And we are called to be co-laborers with God in a continuing divine metamorphosis as he brings forth the new."[49] In this sermon Marsh ties faithful discipleship to living conscious lives full of creative openness to God's gracious presence. When any of us assume that we have exhausted God's dream we are guilty of blasphemy, a blasphemy that is challenged by God's ringing affirmation, "I make all things new!"

CONCLUSION

It is significant that in the black Presbyterian tradition, where transformative grace, sometimes explicit but oftentimes implicit, is the basic motif, each member in the household of faith seeks to make the connection between God's freely given gift of sacred life-giving power and the redeeming love that enables creative resistance against precarious, death-dealing boundaries imposed by church and society. Being created in God's image, women, men, and children of African ancestry are under eternal compunction to set primary importance on reflecting God's glory in the dailiness of life. In other words, according to our kinship with God, we must stand firm and fight with all our might against oppositional powers and principalities that try in any way to tamper with the essence of our well-being. Thus, for black Presbyterians, the framing of grace as inevitably transformative prevents us from choosing a life lower than God ordained. Transformative grace begins and ends with God's union with humanity. This union is created by God, sustained by the love of Christ, and made continuous, morning by morning, by the Holy Spirit. We have been gripped by God's Spirit, touched by divine love, and redeemed by grace. God has each of us in God's embrace. All in all, transformative grace functions for hard-pressed Christian people on a shrinking globe as a mandate for thankful, creative living.

10

ALWAYS REFORMING,
ALWAYS RESISTING

Kristine A. Culp

"Résister." She carved the word into the stone. Marie Durand, an eighteenth-century French Calvinist, etched this word into the chamber of the fortress in southern France where she was imprisoned for her faith. Resist—resist tyranny, it implied. She was not, herself, a political insurgent. Rather, Marie Durand was an activist in the sense that it took the full force of her life to resist powers that would bind her conscience and constrain worship of God. During thirty-eight years of captivity, she never stopped singing the Psalms, studying the Bible, and writing to secure provisions needed for the well-being of herself and the other women prisoners.

In the mid-twentieth century, other French Protestants took Marie Durand's "Résister" and the experience of the persecuted Huguenots in general as a rallying charge. In 1935, writer and antifascist activist André Chamson took up Durand's call in relation to the threats of his time and challenged Reformed leaders to resist both Nazi tyranny and their own anti-Judaism.[1] Subsequently, remote mountainous areas of France that once sheltered French Calvinists from relentless persecution at the hands of the church and monarchy again provided shelter: this time to French-born and refugee Jews who fled Nazi brutality. Freedom fighters in the Cévennes, the stronghold of the French Reformed church, sang of defying the German occupiers and writing "Résister" across the flags of France.[2]

In the twenty-first-century United States, the tyrannies we face are not so immediately a matter of life and death as they were for Huguenots under the French Catholic monarchy and for Jews under Nazi rule. We *do* know violence and viciousness, often wrought in the name of religion and ethnicity. And every regime and culture can be measured in terms of more or less tolerance of religious, racial, and cultural diversity. Nonetheless, in our day the worth of tolerance and human dignity are generally acknowledged. Yet tyrannies and idolatries have by no means been eradicated from our lives; we ourselves consume them, conform to them, and are implicated in them by what we take for granted and fail to question.

In our day, any sense of the glory of God is already shaped by the mediation of a market economy (as it would be mediated by any economy) and, almost inevitably, becomes entangled with the market's cultivation of consumption as a dominant way of engaging the world. Any notion of God's truth is already shaped by the global flow of language and images and, almost inevitably, becomes appropriated and spun into byte-sized, quickly assimilable, media-ready information. Any construal of a well-ordered kingdom of Christ is already shaped by the relations and patterns that order our lives and, almost inevitably, becomes distorted by grotesque rifts in wealth and by tenaciously entrenched patterns of power and privilege. In twenty-first-century North America, the immediate consequences of our day's tyrannies and idolatries are not as dramatic as those suffered by Marie Durand. The effects tend to cumulate more quietly, for example, in inadequate health care, housing, and schools. The effects are deadly in more dispersed ways, such as in pressures to consume and keep up, and in contaminated food, water, and air. Indeed, the questions of what and how to resist may be more difficult to answer in our day.

A TESTIMONY AND A THREEFOLD CALL

Behind the testimony and call of resistance is the assumption that creaturely life remains ambiguous; that is, it is always being corrupted and yet made glorious. Theology's work is, in part, to diagnose the ambiguous condition of personal and social life. At their best, Protestant theologies in general, and Reformed theologies in particular, are fed by the sensibilities to resist idolatry, to marvel at the abundance of divine mercy, and to find life's fullness in glorifying and enjoying God. At their worst, Reformed theologies have cut themselves off from these wellsprings of faith: they have lost the interrelatedness of protest, mercy, and praise; ongoing theological renewal and reformulation have been eschewed; and "protest" itself has taken vicious forms of persecution of heretics and tyrannical imposition of order and orthodoxy on others. Without resistance as a testimony of faith and religious calling, Protestant theology cannot be properly "protestant" and Reformed theology cannot be rightly reformed.

How, then, shall we take up Marie Durand's word? Her word can, first, be received as a testimony of faith, a testimony to how faith is sparked and oriented by resistance. To resist is a basic religious sensibility. It is marked by protest against the diminution of God and life, a protest that seems to surge from the depths of our being and that reorients life and worship.

To resist is also a call. Marie Durand's word must be heard as a summons to the work of transformation. More specifically, to resist demands naming and defying idolatry and indignity in individual, ecclesial, and sociopolitical life. Here, theology contributes to efforts to bring about the well-being of life by diagnosing the current situation, unmasking idolatry, and articulating a vision of the flourishing of life before God.

The call to resist is threefold. Marie Durand resisted both idolatry proper, that is, encroachments upon the divine image and authority, and tyranny, the perpetration of inhumanity by authorities who thereby usurp divine judgment. "Résister" calls us not only to defy idolatry proper but also to resist idolatry broadly understood, that is, to resist also human indignity and the degradation of life, and thereby the diminishment of God as the source of all life and goodness. To take up the call of "Résister" requires, third, that theology itself must be subject to critique and ongoing reformation. Idolatry and tyranny are not only external threats; our own lives and thought are implicated in them. Contemporary feminist and womanist theologians have made this third point through their critiques of the idolatries and potential viciousness of theology itself, to the extent of subjecting their own theologies to ongoing critique.

To take up "Résister" in our day, this chapter uses historical-theological resources in mutually critical relation with diagnoses of social-cultural-political situations. The first section looks at Marie Durand's testimony of resistance in order to root theology in concrete struggles to live fully before God. The remaining sections take up the threefold call to resist. The second section focuses on John Calvin's diagnosis of idolatry and indicates how this diagnosis informed the 1934 Barmen Declaration. In the third section I turn to the French Reformed response to Nazi tyranny and anti-Judaism, and in the fourth section to the thoroughgoing idolatry critique of contemporary feminist and womanist theologians. By the end, it should become clear that ongoing resistance and reformation are not only the subject matter of this chapter; they are what I believe feminist theologies at their best are about and what I hope to instantiate in my own work.

MARIE DURAND: "RÉSISTER" AS TESTIMONY

Marie Durand was arrested by the French authorities for professing the "so-called Reformed Religion." At the time of her arrest in 1730, she was nineteen, newly married, and living in her family home in Le Bouchet, a remote hilltop hamlet just west of the Rhone River and about halfway between the cities of Lyon and Avignon. The year before, her father had been arrested and imprisoned. Although professing the Reformed faith was reason enough to be imprisoned indefinitely under French law, clerical and civil authorities were especially interested in the Durand family: her older brother Pierre was a Reformed pastor.[3]

The royal Declaration of 1724 ordered the execution of all Reformed preachers and the imprisonment and loss of property for all who professed the Reformed faith. Moreover, any parents whose children were baptized or married outside *the* Church, or any persons who attempted to comfort or exhort their dying brothers or sisters in the "so-called Reformed Religion," were subject to the galleys—forced labor and life in chains aboard a ship—or to life imprisonment. Louis XV's advisors thought this declaration would finally extinguish the Reformed religion in the kingdom. Instead it inspired resistance. In 1726 Pierre Durand was ordained at the first National Synod to be held in France in sixty-six years. He preached, administered the Lord's Supper, and performed four hundred marriages, all in homes and outdoor gatherings in secluded places since all Reformed temples had been demolished or forbidden. When he eluded the authorities, they arrested his father and then his sister Marie. In 1732, after a sizeable price was put on his head and he was betrayed, Pierre Durand was arrested. At his trial he explained that he thought the Declaration's prohibitions pertained only to "those who foment revolt, against which I have always preached." He continued, "I do not believe it was ever the king's intention to forbid his subjects to worship God according to their conscience."[4] He was sentenced to death nevertheless and is reported to have walked to his execution singing the Psalms.

To resist, for Marie Durand as for her brother, was not to revolt but to defy idolatrous encroachments on a person's faith in God, including those sanctioned by legal and religious authorities. To resist was part of ordering one's life in response to God, for to worship God in all one's days and with all one's powers required eschewing false authority and worship. To resist was also to persist in seeking to live rightly before God despite persecution and threat of death.

Every French Protestant lived under the pervasive threat of persecution and possible death, especially after the 1685 Revocation of the Edict of Nantes. Certainly, persecution was not new to the Durand household. Marie's father, Étienne Durand, marked one doorway in their house with the plea "Have mercy upon me, Lord God, May 1694." Two years later, he engraved another set of words over the kitchen fireplace: "Praise be to God." The Durand family grew up under the plea for mercy and the praise of God. In 1719, when Marie was not quite eight years old, soldiers raided a neighbor's home where a group had gathered to worship in the forbidden faith. The house was destroyed. Marie's mother was taken away, never to be heard from again, as were an uncle, cousins, and family friends. Her brother Pierre, who was probably leading the service, managed to slip away and eventually entered Switzerland, where he studied for the ministry. Soldiers occupied the Durand home for the next three weeks. After they left, Marie and her father made a life together. He retrieved the Bible from its hiding place in the wall, and, pulling the curtains and bolting the door, began to teach Marie about Scripture, prayer, and the Christian life. He told her the history of the persecuted Calvinists. She memorized some of the psalms of exile and learned to read the Bible and write out parts of it.

By the time she was imprisoned in the Tour de Constance, Marie Durand was better educated than the other prisoners (two-thirds of the women did not know how to sign their names); indeed, she was probably better educated than most people of her time. Apparently she was also an indomitable spirit. She instructed the children who had been imprisoned with their mothers and often led psalm-singing and read Scripture. She corresponded with pastor Paul Rabaut and with the Walloon church in Amsterdam, securing the prisoners' survival with needed funds and supplies. From that smuggled correspondence as well as from extant letters to her niece, we know more about Marie Durand's persistent faith. Biblical images and language suffuse her letters, as does a sense of God's merciful and providing power. For example, in a 1755 letter to her niece, she refers to Mara in the book of Ruth (1:20) to give voice to the bitter disappointment she and the other prisoners had suffered. And yet, despite the "constant murmuring of our flesh," she urges patience and endurance: "Seek the reign of God and his justice, and all things will be given to us below. . . . [God] will have pity on his desolated Zion and will restore it in a renewed state on earth."[5]

The plea for God's mercy and the praise of God's beneficent power that marked the Durand family home were written again across the whole of Marie Durand's life. The editor of her letters, Étienne Gamonnet, comments that she "subscribed perfectly" to Calvin's sense of God as the fountain of all truth, knowledge, goodness, justice, judgment, mercy, power, and holiness.[6] Perhaps Gamonnet effuses in his eagerness to portray her as an epitome of Reformed faith. Then again, perhaps we can better understand the sustaining source of which Calvin wrote through Marie Durand's testimony. Unrelenting tyranny, confinement, suffering, as well as sometimes fleeting health and not-so-fleeting despair, stripped her life of all but the essentials. They did not, however, separate her from God, to whom she prayed for deliverance, even when she lost the capacity to hope in it, and whom she praised as the merciful source of all that is, even when her own existence was nearly unbearable.

Yet what Marie Durand inscribed in the Tour de Constance was neither a plea for God's mercy nor praise of God. To the inscriptions by her father she added another: "Resist." Resist what is not of God or of the reign and justice of God. Her testimony echoed John Calvin's protest that "we are not our own, we are God's" and Martin Luther's thundering "God alone." This sensibility of fundamental protest is one of the wellsprings of Protestant faith. It is more than revolt, more than negation, more than a political stance; it is an undeniable faith conviction, an orienting religious experience. "Résister" testifies to the inviolability of God and calls for the alignment of life in response.

In Marie Durand's faith and struggle, the conviction of the inviolability of God was inseparable from the conviction of the inviolability of human dignity. To put it differently, she confronted the violation of *both* tables of the commandments, the violation of the double command to love God and neighbor. She resisted both idolatrous presumptions about God and tyrannous distortion and disregard of human life. As Gamonnet explains, "To annihilate being is the law of all tyranny; to crush all intellectual and religious life that rises up, to break hearts at the same time as spirits and wills. It is against this attempt by the authorities, more than for survival or safeguard of heritage, that Marie Durand had to 'resist.'"[7]

A CALL TO RESIST IDOLATRY

Marie Durand's life of testimony exemplified the counsel John Calvin had given to the French Protestants two hundred years earlier: "See that you take courage to separate yourselves from idolatry and from all superstitions which are contrary to the service of God, and to the acknowledgment and confession which all Christians owe to him, for to that we are called."[8] Protest against idolatrous political power dates to the beginning of Calvin's work. His 1535 prefatory address to the *Institutes of the Christian Religion* poses "a very great question" to King Francis I of France: "how God's glory may be kept safe on earth, how God's truth may retain its place of honor, how Christ's kingdom may be kept in good repair among us."[9]

More than likely, Calvin did not expect Francis to answer; his polemical address was itself already a response to the king's brutal retaliation against French Protestants after the affair of the placards in late 1534. (Whereas Luther nailed one copy of his Ninety-five Theses on Wittenberg's cathedral door as a call to public debate, this French group, working clandestinely under the cover of night, posted placards condemning the "idolatry" of the Roman mass throughout Paris and north-central France. Legend has it that the coverage was so thorough that the king awoke to find a placard posted on his bedroom door.) King Francis responded to the affair of the placards as a political problem, a matter of anarchy, as well as a religious problem, a matter of heresy. Three months after the affair, in a spectacle that involved all the trappings of court and church in a grandiose procession of relics and the sacrament, and following high mass at Nôtre Dame, the king denounced the Protestants and oversaw the public burning of six of them. Persecution intensified after that, causing Calvin to flee France.[10]

Calvin essentially agreed with the placards, namely, that the sacrament had become an idol and the Roman mass was false worship, and went on to say that the Roman church itself was false and its prelates greedy and self-absorbed.[11] In addition, by addressing the king with the question of safeguarding God's glory, Calvin tacitly extended the critique of idolatry from ecclesial symbols, practices, and hierarchy to include the political powers that upheld them. His own answer to the "very great question," provided eventually in his writings and through Geneva's consistory, academy, and magistracy, was to demonstrate how personal, ecclesial, social, and political existence can indeed "advance toward holiness" by adhering to the gospel.[12]

The French monarchy itself seemed to regress from holiness—at least by any Calvinist or humanist standard—by the time of the 1573 Massacre of St. Bartholomew's Day, in which ten thousand Huguenots reportedly died in Paris alone. The next generation of Calvinist leaders, faced with such changing cultural and political situations, argued explicitly for political resistance to Catholic monarchies. "Instead of being called to overturn statues and altars," historian Carlos Eire explains, "Christians were now being called upon to overturn governments."[13] The relation of Calvin and Calvinists to political resistance and revolution has been much debated by historians and political theorists and cannot even begin to be summarized here. Nevertheless, two basic observations about the call to resistance have particular theological relevance for our situation. To resist is a *call* to engagement, not a political program or polity. This call, moreover, assumes an underlying diagnosis of idolatry.

At its best, Reformed thought offers a *call to* resist idolatry with confession and social-cultural-political engagement, not a *program for* political transformation. It poses "a very great question" and struggles to answer it in every age and situation. By contrast, the presumption of an unchanging, monolithic Reformed polity or political theology is fraught with peril: when Reformed authorities have sought to rule church, society, or state as though they had sole purchase on the rule of truth and righteousness, they themselves have become tyrannical. Witness harsh condemnations of outsiders, witness the restriction of women to spheres of domesticity, and, more particularly, witness Calvin against Sadoleto, Puritan witch trials, and South African apartheid. These instances are perhaps easy, even overcited, targets of criticism, but they serve as sobering cautions nonetheless. Calvin's "very great question" cannot be answered once and for all but must be asked again in every age and situation. It calls us to take our place in history seriously, to take responsibility for the power that we have, and to work for justice and truth within the institutions and relationships of which we are part.

For Calvin, idolatry was not merely the problem of the French church and monarch: it was the root problem of human life. When Calvin examined human life, from individual consciousness to religious and political life, he made the diagnosis, informed especially by the Hebrew prophets and Deuteronomic law, of idolatry: "Man's nature, so to speak, is a perpetual factory of idols."[14] Insofar as idolatry is a "common vice" pursued through the ages, the French clerics were no different from everyone else. Calvin had special contempt for them because they, purporting to be guardians of God's truth and salvation, seemed to deceive others on purpose, and because their idolatry seemed particularly perverse—not only did they purvey false doctrine; they conveyed it with superfluous rituals and a multiplicity of images and relics.

In book 1 of the *Institutes*, Calvin provided a sort of ethnography of human life and religion. "Each man's mind is like a labyrinth," he observes, "so it is no wonder that individual nations were drawn aside into various falsehoods; and not only this—but individual men, almost, had their own gods."[15] Calvin mapped the pervasive human tendency to worship and to create ways of worshiping. In a back-handed compliment to humankind, he notes, "Man's mind, full as it is of pride and boldness, dares to imagine a god according to its own capacity." Furthermore, humans fashion images of the gods they imagine in order to provide assurance of divine presence. "Daily experience teaches that flesh is always uneasy until it has obtained some figment in which it may fondly find solace as in an image of God."[16] Even when the creators of these images intend to distinguish between God and the image they have fashioned for God, inevitably the images limit their understanding of God and, effectively, limit God. Thus, Calvin indicated an array of inclinations behind the manufacture of idols—sometimes cleverness or pride, sometimes fear, sometimes ignorance, sometimes naiveté, sometimes wickedness, and sometimes sheer perverseness.

Idolatry is rampant, multiform, and tenacious. It diverts energy from the deepest inclination and highest purpose of human life: to know and honor God. We are labyrinthine, full of multiple dimensions and conflicting desires that do not easily coalesce. Here, Calvin's diagnosis probed further, turning from an ethnography of idolatry and piety to a theological etiology of human capacity and incapacity. His etiology offers at least the explanatory power of Freud's or Marx's, and his "idolatry critique" is arguably as suspicious.[17]

Why are humans so prolific and tenacious in their idolatry? In short, because we want to worship; it is the characteristic that distinguishes human life from all other forms of life. Our lives bear the indelible inscription of God, Calvin insisted. We yearn to know and honor what exceeds and sustains our lives—the source of all goodness and righteousness—but we are incapable of reaching it on our own. Humanity has "an awareness of divinity" or a "seed of religion," and, closely related, a sense of the distinction between good and evil; these, in turn, incline us to seek to know and honor God, the author of all life and goodness. Yet however deeply this sense is imbedded in us, what we sense remains vague and fleeting at best. Often, we lose track of the fact of having this sense itself. But, whether we are aware of it or not, we fasten our seeking and our honor upon something.

Because of our weakness, we inevitably fall back on more tangible and immediate assurances—on small gods of vindication, comfort, stability, control, privilege, revenge. Whatever we seek and honor unavoidably shapes our lives. Idolatry, then, is far more seductive and dangerous than false opinion or unjust action alone. To use contemporary medical metaphors, it is more like a cancer or an HIV epidemic than a wound or infection, and it can only be adequately diagnosed and countered with help of the rescuing and redeeming power of God.

On our own, Calvin explained, we can reach neither to God's full glory nor to our own. However, God reaches to us. God coaxes and teaches us, accommodating our inability through the witness of Scripture, the gospel of Christ, the work of the Spirit, and the work of the church. Divine accommodation provides for true knowledge and worship of God and thus enables us to struggle against false gods and false existence. True piety is, then, the opposite of idolatry. To acknowledge and confess God truly is to align one's entire life with God and to resist competing claims for honor and obedience. We confess that the power of life belongs to God and not to us, and yet we accept responsibility for eschewing idolatry and aligning every dimension of our lives with God—personal, ecclesial, social, cultural, political, economic. Because of this tension between divine sovereignty and human responsibility, we Protestants are, at our best, venturesome folks who are impatient with falsehood and injustice and who can be uncompromising agents of change; at our worst, we fear God and our responsibility, and we evade this tension by creating and submitting to authoritarian religious and political regimes.

The notion of idolatry's pernicious tenacity and its dialectical opposition to true piety lay behind Calvin's counsel to French Protestants, noted earlier in this chapter, that they separate themselves from idolatry and render due acknowledgment, confession, and service to God. It was this counsel, this understanding of idolatry as the root problem of human life, that the German Confessing Church sought to follow in the 1934 Theological Declaration of Barmen, perhaps the most famous example of resistance to idolatry in twentieth-century Reformed theology.[18] The document declared the independence of the church from "any alien voice" and proclaimed the church's "sole dependence" on God and on the Word of God as the source of truth. Barmen "repudiate[d] the false teaching that there are areas of our life in which we belong not to Jesus Christ but to other lords, areas in which we do not need justification and sanctification through him." Barmen also rejected as false the idea that the state "should and could become the single and totalitarian order of life," thus usurping the church's vocation as well.[19] That the Confessing Churches understood themselves to be resisting the alien voice and illegitimate claims of the Nazi regime was obvious enough, if never explicitly stated— obvious enough that Barmen became a rallying point for the church's struggle against Hitler and obvious enough to mark many of the signers of the declaration in the eyes of the secret police.

According to Confessing Church theologians Karl Barth and Dietrich Bonhoeffer, to confess—to be the Confessing Church and to confess the gospel and the lordship of Christ—entailed an active, uncompromising stance. Under a totalitarian regime that demanded ultimate loyalty, the Confessing Church eventually faced the same alternatives that the persecuted French Huguenots had: either to flee or to remain while avoiding false worship, even at the cost of one's life. The option they all rejected was to avoid persecution by professing inner allegiance to what they understood as the true faith while outwardly appearing to be faithful to the "alien" power, be that the French Catholic church and monarchy or the Reich church and National Socialism.[20] As Carlos Eire explains, "Calvin would admit no separation between private belief and public behavior." For Calvin's political heirs, "this principle of confessional integrity went beyond mere passivity: It also called for an aggressive public rejection of the many social norms that supported 'idolatry.'"[21] This Reformed principle helps us to understand the power of Barmen's confession as well.

Yet for all of its power to orient courageous protest, Barmen had serious shortcomings. Its protest remained church centered, focused on the constriction of the church and Christian conscience by an alien power. It evaded explicit condemnation of Hitler and Nazi totalitarianism, and, as Bonhoeffer and, later, Barth recognized, did not even approach the so-called Jewish question. It failed to protest the most heinous aspect of the Nazi regime: its propagation of virulent hatred of Jews, a propagation that would escalate, horrifically and relentlessly, in the few short years after Barmen into a massive, systematic program of extermination. We must ask, albeit with the clarity of hindsight, whether Barmen's understanding of idolatry was broad enough, whether its theology effectively removed God from history, whether it truncated the moral heart of Jewish and Christian traditions by emphasizing the first table of the law to the diminishment of the second, and to what extent its focus on hearing the Word of God alone hindered its ability to hear the claims of suffering humanity. These questions lead to the second aspect of the call to resistance.

A CALL TO RESIST THE DENIAL OF HUMAN DIGNITY AND THE DEGRADATION OF LIFE

The call to resistance must be understood as a call not only to defy encroachments upon divine authority, as suggested above, but also to resist the denial of human dignity and the degradation of all life, and thereby the distortion of God as the source of all life and goodness. The Nazi regime was not merely idolatrous because its "alien power" contravened the authority of God and the church, but also because it presumed to know the worth of life, to determine what was worthy of worship and honor, and to judge between life and death. The death camps represented, among other things, a pernicious, thoroughgoing denial of the dignity of human life and, in this way, a denial of the God of life.

The commitment to the inviolability of human dignity and life ought not be separated from the confession of the inviolability of God. Each commitment must correct and extend the other: resistance to idolatrous limitations of God must inform an expansive notion of human well-being, and resistance to hatred and human indignity must likewise shape a capacious understanding of God. Marie Durand resisted both idolatrous presumptions about God and tyrannous distortion and disregard of human life; she confronted the violation of *both* tables of the commandments, of the double command to love God and neighbor.

Marie Durand's full legacy is more evident in the French Reformed who rallied to her call in the mid-twentieth century than in the Barmen Declaration. They resisted the power of the Nazi regime and explicitly resisted the degradation of human life and dignity. Furthermore, their solidarity with the persecuted Jews led them to deepen their understanding of the love of neighbor, to address love of enemy by defying the destruction of life, and to confront the limitations of their own faith.

As I noted at the beginning of this chapter, in 1935, writer and antifascist activist André Chamson took up the call "Résister" in relation to the threats of his time, urging the Reformed Church in France to resist both the threat of Nazi power and the longstanding scourge of Christian anti-Judaism. By the early 1940s, remote, mountainous areas that had once sheltered French Protestants from persecution were defying Vichy rule to shelter French-born and foreign-born Jews. As Nazi atrocities multiplied, Reformed pastors and people intensified their efforts and joined with other persons of goodwill to make the region of the Cévennes, the population center and historic stronghold of the Reformed Church, an area of refuge.

In and around the Cévennes, the struggle and faith of the Huguenots under persecution are remembered vividly, not only within the Reformed Church but in the culture in general. (Marie Durand had grown up just to the north and was imprisoned just to the south of the region.) According to historian Philippe Joutard, this memory resulted in "an instinctive solidarity" with those who are persecuted, especially the Jews. He views this sense of solidarity as "the decisive phenomenon" behind fairly widespread Cevenol efforts to shelter Jews from persecution and death.[22] Many in the isolated Cévennes had never met a person of Jewish faith or ancestry; they knew the Jews rather as the people of the Bible and as those whose psalms of suffering their ancestors had sung as their own. But with knowledge of deportation centers as near as Lyon and Toulouse and with word of the death camps, "the Jewish question was no longer simply a biblical question, but a reality," one Cevenol pastor explained, a reality that addressed their consciences.[23] We might, then, call the profound recognition of the inviolable dignity of humanity and the revulsion at relentless persecution of the Jews "a seed of religion," a testimony of conscience, "a sense of divinity."

Felt solidarity with the suffering humanity of Jews was decisive. But there were other factors that inclined the Cevenol pastors and people to resist both Nazi power and Christian anti-Judaism. These factors are instructive for any adequate response to the call to resist. First, the Cevenols obtained the best information possible about the nature of the Nazi threat: information channeled through Switzerland told them of Hitler's "final solution" before most persons anywhere else knew or were prepared to believe it. Second, their leaders, especially Marc Boegner, president of the Protestant Federation in France, kept up the call to resist from the mid-thirties to the end of the war. Third, congregations, neither funded by the state nor subject to a vast ecclesiastical hierarchy, were autonomous enough to pursue resistance activities at their own initiative, without need for authorization from a bureaucracy or hierarchy, and with needed secrecy. Fourth, they had some time and they used it to prepare themselves: already by 1933 they started to address the Nazi threat and the so-called Jewish question and did not come under Vichy rule with its censures and deadly sanctions until 1940. Most of all, they deepened their "instinctive solidarity" with biblical study and theological reflection and, through these, readied themselves for active solidarity and resistance.

Biblical texts were engaged freshly in light of the situation, and much of this engagement served to unmask Christian anti-Judaism. Among the texts that figured prominently was the parable of the Good Samaritan with its question of who is my neighbor. North of the Cévennes, in the village of Le Chambon that would shelter hundreds, possibly thousands, before the war's end, the Protestant temple had "Love one another" inscribed across its doorway. Pastors Éduard Theis and André Trocmé preached that nations and individuals must resist evil (*le mal*, which also connotes "harm") with all their power, and particularly the hatred and destruction that Nazi Germany represented. Moreover, they preached, in Philip Hallie's words, that "in attacking evil, we must cherish the preciousness of all human life." Here again is the call to resist not only the encroachment of divine authority but also the degradation of life. Trocmé and Thies addressed Jesus' radical command to love the enemy in terms of resisting the destruction of life. "To be against evil is to be against the destruction of human life and to be against the passions that motivate the destruction." However, Hallie notes, "the sermons did not propose a neat blueprint for fighting hatred with love." Rather, beginning in the late 1930s as Nazi evil increased, Theis and Trocmé preached "an attitude of resistance and of canny, unsentimental watching for opportunities to do something in the spirit of that resistance." And, "opportunities soon came," as Hallie elaborates in his account of Le Chambon's resistance, *Lest Innocent Blood Be Shed*.[24]

Pastors in the Cévennes also deepened their instinctive solidarity and readied themselves for active solidarity and resistance by thinking theologically about Nazi power and Christian anti-Judaism and by examining the theological and cultural "logics" that underlay them. Articles in the *Revue du Christianisme social*, a journal well circulated among Reformed pastors, had addressed the German situation and Christian anti-Judaism regularly since 1933, as had a more popular church publication. Karl Barth's prophetic "No" was much admired and his writings widely read, but they were also met with vigorous theological critique. At dispute was never the denouncement of Nazi tyranny but the theological grounds for doing so. French theologians critiqued Barth's "métaphysique de l'Intemporal," his "disdain of history," his construal of God as "pure will" who is seemingly "a rigid vertical line that nothing can bend," and an apparent "misanthropy," in the strict sense of a distrust of all people.[25] In contrast to Barth's revelationism, these theologians and pastors engaged the Bible and theology to immerse themselves in the events of the day, struggling to wrest meaning and wage resistance to the hatred, idolatry, and inhumanity that was so evident around them.

After the death camps, after the killing fields, after chattel slavery, after the formal end of global colonialism, and in the face of other old and emerging regimes of oppression and death, we must continue to cultivate a sense of solidarity with suffering humanity, to deepen it by critical biblical and theological engagement, and to sharpen it not only through a Calvinist "idolatry critique" but also through the use of contemporary critical theories. This instinctive solidarity is perhaps the "awareness of the divine," the testimony of conscience, that is most relevant in our day. But, unlike the forms of Reformed theology that foster distrust of our deep, albeit fleeting, sensibilities of the good and the divine, we must, rather, use Scripture, reason, theology, and concrete action to magnify as well as to suspect these sensibilities. Through these means, we must further understanding of our ambiguous lives, our humanity and inhumanity; nurture our repulsion at injustice and evil; and encourage our call to seek the righteousness of God and the well-being of humanity.

A CALL TO CRITIQUE THEOLOGY'S OWN IDOLATRIES

The French Reformed pastors found that to receive the call "Résister" from Marie Durand and other persecuted Huguenots required that their own theologies change: they had to uproot deeply entrenched anti-Judaism from their own theology and culture. They had to turn their Huguenot heritage of protest back on their own theology. To take up "Résister" today likewise requires that theology itself be subject to internal critique and ongoing reformation. Like the pastors in the Cévennes, we must uncover the idols—the ideologies that constrain the flourishing of life before God—in our own theologies, institutions, and practices. However, we do not face one overwhelming, external threat, such as Nazi tyranny. The idols of our day are all around us—intermingled in the way we speak and think, with where we live and work and worship, in what we buy and eat. We uphold and advance these idols in everyday language and relations and the most prosaic of activities. As Calvin reminds us, idolatry is both commonplace and extremely dangerous. I do not consciously choose to affirm white privilege or to dishonor the poor, to give examples, but I nevertheless participate, advertently and inadvertently, in patterns of engaging the world that effectively uphold such choices. And, by being so "honored," these idols accumulate the power to describe and organize "reality," and thus they are, in a manner of speaking, more able to compel us to bow down. We must, therefore, extend our resistance to ourselves and our theologies, to our own presumptions and idolatries, the falsehoods and injustices in which we advertently and inadvertently participate, even as we are resisting other idolatries and tyrannies.

Resistance to idolatry—without and within Christian theology, institutions, and practice—has been foremost among the concerns of feminist and womanist theologies. For example, Mary Daly's classic 1973 book, *Beyond God the Father*, put the matter of idolatry simply: "If God is male, then the male is God." Her pithy statement implies all three aspects of idolatry. One, defining "God" as male is idolatrous in the narrow sense: the divine is falsely and reductively pictured as male. Two, elevating the male and thereby subordinating women is tyrannous and presents a false picture of humanity. And three, any theology that endorses this definition perpetuates and promotes a false picture of "reality." More specifically, Daly's iconoclastic critique focused on how theologies have fixed and objectified "God" in static symbols, especially but not only male ones, and how these theologies in turn have legitimated oppression and subordination. "The symbol of the Father God, spawned in the human imagination and sustained as plausible by patriarchy, has in turn rendered service to this type of society by making its mechanisms for the oppression of women appear right and fitting."[26]

Sallie McFague likewise attends to the power of language about God to wreak harm—or good. She is less concerned with the idolatry of alien powers than with the idolatries of familiar powers, in other words, with idolatries perpetuated every day by theologies that are no longer adequate to our situation (if they ever were). She critiques theologies that are "idolatrous," "irrelevant," and potentially dangerous for "the continuation of life on our planet" and offers alternative models of the relation of God and the world that uphold the survival and thriving of all life.[27] Like Daly, McFague rejects fixed language for "God" but not, as for Daly, because it stifles participation in a dynamic ontology of gynocentric becoming. Rather, in a move that can be understood as quintessentially Protestant, McFague says that language about "God" is always inadequate. If language for God appears to be fixed, it is because the metaphorical character of all God-language, indeed of all language, has been forgotten. For, as McFague insists, seeming to take a page from Calvin himself, we forget that the metaphors we use are metaphors. We forget as well that they inevitably limit our understanding and, thereby, effectively limit God. Moreover, metaphors that may have been relevant in one context can become irrelevant, idolatrous, and even dangerous in another. Thus, we are always having to re-form our ways of speaking about God.[28] Here, the task of the internal, ongoing reformation of theology is shaped by the call to resist both idolatrous limitations of "God" and the degradation of all life. In McFague's work, the rejection of patriarchal, triumphalist, and imperialist metaphors for God informs an expansive notion of human well-being as inseparable from the well-being of all life. At the same time, resistance to the idolatrous degradation of life and a correlative reverence for life as a glorious gift of God inform capacious models of and for God.

Womanist and feminist theologians have pursued diverse strategies for identifying and resisting idolatry internal to Christian life and thought. Iconoclasm—whether it be Daly's ontological rupture of static symbols or McFague's constructivist displacement of idolatrous metaphors and models—has been a prominent approach. Others, like feminist social ethicist Beverly Wildung Harrison, have resisted problematic construals of divine power. She sounds the classic Reformed theme of divine sovereignty, but in a way that questions historic construals of divine authority. God is "beyond our manipulation and control," she writes, but "does not aspire to control us or require our obeisance."[29] However, Harrison's primary strategy for resisting theological idolatries has been to trace theology's collusions with ideologies and practices that constrain, sometimes viciously, the well-being of life before God. She, along with others, has tracked and resisted theology's complicities with cultural, racial, and gender dominance, with rampant consumerism and capitalist exploitation, with imperialism and colonialism, and with misogyny and homophobia.

Another theological strategy, one followed partly in this chapter, is to thematize resistance as integral to Christian faith and to survival. For example, womanist theologian Delores Williams has explored the continuity of Hagar's story with those of African American women as narratives of survival and resistance.[30] Katie Geneva Cannon explores how enslaved African Americans and their descendants have survived the dehumanizing "blight" in the dominant culture and religion by creating a counterculture through folklore, spirituals, and prayer.[31] In her essay in this volume, Cannon traces the power of transforming grace among black Presbyterians in the face of racist idolatries in the larger Presbyterian Church. We might compare her strategies for resisting idolatry with Calvin's approach and suggest that Cannon is charting ethnographies of idolatry and of "true piety."

ALWAYS REFORMING, ALWAYS RESISTING

To take up "Résister" in our day also implies that, as for the French Reformed under Vichy rule, resistance to theology's own idolatries will occur alongside active resistance and political struggle. Critical consciousness and concrete resistance require and further each other. "If concrete practices of resistance flag," Harrison warns, "the critical consciousness generated by those practices will also wane." Moreover, Harrison argues, "what is authentic in the history of faith arises only out of the crucible of human struggle."[32] Her words ring true for Marie Durand and the persecuted Huguenots, for Calvin, and for the resisting Reformed at mid-century. Feminist and womanist theologies have likewise insisted that there can be no real reformation of Christian theology and life apart from concrete resistance to oppression, repression, and exploitation. At the same time, they insist, genuine struggles for transformation will always include uprooting the distortions internal to our own lives and thought.

Marie Durand's day-to-day resistance was waged at the most basic of levels in her struggle to eat, keep warm, be clothed, maintain community and communication, and worship without constraint. She took nothing for granted but the constancy of God and the responsibility to do what she could. In our day, the sheer struggle for survival of mind, body, and spirit is waged throughout the world's villages and cities. The deadly effects of our day's idolatries are seen in places where the basic goods of life cannot be taken for granted, where it is a struggle to keep a child safe from violence and well-enough fed, where decent housing can neither be afforded nor found, where access to minimal health care or education cannot be assumed, where the lack of hope numbs minds and spirits. The effects of our day's idolatries also cut across relative privileges. They are seen in interpersonal abuse and violence, substance abuse, ragged relationships, lack of viable common life, contaminated food and water and air, and relative inability to access or effect political processes. To resist is to gain a toehold against the seemingly insurmountable accumulation of such ravages. In such contexts, to resist may mean marches and international coalitions, but it more likely involves an accumulation of daily resistances equivalent to the Durand family's persistence in faith, to Marie's being taught to read by her father and in turn teaching imprisoned children, and to writing her testimony in letters and in stone.

At their best, womanist, feminist, and Reformed theologies emerge from and fund a continuous this-worldly conversion. Our calling, as Christians and also as womanists and feminists, is not simply to endure the ambiguity of life by navigating it well, and certainly not to evade or escape it. Rather, our call is to resist, that is, to struggle to live fully and responsively to God in the midst of the ambiguity of life by resisting idolatry, even when that entails resisting our own theologies and institutions. Theology itself becomes idolatrous when it pretends to possess final truths apart from historical and cultural influences. Feminist and womanist theologians suggest that we ought to construe theology more modestly, as neither being a closed system nor having a final point of closure, but as requiring ongoing reformation and resistance.[33] That does not mean theology's work is less demanding, however. The call to safeguard the glory of God, to seek the truth, and to align our thought and lives with what is worthy of honor and reverence is a never-ceasing, though always-proximate task.

If Marie Durand did not indicate how "Résister" must also be directed to Reformed theology and faith itself, this reflexive aspect of the call to resist was already implicit in the older slogan *ecclesia reformata sed semper reformanda*, "the church reformed but always being reformed." Beverly Harrison observes that this "continuously reforming theological stance . . . was, at best, our tradition's rhetorical ideal, even when honored more in the breach than in the practice."[34] I suggest that feminist and womanist theologians have tried to honor this stance, not only in the breach but also in the practice of resistance, as did Marie Durand and the mid-twentieth-century Reformed resisters. Moreover, they have done so by making explicit, in their theologies and with their lives and struggles, the connection between the call to resist and the calling to be reformed. If we exegete these old slogans well for our day, "Résister" and "semper reformanda" can continue to spark and guide a venturesome faith and a theology that never ceases its attempt to bear truth amidst the ravages and glories of life.

11

BETWEEN VOCATION AND WORK

A Womanist Notion of a Work Ethic

Joan M. Martin

To speak of a work ethic is not to ask how much work a people did, or even how much work they thought they should do, although the latter is getting tolerably close. It is to ask of a people what meaning did work have in their own conceptualization of their social existence. In this sense, the work ethic of a people is so securely bound to their collective *Weltanschauung* [worldview] as to make meaningless any attempt to transcend a given collective experience. Thus the alteration of social relations embedded in slavery would precipitate a change in the very meaning of the concept of work itself.[1]

These words crystallize my interest in the meaning of work and moral agency in African American historic existence and in our contemporary "worldview," and support my intuition that work was not and is not an individualistic endeavor. From my first free-enterprise selling of Christmas cards at age nine, to my ordination, through today, my life continues to be shaped by experiences as a daughter in a family whose parents gave their children a legacy of meaningful work. My parents impressed upon me that hard, decent, and honest work, coupled with a good education and a deep faith in Jesus, were sufficient to gain respect in the world. And they tried their best to model what they believed, particularly as African Americans in what they considered to be a society rendered unsafe by white supremacist racism, about an abundant life given by God.

I learned that work and labor are measured by the survival and nurture of self, family, and community, rather than by individual economic success or other values of the dominant society. The dominant social values do not liberate communities of black people and poor people, but oppress them on the basis of economics and class, gender, and race. In this essay I explore the complex origins of African American Christians' work ethic, and in particular this ethic as it emerged through the lives of enslaved blackwomen.[2] By placing the words and experiences of enslaved and ex-enslaved women at the center of the work ethic discussion, I attempt to uncover the connection between "calling" and "work" that has often remained theologically abstracted from concrete personal and social history. In seeking the meaning of enslaved blackwomen's reality in relation to Christian faith and the work ethic that evolved in the Protestant ethos of the United States, I interweave three themes: Protestant social teachings on work and vocation and the biblical perspectives underlying them, the historical development of the work ethic in the United States, and the interface of these traditions with the lives and experience of enslaved blackwomen.

BIBLICAL AND THEOLOGICAL PERSPECTIVES ON WORK

Work is part of the relationship between God and humanity. First there is the work of God—creation and redemption (liberation)—which the Bible attributes to God alone and which consequently encompasses God's covenantal relationships with humanity through Israel and beyond (Gen. 1–2; Ps. 8:3; 33:6; 104:24; 148:5; Isa. 43:24ff. and Isa. 53). Second, there is the realm of human work—that is, all the work that humans do to meet basic needs and to live socially (Gen. 1–2). Such work is necessary. By *necessary*, I mean work that is for the maintenance and reproduction of human life, mediating between our relationship to nature for the satisfaction of life's basic needs and our relationship as culture-creating-building-sustaining beings. Even "at the beginning of creation there was no work-free age . . ." and only "after the Fall is work cursed by toil, pain, and uselessness," according to Jürgen Moltmann.[3] (Of course, it is important to remember that the church has traditionally read Gen. 3 as justification for the view that Eve's sin is blamed for work becoming "toil.") Third, when the faith community and its members live and work in and for the "kin-dom" of God (Mark 16:20), such participation in work is a participation "in Christ." This is a metaphorical faith understanding of work: the community of faith "works" in the cause of the gospel or shares in "the work of Christ" (Phil. 2:30).[4]

The different historical and economic situations of the several biblical traditions and the ideological commitments present in those traditions yield diverse perspectives on work. As depicted in the Pentateuch and the "historical books" of the Hebrew Bible, human labor in Israel's nomadic and agricultural life is self-supporting, communal (in the sense of extended kinship relations and within the context of community), and meaningful. This is true even when work is viewed as toil done "by the sweat of their brow" in such narratives as the story of Cain and Abel, the story of Noah and the Flood, the Abraham and Sarah cycles, and the narratives of Judges, Samuel, and Kings. In Exodus 1–2, the Israelites find themselves in slavery and conscripted for the public work projects by Pharaoh. In 1 Kings 5 and 9, it is clear that King Solomon has created a forced labor system utilizing Israelites or foreigners within Israel's borders to build the Temple and the king's house. Likewise, the Prophetic literature denounces the oppression of the poor through unjust labor systems and their products (Isa. 31:3) and the idle rich (Amos 6:3–6), while the Psalter raises the concern of Israel's faithfulness through its work while the nation is in exile. Ecclesiastes and Proverbs, as examples of Wisdom literature, often commend the proper work attitude as that of diligence and care in one's labor as well as the most fruitful way of securing an identity as God's people (Prov. 6:6–11; 12:24).

The New Testament—both Synoptic literature and epistolary works—contains multiple meanings and uses of human work. In the Synoptic parables, daily work themes and activities become the context for metaphors of the new reign of God (Matt. 13:1–23; 20:1–16; Mark 4:1–20; Luke 8:4–18; 13:20–21). Pauline and deuteropauline letters stress work and daily living, a cheerful attitude toward work, and the condemnation of idleness (Col. 3:23; 2 Thess. 3:10–12). Further, the daily work of Christians is addressed in household codes of Paul (Eph. 6:5–9; Col. 3:22–4:1) and in the letters of 1 Timothy, Titus, and 1 Peter. They pertain to familial relationships, including the master-servant/master-slave relationship. Within the context of daily life, there is the opportunity to see one's work as a faithful response to God. Work for the Christian is a vocation—that is, a vehicle through which one is to be obedient to God, who is the Christian's master. In this view of work, Paul in particular is underlining the double use of the term vocation, or calling. Persons are "called" into new life by God through repentance and faith and into the life and work of the church. This is the foundation from which Christians become "workers" in whatever they do in daily, "secular" activity.

WOMANIST REFLECTIONS ON THE BIBLE, ENSLAVED WOMEN, AND WORK

In the Protestant tradition, laity and scholars alike turn to the Bible because it serves as the fundamental source of theological and ethical reflection in two ways. It is the repository for the archetypal, generative, and organizing myths of the community of faith in which the community finds its memory and purpose for the past, present, and future. Furthermore, the Bible is the paramount and first source for "doing theology" for most members of the churches—the "textbook" (written and oral/aural) for conversion and faith experiences, church school education at all levels, preaching, and group and individual meditation. This is particularly true of African American Christian women historically, and it still holds true for contemporary blackwomen. But why is this the case, given critical studies and interpretations of the Bible from African American liberation scholars that document and demonstrate the use of the Bible as an ideological tool to foster and perpetuate white supremacy, colonialism, and the subjugation of black Americans? Why is this the case, when feminist scholars have more than adequately analyzed the prevailing patriarchalism and misogyny of the biblical traditions and texts? Both groups of scholars have drawn upon a formidable array of disciplines and methods in their work. What accounts for blackwomen's allegiance to the biblical witness—an allegiance that has been neither uncritical nor unsophisticated in the face of racism, sexism, and classism in this society?

Womanist biblical scholar Renita Weems has suggested that the answer to this question is very complicated indeed. Owing to the historical experience of blackwomen's oppression, the Bible needs to speak with existential authority to the experience, identity, and values of blackwomen, and provide a "life guide" that sustains hope and strength in blackwomen's struggle for authentic personhood. For Weems, this complex encounter with the Bible and the Christian God is a matter of "reading the text" from one's social location. At the same time, blackwomen must be cognizant and critical of the social locations of the biblical narrators and of the interpretative voices in the dominant culture both historically and currently (including those voices within the black male and white feminist Christian community).

Weems advocates a blackwomen's biblical hermeneutic grounded in neither an African American liberationist perspective nor a white feminist analysis alone. Her womanist hermeneutic comprises three elements. First, it is a hermeneutic that seeks to "uncover whose voice [blackwomen and marginalized people] identify with in the Bible—female as opposed to male, the African as opposed to the non-African, the marginalized as opposed to the dominant." Second, "it has equally and more precisely to do with examining the *values* of those readers and the corroboration of those values by the text."[5] The third and most important dimension for womanist reflections on blackwomen's lives, the Bible, and work is what Weems calls the "credibility of the text" in its portrait of how human beings relate to one another. That portrait ought to coincide with the way blackwomen have experienced reality and relationships with other people and, as a text, arouse, manipulate, and harness African American women's deepest yearnings.[6]

In the context of liberationist perspectives, neither African American (male) nor feminist biblical and theological interpretation adequately addresses the particularity of blackwomen's lives. Blackwomen's experience of the "credibility of the text" has been best exemplified by the work of Delores S. Williams. While African American and feminist biblical interpretation often focuses on liberation in the exodus event,[7] Williams chooses, not the exodus motif, but rather the story of Hagar, the African female slave of Sarah (Gen. 16:1–16 and 21:9–21). She traces Hagar's presence through the experience of African American enslaved women:

Hagar's heritage was African as was black women's. Hagar was a slave. Black American women had emerged from a slave heritage and still lived in light of it. Hagar was brutalized by her slave owner, the Hebrew woman Sarah. The slave narratives of African American women and some of the narratives of contemporary day-workers tell of brutal or cruel treatment black women received from wives of slave masters and contemporary white female employers. Hagar had no control of her body . . . mother and child were eventually cast out of Abraham and Sarah's home without resources for survival. The bodies of African American women were owned by their masters . . . raped by their owners and bore children whom slave masters never claimed . . . children and their mothers whom slave-master fathers often cast out by selling them to other slave holders. . . . Hagar resisted the brutalities of slavery by running away. Black American women have a long resistance history that includes running away from slavery in the antebellum era. Hagar, like many women throughout African American women's history . . . had a personal and salvific encounter with God.[8]

Williams understands that Hagar, the enslaved woman, is bound by a context in which her "story is and unavoidably has been shaped by the problems and desires of her owners": Abraham's need for an heir in light of God's covenant promise and Sarah's barrenness as a defining reality of her femaleness.[9]

Of the many issues raised by Williams regarding blackwomen's biblical hermeneutic, I want to direct attention to two critical issues that foreground my project of blackwomen, work, and moral agency. The first issue is enslaved women's experience of God. Williams notes that in the initial meeting between Hagar and the angel, Hagar is in the wilderness by way of her own momentary volition (resistance as flight from ownership and abuse) and fight for survival. As a result, "the angel of the LORD found her by a spring of water in the wilderness, the spring on the way to Shur" (Gen. 16:7). Following the conventions of the biblical text, Williams suggests that this angel *is* God.[10] Although God is not portrayed in a liberatory light, still seeing Hagar as Sarah's property, God is personally present to Hagar in her concrete plight and seeks the immediate and long-term survival and flourishing of Hagar and her yet-to-be born child.[11] In using the work of Phyllis Trible, Williams remarks about the twofold encounter with God: "Hagar is the only person in the Bible to whom is attributed the power of naming God [El Roi], who has ministered to her and empowered her in these surrogate roles."[12] In the second meeting with God (Gen. 21:17–19), God again asks Hagar a question, but does not permit her to answer it. This God is transcendent—one who calls to Hagar from the heavens, reminds her of God's promise (including Ishmael's future as the father of a great nation), opens Hagar's eyes to the presence of a well in the desert, and ensures the child's survival. Thus the God who meets enslaved women of African descent in the wilderness cannot simply be identified from the perspective of the dominant group, in this case, Abraham and Sarah the slave owners. God works redemptively in Hagar's life independently of the desires and problems of her owners.

The second issue concerns Hagar's choice to resist oppression. Although some could see Hagar's flight from Sarah as reactive, Williams posits that Hagar's act of escape is proactive. It is not a "heroic" act according to contemporary notions of heroism as exemplified in either a terrorist holy war or a preemptive war to secure a nation against another sovereign people. Hagar's act is proactive because in flight, in the present knowledge that she is the property of another, she seeks a different outcome for her yet-to-be born son. Hagar seeks to be enslaved no more and to act upon that choice. Her decision to flee is conscious and self-determined. It was not the decision of either Abraham or Sarah as her owners. So too was her decision to return to enslavement for the sake of her child at the command of the angel of the LORD. It was a conscious and self-determined decision made *in light of* God immanently present *with* her in her suffering and her survival in the wilderness. This presence and promise was sufficient to empower Hagar to endure in the interim. Williams's womanist rereading and reappropriation of the biblical story points to blackwomen's trust that God's presence, God's power, and God's promise could fuel their work to maintain physical life and find hope for the future.

A womanist reading of the exodus narrative also yields insights into work. In African American liberation theology, the exodus story focuses on the relationship between God and Moses, not the midwives Shiphrah and Puah. But a womanist hermeneutic notes that the story begins with the actions of these midwives in responding to the oppression of the Egyptian king over the Hebrews, women who can be recognized by ethnicity, by class (that is, work) orientation, and by solidarity with other women. They are multiply oppressed people as Hebrews, as Hebrew women, as "domestic workers," and as home healthcare workers. Moreover, their action is prompted by their faith. They, like Moses later in the narrative, become deliverers of their people,[13] and by their actions are in solidarity with the Hebrew women and their God.

The work of the midwives subverts dominant understandings of work. Taskmasters were set over the Hebrews "to oppress them with forced labor" and to make their lives "bitter with hard service in mortar and brick and in every kind of field labor" (Exod. 1:11, 14). It seems the forced labor of the Hebrews was, according to Pharaoh, the appropriate work of common people (the Hebrews outnumbering the Egyptians) who labored for upper classes, the priests, and god-king. Indeed, large economic enterprises—work supporting empire building—were connected to the state religion, its cult(s), and its gods in the ancient Near East.[14] That work maliciously exploited the labor of others, often in a death-dealing fashion. Pharaoh had sought the work of the midwives as part of his exploitative, imperial scheme, but they refused to participate in their own exploitation and that of the Israelites. Instead, they chose to place their labor—its skills and its knowledge—on the side of the Israelite God whose work would be revealed in the redemption of Israel.

Shiphrah and Puah, courageous in faith, in solidarity with others, and empowered with the skill of their craft, positively respond to the God of the Hebrews and thwart the will of Pharaoh. By doing so, they work to ensure the survival of the Hebrew people. (Survival of the Hebrew people is later placed in the hands of Moses, a development that raises thorny issues about women's traditional domestic role related to birth, children, and status in patriarchal culture, and about the controlling of women's subversive power). The midwives' "fear of God" compels them to risk and act. According to Cheryl Exum, "to 'fear God' does not simply mean to be afraid of God or God's punishment; it is, on the contrary, a far broader theological concept, having at its center the element of *mysterium tremendum* and extending to conduct which is guided by basic ethical principles and in harmony with God's will." Exum reminds the reader that in the Wisdom literature this sense of awe, "the fear of God," is the beginning of knowledge, a knowledge that is not the exclusive prerogative of the Israelites. In other words, one needs right knowledge and relationship with God.[15] Such faith and action are not unlike the stance taken by Sojourner Truth in the face of an arrogant proslavery woman, and Harriet Jacobs in opposition to Dr. Flint.[16]

From a womanist perspective, right knowledge and reflexive action on the part of the Hebrew midwives and enslaved women were more acutely faithful to an understanding of God than claims of either Pharaoh or the proslavery "Christian" women. Pharaoh thought himself to be divine and was worshiped by the Egyptians as god. The midwives, however, "feared [the] God" of the Israelites. Similarly, the proslavery women assumed they knew God's intention was the enslavement of African Americans while Truth countered with a different claim about God's identity. As it turns out, Pharaoh is no god at all in comparison with the God of the Israelites, but is in fact a god of oppression and death. Likewise, it turns out that the god of proslavery Christianity is also one of oppression and death in the sensibilities of enslaved women such as Truth and Jacobs.

The God who stands in the background behind the Hebrew midwives and the One who stands behind Sojourner Truth is the God and Creator of life. This God is the One who in the creation of the cosmos creates human beings and fashions them after God's own likeness. Moreover, it is the same God who covenants with humans (Abraham, Sarah, and Hagar's descendants) to empower them in specific times and in specific ways according to God's expanding purpose. God is able to have relationships with the lowliest in life's stations according to the world's standards, and to use their work for God's redemptive aims.

A womanist reading uncovers a new dimension of blackwomen's theo-ethical understanding of God. It appears from the dialogue between the biblical and enslaved narratives that the interaction between faithful women and a faithful God calls forth the expansive moral agency of each. Each party calls the other into greater fullness of being in a relationship to affirm, defend, and perpetuate life as the divine purpose of God and the creaturely purpose of women. For the midwives to have such a knowledge of God is also to have a knowledge of God's relationship to the ancestors of the Hebrews—Abraham and Sarah, Isaac and Rebekah, and Jacob, Leah, and Rachel. The same is true of Sojourner Truth, and particularly Harriet Jacobs, who join their knowledge of God to the knowledge of their ancestors and ancestral ways. For Truth, it is the connection between her mother's name, Mau Mau, and her mother's admonishment to recognize that there is but one Being greater than all. For Jacobs, it is the integration of the power of her parents' spirit of freedom and the power of God that launched her on her escape to freedom. The blackwomen's theo-ethical insight is that remembrance of the past, faithfulness in the present, and just moral activity by God and persons of faith together work to restore a degree of moral harmony in the universe.

In the context of enslaved women's lives, midwifery was itself work that affirmed life and assisted persons and communities through the life cycle. It served as basic medical support to women in pregnancy and birth—that is, in bringing forth new life. Ex-enslaved woman Aunt Clara Walker recounted for her interviewer, "When I was thirteen years old my ol' mistress put me wid a doctor who learned me how to be a midwife. Dat was cause so many women on the plantation was catchin' babies. I stayed wid that doctor . . . for five years."[17] Yet, midwifery was actually broader in scope in traditional societies where midwives served as the "medicine" women of their communities and cultures, often acting as nutritionists, herbalists, physicians, leaders of sacred rituals, and counselors. They were teachers, healers, and leaders who sought to empower the health and welfare of their clients and communities. Midwives understood the cultural and countercultural aspects of their work setting and the community. This knowledge enabled them to engage in successful subterfuge against structural oppression.

Economically, slaveholders had a relative self-interest in protecting the health of pregnant women as well as others in their labor force; utilizing midwives instead of a doctor also cut operating expenses.[18] Midwives also provided life-giving support to postpartum women and instructed other enslaved women who would attend the newborn and its mother on their own or neighboring plantations. Midwives served vital communication roles in enslaved communities, sharing news from one plantation to another in the respective slave quarters. As moral agents in their slave communities, they confronted both life and death, wellness and sickness.

In the United States, slaveholders and the system of slavery appropriated enslaved women's work more often than not. Their labor, however, was often placed in service of enslaved individuals (especially children) to help the community affirm and sustain life in the midst of oppression and in the hope of freedom. This latter work, like that of the Hebrew midwives, sought to participate in the purpose of God's work in creation and in redemption—life given, preserved, and enjoyed in the presence of the Creator. From the vantage point of the biblical and enslaved narratives in dialogical reading, a womanist understanding of work connects the work of God and the work of humanity.

NOTIONS OF "WORK AND CALLING"

To explore the theo-ethical roots that gave rise to the notion of a "work ethic" in Protestant thought, I turn to the early Protestant Reformers Martin Luther and John Calvin. They gave Western Christianity the first positive interpretation of work applicable to all persons in every socioeconomic, political, and occupational status. In doing so, they rejected the classical Greek view of human labor in which work had no spiritual significance and gave honor and dignity to all work diligently done. Moreover, first Luther and then Calvin rejected the contrast between the highly privileged calling of the religious life and the less esteemed calling to toil in the everyday world that had come to dominate the medieval Church. Ordinary human labor became spiritually significant for every Christian. Martin Luther proclaimed the recovery of "the priesthood of all believers" in the Leipzig Disputation of 1519 and in "An Appeal to the Ruling Class of German Nationality . . .":

> [T]here is no true, basic difference between laymen and priests, princes and bishops, between religious and secular, except for the sake of the office and work, but not for the sake of status. They are all of the spiritual estate, all are truly priests, bishops, and popes. But they do not all have the same work to do. . . . A cobbler, a smith, a peasant—each has the work and office of his trade, and yet they are all alike consecrated priests and bishops. Further, everyone must benefit and serve every other by means of his own work or office so that in this way many kinds of work may be done for the bodily and spiritual welfare of the community, just as all members of the body serve one another [1 Cor. 12:14–26].[19]

Theologically and ethically, the godly life of monasticism is posited as the vocation of all people. Yes, labor is part of the human condition, a necessity for individual and collective survival. However, it is now affirmed as part of humanity's very purpose. In Luther's thought, vocation emerges as an outcome of justification by faith. As justified persons, Christians live in "two kingdoms"—the kingdom of heaven in which we have our relationship to God through faith, and the kingdom of earth in which we have our relationship to our neighbors. The kingdom of earth is the locus of vocation and Christian liberty in which we are free, through grace, to respond to God's command to love our neighbors through our station in life. Here, "stations" in life are the inherited social classes, professions, and immutable forms of the orders of creation divinely instituted by God and into which we are born. One's station in life, one's occupation, and one's vocation are, therefore, for a lifetime, and not to be changed.[20] Luther firmly believed that vocation is lived out through the organic human relations of marriage and family life, the community of believers, and the economic-political order, as well as through one's occupation or profession. Put straightforwardly, our human vocation is spiritual in the concrete and particular ways we are "the servants of all." Work is thus part of who and what God calls us to be and do.

John Calvin gave additional nuances to Luther's notion of work as a positive human activity. According to Calvin,

> [T]he Lord bids each one of us in all life's actions to look to his calling . . . he has appointed duties for every man in his particular way of life. And that no one may thoughtlessly transgress his limits, he has named these various kinds of living "callings." Therefore each individual has his own kind of living assigned to him by the Lord as a sort of sentry post so that he may not heedlessly wander about throughout life.[21]

The first goal of work is obedience to the calling of God, who has given each human a calling. To be obedient in and to one's calling is, therefore, a means of glorifying God. However, it was also important to Calvin that a person determine before entering an occupation, craft, or profession their fitness to undertake it. Here is a significant change from Luther's notion. Calvin further asserts that "Scripture leads us by the hand . . . [and] warns us that whatever benefits we obtain from the Lord have been entrusted to us on this condition: that they be applied to the common good of the church . . . liberally and kindly . . . and [we] are required to render account of our stewardship."[22] This responsible stewardship of gifts is the second goal of work in Calvin's thought. Given that church and society in Geneva were one, work became a religious "duty" or obligation that glorified God and exemplified love of neighbor and good stewardship.

Neighbors for Calvin even include those whom we do not know and those we consider enemies, because of the bond between us forged by our creation in God's own image.[23] Thus, Calvin understood work and vocation in light of his doctrine of creation. Being made in the image of God is a mandate to engage in purposeful action in human society through the work of shaping and governing God's creation. Because God's image resides in us, God's providential care of all of creation is a template for our Christian calling. Human life is precarious, contingent life. But Calvin realized that such contingency has purpose: humans are created as social beings unable to be sufficient unto our selves and therefore mutually dependent upon one another. Such a state indicated to Calvin that God's purposes include the bond of the human race in common need and in mutual service. Our vocation and calling are in light of these purposes for *common good*—a notion for him related to being "the members of the body."[24] This aspect of Calvin's thought is useful for womanist constructions of work and calling.

In contrast to Luther, Calvin thought there existed some guarded latitude in changing one's occupation. One calling could be exchanged for another as long as it was in the service of God's glory.[25] Such change could theoretically be made by the discernment of how and where one's talents, as gifts from God, could best be effective in service to others. However, generally Calvin agreed with Luther that any attempt to alter one's social position, and therefore one's calling, was sinful.

Calvin's understanding of the divinely ordered society also distinguished his view of vocation from Luther's. Calvin's theology assumes responsibility to God on the part of secular and ecclesiastical authority alike, and proposes the effectual operation of the will of God as the goal of good governance.[26] In Calvin's Geneva, two elements were important. First, Calvin conceived of human society as a Christian social organism (the body). Hence, "the Christian society, the society which strives for earthly justice, looks to divine law to be reconstituted as just, thus imitating the self's interaction with God's saving grace."[27] He further understood the church to be the model for human social interaction.[28] In this, he differed from Luther's understanding of the relationship between the church and the state and the respective role of each. The reality of sin necessitated, for Calvin, proactive opposition. Every member of the church, and therefore of society (a confused and often blurred distinction in Geneva), was to assume a social role through subordinating self-love to the love of God and others. Therefore, the meaning of work took on the added dimension of the positive effort of the redeemed community to transform the world through coordinated human effort.[29] This transformationist element in Calvin's thought is also of some use for womanist constructions.

A WOMANIST READING OF THE THEOLOGY OF VOCATION AND WORK

Although the world of enslaved women did not directly parallel that of the Reformation, a womanist reading can raise several issues pertaining to the operations of economic structures and the exploitation of work and persons in this world. Despite the positive affirmation of daily work as part of the Christian vocation and life, work in the theologies of Luther and Calvin is problematic.

Neither wrote from a perspective that seriously understood the economic stratification and the division of labor in which menial work was generally also exploited work. Luther and Calvin seemed to have little sense of the morality of the political economy. The way in which economic relations structured social life and work was changing around them, but it was not yet fully seen as a contingent human construction rather than a divinely order element of creation. The material conditions of living—as shaped by the relationship of people to production and production's role in shaping all areas of human life and social relations—were not an issue for theological or ethical scrutiny except as they related to issues of Christian charity and personal responsibility. Rather than asking whether the economic relations themselves were just or unjust, Luther and Calvin both clung to the notion that "economic behavior can be regulated by [individual] moral restraint."[30]

Luther and Calvin wrestled with the ambivalence of the Christian tradition that had a concern for the plight of the poor but also viewed the poor as those persons unwilling to work. Luther, a former Augustinian monk, and Calvin, a trained lawyer and academic, were both products of this tradition and history. As a result, neither theologian questioned how the class and social location in which he was embedded shaped his notions of work and moral agency, wealth, and poverty. This lack of self-scrutiny seems to have contributed to an inability to acknowledge the reality of some work as exploitation or "drudgery" and the relationship of exploited work to poverty. Instead, Calvin and Luther distinguished between the deserving and the undeserving poor, and maintained Christianity's traditional mixed view of the poor—that is, as Christ's brethren and as lazy sinners. The deserving poor were to receive the church's charity. The undeserving were those who, in the eyes of the Christian social organism, refused to work—those who were fit to work but idle. As Luther comments, "It is not fitting that one man should live in idleness on another's labor, or be rich and live comfortably at the cost of another's hardship, as it is according to our perverted custom. St. Paul says, 'whoever will not work shall not eat.'"[31] Social control and social responsibility were commingled in Calvin's Christian social practices in Geneva, reflecting this traditional view of work and the poor.[32] However, "as time went on, business-minded magistrates began to question the traditionalist program of Calvin. . . . The poor were described solely as idle and lazy, and relief degenerated to mere social control by the beginning of the seventeenth century."[33]

However, Calvin came closer than did Luther in understanding unjust economic practices such as usury and slavery. In his commentary on Ephesians 6:5–9, "Calvin does not confine himself to criticizing cruel masters or indolent slaves. He proceeds to attack the whole institution of bondservant as 'totally against the order of nature,'" though without calling for its abolition.[34] From a womanist perspective, Calvin's doctrine of Christian freedom had within it the seeds for a later understanding of humanly constructed social structure.

The notion of work and calling as positive goods subordinated to the well-being of the commonwealth in obedience to the light of God's grace seemed to be only possible in limited periods and geopolitical enclaves such as Geneva. As church authority over social affairs waned across Europe in the succeeding generations, the Protestant theology of work was open to ideological social use. By upholding an unambiguously positive notion of work as vocation without criticizing the social relations of the changing political economy, the Protestant tradition was left with no theological or moral recourse for challenging exploitative work. Indeed, because there was virtually no notion of a "calling" to transform unjust human structures, despite the fact that such institutions were seen theologically as the result of the Fall into sin, little thought was given to the notion of the social structuring of work.[35] Vocation remained abstracted from the material conditions of life and systems of exploitation. The legacy of an enslaved woman's work ethic, on a womanist reading, identifies the incipient danger of theologizing, mystifying, and romanticizing all forms of work as theologically and morally "good."

THE EMERGENCE AND CONVERGENCE OF THE "PROTESTANT ETHIC" AND THE "WORK ETHIC"

With the establishment of Puritan enclaves in the British colonies a scant seventy years removed from Calvin's Geneva, a new generation of Calvinism transformed its theological heritage into a New World–building enterprise. The Puritan theology of work stressed the religious and civic virtues of frugality, diligence, postponement of gratification, abstinence, sobriety, moderation, and stewardship. From the writings of English Puritan Richard Baxter, a vivid picture emerges of the conjoined religious and civic nature of vocation:

> The callings most useful to the public good are the magistrates, the pastors, and teachers of the church, the schoolmasters, physicians, lawyers, etc., husbandmen (ploughmen, graziers, and shepherds); and next to them are mariners, clothiers, booksellers, tailors, and such others that are employed about matters most necessary to mankind.[36]

Similar themes run through the writings of other Puritans such as Governor John Winthrop and Rev. John Cotton.

The emerging new middle class in England formed the group that would organize the religious, commercial, and adventure-seeking endeavors in the British colonization of North America. In New England, the primary reason for colonization at first was Puritan religious freedom. The southern British colonies, especially the Virginia colony,[37] began as business ventures or new life beginnings for adventure seekers and the indentured poor. In the northern colonies, Reformed theology and ethics were privileged, with its transformative elements establishing the nature of civil and economic life. This included the Reformers' emphasis on the communal meaning of work. The southern colonies, however, emphasized settlement and the discovery and exploitation of natural resources for English economic development. The introduction of slavery, free wage, and indentured servitude, as well as emerging notions of productivity, shaped the drive to colonize North America. Thus, notions of a work ethic grew from a complex confluence of religious, economic, and social factors.

According to Mechal Sobel, Scots, Scotch-Irish, Huguenots, and "vexed and troubled Englishmen" brought to the colonies a mix of religious and economic outlooks and values: Catholic as well as Protestant, agrarian and working class as well as merchant, artisan, and middle-class.[38] Given that the colonial settlement occurred during a period of intense upheaval—familial, geographic, social, and in some cases, economic—new worldviews, values, and patterns were created and meshed with traditional ones. In the colonies, and later in the nation, a certain work ethic emerged that posited "hard work, self-control, and dogged persistence" as the virtues necessary in order for most anyone to lead a successful life in America.[39]

In the United States, the religious roots of the work ethic were now joined with transvalued social and economic interests—earthly reward, class mobility, and the fulfillment of ambition—in the growing "economic democracy."[40] In this way, the use of the work ethic in the antebellum North was an attempt to acclimate working-class European immigrants into its industrial capitalism.[41] Throughout the nineteenth century, the term *work ethic* became

> synonymous with the idea of social order . . . representing a complex ethical statement of the interrelationship between the individual, what he or she produced, and society. It represented an ideal situation in which individuals received, not just payment, but ethical and aesthetic enrichment for their work as well. . . . [I]t is the idealized relationship between individuals and their labor.[42]

Embedded in this ideal work ethic were biblical, Reformation, and Puritan notions of work as manual labor, craft, and mercantile entrepreneurship. According to James B. Gilbert, this "traditional work ethic depended upon the type of environment that existed in a small town or village, where each citizen could learn the values of community through the contribution of his labor."[43] This is the notion of work that Max Weber found intriguing in *The Protestant Ethic and the Spirit of Capitalism*. While the term *Protestant ethic* for Weber meant a worldview—a way of seeing one's work and life as ordered by God's call—the more modern meaning of work ethic was secularized. According to Ernst Troeltsch, Weber's view gave "rise to that ideal of work for work's sake which forms the intellectual and moral assumption underlying the modern bourgeois [industrial] way of life."[44] Not among the least important elements embedded in the secularization of the work ethic were its assumptions about individual responsibility and autonomy. In the developing ethos of the United States, shaped by the Industrial Revolution, capitalism, and democratic individualism, the work ethic followed more the cultural identity of the nation than formal Protestant theology.

In the antebellum South, slaveholders' Christian ideology attempted to inculcate in the enslaved a sense of duty to their slave master or mistress. Enslaved blackwomen were judged and held morally accountable under the rubric of "obedience to your master" by the slaveholding community. However, within the enslaved and later emancipated community, different ethical values and moral conduct were articulated and lived out relative to the contradictions, circumstances, problems, and possibilities of the larger society. These ethical constructions were neither "identical with the body of obligations and duties that Anglo-Protestant American society requires of its members,"[45] nor always dependent on its basic assumptions.

The slaveowner's own work ethic is a no-less-complicated issue than the work ethic of enslaved women. Southern planters often appealed to the same values regarding work as their northern counterparts. The persons settling and planting in the South were drawn from the same English classes as were the Puritans—"pious, hardworking, middleclass, accepting literally and solemnly the tenets of Puritanism—sin, predestination, and election."[46] In that sense, the southern "work ethic" upheld the general American ethos about work evident at the time. Yet a southern attitude also existed that militated against the work ethic as derived from Puritanism. An interest in business and investment in plantation economics was tempered by a notion of leisure that defined labor itself as leisurely— that is, "the first end of life is living itself."[47] Eugene Genovese took this sentiment even further in his Marxist analysis of the "southern ethic":

> The planters commanded Southern politics and set the tone for social life. Theirs was an aristocratic, antibourgeois spirit with values and mores emphasizing family and status, a strong code of honor, and aspirations to luxury, ease, and accomplishment. In the planters' community, paternalism provided the standard of human relationships, and politics and statecraft were the duties and responsibilities of gentlemen. The gentleman lived for politics, not, like the bourgeois politician, off politics.[48]

This move away from the Puritan work ethic severed the bond of common need and mutual service that Calvin posited across the whole human race, and it captures the contradiction of slavery and enslavement in an economic and social environment with deeply held biblical, Reformation-Puritan, and democratic foundations.

A READING OF THE NOTION OF A "WORK ETHIC" THROUGH THE LIVES OF ENSLAVED WOMEN

A womanist examination of the American "work ethic" from my reading of enslaved women's narratives must address two issues. First, I will examine the social norms that are taken for granted in the general notion of a work ethic. Second, I will raise questions about the theological and ethical doctrines concerning work.

The work ethic encompasses moral action, ethical reflection, and a social ethos that informs the development of individuals and communities. Intrinsic to the idea of the work ethic is the privileging of labor over leisure and idleness. Human activity and behavior ought to be systematically organized, or at least directed, toward a positive goal through human labor. Indeed, work itself becomes a positive moral good and moral end. The work ethic "gives a special nuance to the word 'duty' and creates an infectious model of an industrious life . . . it is not a single or simple idea. Rather, it is a complex of ideas with many roots and branches."[49]

The work ethic carries social and economic assumptions, one being that the opportunity to work, and the opportunity to achieve through work, create personal well-being. This "opportunity" is assumed to be normative, available, and functional for all persons or members of society at large. In such thinking, opportunity inherently means access to resources and power with which to act independently for one's own welfare and that of the common good. Given favorable conditions of talent, resources, and opportunity, work leads to self-fulfillment.

There is nothing in this assumption that acknowledges the existence of social relations of domination and subordination. However, the truth is that by the mature period of the antebellum, slaveholders and the enslaved existed in relationships marked by a complex set of negotiated customs and conventions within the larger framework of domination and subordination. Slaveholders certainly had structured normative positions of dominance and power; generally, enslaved persons were relatively powerless. Enslaved persons lived in a relationship of enforced and reinforced dependency,[50] in the sense that their reliance on slaveholders was neither of their own choosing nor mutually defined. Considering this situation, enslaved persons' relation to work was not a relationship of opportunity, or potential achievement, or possible personal fulfillment. Their relationship to work did not come with access to the economic, social, legal, and political resources from which further access could be turned into opportunity. Independence and the opportunity to acquire power through knowledge, education, skills, tools, and economic resources are prerequisites for the possibilities of achievement and personal fulfillment attainable through work. The nature of the one-way, enforced dependency in the slaveholder-enslaved relationship (and solidified in objective structures of law, economics, and politics) reveals the near impossibility of *opportunity* as a key concept in the meaning of work in the lives of the enslaved.

A related and deeper manifestation of the notion of opportunity is revealed when one considers that the meaning of work is an *inherited* meaning and is experienced not just by individuals but by cultures and classes of people. As such, inherited meanings are resources—cultural capital—that through their operation as inheritances condition moral value. These prerequisites to acquisition and use of power should be seen themselves as cultural inheritances. Working with this deeper meaning of opportunity, the notions of inheritances and dependence become more complex.

The slave narratives of Harriet Jacobs and Lucy Delaney speak of such inheritances. Jacobs's father, although enslaved, was considered to be a carpenter of such skill that his owner permitted him to "hire out," and even manage his own affairs with relative freedom. Jacobs's father provided his children with clothing, extra niceties, and, most important, "a feel[ing] that they were human beings."[51] Jacobs's inheritance included an experience of relative self-esteem related to work by her father (and grandmother); the fulfillment of life's basic needs; and a knowledge of the meaning of freedom. Lucy Delaney had been born free, and was later kidnapped and sold into slavery. Like Jacobs, she labored as an enslaved child and woman. However, she had not been taught as a child the domestic arts of sewing, laundering, cooking, and housekeeping. (As an enslaved child, she had been a nursemaid.) Nevertheless, like Jacobs, she had an inheritance of the meaning of freedom that empowered her in her flight for freedom.

Both these enslaved women inherited different meanings and experiences from their families regarding work, legal and relative freedom, and knowledge and skills on the basis of which opportunities could be sought and created. Their experiences exemplified the relative maneuverability of the dominated who had access to the resources valued by society (but not intended for the enslaved) that could be used as leverage for opportunities. These inheritances were not, however, the norm for most enslaved women. Most enslaved women did not have parents or grandparents who were freeborn or freed. Most enslaved women were not in a context in which they could become literate. Indeed, they were forbidden to gain the skills of literacy by law. Moreover, most enslaved women were not in a position to utilize what marketable skills they had to hire themselves out to earn money or to live relatively independent lives. As noted by William Harris, "by confining slaves to unskilled, rural tasks requiring no formal education or training, slavery, it is said, left blacks unprepared for any productive role in the growing cities of the nation."[52]

It would seem, then, that in situations of group dominance and subordination such as slavery, enforced dependency thwarts truly meaningful work and thus moral agency as judged by the dominant social and economic norm. At the same time, it seems equally true that there did exist among the enslaved those who gained relative opportunities, knowledge, and skills, and so gained a small measure of distance from the vicissitudes of oppression. This would involve a relative ability to influence the powerful, but rarely the opportunity to exercise consistent power from a structured position so as to be able to represent the enslaved. Such situations gave an individual "influence," and perhaps were a contributing dynamic to the development of intragroup socioeconomic/class relations and divisions.

A second underlying assumption embedded in the work ethic is that no matter what the nature of the work and of the person who does it, all work and all workers are equally valued. But enslaved women's narratives indicate that this assumption is not true. Aunt Sally, a fugitive slave who returned to hire herself out and purchase her freedom when her slaveowner was in financial trouble, recalled that hiring oneself out brought the accusation of being uppity and uncontrollable as a slave. She understood that it was not a good thing for a slave to look self-reliant and independent.[53]

It is clear that when work is considered valuable in itself and as a crucial element of positive human identity, it is contradicted in exploitative, objective structures like chattel slavery. According to C. Vann Woodward, a historian of Southern culture, notions about the meaning and value of work ranged from subsistence farmers' need to feed and clothe themselves to the middle- and upper-class farmers' associations of manual labor with a degraded social status. He writes, "Much [of the] work in early America required of all people was crude and hard, and little of it anywhere could honestly be characterized as stimulating, creative, or inherently enjoyable. Those who wrote of its joys and rewards probably had a larger share of work that could be so characterized than those who failed to record their impressions."[54] Woodward also asserts that "neither the hired man nor the slave (who generally did the same work) shared the dignity and honor conferred by myth on the yeoman."[55] In either case, the contradiction in the value and meaning of work was not lost on enslaved persons. The awareness of this contradiction was captured in a slave song:

Missus in the big house,
Mammy in the yard,
Missus holdin' her white hands,
Mammy workin' hard.
Missus holdin' her white hands,
Mammy workin' hard.[56]

This contradiction unfolds further. On the one hand, enslaved people knew that their owners valued their work. On the other hand, the work done by most enslaved people was manual labor—work that according to Woodward was "crude and hard." It was work that had historically been done against their will and for the profit of another. Enslaved people knew that they were as valuable as any property owned by a slaveholder. Yet it was also abundantly clear that as slaves they were instruments of production and were considered tools. They were the "things" that were bought and sold to do the kind of work understood to be drudgery and toil. The social and religious conviction of slaveholder was that the work slaves did was the work they were created by God to do. In Moltmann's words, "work itself was enslavement." This double meaning of identity and work was not lost on the enslaved. Elizabeth Kleckley records witnessing her first slave auction when she was seven years old: "[M]aster had just purchased his hogs for the winter, for which he was unable to pay in full. To escape embarrassment it was necessary to sell one of the slaves. Little Joe ... was selected as the victim. ... He came in with a bright face, was placed in the scales, and was sold, like the hogs, at so much per pound."[57] Kleckley's recollection is sobering. It captures the contradiction that slavery and enslavement posed to the biblical, Reformation-Puritan, and democratic foundations of the American work ethic. It is no surprise then that the investigations of enslaved peoples' lives have focused not on the meaning of work as exemplified in traditional formulations of "the work ethic" but on how they lived their lives beyond their work.

In this chapter I have attempted to survey the sweep of cultural, religious, and economic factors shaping American Protestant notions of work and calling, and suggest an interpretation of the work ethic from the perspective of enslaved African Americans. I have called into question the romanticization of both the Reformation (and its latter Calvinist-Puritan) notions of work and calling and the secularized "work ethic" of the nineteenth and early twentieth centuries in America. Maintaining that there existed an enslaved women's work ethic thus presents a historical and theological paradox. Yet the dominant cultural notion of a work ethic still plagues the theological and socioeconomic sensibilities of African American, female descendants of the enslaved in our struggle for quality of life, freedom, and liberation, thus justifying an attempt to retrieve an enslaved women's work ethic from a contemporary womanist perspective. In reflecting on their words and actions, I have found four characteristics of this work ethic that can guide contemporary blackwomen and other people: 1) a theological and ethical belief in God as the God of life, freedom, and protection; 2) womanish moral authority, instruction, and action as an intergenerational dynamic for communal maintenance, solidarity, and empowerment in the context of oppression; 3) a struggle for self-determination in the use of one's labor, especially sexual and reproductive labor; and 4) a work-related attitude of self-reliance and confidence in one's learned skill and craft. I contend that these characteristics point toward a work ethic that has as its goal the move from mere survival to abundant life, freedom, and human wholeness in the face of and in opposition to oppression and evil. African American, female descendants of the enslaved live in the eschatological hope of meaningful work for all. This hope is communal rather than individual, and aims at communion, the fullest expression of faith and life in God, and the authentic community of mutuality. Community and communion are created and re-created as a result of the work of God's creating and justifying grace and our work of vocation.

12

THE GRACED INFIRMITY
OF THE CHURCH

Amy Plantinga Pauw

I remember sticky summer Sundays in my grandmother's Reformed church in Wisconsin. Like the other women in the congregation, she was not allowed to speak in worship, except to join in unison recitations of the Ten Commandments and the Lord's Prayer. At the Lord's Supper, I watched her receive the bread and wine from a phalanx of white men in dark suits, who would stand, hands folded, guarding the communion table until the minister in his long robe gave the authoritative nod to distribute the elements. As far as I could tell, my grandmother had thoroughly internalized the theology behind these liturgical arrangements. Along with her communion wine, she drank in potent assumptions about gender and grace, about divine rule and male authority. Denied the possibility of holding ordained office, or even the right to vote in congregational meetings, my grandmother was largely shut out of the communal discernment of God's call to ecclesial faithfulness. Yet the church was at the center of her life. She was baptized, confirmed, and married in the church; it was there that she lived out her years, raised her children, buried her husband, and ultimately was buried herself.

My grandmother's story is a common one. Life in the church has often been a jumbled experience of nurture and repression, identity formation and alienation for women. How do the resources of Reformed theology make sense of women's ambiguous ecclesial experience and empower them to seek the church's faithful transformation? How do feminist and womanist insights contribute to the ongoing formation of Reformed ecclesiology?

THE "INFIRMITY AND WEAKNESS" OF THE CHURCH

A Reformed narrative of the church has no Eden. The church on earth has always existed "after the fall," often in the midst of great religious and political turmoil. The perception of scandalous failings in the established church significantly shaped Reformed ecclesiology from the beginning. The first Reformed theologians had to accommodate the conviction that dissent from the visible church in their time was a Christian duty because of its oppressive abuse of the sacramental system and its failure to proclaim the Word. According to John Calvin, God has entrusted the church with the "power of the keys" (Matt. 16:19), but Christian communities can so abuse this trust that in them "Christ lies hidden, half buried, the gospel overthrown, piety scattered, the worship of God nearly wiped out."[1] Thus Reformed ecclesiology is rightly marked by a stark recognition of the church's fallibility. As Karl Barth notes, Calvin's "energetic attempt to make Protestantism historically functional" required that he give "to this fellowship in Christ . . . an earthly form that takes into account as much as possible human infirmity and weakness."[2]

Because there is no Edenic church, Reformed theology rejects restorationist wistfulness for pre-Constantinian or premodern forms of ecclesial existence. While the great company of Christian saints deserve our respect and gratitude, they suffered from "human infirmity and weakness" as much as we do, and provide no perfect blueprint for Christian community. "We do not receive uncritically whatever has been declared to men under the name of the general councils," asserts the 1560 Scots Confession, "for it is plain that, being human, some of them have manifestly erred, and that in matters of great weight and importance." Significant elements from the church's past may deserve retrieval, but no "policy or order of ceremonies can be appointed for all ages, times, and places."[3] Attention to the enormous diachronic and synchronic breadth of the church's life and witness serves as a hedge against perennial tendencies to absolutize features of the church's existence in particular historical and geographical contexts. This insistence on the relativity of Reformed liturgies, polities, and even confessional standards becomes ever more important as the "center of gravity" of global Christianity has shifted away from western Europe, the birthplace of the Reformed tradition.[4] The central Reformed task is not the maintenance of a historic tradition but the prayerful, communal discernment of the *present* form of ecclesial faithfulness, which across time and culture may involve institutional change, even novelty.

Reformed theologians have been adamant about the importance of remaining in the fellowship of the earthly church, not because the church is spiritually exemplary—a community of character in a society morally adrift, a city of peace in a world of violence—but because God has given the church the gospel and has promised not to give up on it. Commenting on the Apostles' Creed, Calvin notes that the church is properly an article of belief, "because often no other distinction can be made between God's children and the ungodly, between his own flock and wild beasts." The American Reformed theologian Jonathan Edwards extends this bestial metaphor even further, comparing the church to Noah's ark: just as the door of the ark "was open to receive all sorts of creatures—tigers, wolves, bears, lions, leopards, serpents, vipers, dragons—such as men would not by any means admit into the doors of their houses," so likewise "Christ stands ready to receive all, even the vilest and worst."[5] Because of the constitution of the earthly church, Calvin insists, we do not properly believe *in* the church: "We testify that we believe *in* God because our mind reposes in him as truthful, and our trust rests in him."[6] The earthly community of believers is God's gracious accommodation to our spiritual weakness, and we place ourselves in spiritual peril by abandoning the visible church because we can rely on finding there God's grace and mercy. Though God's Word and Spirit are given to the church, they do not thereby become the church's possessions. Christian trust rests finally in God, not in the church.

As the body of Christ in the world, the church is a broken and diseased body, mirroring the ills and divisions of the larger society. Yet it remains a mysteriously powerful channel of God's grace to us. The church is a nursery of piety, where Christians are schooled by worship, teaching, and discipline into deeper communion with Christ and each other. Our incorporation into Christ by the power of the Holy Spirit gives every Christian a share in Christ's threefold office of prophet, priest, and king. In the work of teaching and preaching, however ordinary, we share in his prophetic anointing. Despite our continuing sinfulness, we are made priests in Christ, offering our whole lives to God. Though we continue to live under the cross, pummeled by suffering and failings, Christ in his kingly office "arms and equips us with his power, adorns us with his beauty and magnificence, enriches us with his wealth."[7] This participation in Christ endures throughout the contingencies of the church's history, as the peace and faith of the church are negotiated and risked. In union with Christ, by the power of the Holy Spirit, the cracked earthen vessel of the church continues to be a means of grace—a locus for worship and for personal and social transformation.

The church is a centrally important locus within a Reformed theological framework because Christian purification and transformation are understood to extend over lifetimes. God's grace works to eliminate human sin by creating ecclesial space where sin can be exposed, repented of, and forgiven. The confession of sin in Reformed worship recognizes the corporate sin of the church body as well as the personal sin of individual members. Like the Jewish community at Yom Kippur, the Reformed church "proclaims to itself and to the world its reliance upon God's forgiveness and reconciliation."[8] The church is called into existence by God and sustained *as a community* by the power of divine mercy. Throughout the centuries, Reformed church leaders have attempted to infuse the visible church with a measure of visible holiness. However, the Reformed stress on sanctification is less an indicator of the success the church has had in achieving this holiness than it is painful evidence of how much it needs the ongoing sanctifying work of the Holy Spirit.

Reformed ecclesiology is firmly anti-Donatist.[9] Even in communities that meet Calvin's definition of a true church—where the Word is proclaimed and the sacraments are rightly administered—church leaders are understood to be sinners. They too are assailed by weakness and doubt, and are justified not by their holiness but by God's grace. Church leaders need God's forgiveness as much as anyone else and do not deserve our blind obedience. Nor do ministers of the gospel necessarily tower over other Christians in wisdom or spiritual maturity. Calvin's frank appraisal of the ordinariness of pastors bears repeating: "When a puny man risen from the dust speaks in God's name, at this point we best evidence our piety and obedience toward God if we show ourselves teachable toward his minister, although he excels us in nothing."[10] This ecclesial realism has fostered distinctive understandings of church office in Reformed communities. Ordination in Reformed communities is not intended to establish a hierarchy of clergy over laity. The church is a community of practice, and the religious practices of the *whole people*—such as prayer, forgiveness, healing, giving, and witness—are what define and sustain congregations and larger ecclesial traditions. Church office is understood as a routinization of the various practices of the community, a way to ensure that they are always available to the church's members. Members defer to ordained persons out of respect for their *office*, not because of something intrinsic to their person. In keeping with this understanding, Reformed communities ordain deacons and elders, as well as ministers of the Word and sacrament, so that the authority of ordained office is shared within every congregation.

The abuse of clerical power in sixteenth-century Europe made Reformed communities wary of undue deference to those with authority in the church. As Calvin declares, "if we simply grant to men such power as they are disposed to take, it is plain to all how abrupt is the fall into tyranny, which ought to be far from Christ's church."[11] He thought the hierarchs of the church in his day, and especially the pope, were usurping the place of Christ. As the 1566 Second Helvetic Confession teaches, "Christ the Lord is, and remains the only universal pastor, the highest Pontiff before God the Father."[12] Clerical power can be dangerous and has to be kept carefully in check. The conviction that all pastors have the same standing in the larger church grounds the general Reformed rejection of an episcopal polity.[13] Fear of clerical tyranny has fueled both thoroughly congregationalist impulses in some Reformed communities and careful systems of checks and balances in more connectional Reformed polities. The structure of Reformed communities at all levels reflects the desire for institutional forms that can nourish a strong sense of Christian identity and unity without stifling dissent within the church.

Reformed feminists and womanists can applaud their tradition's recognition of the infirmity and weakness of the church and its suspicions about

inordinate clerical power. However, it is clear that these salutary ecclesiological principles did not thwart the reclericalization of Reformed churches
and the concentration of male ecclesial power. Like other manifestations of
the visible church, Reformed congregations and denominations have historically been "hierarchical institutions whose leadership has been in the
hands of males, with male control of the language, space, and functions
of church life."[14] With few exceptions before the 1950s, the assumption
in Reformed communities has been "that women should be silent in the
church, subordinate to male authority, submissive to doctrine and church
order, and satisfied to function within their proper 'sphere,'" though the
way in which this sphere was defined varied dramatically according to a
woman's race and social standing.[15] Calvin's prophecy about the tyrannical results of "simply granting to men such power as they are disposed to
take" has come true for women in Reformed communities. While many
(but not all) Reformed denominations now ordain women to the three
offices of deacon, elder, and minister, genuine partnership between men
and women in ministry remains elusive.

Friedrich Schleiermacher liked to refer to the church as a "common life"
and called for Christians to "sink themselves in the common life, allowing
it to work on them in a life-giving way."[16] On the one hand, Schleiermacher's phrase helpfully reminds us that the Christian life is a visible, material life. Christian discipleship is about the patterns and practices of our
lives as embodied creatures, and that is first of all a public and communal,
not an interior and private, matter. Spirituality and materiality should not
be falsely opposed. Schleiermacher's communal vision of Christian life
resonates with feminist and womanist depictions of human beings as
embodied persons embedded in webs of relationships. The church is a
"common life" because we all have our being in community. Too many
expressions of Christian faith, especially in the North American context,
have exaggerated human independence and individualism. The Reformed
insistence on the covenant as the focus of God's redemptive activity and
on the church's preaching and sacraments as communal means of grace is
a welcome corrective, reminding us that the life-giving power of Christian
faith is nurtured and experienced in physical human community.

On the other hand, as Kathryn Tanner points out, "assuming the social
constitution of the self does not, all by itself, however, specify the *sort* of society that *should* constitute the self."[17] The society of the church has often incul-
cated "womanly" virtues of passivity and unquestioning obedience to male
authorities. Reformed women have found that "sinking" into the common
life of the church has the potential to suffocate or silence them. Many women
have gifts for ministry that are never recognized or encouraged by their
communities. For them and for other groups of people unjustly excluded
from ecclesial power structures, either by policy or practice, affirmation of

personal agency and creaturely dignity has had to be obtained largely outside the walls of the church. The growing number of women serving as pastors and seminary professors in at least some Reformed communions is gradually producing changes in curricula and church life, but progress is uneven and often difficult. Many women in Reformed communities around the globe still find themselves "defecting in place,"[18] participating in church life, while inwardly dissenting from its various manifestations of male authoritarian rule.

For women of color, doubly marginalized in largely white Reformed denominations, the task has often been to find or make "a place out of no place." Katie Cannon, the first black woman ordained in the Presbyterian Church, grew up in an all-black synod in North Carolina. The color barriers between white and black Presbyterians were so absolute that she simply assumed as a young girl that the Presbyterian Church was a historic black denomination. "Imagine my surprise," she says, "the first time I attended General Assembly!" The church was at the center of her family's life, and by the time she was three she knew all the Bible stories like she knew her name. But her place in the Reformed community grew more complicated as she pursued her calling as a minister and ethicist. As a graduate student at Union Seminary in New York she felt deeply torn by the allegiances of gender and race. To succeed in the predominantly white world of theological education, she felt she had to become an "honorary white person," relinquishing the black community that had nurtured her. At the same time she encountered sexism from her African American classmates, who challenged her assumption that God would call a woman into ministry. Even her extended family embraces her little brother, also a Presbyterian minister, as the quintessential southern black preacher but regards Katie, a *woman* minister, as an enigma.[19]

Reformed realism about racism and other perennial forms of human sinfulness cuts off any escape into a "cosmic sisterhood" of women liberated from the bonds of patriarchy. "Women-church" is at best a provisional strategy for Reformed women, who are convinced that there is no pure community of the redeemed, where only life-giving, sanctified texts, rituals, and relationships are present. Reformed feminists and womanists are rightly suspicious of feminist liturgies that are content to "honor women in all their diversity as imaging the divine and as engaging in divine activity,"[20] as if the only spiritual transformation women needed were the reaffirmation of their Godlikeness. From a Reformed perspective, those attacking the sin of the patriarchy are always themselves subject to error and sin. In the last decades, white women have learned to their sorrow and shame that "commitment to feminism does not . . . automatically entail willingness to relinquish race, class and religious privilege—or even to acknowledge they exist."[21] As Judith Plaskow remarks elsewhere, "*there is no reason* why becoming feminists should suddenly free us from the other forms of hatred that mark our world or the groups to which we belong."[22] In combating corporate sin in the church, determined resistance must always go hand in hand with humble confession.

THE CHURCH AND ISRAEL

Christian feminism has been justly criticized for using Judaism as a negative foil for its emancipatory claims. As Katharina von Kellenbach notes, feminist approaches to Jesus have tended to see his attitudes toward women not "as a result of his Jewishness but rather as a consequence of his disassociation and alienation from Judaism."[23] In this way feminism has mirrored the broader Christian proclivity to depict Christianity "as a vibrant, revolutionary, future-oriented, young movement," in opposition to the "degenerated, rigid, lifeless, narrow, legalistic and bureaucratic tradition" of Judaism.[24] While Reformed theology has often succumbed to portraying Israel as the rejected people of God, or at least as the people of God in a "passing form,"[25] Reformed understandings of the church also provide resources for a different approach.

Old Testament Israel is often referred to as "the Church" in early Reformed writings, and the ecclesiological significance of this should not be underestimated. The paradigm for the church's self-understanding is not an idealized community of Christian disciples, but the believing community of Israel, struggling and often failing to respond adequately to God's covenant faithfulness. As George Lindbeck asserts, Christians have generally "either assumed with the Catholics that the church does not sin in itself but only its members, or, with the Protestants, that it ceases to be the true church when it does."[26] Reformed Christians have often followed the Protestant party line on this point. But when Reformed theologians have identified the church with Old Testament Israel, they have opened a way for honest acknowledgment of ecclesial shortcomings. This fundamental commonality between the two communities discourages invidious comparisons of them as disobedient and obedient, faithless and faithful forms of the people of God. The church hears the judgments and promises of the Old Testament as God's Word to them. The idolatries of Israel are snapshots from the church's family album. Both Israel and the church struggle to be obedient and faithful; both often fail.

Though it is not unique to them, Reformed Christians have emphasized the positive or third use of the Law of Israel as a guide for faithful Christian life before God. In contrast to churches in which members sit during the readings from the Law, and then stand for the gospel readings, Reformed Christians often sit during gospel readings and stand to recite the Decalogue following the sermon, as a sign of their gratitude to God and their desire to live a holy life. The obedience that God required from Israel is not essentially different than the obedience God requires from Christians, and Christians are not essentially better at rendering it. Commenting on Isaiah 9:13, "The people did not turn," Calvin warns,

> This rebuke applies not to the Israelites only but to us also. . . . Justly, therefore, might the Lord address to us the same expostulation, and assuredly he addresses us by the mouth of Isaiah; and we ought not to look for another Prophet to threaten new chastisements, seeing that our case is not different from that of the Israelites, and we are involved in the same blame with them.[27]

This resolute identification of the church with Israel as a needy people of God, guided by the law and sustained by divine grace and forgiveness, creates a hedge in Reformed theology against Christian triumphalism.

What joins Israel and the church together even more than their common sinfulness and respect for the law is their trust in the consistently gracious character of God. Consider the declaration of Marie Dentière, one of the first Reformed theologians, when comparing God's deliverance of the Genevans from their Catholic enemies to the deliverance of Israel from Egypt: "Their God, is he not also ours? Yes, certainly! Is he less than he has been? No! The God of Abraham, of Isaac, of Jacob, and of the other patriarchs and prophets, is he not our own?"[28] The God of Christian faith is also the God of Israel. The God whose promises Christians rely on through their union with Christ is also the God of Abraham, Isaac, and Jacob.

The logic of Reformed reliance on God's covenant faithfulness despite obstinate human sin invalidates the distinction often made in Reformed theology between Old Testament Israel and contemporary Jews. According to this distinction, God's grace to Israel is withdrawn after the coming of Christ: by their lack of faith, Jews forfeit their covenant standing. But as Calvin notes in his commentary on Isaiah 37:35, the source of stability and hope in Israel's covenant relationship is divine steadfastness, not human merit: God "will be their [the Jews'] defender, not because he finds any cause in them, but rather because he looks to himself, . . . that he may adhere firmly to his purpose not to cast away the posterity of Abraham which he adopted."[29] If God were at some point to abandon the covenant made with the Jews, then God's trustworthiness in general would be called into question. Both Israel and the church are called into being through God's electing mercy and sustained by God's promises and forgiveness, not by their right belief or behavior. What has been termed the "perseverance of the saints" in Reformed theology is really the perseverance of God, who, in defiance of all human meritocracies, justifies the sinner and saves the undeserving.

If, to paraphrase Dentière, "our God is also the God of Israel," then the church is not to see itself as the exclusive focus of God's love and covenant faithfulness. As Romans 9:4 insists, to Israel belongs "the adoption, the glory, the covenant, the giving of the law, the worship and the promises" of God. In the mystery of God's electing grace, Israel is the root, the cultivated olive tree; we Christians are the wild branches, grafted in. To acknowledge our roots as the church of Jesus Christ is to cultivate humility, to refuse to see ourselves as the religious community into which all others are destined to be absorbed. Reformed theology has clearly stated that God, not the church, is the agent of salvation, and that God's ways are not our ways. What Christians do know is the unfathomable depth and breadth of God's mercy shown in Jesus Christ, and this provides grounds for a wide eschatological hopefulness.

The laudable effort of the church to repudiate its long record of anti-Judaism does not imply that it is wrong for Christians to criticize Israel, either in its ancient or contemporary manifestations. The appropriate Christian desire is to identify with Israel's sin, not to deny it. This means seeing in Israel's history various forms of chauvinism that we Christians can readily identify with. For example, the church hears with Israel God's insistence to show hospitality to the strangers in their midst and refuses to paper over Israel's failures in this regard. Yet in denouncing Israel's failure to welcome the Other, the church shines the spotlight on its own exclusions and inhospitality. In pointing out the sins of Israel, the church confesses them as its own.

Womanist readings of the Old Testament, however, have shown that this approach is too simple. The larger narrative of Israel, especially the story of Israel's exodus from slavery in Egypt, has been an important paradigm for Christian self-understanding in the black church. As Thomas Hoyt notes, "Through hearing and reading the story of the Jews, blacks were enabled to perceive the activity of God in their own community."[30] But Delores Williams and other womanist theologians have challenged black theologians' uncritical identification with Israel's story:

> Have they, in the use of the Bible, identified so thoroughly with the theme of Israel's election that they have not seen the oppressed of the oppressed in scripture? Have they identified so completely with Israel's liberation that they have been blind to the awful reality of victims making victims in the Bible?[31]

Williams points to Hagar, the Egyptian slave oppressed by her Israelite mistress Sarai, as a biblical figure with whom African American women find special resonance. By lifting up Hagar, Williams deftly shifts the theological focus from Israel to one of Israel's victims.[32]

This shift invites careful ecclesiological reflection. Reformed Christians are called to *identify with* Israel's sin as proclaimed by the prophets, not to exonerate ourselves from it. But we are also called to *identify* sin that lies hidden and unacknowledged in the "official" narratives of both Israel and the church. We are sometimes called to write unauthorized biographies of the religious communities to which we belong. To do this, we have to leave the winners' circle and identify with the victims of Israel and the church. The victims of a religious community are often the ones best able to testify to its hidden violence. Those who are perched on the margins or outside the circle of a faith community often have the best sense of the *missing* chapters in its constructed history. Since womanist theologians find a natural identification with the oppressed and marginalized in Israel, they may also be in an ideal position to write unauthorized biographies for the church. But as Delores Williams's rhetoric suggests, the identification with Hagar is an unstable construction, because of "the awful reality of victims making victims." Womanists and feminists who claim the freedom, life, and hope of Christian faith can never assume that they have adequately heard the voices of all the brothers and sisters "in the wilderness." They can never assume kinship only with Hagar and not also with Sarai. Like King David, outraged after listening to Nathan's parable about the poor man and his lamb (2 Sam. 12), Christian feminists and womanists may be better able to acknowledge their own victims through the exercise of identifying with the victims of Israel.

VISIBLE AND INVISIBLE

Reformed ecclesiology has followed Augustine in positing, within and beyond the visible church, a church invisible to all but God, composed of the elect saints from every time and place. Forged in the fire of the Donatist debates, Augustine's understanding of the church rejected rigorist conceptions of Christian community that would confine its membership to the truly holy. It was a given for Augustine that the visible church is a mixed body, and he repudiated the violence and hypocrisy of premature human attempts to separate saints from sinners. The notion of an invisible church can be useful in resisting the pretensions of any particular historical form of the church, without denying that the church's eschatological future as God's sanctified people is in some measure present already in its visible life. However, when allied to a theology of double predestination, the notion of an invisible church presents serious theological liabilities.

In the face of the splintering of the visible church in sixteenth-century Europe, Protestant Reformers took different ecclesiological paths. Anabaptists returned to rigorist conceptions of the church: the "true" church is the gathering of the children of light, both on earth and in heaven. Reformed theologians reappropriated Augustine's distinction to identify the "true" church with the invisible church of the elect, its membership past and present determined by God's secret decree. The shadow church of the truly elect always stood in some tension with the Reformed emphasis on the importance of the visible church. Pastors are to preach the good news to all and benevolently pray for the salvation of all members of the visible community. But in the end, as Brian Gerrish notes, it seems that ministers will have been more benevolent than God,[33] for not all who have been ardently preached to and prayed for were from eternity chosen by God as members of the invisible church. When the primary appeal to the invisible church is to establish God's eternal partiality towards some, the significance of the comfort and spiritual nourishment provided by the *visible* church is greatly diminished.[34]

In the contemporary context, the concept of the invisible church serves to remind us that the church is a community we have neither created nor chosen: in the words of the 1563 Heidelberg Catechism, it is *Jesus Christ* who "gathers, sustains and preserves the church."[35] Reformed communities have flourished in a variety of social incarnations: state-sanctioned religion, culturally established institution, and voluntary association. All these sociological forms bring their own problems. The voluntary association model that dominates in the contemporary period risks portraying the local and denominational church as a competitive franchise, oriented toward satisfying customers' spiritual needs. Yet human sin has also proven adept at warping other ecclesial forms around the achievement of particular human ends, be they social control, political stability, or the maintenance of cultural and racial privilege. The notion of the invisible church reminds us that the church does not exist to serve its own ends; the church exists because of God, not because of us.

Nor is the church an end in itself. It is a pilgrim community pointing ahead of itself to the fulfillment of the reign of God already inaugurated in Jesus Christ. However much we love the church and have been nurtured by it, it cannot command our ultimate loyalty or obedience. For women, ethnic minorities, homosexuals, and others who have felt disenfranchised from the church or who have made wrenching decisions to leave their denomination to seek refuge somewhere else, the doctrine of the invisible church is a comfort. We are Christians because God has called us and claimed us, not because the visible church has given us its stamp of approval.

THE CHURCH AS MOTHER AND BRIDE

Mother and bride are prominent images of the church in Reformed theology.[36] These images of the church present problems in the contemporary setting, not the least of which is their tendency to reinforce normatively masculine images for God. Yet, in revised form, they are still worth pondering. At its best, the Reformed tradition has held these two ecclesial images of mother and bride not only in tension but also in paradoxical relation: the church as a gasping, panting mother is on her way to becoming the pristine bride of Christ. The maternal image describes the visible church on earth, while the image of the church as bride is an anticipation of its eschatological state.

As mother, the church is engaged in the hard and messy work of forming Christians. Believers are conceived in her womb, nourished at her breast, and guided and instructed by her throughout life. The Lord's Supper is God's merciful accommodation to human weakness: nourishment in the wilderness, a visible means of grace, a tangible symbol of the forgiveness and presence of God for those on the journey of faith. In her ministries, the mother church provides the visible structures within which the grace of Christ is conveyed to believers who remain needy sinners throughout their lives. The image of the church as mother is an important corrective to Reformed portrayals of the church's authentic ministry as primarily a recital of God's saving deeds, a matter of standing above the fray of daily experience and witnessing to the timeless truths of the gospel. By contrast, the image of mother reminds us of the redemptive significance of the church's daily life in the world, as it negotiates material issues of community. The church not only recites or displays God's salvation—it mediates it through attention to the ordinary tasks of kindness and nurture so often denigrated as "women's work": meals prepared and served, newcomers welcomed, the sick visited, clothing and food collected and distributed, Sunday school classes taught. The church's "means of grace" are not restricted to the ordained ministries of Word and sacrament. In the communal practices of the laity, the healing mercies and forgiving love of Christ are communicated both within the "common life" of the church and far beyond it.

The church is also the bride of Christ. According to Ephesians 5, she has been washed of water by the Word, and presented without a spot or wrinkle before her bridegroom. In the imagery of Revelation 19, the church as holy bride has been "clothed with fine linen, bright and pure," transformed by a divine grace that is reflected in all her righteous deeds. The Lord's Supper is the joyous marriage supper of the Lamb, a feast of love for the redeemed family of God, a visible manifestation of the communion of the faithful. The work of the Holy Spirit in the church is progressive, so that its members are "daily advancing" in sanctification. The image of the church as bride does not signal a retreat from harsh material realities, as if the advancing holiness of the church rendered issues of power, race, and difference peripheral to the church's "real" identity. As Letty Russell insists, the church is a community of hospitality "bought with a price." "The struggle of Jesus to overcome the structures of sin and death constitutes both the source of new life in the community and its own mandate to continue the same struggle."[37]

The eschatological image of the church as bride provides a framework for considering the four "marks" of the church confessed in the Nicene Creed: the church is one, holy, catholic, and apostolic. It is evident that these marks are not an empirical description of ecclesial reality. The church's drive to be one has often led to conflict and schism. The church's holiness has been persistently marred by sin. The church's catholicity has been fragmented by partisanship and heterodoxy. The church's apostolicity has been compromised by a refusal to repent and listen to others. Yet as the bride of Christ the church is called to participate now in the eschatological promise of the four marks. James Evans helpfully correlates these marks with the central Christian ministries of gospel proclamation, fellowship, service, and teaching.[38] The church is one as it centers its life around proclaiming the gospel, forging a unity that respects racial and cultural difference. The church is holy as it finds joyful communion as members of Christ's body, a genuine fellowship of the flesh. The church is catholic as it moves beyond itself through open-handed service to provide a welcome space for all. The church is apostolic as its teaching and practice express faithfulness to the gospel across time. The church claims these marks in hope as it leans forward into the reality promised by God's transforming grace.

The ecclesial images of mother and bride belong together. By itself, the maternal image for the church risks complacency, because it fails to capture the dynamism of the Reformed view of Christian life. Christians strive by God's grace to grow into a mature life of gratitude and holiness, despite turbulent spiritual emotions and repeated moral failures. They stand on tiptoe, yearning for anticipations of the eschatological promise of full communion with God. Likewise, by itself the image of the church as bride risks arrogance, by obscuring the fact that the earthly church remains a community of confession and forgiveness. To claim that the church, either in its individual members or in its communal forms, is already "without spot or wrinkle" in its earthly pronouncements and actions is to fall victim to pride and idolatry. The faithfulness of the church remains a work in progress. Together, the images of mother and bride encourage a humble hopefulness for the church's common life in the world.

A COMMUNITY OF GIFT AND ARGUMENT

Some nineteenth-century American Presbyterians promulgated the doctrine of the "spirituality of the church." They argued that the church was not to become involved in social and political matters because its mandate was spiritual: to proclaim the gospel. But by claiming that slavery was a political issue that the church should leave alone, the promulgators of the "spirituality of the church" were not being apolitical: they were defending the institution of slavery. Like all other social entities, the church is a political body because it possesses and uses social power. As Wallace Alston asserts, "politics is the means by which the mission of the Church is discerned and done in the formal and informal processes of its institutional life. . . . The politics of the church are those patterns of human association that enable the church to reflect on and to participate in the politics of God, that is, in God's renovating activity in the world."[39] Politics is an inescapable dimension of the life of the church.

Not surprisingly then, the church has always been a community of argument, as the New Testament writings readily attest. Different voices in the church, even sensitive and discerning voices, often fail to harmonize. Theologians who extol the peace and unity of the church above all else are usually dodging some hard political questions about ecclesial power structures and channels of religious authority. From a Reformed perspective, the church *must* be a community of argument. "There have at all times been great contentions in the Church," declares the Second Helvetic Confession, "and the most excellent teachers of the Church have differed among themselves about important matters."[40] All the church's members are prone to error and sin, and therefore decision making must be prayerful and collaborative. Voices from the entire household of believers must be heard— voices from the kitchen as well as voices from the study. Furthermore, those in the kitchen should be encouraged to gain more knowledge of the tradition, and those in the study should do some kitchen work. Listening to each other through protracted arguments over difficult issues is the only way forward.

The Reformed communion has been one of the more schismatic bodies in the Christian tradition, and it has sometimes seemed as if it were *only* a community of argument. The self-righteous determination of Calvinists convinced they are doing God's will has few equals in the Christian tradition. But if the church were not also a community of gift, there would be no reason to stay and argue. In ways both obvious and mysterious, the church is itself God's gracious gift to us, and it exists as a community in which we receive the gifts of God's grace. Letty Russell attests, "It is impossible for me and for many other alienated women and men to walk away from the church, . . . for it has been the bearer of the story of Jesus Christ and the good news of God's love."[41] In church, like nowhere else, we drink in the good news of the gospel, the stories of God's people, the rhythms of the liturgical year, the disciplines of prayer and Bible study, the challenge of local and global mission. We find in the church's worship and fellowship sources of hope, strength, and consolation. This community centers our lives, calling us to confession and praise, and connects us with God and each other. The church is where we bring our children—both daughters and sons—hoping that they too will enter into its arguments and receive its gifts.

13

THE GIFTS OF GOD FOR
THE PEOPLE OF GOD

Christian Feminism and Sacramental Theology

Leanne Van Dyk

In the prologue to *The Canterbury Tales*, Chaucer suggests that nesting birds are so filled with praise for the Creator that they sleep with eyes opened, so as not to lose a moment for praise. In his preface to the French Bible translation of his cousin Robert Olivétan, John Calvin remarks, "It is evident that all creatures, from those in the heavens to those under the earth, are able to act as witnesses and messengers of God's glory. . . . For the little birds that sing, sing of God; the beasts clamor for God; the elements dread God; the mountains echo God, and the fountains and flowing waters wink at God. . . ."[1]

Creation, it seems, from the perspectives of a medieval poet and a sixteenth-century Reformed pastor, strains with eagerness and longing for the glory of God. The created world perceives the presence and reality of God with a clarity human beings often lack. The Psalms express this in Hebrew poetic form: "The heavens are telling the glory of God and the firmament proclaims God's handiwork" (Ps. 19).

Human experience of God, however, is marked by ambiguity, darkness, loneliness, and loss. The little birds, the flowing waters, and the expansive heavens seem to have a much more direct apprehension of God. Yet human beings continue to long for God. The intense longing of the human soul for its deepest need, a need sometimes identified as comfort, connection, forgiveness, grace, love, safety, home, or God, is obscured and frustrated by personal, communal, and social barriers. Some people, faced by such daunting barriers to the simple, spontaneous praise of the little birds and expansive heavens, find shelter in religious traditions that prescribe both their expectations and experience. Others abandon the hope for God or any transcendent compass and resort to the moral equivalent of a flat-earth cosmology. Others continue the search, exploring an always-expanding list of options and exercises that may fill the void.

The Christian tradition, in its many cultural and historical particularities, has always known about the deep longing of the human heart for God. The traditions of Christian mysticism and contemplation that flourished in medieval times; the poets who penned the hymn texts of all the centuries of Christian worship; and the introspective spiritual autobiographies of Augustine, John Wesley, Teresa of Avila, and Simone Weil are specific examples of a various yet common longing for God.

One important way that Christians express their longing for God is through a celebration of the sacraments in Christian worship. From the very earliest days of the young Christian community, the meal of remembrance and hospitality that became known as the Lord's Supper and the ritual washing and incorporation into the community that became known as baptism were tangible, physical acts of worship that expectantly awaited the gracious presence of God.[2] One of the scars that marks the history of the church is the way that the sacraments have been diverted from such expectant hope for God's grace to an instrument of exclusion and silencing. My task in this chapter is to explore Christian sacramental theology and look for construals and implications that contribute to the flourishing of all people, most particularly women, and that contribute to the sustenance of the created world. The construals that I will explore are located in the broad Reformed tradition but focus especially on John Calvin. The thesis I wish to demonstrate is that Reformed theology contains a sacramental richness that is deeply supportive of women's and earth's flourishing. Although these deep supports went largely unnoticed in classic Reformed formulations, a key task of a Reformed feminist theologian is to make explicit these implications of Reformed sacramental theology for women's wholeness. It is my cautious hope and my firm resolve to claim what riches the Christian tradition does contain with respect to the dignity and full personhood of women.

SACRAMENTS AND THE CHALLENGE
OF CHRISTIAN FEMINISM

Even a cursory glance at the history of the church reveals a long series of polemical hot spots concerning the sacraments. Vigorous disagreements have emerged over the number of ecclesial sacraments; the purpose of sacraments; the role of clergy; the understanding of divine agency and human receptivity; the relationship between language, symbol, and reality; and a wide variety of other issues.

One way to organize the discussion is to suggest a rough typology of sacramental approaches. There is the "strong" sacramental view, namely, one that assumes that God self-discloses, reveals, and acts in the particular sacramental rites in the worshiping community. For Protestants in the Reformed tradition these sacramental rites are baptism and the Lord's Supper. A contrasting "general" sacramental view posits divine self-disclosure in any of a number of sacred rituals or rites although it is not clear, in this view, how baptism and eucharist are each unique as a particular locus of divine agency. Yet another perspective on sacraments might be called the "experiential" view, one that avoids both modest and strong claims on divine agency and focuses instead on human self-awareness in sacred rituals.

Calvin's own sacramental theology does not demand a strict choice from these three sacramental views. Certainly, Calvin assumes the priority of the "strong" sacramental view, the view that weights divine initiative and the particular grace of baptism and communion. However, the more "general" sacramental view is also acknowledged as part of God's palette of self-communication. Calvin argues that God can use all creation to amplify God's glory. A rainbow, for example, can sacramentally underline the promises of God. Calvin turns aside any objections:

> Therefore, if any philosophizer, to mock the simplicity of our faith, con-tends that such a variety of colors naturally arises from rays reflected upon a cloud opposite, let us admit it, but laugh at his stupidity in fail-ing to recognize God as the lord and governor of nature, who according to [God's] will uses all the elements to serve [God's] glory.[3]

It all depends on one's perspective, Calvin points out. The Christian believer sees in the rainbow the promises of God and is not embarrassed to say so. This is a sacramental moment in that broader sense of the word: the entire created order as sacrament of God's presence and action.

In addition, the "experiential" component of the sacraments is not absent. Calvin defines a sacrament with the human experience well in mind. He says a sacrament is a visible sign by which God "seals on our consciences the promises of [God's] good will toward us. . . ."[4] Calvin's concern here is that believers receive the support, encouragement, and care they so desperately need. Without the tender, attentive care of God, believ-ers would "tremble, waver, totter, and at last give way."[5] It is precisely because God knows we need help maintaining confidence, balance, and sturdiness that God provides us with the unique grace of baptism and com-munion. These experiential aspects of the sacraments are also a concern of Calvin's sacramental theology.

This brief survey of Calvin's sacramental theology reveals an interest-ing range of aspects. It assumes an emphasis on the "strong" view of the sacraments, with its stress on divine initiative and agency. Clearly, for Calvin, a sacrament is an act of Christian worship by which God gifts the community with a particular grace. Yet Calvin openly acknowledges the sacramental potential of all creation as revelatory of God. The list of poten-tially sacramental created realities is as diverse as human experience itself. Rainbows, mountain peaks, shared meals with friends, laughter, conver-sation, embraces, and baby smiles are certainly part of that list. Although Calvin does not explore and expand in detail the notion of the "sacramental reality of all of life," his clear acknowledgment that God can surely self-reveal in a wide variety of ways is striking.[6] In addition, the experiential aspect of sacramental grace is a consistent interest in Calvin's treatment of the sacraments.

Although John Calvin is not the beginning and end of the Reformed tradition, his sacramental theology can reasonably be claimed as the most expansive and creative of the classic Reformed tradition.[7] Thus, it is discouraging to note that in spite of the conceptual range of Calvin's sacramental theology, the story of women and Reformed sacramental practice has not been characterized by the kind of openness and hospitality that is at least implicit in the tradition. Christian traditions, including traditions identified with Reformed theology, have instead been marred by blatant and subtle diminishments of women. The exclusions and limitations are many, from entrenched social patterns to petty restrictions.[8]

These oppressive ecclesial patterns exist, of course, against the backdrop of global cultural discrimination of women. In many cultures, women's physical, psychic, and spiritual safety is utterly at risk. In 1993, the United Nations General Assembly, concerned by the growing global violence against women, adopted the Declaration on the Elimination of Violence against Women. Since then, the U.N. has continued its efforts to collect information on violence against women, to research its causes, to recommend measures to combat violence against women, and to work together with groups seeking justice for women. Some of the research that followed the 1993 Declaration was reported at the Beijing Conference in 1995. The Secretary-General at that time, Boutros Boutros-Ghali, said that the fate of women and girls on a global scale is more precarious than ever. The areas of risk for women include the home, where domestic violence touches the lives of women at all socioeconomic levels; the community, where rape, sexual harassment, and labor exploitation occur; and the state, which sometimes tolerates injustice against women in the courts of law, as well as violence against women in situations of warfare and imprisonment.[9]

The church, both at denominational and congregational levels, has often risen to the challenge of seeking full human rights and protections for at-risk people, including children, the elderly, women, the poor, the disabled, and the sick. Countless congregations tell their own stories of Habitat for Humanity teams, food pantry volunteers, mentors for struggling families, and political efforts for legislation with attentiveness to the needs of the poor and sick. Ecumenical church agencies have also committed themselves to advocacy and action on behalf of at-risk people. The World Council of Churches has declared the years 2001–2010 as the Decade to Overcome Violence. Although these efforts are encouraging, it must also be admitted that the church has often either turned away from women's risks, judging these to be unimportant or defended exclusionary patterns on biblical, theological, or philosophical grounds.

Women's marginalization in the broader culture and in the church impacts the authentic expression of sacramental theology. Central to baptism and communion are the themes of hospitality, inclusion, nourishment, community, and forgiveness. When the church is deaf to the voices of women, children, powerless men, and other peoples at the margins, the health of its faith and witness is compromised. Sacramental vitality can be a lived reality in the church only when women are fully included in leadership and ministry and fully valued as human persons.

Clearly, the challenge for Reformed feminist and womanist theologians is daunting. Sacramental vitality in its fullest and liveliest potential is possible only in communities of reconciliation, mutual support, and hospitality. Yet the strongest and thickest walls against women's leadership in the church have traditionally been raised between the sacraments and women. This is the case not only in the Reformed tradition but also in the Roman Catholic Church, the Orthodox Church, and the burgeoning Christian churches in the southern and eastern hemispheres, especially the charismatic and Pentecostal churches.

A rich sacramental, ecclesial life requires strong commitments to the flourishing of women; moreover, a rich sacramental life and the flourishing of women are deeply congruent and mutually supportive. To support this claim, careful sociological data on the features of congregational life that might encourage particular patterns of flourishing would be helpful. But our approach here will be one of conversation between a Reformed understanding of the sacraments, especially as expressed by John Calvin and the challenges, questions, and contributions of Reformed feminists and womanists to classical or traditional understandings of Reformed sacramental theology.

Some feminist and womanist theologians would view this method of conversation between the classical Reformed tradition and contemporary feminist theology as overly optimistic. They might challenge this approach with a reality check: feminist and womanist theologians often find the classic theological traditions deeply contrary to the commitments of feminism. And the classic theological traditions have often resisted both correction and a reception of marginalized voices. It would seem that the vision of mutuality and reciprocity between classic theological traditions and the advocacy voices of women and peoples of color is either naïve or utopian or both.

Yet recent feminist literature suggests openness to a form of feminist theology that is not only oppositional and constructive but also perhaps "traditional" in a new sense. In an intriguing and suggestive essay, Kathryn Tanner proposes that "every element in service to a patriarchal cause has at least some potential for alignment with a feminist one."[10] Realizing this potential requires a twofold process of "disarticulation" and "rearticulation," a process of "un-saying" and "re-saying." The possible continuities between classical theology and feminist theology are expressed by Serene Jones as well. She defines Christian feminist theology as "a theology that articulates the Christian message in language and actions that seek to liberate women and all persons, a goal that Christian feminists believe cannot be disentangled from the central truth of the Christian faith as a whole."[11]

Continuities and shared visions between classical theology and feminist theology are especially evident in sacramental theology because both have a social vision. The challenge for Christian feminist and womanist theologians is to articulate a social vision that replaces patriarchal assumptions of exploitation and domination with a vision of a social order that affirms the full humanity of all persons, including women, and that is dedicated to the flourishing of all creatures, including the earth. Kathryn Tanner recommends an engagement with traditional theology partly for pragmatic and strategic reasons. The more feminist theology engages with the tradition, the more influence feminist theology will have. She says, "The influence of feminist theology is strengthened to the extent it wrestles constructively with the theological claims that have traditionally been important in Christian theology; the more traditional the material with which it works, the greater the influence of feminist theology."[12] It is that vision and hope which motivate the conversation between classic Reformed theology and feminism in this chapter.

In recent years, a renewed interest in sacraments, liturgy, and worship has signaled an opportunity for Reformed feminist and womanist theologians.[13] Because baptism and the Lord's Supper are brimming with affirmations of community, relationality, bodies, feasting, transformation, healing, wholeness, inclusion, and hospitality, Reformed feminist and womanist theologians see natural connections with feminist concerns. A sacramental theology with roots in the broad Reformed tradition turns out to be strongly congruent with the passions of feminist theologians. A brief overview of Calvin's sacramental theology reveals three themes that demonstrate the shared social vision of Reformed theology and feminism. An explication of those three themes follows.

Theme One: Sacraments as Divine Gift

Fundamental to the Reformed tradition is the simple affirmation of the divine origin of all goodness. God is the "fountain of all good," says Calvin,[14] and we are to receive all good things as from the hand of God. The good gifts of God include, for Calvin, the sacraments. In his *Institutes of the Christian Religion,* Calvin understands baptism and the Lord's Supper as gifts of God to support and nourish the faith of the community. He says that God, like a caring and attentive parent, provides for us in ways that we can uniquely receive and understand. Employing his doctrine of accommodation, Calvin explains that God "tempers" God's divine self to meet our frail condition; that God "condescends" to us so that our faith will not fail under the weight of our own finitude.[15]

Calvin expands his efforts to convey the gift character of the sacraments with additional metaphors. The sacraments are like pictures, seals, exercises, promises, visible words, mirrors, and pillars. All of these images are intended to emphasize the sheer bounty of God's generosity. Calvin says, for instance, that the sacraments are like mirrors into which we look to see the riches of God's grace, which God "lavishes upon us."[16]

Sacraments, then, are divine gifts, given for the purpose of support and encouragement. Furthermore, they are particularly apt gifts—they are given in God's mercy because God knows we need encouragement in ways that suit our own creatureliness. We are earthly creatures, Calvin points out, so we need earthly encouragements. God "feeds our bodies through bread and other foods"; God "illumines the world through the sun"; and God "warms it through heat."[17] Calvin insists that sacramental elements are simply common things.

Reformed theologian David Willis notes this feature of Calvin's sacramental theology as well. "The Lord's Supper is a 'sacred action' because of the use the Holy Spirit makes of ordinary bread and wine, their breaking and pouring and chewing and swallowing, to be the instruments of Christ's presence and consequently of renewed repentance, forgiveness, and walking in newness of life."[18] Willis then offers the rather striking remark that, for Calvin, the traditional Catholic view of transubstantiation does not take the elements too seriously; instead, it does not take them seriously enough![19] The undiluted claim of a Calvinian understanding of sacramental grace is that these utterly ordinary elements are exactly what the Holy Spirit uses to unite us to Christ.[20] Calvin makes the further claim that not only are the sacramental elements themselves common, ordinary earthy things used by the Spirit for our good, but that we receive the divine grace God intends to give us in our own bodies. He says, "It is therefore a special comfort for the godly that they now find life in their own flesh."[21] I take this remark of Calvin as a somewhat surprising acknowledgment of embodied knowing and experience.

Serene Jones further radicalizes this understanding of the elements as common, earthy things. She notes that sacramental elements are not only earthy; they are *temporary or transient.* They must be received and enjoyed when they are given. Because of their very ordinariness, "they mold, they decay, they are digested; they are impermanent, changing, and yet they give life."[22] The transient character of the sacramental elements signals three things that are congruent with feminist concerns.

First, the gift must be recognized as gift. Common, earthy things like water, bread, and wine are fundamental to the sustaining of life. In most cultures, it is the women who draw the water, who bake the bread, who crush the grapes. Women's work, especially in traditional agrarian and tribal cultures, is consumed with the constant toil of sustaining the life of the community. These gifts of labor that produce the food and fetch the water often go unnoticed, unrecognized. Reformed feminist and womanist theologians who affirm Calvin's emphasis on the gift character of the sacraments given in common, earthy, and transient elements also point out the importance of *recognition*. The gifts of God for the people of God must be noticed, both in the sense of divine gracious origin and human labor.

Of course, a recognition of the gifts of the common, earthy elements is not an implicit justification of the often-grueling patterns of women's work. A thorough cultural critique is necessary and concrete political action required to address the inequities of women's work. This is most acute in womanist theologians' accounts of slavery, an unjust institution that conscripted the work of women.[23] Recognition and gratitude for the gifts of earthy sacramental elements does not dismiss the hard work of cultural critique and political action.

Second, the gift must be received. God said to Moses, "I am going to rain bread from heaven for you, and each day the people shall go out and gather enough for that day" (Exod. 16:4). Exodus 16 tells the story of the manna that God sent to feed the people. Those who received the gift each morning were fed. Each had enough and was satisfied. Those who attempted to hoard the gift discovered it "grew worms and became foul." Divine gifts are not to be saved, guarded, hidden, or controlled. They are to be received each day in their own particularity.[24]

One of the contributions of feminist and womanist theology is a reclaiming of the simple gifts of earthly life. The physical joys of nursing an infant, running a 10K race, hugging a lover, feeling strong, and countless other small gifts of physical existence are noticed and celebrated in feminist and womanist writings. In these writings, the tendency in some streams of the Christian tradition to devalue physical and earthy experience is decisively rejected. Instead, physical embodiment is celebrated. Convinced that these affirmations are not only deeply healing to women but also resonant to the truest notes of the Christian faith, feminist and womanist theologians insist on the worth of bodies and then seek to draw out the ethical implications of that insistence. In a culture with unrealistic and often dangerous ideals of beauty, feminist and womanist theology calls into question prevailing cultural norms and articulates a theological, social, ethical, and political alternative.

One implication of the insistence of receiving with joy the gift of bodies is recognizing as well the worth, beauty, and dignity of differently abled bodies, chronically ill bodies, and other bodies not deemed valuable by our culture. A sacramental ethic that takes its cue from Jesus, who gathered his disciples around his own "broken body," is alert to the subtle diminishments around "difference" that often occur in communities. Receiving the gift in particularity and gratitude can be a prophetic and political act when the physical and spiritual strength of racial-ethnic women is declared, when the wisdom of wheelchair mobile women is asserted, when the dignity of elderly women is protected. These are sacramental instincts by which the gift is received.

Third, the gift must be confidently anticipated again and again. Confident anticipation is an active, not a passive, mode. It includes desire and longing for the gifts of God that sustain and nourish us. One of my seminary students once exclaimed to me, as we were both walking into the seminary chapel for our community's weekly Lord's Supper celebration, "I'm starving!" His exuberant expression of his hunger and thirst for God strikes me as a fitting example of anticipation.

Perhaps partly because African American slave women had to wait so long for their day of freedom, the themes of hope and anticipation run deep in the tradition of black spirituals. Hope and anticipation run deep in contemporary womanist theology. Emilie Townes names the hope that continues to challenge and inspire African American women in their struggle for justice in a North American culture still deeply scarred by entrenched racism:

> Hope, that which scares us and yet prepares us, gives us the wisdom to know that God is not through. Our task is to take the challenge that hope gives us—the joy along with the disappointment—and to work *with* God until our lives begin to pulse with something vaster and greater than anything we have known before.[25]

If a keen appetite for sacramental grace is a part of Christian worship, then whetting the appetite for those divine gifts is one of the challenges of Christian pastors and worship leaders. Worship is not primarily for the purpose of being interesting, relevant, entertaining, meaningful, uplifting, or inspiring. Paul Wadell gives a stinging rebuke to worship trends visible in some Christian communities: "When liturgy becomes entertainment, our worship becomes as trivial as our lives."[26] The primary purpose of worship is to bring honor, gratitude, and praise to God; a secondary purpose is to whet the believer's appetite for God's grace in the waters of baptism and at the feast spread before us at the Lord's Table.

Because sacramental grace is given to us through earthy, transient elements; because we cannot hoard and control sacramental grace; and because we need the nourishment and sustenance supplied by sacramental grace, we must anticipate the gift, always in confidence and joy that it will be given to us. The gift character of the sacraments marks off hierarchical or authoritarian sacramental policies and practices. The community of faith must exhibit the virtues of a gift-receiving people, virtues that include the habits of recognizing the gift, receiving the gift, and anticipating the gift again and again.

Theme Two: Sacraments as Pointing to Christ

The second theme in Calvin's *Institutes* relevant to feminist and womanist commitments is the clear emphasis on the referential function of the sacraments. The sacraments *point* not to themselves but to Jesus Christ. The sacraments are divine gifts, to be sure, but they are gifts with a purpose— to reveal Christ to the believer so that the life of faith may be built up. Not only do sacraments reveal Christ, but in the Reformed tradition Scripture and the preached word also reveal Christ. There is a deep unity between the preached or written word and the sacraments. *Both* "set forth Christ." Calvin explains: "Therefore, let it be regarded as a settled principle that the sacraments have the same office as the Word of God: to offer and set forth Christ to us, and in him the treasures of heavenly grace."[27]

This strong referential character of the sacraments and the preached word to Christ seen in Calvin's sacramental theology is complexified by other theological traditions. Writing from within a Roman Catholic tradition, theologian Susan Ross highlights the inherent ambiguity of the sacraments. She says, "Sacramentality is an inherently *ambiguous* reality, and the dangers of overstating either its disclosive or concealing powers are great." Drawing on the work of Paul Ricoeur, Ross goes on to offer a dialectical understanding of sacramental referencing: "[S]acramentality means that created reality *both* reveals *and* conceals the presence of God."[28]

Ross identifies three kinds of sacramental ambiguity: 1) *metaphysical ambiguity*, which takes the form of questioning dominant Western philosophical categories that have marked traditional Christian theology; 2) *expressive ambiguity*, which is alert to multivalent layers of symbolic meaning; and 3) *moral ambiguity*, an awareness of the deep failures of the Christian tradition, including the sacramental traditions. Ross says, "Like their colleagues in biblical, historical, systematic, and moral theology, feminist sacramental theologians are confronted with a tradition that both draws and repels, invites and excludes."[29]

Reformed feminist and womanist theologians perhaps have a greater affinity to Ross's complexified referential character of the sacraments than to Calvin's straightforward assertion that the sacraments "present Christ." Surely exclusions and diminishments of women, racial-ethnic groups, and other marginalized people at the Lord's Table and before the waters of baptism obscure Christ rather than present Christ. Reformed feminist theologians might rightly point out that the particulars of sacramental practices matter here. The theological claim that sacraments present Christ is abstract, whereas each sacramental rite is particular. Surely, Reformed feminists might say, exclusionary practices that target, even inadvertently, women and other people standing outside the margins of power and influence exclude Christ as well.

Such a feminist critique of the classic Calvinian affirmation that the sacraments present Christ is helpful in that it focuses attention on the crucial importance of the particular. Feminist and womanist theology does not remain content with the general, the vague, and the universal. The particular, concrete, experienced, and contextual realities are theologically relevant as well. This concern for the particular that is characteristic of feminist theology opens up a wide range of questions. Open for examination are the liturgies of the sacraments. Are they beautiful? Are they expressive of the whole people of God? Are they inclusive in their portrayal both of human persons and of God? Open for examination is the architecture of the church. Is it fitting? Does it invite wonder, reverence, and hospitality? Is it accessible for persons in wheelchairs or assisted by walkers? And open for examination is the manner of partaking of the sacraments. Are three tiny droplets of water used for baptism? Or is there room—literally, room!—in the church for an abundance of water? What does our choice of sacramental elements convey? What does our manner of receiving those elements convey?

In these examples, the feminist critique of the classic Calvinian affirmation that the sacraments present Christ is at work in that it calls our attention to the particular. Yet another Reformed feminist critique might turn in the direction of affirming the Calvinian dictum. A brief overview of Calvin's thoughts of sacramental grace will clarify this possibility: Calvin himself considers the problem of particularities that might hinder sacramental grace. He does this by reflecting on the problem of unworthy clergy and the problem of ungrateful participants. He answers, in line with Augustine, that unworthy clergy cannot make null and void the promises of God. Clergy, in short, do not control sacramental grace. Ungrateful participants will not receive sacramental grace, however—at least, not the fullness of sacramental grace—because they turn away and resist it. But, Calvin adds, "For what God has ordained remains firm and keeps its own nature, however people may vary."[30]

Still following Augustine, Calvin identifies two errors in approaching the sacraments.[31] Both of these errors have to do with the particularities of the sacramental rites. First, we must not be suspicious of the efficacy of the sacramental elements. Calvin says we must not "receive the signs as though they had been given in vain." In other words, we must not be excessively cynical. Reformed feminist theologians might well be cheered and encouraged by Calvin's advice. Even when the particularities of the sacraments are marred by sexism, even when the celebration of the sacraments is obscured by human pride and power, the signs are still connected to sacramental grace, by God's goodwill and not by our own. Grace gets through. This is a Reformed theological insight worthy of feminist and womanist support.

The second error Calvin identified with respect to the particularities of the sacramental elements is that we must not transfer to the elements what properly belongs to Christ alone. In other words, we must not be excessively vigilant. It is not the case, cautions Calvin, that the visible signs and the sacramental details surrounding the sacramental elements, such as the clergy or the liturgy, can claim the credit for the divine grace that is given. Thus, neither an "agnosticism" concerning the divine promises contained in the sacramental elements is appropriate, nor a zealous protection of the elements *as if* divine grace depended on them. Reformed feminist and womanist theologians can support this Calvinian insight as well. When the divine gift of sacramental grace is clearly located in God's good pleasure toward human persons and not in the structures of church tradition, peoples of all exclusions and diminishments can perhaps find the courage and persistence to claim their rightful place at the table and besides the flowing waters.

Theme Three: Everything Depends on the Holy Spirit

The third theme so prominent in Calvin is the centrality of the Holy Spirit. Everything, for Calvin, depends on the Spirit. The preached word will not set forth Christ without the action of the Holy Spirit. The sacramental word will not set forth Christ without the action of the Holy Spirit. Calvin says bluntly that "they are of no further benefit unless the Holy Spirit accompanies them."[32] This implies that the means of grace in the preached word, in the waters of baptism, and in the bread and wine of the Lord's Table are not under the control of the church, the minister, or the gathered people. The means of grace in the preached and sacramental word are always a fresh gift of God through the Holy Spirit.

Calvin's comprehensive vision of the work of the Holy Spirit includes his attention to the subject of "union with Christ." Some Calvin scholars suggest that this nuanced phrase is the best candidate for a "central idea" in Calvin's theology.[33] Through faith, itself a gift of the Holy Spirit, the believer is united with Christ in such a way that "we are united with him more closely than are the limbs with the body."[34]

Feminist and womanist theologians may wish to raise concerns about this theme in the Reformed tradition. Calvin clearly understands union with Christ as constituting the very identity of the Christian believer. But feminist theologians hear "union" language with some suspicion. The language of union can sound like the loss of self. In a society that exerts strong pressures for conformity, one of the cultural challenges for girls and young women is self-differentiation. In spite of sustained and vigorous critique by observers of American culture, cultural messages to girls continue to advance passivity, weakness, silence, deference, and dependence. These cultural messages are seen most starkly in media advertising.[35]

No simplistic claim is being made that Reformed theology threatens the self-differentiation of girls and women. But awareness of the conceptual and psychic challenges for women in traditional theological language is important. For example, if girls and women are subtly reinforced in passivity and dependence by the engines of advertising, how can the language of faith resist and subvert those negative messages? If "union with Christ" is expressed in language that reinforces passivity and dependence, the conceptual link is inevitable. Reformed feminist theologians, at the very least, are alert to subtle links between traditional Christian language and the marginalization of women. They are also motivated to rearticulate, recast, reframe, and reclaim traditional Christian doctrine precisely so that the church as a whole, women and men, can flourish as a community of care and respect.

Feminist and womanist theologians can reclaim the language of "union with Christ" in several ways that avoid the dangers of passivity and loss of self. Womanist theologians, for example, have emphasized the solidarity of Jesus Christ with black women in their suffering. Following Jesus may require a subversive, radical discipleship. "We must live our lives, both publicly and privately, in the same subversive manner that Jesus Christ led his," says Diana Hayes.[36] She closely relates black women's struggles for truth and justice with Jesus Christ's struggles for truth and justice. Hayes does not employ the classic Calvinian language of "union with Christ," but her language is a close theological neighbor. Both feminist and womanist theologians can link the language of "union with Christ" with other Christian theological, biblical, and ethical themes that clearly value the individual worth of each child of God.

Another issue that emerges in a consideration of the role of the Holy Spirit in the sacraments is the nature of the reception of that sacramental grace. Human beings are the ones who both need and receive sacramental grace. How, exactly, does that happen? Frequently, the Christian theological tradition has emphasized metaphors of *hearing* the word of God and, in that way, receiving God's grace. Other metaphors are common as well, including the image of sight or images of hearts being filled, warmed, or changed. Feminist theologians wish to value and notice the particular and existential nuances of women's religious experience and so are interested in the best ways of expressing the reception of sacramental grace.

In a fascinating chapter in their recent book *Truth in Aquinas*, coauthors John Milbank and Catherine Pickstock make interesting links with this issue. Chapter 3 examines Aristotle's ancient theories of sense, knowledge, and truth as expounded by Thomas Aquinas. Critical of modernity's excessively elusive and theoretical understandings of truth, Milbank and Pick-stock seek a new reading of Aquinas. In so doing, they seek to avoid modernity's faith/reason split and to affirm the accessibility, reality, and practicality of truth.

In a philosophically nuanced argument, Milbank and Pickstock describe a "sensorial access to truth" in the sacraments. They are referring to the way the earthy, common elements of the sacraments elevate the sensory over the intellectual. Drawing on Aquinas's reading of Aristotle's *De Anima,* the authors focus on touch and taste in particular. Contrary to the main current of Western intellectual thought, Aquinas sees these lowly senses as the receptors of truth rather than obstacles to truth. Substantiating this claim is the incarnation, in which an "ontological revision" occurs in "such a way that the lower senses now instruct in truth the higher reason."[37] It is fitting that in the incarnation "Christ should mediate to us what is most certain in itself, namely, divine truth, through what is most certain for us, namely, the directly touchable by the senses."[38]

Tasting, especially, is a "more intimate mode of touch."[39] Remarkably, Christian worshipers in the Lord's Supper encounter God through the "most intimate and discerning touch of all, which is that of the tongue in taste."[40] Aquinas recognizes in his commentary on Aristotle that the senses of sight and hearing are more comprehensive: one can survey a river valley from the top of a hill alongside many other viewers whereas touch is more limited.[41] Aristotle's point, as understood by Aquinas and related by Milbank and Pickstock, is that the particularity and immediacy of touch and taste equip those senses with a sensory access to truth.

Reformed feminist theologians concur with Milbank and Pickstock's remark that "our sacramental re-education is not primarily a matter of looking."[42] Although some feminist philosophers and theorists might disagree with Aquinas's theory of truth as reappropriated by Milbank and Pickstock, this contemporary support for feminist interests in the rich variety of human lived experience, including the intimacies of taste and touch, as receivers of God's grace in the sacraments is noteworthy.

AMBIGUITIES AND TENSIONS

Reformed feminists are faced with a familiar quandary in approaching the theology and practice of the sacraments in the Reformed tradition. There is much to celebrate in Calvin, Zwingli, and contemporary Reformed thinkers. Themes of the hospitality and generosity of God abound in classic Reformed theological sources and can readily be incorporated into contemporary feminist thought. But strong tensions are felt even in endorsing the most amenable theological themes. For it has been the experience of women that the brightest and best affirmations of the Christian faith have often been turned against them in countless trivial and entrenched ways.

Both the theology of sacraments and the practices of the sacraments bristle with ambiguity and tension for Reformed feminists. Not content only to correct the glaring denials of women's gifts and voices in the church, feminist theologians are also alert to subtle exclusions. They note the chasm between the claims of the church for welcome and acceptance and the lived practices of the church that encode multilayered limitations.

The sacramental liturgies and the sacramental elements themselves are one area of ambiguity and tension that require careful feminist evaluation. In North American feminist conversation, the traditional sacramental elements have been challenged. In the 1993 Re-imagining Conference in Minneapolis, the conference leaders planned a ritual for participants that included the symbols of milk and honey. The interpretation of this event was widely diverse. Some saw it—and denounced it—as a pagan ritual. Others understood the milk-and-honey ceremony to be a creative, symbolic reference to women's generativity and community. In any case, the question of what constitutes a sacramental element was raised.

Reformed theologian Michael Welker observes, without reference to Re-imagining and the particular controversy that erupted there, that it is a mistake to focus exclusively on the elements of the Lord's Supper. The sacramental elements are not, in fact, equivalent to the sacrament itself. Rather, the whole "symbolic nexus of actions" together constitute the sacrament. In the case of the Lord's Supper, this nexus includes the taking, the sharing, and the distributing of the elements as well as the invitation to take, eat, and drink. Most broadly considered, it includes the forms of the community gathering together, passing the peace, welcoming the stranger, and being sent out into the world. The Lord's Supper is an interconnected web of meaning, not merely a single moment of consecration or distribution of the elements. Welker notes that part of this interconnected web of meaning is "mutual acceptance and a basic will for justice."[43] Reformed womanists and feminists endorse this reminder of Welker. Although it does not solve the fierce controversy that surrounded the Re-imagining ritual, it does serve to reframe the question in a larger sacramental context.

In the sacrament of baptism, the whole symbolic nexus of actions includes not only the liturgical and sacramental actions themselves but the patterns of catechesis, welcome, and incorporation of the baptized person into the community. This implicates a wide range of issues, including those of welcome, justice, forgiveness, and reconciliation.

Ambiguity clusters around the wonderful Calvinian theme of feasting at the table of God's hospitality in the Lord's Supper as well. The Lord's Table has long been undermined by the exclusion of women as ordained clergy. There are still many Protestant denominations with roots in the

Reformed tradition that continue to restrict ordained ministry to men. The argument over women's ordination has tended to focus on the interpretation of a few Pauline texts and on essentialist understandings of both women and men. A distinctly Reformed feminist approach might illuminate the issue of women's ordination in a new way by stressing the implications of a Reformed sacramental theology for hospitality at the table. Such hospitality implicates "both sides" of the table. There are multiple ways of imagining the fullness of sacramental hospitality, including the picture of an ordained clergywoman distributing the feast on one side of the table and all hungry people coming forward on the other: women, men, children, the differently abled, and the poor.

Feasting images, so evocative of nourishment and comfort, are also an ambiguous image for young women struggling with eating disorders. No causal link is being claimed here between the Reformed tradition and this particular disorder. I am simply acknowledging the thick tangle of issues surrounding food for many young North American women.[44] An ecclesial tradition that rightly celebrates the banquet of God's grace at the Lord's Table must, at the very least, be aware that such language is threatening, not inviting, to those who often suffer in silence, not daring to name their awful secret. The work that must be done on behalf of girls and women in North America includes a massive shift in attitudes toward women and women's bodies. This task finds its theological support, in part, in sacramental theology, with its clear affirmation of the materiality, the bodiliness, the very stuff of life.

Tension also is felt in Reformed sacramental theology around the images of community. Community, that buzzword of contemporary church life, is a sacramental reality. The sacraments, baptism and the Lord's Supper, both presume and constitute community. Baptism brings the infant or the adult believer into the life of the community, which is the body of Christ. The Lord's Supper is a feast of the community of believers, a celebratory event that shapes, forms, and creates community. Yet, for women in the church, the community has often been characterized by repressive structures of power and authority, not shalom, acceptance, and mutual correction. The community-forming power of the sacraments can be realized more completely in the church when old, familiar habits of social limitations based on gender, race, giftedness, age, and sexual orientation are recognized and rejected. In many Christian communities, this most basic step has not yet been taken.

Even the sacramental theme of gratitude, so central in Calvin's theology, can cause tension for women. The call for justice, dignity, and respect made by women, perhaps especially black women, are sometimes countered by church leaders with the admonition to gratitude. Feminists and womanists may wonder if gratitude is evoked by those in power in order to avoid the hard work of prophetic action for justice and reconciliation. The gifts of God for the people of God are received with open hands and hearts by feminist Christian believers, along with all Christian believers. But gratitude to God can only fully flower in a community of compassion, justice, and truth telling.

One of the traditional moments in Christian worship is the call to confession. In most worship liturgies, the prayer of confession comes before the sacrament of the Lord's Supper. The classic prayer of confession in the Anglican *Book of Common Prayer* contains one of the most profound of these prayers: "We have sinned against you in thought, word, and deed. We have not loved you with our whole heart or our neighbor as ourselves. Truly, there is no health in us." However, in recent years, prayers of confession have been widely dismissed from worship services in churches across the political spectrum. Perhaps the rejection of the prayer of confession is one of the few things that progressive and conservative churches agree on! Yet feminist and womanist theologians ought to call the church back to confession. The prayer of confession disciplines the church to examine its habits, its assumptions, its practices. The prayer of confession, sometimes seen as negative self-abasement, ought to be a moment when the whole church, including the powerful and the comfortable, speak the truth to God and one another. Truly, there is no health in us.

This chapter has explored primary sacramental themes in the Reformed tradition with feminist commitments to the wholeness and health of women and communities clearly in mind. Calvin's interest in emphasizing the gifts of God in the sacraments, pointing and connecting believers with Christ for their encouragement and comfort, finds common cause with the commitments of feminists and womanists for health, wholeness, and transformation in community. However, all the familiar ambivalences that feminist theologians learn to negotiate are still present. One reason for hope for Reformed feminist theologians is the recognition that tradition is never finished, never static. The Reformed tradition, too, is always arguing, exploring, changing, stretching, and challenging received concepts and ideas. The Reformed tradition is an ongoing conversation, one which now includes feminist and womanist theology. This inclusion has not come by gracious invitation but by the persistence and passion of feminists and womanists who are convinced the church is called to more, better, and higher response to God's grace. It is this grace that the sacraments celebrate, enact, and invite all to claim.

14

SOME LAST WORDS
ABOUT ESCHATOLOGY

Amy Plantinga Pauw

Reformed eschatology has not always been modest. From the elaborate covenant dispensations of Johannes Cocceius to the vivid apocalyptic speculations of Jonathan Edwards, Reformed theologians have sometimes combined epistemological confidence with a fertile imagination in their reflections on the last things. But the authors of this volume embrace the restrained, sober strand in Reformed eschatology: a Calvinian reticence about bold eschatological claims. Eschatology is for us a posture of trust and hope, grounded in the conviction of God's faithful and transforming presence; it is not a timetable or a set of metaphysical explanations. In these last pages, we articulate the reasons for our eschatological modesty and give shape to the eschatologies that are reflected in the preceding chapters.

From womanist and feminist perspectives, eschatology presents special doctrinal dangers. Those who control the dominant theological discourse tend to attach the polarizing labels of orthodox and heterodox, faithful and unfaithful, to people as well as to doctrines. In eschatology, these theological polarizations are given eternal significance: they claim to define who belongs to God's chosen and who belongs to the eternally rejected. Eschatological doctrine thus has functioned to justify certain classes of people on the basis of their beliefs and morals and to demonize others.[1] The church has often been all too ready to set the guest list for the eschatological banquet.

Eschatological doctrine has been subject to other kinds of corruption as well. It has often been articulated in individualistic, disembodied ways that deny the goodness of communal and bodily existence. It has been a repository for an unmitigated divine wrath that seems to contradict the gospel message of God's creative and redemptive mercy. Perceptive critics of Christianity, following the grand masters Karl Marx, Sigmund Freud, and Friedrich Nietzsche, have decried the political and therapeutic misuses of eschatology: to justify earthly suffering and frustration by the promise of heavenly compensation, or to offer false comfort to those who resent human limitations and deny the reality of death. In short, eschatology has often functioned destructively, serving the interests of oppression and denial. Is it any wonder that feminist and womanist theologians have tended to accent transformation in everyday life, not the afterlife, and to be wary of grand eschatological pronouncements?

Yet we cannot abandon eschatological claims because, as womanist theologian Emilie Townes insists, "God is not through."[2] God is not through righting wrongs and healing our scarred and wounded world. God is not through satisfying our deepest longings for communion and shalom. From our Reformed perspective, Townes puts the eschatological emphasis in the right place: on God's character and agency. Eschatology is not simply a set of brave moral imperatives that human beings adopt in the hope of a better world. Eschatological convictions are grounded in God's continuing faithfulness to the creation that was declared "very good." They take their direction from the new thing God has already done in Jesus Christ. These convictions are alert to the present movements of the Spirit in both familiar and unexpected places. The fact that "God is not through" means there are still many surprises in store; but our eschatological convictions are shaped by the trust that what lies ahead will not contradict the creative, redemptive, and transformative grace already revealed by the triune God.

This trust in God's transformative grace shapes the way we understand the fear of divine judgment that has been a hallmark of Reformed eschatology. Remembering that Reformed trust in the perseverance of the saints is really trust in the persevering mercy of God, we reject the notion that in the last days we will find ourselves in the hands of a vengeful God who is utterly unlike the God we have known in Jesus Christ. We also reject eschatologies in which merciless divine wrath falls only on *other* people, to the supposed increase of the eternal joy of God's elect. We repudiate as well annihilationist fantasies, in which the created order that God declared "very good" (Gen. 1:31) is destroyed or discarded as God's redemptive drama moves on to some heavenly place. These visions of eschatological judgment mirror all too well humanity's destructive powers and violent proclivities, but they contradict our understanding of God's Word in Jesus Christ. God's love toward creatures is neither negated by the power of evil nor constrained by some general law of eschatological deserts. As Karl Barth insists, God acts "in independent self-determination directed and characterised only by [God's] own choice and love."[3] However the promise that "Christ will come again" will find fulfillment, our eschatological hope is that in Christ God will absorb the pain and hate of our world, not recreate them on a cosmic scale.[4]

Yet we do not shy away from the notion of God's judgment. Indeed, God's gracious presence with us shines a light on our sinful lives and opens us up to accept God's judgment. At its root, Kathryn Tanner notes, sin is the creaturely attempt to reject God's gifts of love and union, and to refuse to be ministers of these gifts to others. Divine punishment for sin "is the sin itself *as* punishment," namely, separation and alienation from God.[5]

With this construal, God's judgment is not unrelenting divine retaliation against those who have gotten it wrong; rather, it is intrinsic to the devastating effects of our own sin. God's judgment on us is experienced in the crises produced by our personal and communal destructiveness, whether those be interpersonal, social, or ecological. To fear God's judgment is to resist and repent of this destructiveness and to adopt a posture of openness to God's often discomforting reformation of our thoughts and actions. We hold that there is "no condemnation for those who are in Christ Jesus" (Rom. 8:1). But there is confession, repentance, and transformation.

If there is no escape from divine judgment, neither can there be any denial of the injustice and harshness of believers' actual present experience. Thus lament and resistance are valid expressions of eschatological hope. Lament bears witness to what should not be and therefore to what should be, and what will be, according to God's promises. Lament expresses our agonized awareness that this world desperately needs transformation and that we still await God's will to be done "on earth as it is in heaven." Likewise, resistance against what is not of God or of the justice of God keeps alive the hopes of God's coming reign. Even when it cannot topple regimes of domination, resistance can, in Joan Martin's words, "enable daily sabotage, subversion and protection against the internalization of dehumanization."[6] Together, lament and resistance nurture our hopes for a different world while keeping us rooted in the struggles of this one.

The glory of God is at the center of this different world for which we hope. According to the Westminster Confession, the fullness of human life is met in glorifying and enjoying God, and Christians yearn for the day when the personal and structural barriers to that perfect communion with God are removed. As Jonathan Edwards observed, divine glory and human happiness in fact coincide in God's purposes for creation.[7] When we are finally released from fear, sin, and suffering to find our true happiness in glorifying God, we will have attained "what it was the desire of divine love that we should become."[8] Until then, God's work of at-onement remains incomplete. Putting God's glory at the center of our eschatology is a hedge against our perennial idolatrous tendencies to glory in other things—including our spiritual practices, our confessional traditions, or even the church itself, as if they were the end of the ways of God. Eschatology relativizes all our systems of meaning, even religious meaning, by insisting that these will all eventually pass away, yielding to the ultimate reality of participation in God's glory.

"But about that day or hour no one knows, neither the angels in heaven, nor the Son, but only the Father" (Mark 13:32). There have always been those who claim to know much more than the Bible about this eschatological day and hour, but Reformed Christians have tended toward a healthy agnosticism at this point. John Calvin rejected the idea, common in his time, that the world was just about to end, and along with it he rejected the anxious preoccupation with "signs of the end times." His teachings on the end times were funneled through his doctrine of providence. Joining the doctrines of providence and eschatology in this way can certainly promote quietism and political docility, a willingness to accept the status quo and await patiently end-time transformation. But this combination can also nurture active hope and endurance. Providence, as Reformed theologian Joe R. Jones notes, is "a grammar of a long and meaningful middle."[9] Faithfulness in this "long and meaningful middle" requires an acceptance of physical and intellectual limits and a tolerance for lack of closure. Since it is not given to us to know "the day or the hour" of history's fulfillment, we are to plunge into the struggles and joys of this life, trusting that the world which God is at such pains to sustain and redeem is worth our best energies and efforts. This "long and meaningful middle" is where our eschatological hopes have to be lived out. The Christian task in the present, as Emilie Townes asserts, is "to take the challenge that hope gives us."[10]

For Reformed feminists and womanists, this means that last things cannot be divorced from present things. According to Kristine Culp, Christian discipleship within this kind of eschatological framework will mostly be lived out in "plain, small ways: in each choice and act that refuses to betray the trust of another, that refuses to cease from caring, that refuses to stop doing justice, that refuses to give up hope on this day."[11] We are to be diligent in our "small moves against destructiveness," while recognizing that the final victory over sin and death is a work of grace and, thus, unattainable by human effort in history. In the meantime, as Reformed ethicist Beverly Harrison insists, the church is called to "a praxis consistent with the reign of God": "we are to find ways to be, together, a living parable of hope."[12] Our lives are finally the clearest testimony to the shape of our eschatological convictions.

NOTES

INTRODUCTION

1. Katie Geneva Cannon, *Katie's Canon: Womanism and the Soul of the Black Community* (New York: Continuum, 1995), 18.

2. Adrienne Rich, "Sources," in *Your Native Land, Your Life: Poems* (New York: W. W. Norton, 1986), 5–6.

3. Judith Plaskow, *Standing Again at Sinai: Judaism from a Feminist Perspective* (San Francisco: Harper & Row, 1990), x.

4. Patriarchy is a form of social organization in which power and voice belong to men.

5. Eberhard Busch, "Reformed Strength in Its Denominational Weakness," in *Reformed Theology: Identity and Ecumenicity*, ed. Wallace Alston and Michael Welker (Grand Rapids: Wm. B. Eerdmans Publishing Co., 2003), 21.

6. John Calvin, *The Bondage and Liberation of the Will: A Defence of the Orthodox Doctrine of Human Choice against Pighius*, ed. A. N. S. Lane, trans. G. I. Davies (Grand Rapids: Baker Books, 1996), 29.

7. Rowan Williams, "Doing the Works of God," in *A Ray of Darkness: Sermons and Reflections* (Cambridge, MA: Cowley Publications, 1995), 229.

8. Plaskow, *Standing Again at Sinai*, 1.

9. The first wave of feminism was a nineteenth-century North American movement, consisting largely of middle-class white women. In the 1960s and '70s, second-wave feminism, still led largely by well-educated white women, recognized that what had been named "human" experience and taken to be human understanding has been men's experience and men's understanding of themselves, the world, and God. The third wave of feminism, beginning in the 1980s, continued reflection on feminist concerns, but with greatly increased recognition of the diversity of women's experience and the corresponding need for a diversity of women's theologies.

10. Elizabeth A. Johnson, *She Who Is: The Mystery of God in Feminist Theological Discourse* (New York: Crossroad, 1992), 116. For an example of this difference, see also the volume of essays written by Catholic women theologians *Freeing Theology: The Essentials of Theology in Feminist Perspective*, ed. Catherine Mowry LaCugna (San Francisco: Harper Collins, 1993).

CHAPTER 1

1. Haven Kimmel, *A Girl Named Zippy* (New York: Doubleday, 2001), 173–74.

2. Elizabeth Clark and Herbert Richardson, eds., *Women and Religion: The Original Sourcebook of Women in Christian Thought* (San Francisco: HarperSanFrancisco, 1996).

3. Later in the essay I discuss some of the positive uses of the fear of the Lord. At its best, the fear of the Lord is an antidote to idolatry, selfishness, and anxiety. It might be argued that when Christians lack a sufficient "fear of the Lord" they are more likely to become fearful of other people or anxious about the evils that might befall them. Fear of the Lord is a positive quality. Other types of fear may have more negative results.

4. William J. Bouwsma, *John Calvin: A Sixteenth-Century Portrait* (New York: Oxford University Press, 1988).

5. Julia Kristeva, *Strangers to Ourselves*, trans. Leon S. Roudiez (New York: Columbia University Press, 1991).

6. Luther and Calvin would have preferred to reform the Roman Catholic Church from within, and they separated from it reluctantly after being forced out. They believed that it was not beyond repair but did not hesitate to criticize it quite sharply, in hope that the church would see the light and return to the gospel.

7. See John Kromminga, *In the Mirror: An Appraisal of the Christian Reformed Church* (Hamilton, Ontario: Guardian Publishing Company, 1957), for a discussion of isolationism.

8. Jerome DeJong, "Ecumenicity and the Reformed Church," *Reformed Review* 20, no. 4 (1967): 18.

9. Howard Hageman, "To Unite or Not to Unite," *The Church Herald* (Jan. 24, 1969): 22. Norman Thomas, "Looking Toward Union," *Reformed Review* 20, no. 4 (1967): 41.

10. Scott Hoezee and Christopher Meehan, *Flourishing in the Land: A Hundred-Year History of Christian Reformed Missions in North America* (Grand Rapids: Wm. B. Eerdmans Publishing Co., 1996), 115.

11. Gerald F. DeJong, *The Dutch Reformed Church in the American Colonies* (Grand Rapids: Wm. B. Eerdmans Publishing Co., 1978), 149.

12. Christian Reformed Church, *Acts of Synod of the Christian Reformed Church* (Grand Rapids: Board of Publications of the Christian Reformed Church, 1920), 49–50. My student Roberta Thomassen found this quote while researching the life of Johanna Veenstra, the Christian Reformed missionary in Nigeria.

13. For an example of some of these tensions see Gayraud S. Wilmore, "Identity and Integration: Black Presbyterians and Their Allies in the Twentieth Century," in *The Diversity of Discipleship: The Presbyterians and Twentieth-Century Christian Witness*, ed. Milton J Coalter, John M. Mulder, and Louis B. Weeks (Louisville, KY: Westminster/John Knox Press, 1991), 187–208. Wilmore discusses the conflict in the United Presbyterian Church (U.S.A.) over financial support for Angela Davis, and notes the fear that there would be an "irreconcilable breakdown in relationships between Black and white Presbyterians" (229). He also reports a creative solution to the conflict.

14. See Jane Dempsey Douglas, *Women, Freedom and Calvin* (Philadelphia: Westminster Press, 1985); Mark Chaves, *Ordaining Women* (Cambridge, MA: Harvard University Press, 1997).

15. Wesley Harmsen, letter to the editor, *The Church Herald* (Jan. 13, 1969): 17.

16. Rollo May, *The Meaning of Anxiety* (New York: Ronald Press, 1950).

17. An interfaith conference primarily for women held in Minneapolis in October 1993. Some of the statements and rituals were sharply criticized, particularly

by some members of the Presbyterian Church (U.S.A.) and the United Methodist Church.

18. Susan Hill Lindley, *You Have Stept Out of Your Place: A History of Women and Religion in America* (Louisville, KY: Westminster John Knox Press, 1996), 1–7.

19. *Minutes of the General Synod of the Reformed Church in America*, 1968, 107.

20. Donald Sage Mackay, "The Lost Sense of God," *Christian-Intelligencer* (Feb. 1, 1905): 66–67.

21. See H. Richard Niebuhr, *Christ and Culture* (New York: Harper, 1951).

22. For an example see Cornelius Dolfin, "Fifty Reasons Why Al Smith Should NOT Be President of the United States," *Leader* (July 4 and 11, 1928): 2–3.

23. *Minutes of the General Synod of the Reformed Church in America*, 1925, 957.

24. Editorial note, "The Quiet Sabbath," *Christian-Intelligencer* (Sept. 11, 1918): 874.

25. I use "we" as a rhetorical strategy to encourage both readers and myself to think about these issues in more personal and relational ways. But who is the "we"? At times it refers to everyone in the Reformed tradition; at other times, to the centers of power and influence. The ambiguity is intentional. As a white female minister in the Reformed Church in America, there are times when I am clearly excluded from the center of power and influence. There are other occasions when I am much closer to the center and have the power to exclude other people. The capacity to exclude and diminish other people, even when we are excluded and diminished ourselves, is one of the saddest aspects of the human condition.

26. See Carol Lakey Hess, "Reclaiming Ourselves: A Spirituality for Women's Empowerment," in *Women, Gender, and Community*, ed. Jane D. Douglas and James F. Kay (Louisville, KY: Westminster John Knox Press, 1997).

27. John de Gruchy, *Liberating Reformed Theology: A South African Contribution to an Ecumenical Debate* (Grand Rapids: Wm. B. Eerdmans Publishing Co., 1991), 170.

28. De Gruchy, *Liberating Reformed Theology*, 165–69.

CHAPTER 2

1. John Calvin, *Institutes of the Christian Religion*, ed. John T. McNeill, trans. Ford Lewis Battles, LCC (Philadelphia: Westminster Press, 1960), 1.10.10.

2. In the broad structure of the *Institutes*, Calvin describes our knowledge of this wondrous God in two parts. He first discusses the knowledge that we have a God the Creator, the one who called the world into being and who continues to sustain and direct it. He then describes the knowledge we have of God the Redeemer, the one who comes to us in the midst of our sin and, through the work of Christ the mediator, offers us the gift of faith and the promise of life eternal. It is thus in book 1 of the *Institutes* that we find Calvin's doctrine of creation and in books 2 through 4, the doctrine of redemption. The knowledge of redemption is the revealed truth that, piercing through the blinding shields of our sin, allows us to know Christ and his love. In this way, sin functions as the great divide that separates creation from redemption and knowledge of God found in nature from knowledge of God found in Christ. It is a gulf that in Calvin's theology stretches wide. "The law," however, is one of the few doctrinal themes that actually appear in both his doctrine of creation and his account of redemption. Under the rubric of creation, Calvin describes for us the *natural law* in all its fullness and glory; under the rubrics of redemption, he

outlines its function as the revealer of our *covenant-law* structure. As a topic, it thus binds these two arenas of God's action together, wedding them one to the other.

3. Note here that I am dealing with law defined in a theological context, not law defined in context of secular jurisprudence.

4. Rhona Mahony, *Kidding Ourselves: Breadwinning, Babies, and Bargaining Power* (New York: Basic Books, 1995).

5. Nel Noddings, *Caring: A Feminine Approach to Ethic and Moral Education* (Berkeley: University of California Press, 1984).

6. *Global Woman*, ed. Barbara Ehrenreich and Arlie Hochschild (New York: Henry Holt, 2004).

7. See Karen Baker-Fletcher, *Sisters of Dust, Sisters of Spirit: Womanist Wordings on God and Creation* (Minneapolis: Fortress Press, 1998).

8. It may well be, conversely, that I find feminist aesthetics attractive because I am such a Calvinist!

9. Calvin, *Institutes*, 1.5.9.

10. Ibid., 1.1.3.

11. Ibid., 1.5.1–2.

12. The definition continues, "Now we shall possess a right definition of faith if we call it a firm and certain knowledge God's benevolence toward us, founded upon the truth of the freely given promise in Christ, both revealed to our minds and sealed upon our hearts through the Holy Spirit" (Calvin, *Institutes* 3.2.7).

13. Ibid., 1.5.1; 1.5.10.

14. The propositional content of doctrine needs to remain an important part of any systematic theology, just not an exhaustive one.

15. Calvin, *Institutes*, 1.5.1.

16. It is always surprising to me how often Calvin refers to our dream worlds in his theology. See, for example, his references to our dreams in *Institutes* 1.1.3.

17. For Calvin, in addition to the human/historical realm, there is the angelic realm, the community of glorified saints, and most of all the eternal life of the Godhead. It is important to note these realms in a Reformed doctrine of creation because they make it clear that God is not an item in the inventory list of the universe, in competition with creatures for power, glory, and agency.

18. This concept of creation as dwelling place is important in much Native American thought. My own Cherokee background, I believe, played a crucial role in focusing my reading of Calvin in this direction. See Linda Hogan, *Dwellings: A Spirit History of the Living World* (New York: Touchstone, 1995).

19. Luce Irigoray, *An Ethics of Sexual Difference*, trans. Carolyn Burke and Gillian Gill (Ithaca, NY: Cornell University Press, 1993); *Speculum of the Other Woman*, trans. Gillian C. Gill (Ithaca, NY: Cornell University Press, 1985); and "Divine Women," in *Sexes and Genealogies*, trans. Gillian Gill (New York: Columbia University Press, 1993).

20. Grace Jantzen, *God's World, God's Body* (Philadelphia: Westminster Press, 1984).

21. John Calvin, *Commentary on the Book of the Prophet Isaiah*, trans. William Pringle (Grand Rapids: Wm. B. Eerdmans, 1948), vol. 4, 30.

22. Commentary on Isaiah; Calvin, *Institutes* 1.3.1.

23. For an alternative view, see Sallie McFague, *The Body of God: An Ecological Theology* (Minneapolis: Fortress Press, 1993).

24. Kristeva, Julia, *The Powers of Horror: An Essay on Abjection*, trans. Leon Roudiez (New York: Columbia University Press, 1982); Jacques Lacan, *Ecrits: A Selection*, trans. Bruce Fink (New York: W. W. Norton, 2002).

25. I appreciate Calvin's insistence that creation includes not only "nature"—the natural world as well as the natural features of the human self—but also the activities of human production and culture—the realities that we construct as social beings. From a feminist perspective, these are very important claims. When Christians engage in debates about issues like gender, sexuality, race, or the family, it is not unusual for folks to try settling arguments by insisting that we should just accept "the way God made us," "the true, natural order of things," or "the God-given way." A Reformed doctrine of creation is wonderfully open-ended and permissive with respect to imagining the relations among nature, cultural change, and creativity. Nature and culture are both included in the sphere of God's divine action.

26. Calvin, *Institutes*, 1.16.3.

27. For a powerful discussion of the complexity of using fertile womb metaphors in theology, see Nadine France, ed., *Hope Deferred* (Cleveland: Pilgrim Press, 2005).

28. See Kalbryn McLean's essay on divine providence in this volume.

29. I have been helped enormously in expanding my understanding of Calvin's sense of the law through the work of Fatima Mernissi, *Dreams of Trespass: Tales of a Harlem Girlhood* (New York: Perseus Books, 1994), in which she develops an Islamic feminist account of the role that lines and walls play in the construction of place and personhood.

30. Kristeva, *Powers*, and Lacan, *Ecrits*.

31. Calvin, *Institutes* 1.7.1.

32. Ibid., 1.8.1–2.

33. Ibid., 2.7.4; 2.7.12.

34. Ibid., 2.7.5.

35. The Reformed tradition's discussion of justice is much more complex and nuanced than this brief note implies. See John Rawls, *A Theory of Justice* (Cambridge, MA: Belknap Press of Harvard University Press, 1971); Iris Mario Young, *Justice and the Politics of Difference* (Princeton, NJ: Princeton University Press, 1990).

36. "Now from the grace offered the Jews, we can surely deduce that the law was not devoid of reference to Christ. For Moses proposed to them as the purpose of adoption, that they should be a priestly kingdom unto God" (Calvin, *Institutes* 2.7.1).

37. Ibid., 2.7.3.

38. Ibid., 2.7.6.

39. Ibid., 2.7.8.

40. Ibid., 2.7.10.

41. Ibid.

42. Ibid., 2.7.12.

43. Ibid., 2.7.14.

CHAPTER 3

1. Not only is this clear in the famous opening line of the 1559 *Institutes of the Christian Religion* ("Nearly all the wisdom we possess, that is to say, true and sound wisdom, consists of two parts: the knowledge of God and of ourselves"), but also in the opening questions of the Genevan Catechism of 1542 ("The minister: What is the principal purpose of human life? The child: It is to know God. . . . The minister: And

what is humanity's sovereign good? The child: The very same thing"). See John Calvin, *Institutes of the Christian Religion*, ed. John T. McNeill, trans. Ford Lewis Battles, LCC (Philadelphia: Westminster Press, 1960), 1.1.1. Also see Wilhelm Niesel, ed., *Bekenntnisschriften und Kirchenordnungen der nach Gottes Wort reformierten Kirche* (Zürich: Evangelischer Verlag A. G. Zollikon, 1938), 3, hereafter abbreviated as Niesel, *Bekenntnisschriften*. Niesel translations are mine; for an English translation, see Jaroslav Pelikan and Valerie Hotchkiss, eds., *Creeds & Confessions of Faith in the Christian Tradition*, 3 vols. (New Haven, CT: Yale University Press, 2003), vol. 2, 320, hereafter abbreviated as CC and cited by volume and page number.

2. See Calvin's argument on this point in *Institutes* 1.1–6. Cf. the Westminster Confession of Faith, chapter 1 (*Die Bekenntnisschriften der reformierten Kirche*, ed. E. F. Karl Müller [Leipzig: A. Deichert'sche Verlagsbuchhandlung (Georg Böhme), 1903], 542–43; hereafter abbreviated as Müller, *Bekenntnisschriften*).

3. Niesel, *Bekenntnisschriften*, 42–64. Niesel gives the 1561 version of the Ecclesiastical Ordinances, which contains several amendments and additions to the original 1541 edition.

4. Müller, *Bekenntnisschriften*, 30; CC, vol. 2, 217.

5. Niesel, *Bekenntnisschriften*, 104–5; CC, vol. 2, 399.

6. Müller, *Bekenntnisschriften*, 172; CC, vol. 2, 462.

7. Müller, *Bekenntnisschriften*, 609.

8. Calvin, *Institutes* 4.8.4.

9. Jan Rohls, *Reformed Confessions: Theology from Zurich to Barmen*, trans. John Hoffmeyer (Louisville, KY: Westminster John Knox Press, 1997), 45.

10. See Anthony N. S. Lane, "*Sola Scriptura*? Making Sense of a Post-Reformation Slogan," in *A Pathway in to the Holy Scripture*, ed. Philip E. Satterthwaite and David F. Wright (Grand Rapids: Wm. B. Eerdmans Publishing Co., 1994), 297–327.

11. See Albrecht Ritschl, "Ueber die beiden Principien des Protestantismus: Antwort auf eine 25 Jahre alte Frage," in *Gesammelte Aufsätze* (Freiburg and Leipzig: Akademische Verlagsbuchhandlung von J. C. B. Mohr, 1893), 234–47.

12. Karl Barth, *The Theology of the Reformed Confessions*, trans. Darrell L. Guder and Judith J. Guder (Louisville, KY: Westminster John Knox Press, 2002), 35, 41. Cf. Karl Barth, "Reformierte Lehre, ihr Wesen und ihre Aufgabe," in Karl Barth, *Vorträge und kleinere Arbeiten, 1922–1925*, ed. Holger Finze (Zürich: Theologischer Verlag Zürich, 1990), 227–28. The Lutheran view of the "article on which the church stands or falls" can be traced to the *Smalcald Articles* (1537), part 2, article 1 (*Die Bekenntnisschriften der evangelisch-lutherischen Kirche*, 10th ed. (Göttingen: Vandenhoeck & Ruprecht, 1986), 415–16. See Paul Althaus, *Die Theologie Martin Luthers* (Gütersloh: Gütersloher Verlagshaus Gerd Mohn, 1962), 195.

13. Müller, *Bekenntnisschriften*, 2–6; CC, vol. 2, 209–14.

14. Müller, *Bekenntnisschriften*, 101; CC, vol. 2, 282.

15. See, for example, Gallican Confession (1559), article 3 (Müller, *Bekenntnischriften*, 222; CC, vol. 2, 375); Belgic Confession (1561), Article IV (Müller, *Bekenntnisschriften*, 233; CC, vol. 2, 407–8); Westminster Confession (1647), chap. 1 (Müller *Bekenntnisschriften*, 543).

16. The Belgic Confession (1561), names God as the author "with his own finger" of the two tables of the law. The Bohemian Confession (1609) takes God to be the ultimate author of Scripture, who, through the Spirit's inspiration, causes the prophets and apostles to dictate and promulgate God's words, and who also guarantees that they are faithful amanuenses (Müller, *Bekenntnisschriften*, 233, 453, 546,

862–63; *CC*, vol. 2, 407, 607). For a theological defense of the doctrine of plenary inspiration by a Swiss theologian that is consistent with the Helvetic Consensus Formula, see L. Gaussen, *The Inspiration of the Holy Scriptures* (Chicago: Moody Press, 1949); first published in French as *Theopneustie* in 1840).

17. Müller, *Bekenntnisschriften*, 30; *CC*, vol. 2, 217.

18. The Westminster Confession makes these points in chap. 1, pars. 4–5 (Müller, *Bekenntnisschriften*, 544–45).

19. Westminster Confession, chap. 1, par. 7 (Müller, *Bekenntnisschriften*, 545–46). For a somewhat different account of the rise of the Protestant Orthodox view of Scripture, see Sarah Heaner Lancaster, *Women and the Authority of Scripture: A Narrative Approach* (Harrisburg, PA: Trinity Press International, 2002), 43–63.

20. Calvin, *Institutes* 1.1–6.

21. Ibid., 1.7.4–5; 1.8.13; 1.9.3.

22. Ibid., 4.9.13.

23. Ibid., 1.7.1; John Calvin, *Sermons on the Epistle to the Ephesians*, rev. trans. Arthur Golding (London, 1577; rpt., Edinburgh: Banner of Truth Trust, 1973), 423–24.

24. See B. A. Gerrish, "The Word of God and the Words of Scripture: Luther and Calvin on Biblical Authority," in *The Old Protestantism and the New: Essays on the Reformation Heritage* (Chicago: University of Chicago Press, 1982), 51–68.

25. See Dawn DeVries, *Jesus Christ in the Preaching of Calvin and Schleiermacher* (Louisville, KY: Westminster John Knox Press, 1996), 14–25. The explicit statement "preaching the Word of God is the Word of God" is made in the Second Helvetic Confession (Müller, *Bekenntnisschriften*, 171; *CC*, vol. 2, 460).

26. Barth's well-known doctrine of the "three-fold form of the Word of God" can be found in Karl Barth, *Church Dogmatics* (Edinburgh: T. & T. Clark, 1958), I/1. (Hereafter cited as *CD*.) Emil Brunner argues for a distinction between revelation as the Word of God and Scripture as the norm of Christian doctrine in his *Dogmatics*, vol. 1: *The Christian Doctrine of God*, trans. Olive Wyon (London: Lutterworth Press, 1949), 22–34, 43–49. Both theologians claimed to be retrieving a position closer to that of the sixteenth-century evangelicals, and both blamed Reformed scholasticism for developing the doctrine of Scripture in unhelpful ways. There were many critiques of Barth's and Brunner's revisions of the doctrine of the Word of God. See, e.g., Louis Berkhof, *Systematic Theology*, new edition containing the full text of *Systematic Theology* and the original *Introductory Volume to Systematic Theology* (first published 1932 and 1938; repr., Grand Rapids: Wm. B. Eerdmans Publishing Co., 1996), 137–39, 146, 166; *The Infallible Word: A Symposium by the Members of the Faculty of Westminster Theological Seminary* (London: Tyndale Press, 1946), 42–43, 100, 204–5, 221–25, 229–31.

27. See, for example, Wayne A. Meeks, "The 'Haustafeln' and American Slavery: A Hermeneutical Challenge," in *Theology and Ethics in Paul and His Interpreters*, ed. Eugene H. Lovering Jr. and Jerry L. Sumney (Nashville: Abingdon Press, 1996), 232–53.

28. See the discussion of similarities and differences between the Protestant Orthodox understanding of Scripture and that of feminist theologians in Lancaster, *Women and the Authority of Scripture*, 58–60.

29. Lancaster draws out a different side of Schüssler-Fiorenza's understanding of the canon in relation to the community of interpretation that in fact argues against a canon within the canon (*Women and the Authority of Scripture*, 22–26).

30. The phrase in quotation marks is taken from the Westminster Confession of Faith, chap. 2 (Müller, *Bekenntnisschriften*, 547). See the discussion in Sandra M. Schneiders, "The Bible and Feminism: Biblical Theology," in *Freeing Theology: The Essentials of Theology in a Feminist Perspective*, ed. Catherine Mowry LaCugna (San Francisco: HarperSanFrancisco, 1993), 31–57, esp. 38–39. There are theologians who argue for the nonmetaphorical character of divine speech. For an example of a rather sophisticated philosophical argument for the literal reality of divine speech, see Nicholas Wolterstorff, *Divine Discourse: Philosophical Reflections on the Claim That God Speaks* (Cambridge: Cambridge University Press, 1995). Wolterstorff employs the speech-action theory of J. L. Austin, particularly the concept of "illocutionary" speech acts, to claim that God could make use of the "locutionary" acts of others—especially the human authors of Scripture—to command, promise, ask, assert, etc.

31. Calvin, *Institutes* 1.13.1; 1.14.3; 1.17.13.

32. John Hick, *The Metaphor of God Incarnate: Christology in a Pluralistic Age* (Louisville, KY: Westminster/John Knox Press, 1993), 105.

33. See the excellent discussion of metaphor in Lancaster, *Women and the Authority of Scripture*, 67–74.

34. Calvin, *Institutes* 1.5.5; Friedrich Schleiermacher, *The Christian Faith*, trans. of the 2nd German ed. by H. R. Mackintosh and J. S. Stewart (1928; reprint ed., Philadelphia: Fortress Press, 1976), 735–37.

35. Barth, *CD* I/1:88–120.

36. Barth, *CD* I/1:111–120.

37. Barth, *CD* I/1:55.

38. Barth writes, "Scripture imposes itself in virtue of . . . [its] content. . . . When the Church heard this word—and it heard it only in the prophets and apostles and nowhere else—it heard a magisterial and ultimate word which it could not ever again confuse or place on a level with any other word" (*CD* I/1:108).

39. For example, the whole discussion of the relationship between man and woman in the doctrine of creation is derived from an understanding of key passages in Scripture—the second creation narrative of Gen. 2–3 and numerous places in the Pauline and deuteropauline epistles, among many others. The relationship between these passages as historical witnesses to revelation and the divine command that authorizes ethical norms is not always clear, nor are the grounds on which some passages are given greater weight than others in determining the constructive position Barth develops here. See *CD* III/4:116–240.

40. Of course, this is not to deny that God's Word to the prophet Isaiah, for example, is in fact written down. The point, rather, is that the association of the Word with written words surely invites the misunderstanding that the biblical words themselves constitute the event of the Word of God.

41. The idea that the Word of God is essentially an *event* was important to several twentieth-century theologians, including Karl Barth and Rudolf Bultmann. However, it is probably Gerhard Ebeling who did the most to clarify the meaning of this idea. See Gerhard Ebeling, *The Word of God and Tradition: Historical Studies Interpreting the Divisions of Christianity*, trans. S. H. Hooke (Philadelphia: Fortress Press, 1964), 137, 144, 229–32; Gerhard Ebeling, *Word and Faith*, trans. James W. Leitsch (Philadelphia: Fortress Press, 1963), 305–32, 424–33.

42. There are a number of theologians who also argue for the instrumentality of Scripture as a vehicle of God's self-revelation. See Kathryn Tanner, "Scripture as

Popular Text," *Modern Theology* 14 (1998): 279–98; Sandra M. Schneiders, *The Revelatory Text: Interpreting the New Testament as Sacred Scripture* (San Francisco: HarperSanFrancisco, 1991); Lancaster, *Women and the Authority of Scripture*, 135–36.

43. The now classic discussion of this subject is David H. Kelsey, *The Uses of Scripture in Recent Theology* (Philadelphia: Fortress Press, 1975).

44. John Webster considers but finally rejects the understanding of Scripture that I am arguing for here. He maintains that the problem with all "theologies of mediation" is that they tend to see God as "inert" or "absent" until made present by the mediating means of grace (*Holy Scripture: A Dogmatic Sketch* [Cambridge: Cambridge University Press, 2003], 24–25). If one understands the means of grace as John Calvin does, as an instrument by which *God* performs what is to be performed on the one receiving the means of grace, then there can be no question of an "inert" or "absent" God. In fact, it is precisely the two views that Calvin rejects that would make God inert or absent. In the Roman Catholic view (transubstantiation), the words of consecration abolish the actual distinction between grace and its means (the sacramental elements), and thus God's gracious gift seems to be at the disposal of the priests who can speak the words of consecration. God seems strangely inactive in this view. On the other hand, insofar as Huldreich Zwingli completely separated God's grace from the means of grace, there was no guarantee for him of the divine presence in sacramental actions. Hence, for him there seems to be an absent God. The instrumental view of the sacrament as God's tool for communicating grace avoids these extremes. See Calvin's discussion of the sacraments in *Institutes* 4.14; 4.17–18.

45. A prime example of such a use can be found in Louis Berkhof's *Systematic Theology*. What some might call "proof-texting," Berkhof would see as a justifiable theological use of Scripture since God is ultimately the author of everything within it.

46. Minutes of the General Assembly, 1832, 348, cited in *Presbyterians Today* (March 2005), 14.

47. Calvin explicitly denies that the *Logos* was fully contained within the human flesh of Jesus of Nazareth. See *Institutes* 2.13.4

48. For an example of the Lutheran approach, see the Formula of Concord, part 2, article 5 (*The Book of Concord: The Confessions of the Evangelical Lutheran Church*, trans. and ed. Theodore G. Tappert [Philadelphia: Fortress Press, 1959], 558–63. Perhaps the best example of the nineteenth-century appeal to the historical Jesus can be found in the theology of Albrecht Ritschl, who argues for the theological centrality of the concept of the kingdom of God precisely because this can be grounded in the teaching of Jesus himself. See *The Christian Doctrine of Justification and Reconciliation*, trans. H. R. Mackintosh and A.B. Macaulay (Clifton, NJ: Reference Book Publishers, 1966), 8–13. However, Ritschl was following what he took to be a promising lead in the theology of Friedrich Schleiermacher. See *The Christian Faith*, 125. A more recent liberal theologian who appeals to the "earliest apostolic witness" as the authorizing norm of Christian doctrine is Schubert M. Odgen. See "The Authority of Scripture for Doctrine," in *On Theology* (San Francisco: Harper & Row, 1986), 45–68. On Rosemary Radford Ruether's understanding of the normative use of Scripture, see her *Sexism and God-Talk* (Boston: Beacon Press, 1983), 22–33.

49. Cf. the discussion in Lancaster, *Women and the Authority of Scripture*, 130–36.

CHAPTER 4

1. An earlier version of this chapter was presented at the 2003 convocation of Austin Presbyterian Theological Seminary. Special thanks to my colleagues at Austin Seminary for the suggestions they made in a seminar discussion following the address.

2. Reference to Isa. 40:12. All biblical citations are taken from the New Revised Standard Version.

3. Daphne Hampson, *After Christianity* (Valley Forge, PA: Trinity Press International, 1996), 15.

4. See Matt. 6:9.

5. John 14:16–17.

6. Rom. 8:26–27.

7. John 14:26.

8. "Docetism" is the heresy that argues that the Christ who was fully divine was not fully human.

9. See, for example, Catherine Mowry LaCugna, *God for Us: The Trinity & Christian Life* (HarperSanFrancisco, 1991), and "God in Communion with Us," in *Freeing Theology: The Essentials of Theology in Feminist Perspective*, ed. Catherine Mowry LaCugna (San Francisco: Harper Collins, 1993), 83–114.

10. Hampson, *After Christianity*, 255. To see a photograph of one of these buckles, go to http://www.nobeliefs.com/nazis.htm.

11. See, for example, "Bush Puts God on His Side," by Tom Carver (*BBC World Edition*, Sunday, 6 April 2003); "God on Our Side? What Does Bush's Religious Talk Mean?" by William Saletan (*Slate*, February 1, 2003, *http://slate.msn.com/id/2078011*); and "With God on Our Side" (advertisement http://www.frif.com/new2004/with.html).

12. "Brief Statement of Faith," *Book of Confessions* (Louisville, KY: Office of the General Assembly, Presbyterian Church (U.S.A.), 1991), 10.1.

13. For example, Shirley Guthrie revisits the doctrine of the Trinity in developing an argument for how we are "Reformed by Faith" in *Always Being Reformed: Faith for a Fragmented World* (Louisville, KY: Westminster John Knox Press, 1996), ch. 3.

14. Thus, one of the major christological debates of the fourth century pivoted around the question of whether Mary was *theotokos* (God-bearer) or *christotokos* (Christ-bearer). Chalcedon affirmed the *theotokos*.

15. See *The Christological Controversy*, ed. Richard Norris and William Rusch (Minneapolis: Fortress Press, 1980).

16. Gregory of Nazianzus, "To Cledonius Against Apollinaris" (Epistle 101), in *Christology of the Later Fathers. Library of Christian Classics*, vol. 3, ed. Edward R. Hardy (Philadelphia: Westminster Press, 1954), 218.

17. John 1:14.

18. As Paul puts it in his letter to the Colossians, "[O]ur lives are hidden with Christ in God" (3:3).

19. For example, Hampson, *After Christianity*, 14–19, and Friedrich Schleiermacher, *The Christian Faith* (Edinburgh: T. & T. Clark, 1986), 391–413.

20. Daniel L. Migliore, *Faith Seeking Understanding* (Grand Rapids: Wm. M. Eerdmans Publishing Co., 1991), 64.

21. In other words, God benefits from relationship to us not because God is subject to some external metaphysical principle that dictates that to be more related is

"better" than being less related. Rather, God benefits because God has chosen to be God in this way. As Karl Barth puts it, "[a]lready in the eternal will and decree of God [God] was not to be, nor did [God] will to be, God only, but Emmanuel, God with [humanity]. . . . And in the act of God in time which corresponds to this eternal decree . . . [God] ceased to all eternity to be God only, receiving and having and maintaining to all eternity human essence as well." (*Church Dogmatics* IV/2 [Edinburgh: T. & T. Clark, 1958], 100). (Hereafter cited as *CD*.)

22. See Ps. 139:16.

23. See Heb. 7:23–25.

24. See Rom. 8:26.

25. This is not to suggest that God's essence is exhausted by God's existence, but that God's existence always reveals something of who God really is. This is in contrast to we human creatures, whose acts are not always consistent with our being. Unlike God, we are not free. [For more on this understanding of freedom, see Rigby, "Free to Be Human: Limits, Possibilities, and the Sovereignty of God," *Theology Today* 53, no. 1 (April 1996): 47–62.]

26. I think, in this regard, of the so-called parable of the Prodigal Son in Luke 15. In this parable, the elder son does not seem to understand that the father's generous acts are not only things the father does, but who the father really is. When the elder son asks why the father has not given him his due, the father is uncomprehending. "Son, you are always with me, and all that is mine is yours," he replies, yearning for his son to participate in life with him.

27. Gregory of Nazianzus, Gregory of Nyssa, Basil the Great, and Macrina (sister and teacher of Basil and Gregory).

28. LaCugna, *God for Us*, 93.

29. Ibid., 92.

30. See, for example, Ellen T. Charry, "Dwelling in the Dignity of God: Augustine of Hippo," in *By the Renewing of Your Minds: The Pastoral Function of Christian Doctrine* (New York: Oxford University Press, 1997), ch. 6, esp. 123–25. According to Charry, LaCugna (along with Rahner, Jenson, and Gunton) does not "understand . . . [that] . . . Augustine's soteriology was patristic, not medieval . . . ontological, not functional." The implication of this, Charry explains, is that LaCugna reads Augustine by way of the contemporary "liberal" emphasis on "the realm of action" rather than appreciating him on his own terms.

31. For more on this, see Kathryn Tanner, *Jesus, Humanity, and the Trinity: A Brief Systematic Theology* (Minneapolis: Fortress Press, 2001).

32. This last quotation is something I imagine God might have said to Moses, based on my reading of the story.

33. See *The Wizard of Oz*, script by Noel Langley, Florence Ryerson, and Edgar Allen Woolf (Metro-Goldwyn-Meyer, 1939).

34. See Barth, *CD* II/1, passim.

35. See LaCugna, *God for Us*, passim, my emphasis.

36. See Mark 8:27–33.

37. The rejection of the scandal is seen, along these lines, in the expectation of some Christian believers that Christ's Second Coming will be marked by him showing his "true colors"—not wearing swaddling clothes, not crying out on the cross, but (strongly, ably, powerfully, superhumanly) straightening out the world.

38. See Paul Tillich, "The Escape from God," in *The Shaking of the Foundations* (New York: Charles Scribner, 1976), 38–51.

39. See Ps. 139:7–10.

40. See Tillich, "You Are Accepted," in *The Shaking of the Foundations*, 153–63.

41. For more on Kierkegaard's complex and multifaceted understanding of the categories of offense in relation to the incarnation, see his *Practice in Christianity*, ed. Hong and Hong (Princeton, NJ: Princeton University Press, 1991).

42. I am thinking generally for forty-five years of feminist and womanist scholarship on the subject from Valerie Saiving's work in the 1960s (e.g., "The Human Situation: A Feminine View," in *Womanspirit Rising: A Feminist Reader in Religion*, ed. Carol Christ and Judith Plaskow [New York: Harper and Row], 25–42), to Judith Plaskow's in the 1980s (e.g., *Sex, Sin, and Grace: Women's Experience and the Theologies of Reinhold Niebuhr and Paul Tillich* [Lanham: University Press of America, 1980]), to current work by Jacqueline Grant (e.g., "The Sin of Servanthood, in *A Troubling in My Soul: Womanist Perspectives on Evil and Suffering*, ed. Emilie Townes [New York: Maryknoll, 1993], 199–218), Delores Williams (e.g., "A Womanist Perspective on Sin," *A Troubling in My Soul*, 130–149), and Serene Jones (e.g., *Feminist Theory and Christian Theology: Cartographies of Grace* [Minneapolis: Fortress Press, 2000]).

43. Jones, *Feminist Theory*, 52.

44. For more on this, see my "Mary and the Artistry of God," in *Blessed One: Protestant Perspectives on Mary* (Louisville, KY: Westminster John Knox Press, 2003).

45. Williams, "A Womanist Perspective on Sin," 143.

46. See Rosemary Radford Ruether, *Sexism and God-talk* (Boston: Beacon Press, 1993), ch. 5.

47. From the "Vatican Declaration on the Question of the Admission of Women to the Ministry," section 27 (1976). As cited by Ruether, *Sexism and God-Talk*, 126.

48. Francis Martin, *The Feminist Question: Feminist Theology in Light of Christian Tradition* (Grand Rapids: Wm. B. Eerdmans Publishing Co., 1994), 394, 390.

49. Lest we Protestants become too smug about understanding the maleness of Christ as a particularity rather than a universal, we need be reminded that the majority of Protestant churches and denominations in the world today still do not ordain women. Those that ordain have begun to do so only recently, but this does not mean that clergy women are always getting good jobs or being received as equals in the circle of male colleagues. Discrimination against female ministers in Protestant denominations has, ostensibly, been for hermeneutical reasons rather than because women do not "bear physical resemblance" to Christ. But, on some level, consideration of maleness as "normative," and Christ's maleness as buttressing this norm, has certainly come into play.

50. Daphne Hampson's term, as referenced in Eleanor McLaughlin, "Christology in Dialogue with Feminist Ideology—Bodies and Boundaries," in *Christology in Dialogue*, ed. Robert Berkey and Sarah Edwards (Cleveland: Pilgrim Press, 1993), 308–39, 311.

51. Mary Daly, *Beyond God the Father: Toward a Philosophy of Women's Liberation* (Boston: Beacon Press, 1973), 19.

52. John Calvin, *Institutes of the Christian Religion*, ed. John T. McNeill, trans. Ford Lewis Battles, LCC (Philadelphia: Westminster Press, 1960), 1.17.12.

53. Ibid., 1.17.12–13 and 2.16.2.

54. Ibid., 1.17.13.

55. Interestingly, this is not a problem that pervades Calvin's theology. His doctrine of divine providence, for example, eloquently testifies to God's radically

creative presence in the world (*Institutes* 1.16). "And truly God claims . . . omnipotence—not the empty, idle, and almost unconscious sort that the Sophists imagine, but a watchful, effective, active sort, engaged in ceaseless activity" (*Institutes* 1.16.3).

56. See Rita Nakashima Brock, *Journeys by Heart: A Christology of Erotic Power* (New York: Crossroad, 1991) and Sharon Welch, *A Feminist Ethic of Risk* (Minneapolis: Fortress Press, 1990).

57. Alvin F. Kimel Jr., ed., *Speaking the Christian God: The Holy Trinity and the Challenge of Feminism* (Grand Rapids: Wm. B. Eerdmans Publishing Co., 1992).

58. Alvin Kimel, "The God Who Likes His Name: Holy Trinity, Feminism, and the Language of Faith," in *Speaking the Christian God*, 188–208.

59. Migliore, *Faith Seeking Understanding*, 140.

60. Tanner, *Jesus, Humanity, and the Trinity*, xiii.

61. Annie Dillard, *Pilgrim at Tinker Creek* (New York: Harper's Magazine Press, 1974), 80.

62. Calvin, *Institutes* 1.13.1.

63. John Calvin, *The Gospel According to St. John, 11–21*, in Calvin's New Testament Commentaries, ed. David Torrance and Thomas Torrance (Grand Rapids: Wm. B. Eerdmans Publishing Co., 1959), 202.

64. John Calvin, "The Gospel According to St. John, 11–21," 202.

65. John Calvin, *Commentary on Isaiah 46:3* (Baker Book House, 1984). I am indebted to Amy Plantinga Pauw, who directed me to this citation and discussed with me its implications.

66. From "One of Us?" by Eric Bazilian, sung by Joan Osborne. Lyrics found at http://members.aol.com/drldeboer2/htm/oou.htm.

67. See Ruether, *Sexism and God-Talk*, 1–11.

68. "Kyriarchy" is a word used by Elizabeth Schüssler Fiorenza in *Jesus: Miriam's Son, Sophia's Prophet* (New York: Continuum, 1994). She suggests that "kyriarchy" might be a more helpful way of referencing systemic inequality than "patriarchy" because it reminds us that women (as well as men) abuse power and men (as well as women) are oppressed. It is important to note, however, that Schüssler Fiorenza does not believe everyone is an equal offender in the kyriarchal system. She writes, "Feminist movements and theologies must seek to overcome the oppression of all persons exploited by kyriarchy, women *and* men, but they nevertheless must focus their efforts especially on the liberation of women who live on the bottom of the pyramid of multiplicative oppressions" (*Jesus*, 48).

69. Luke 1:53.

70. Barth, *CD* IV/2:270.

71. One theologian who takes such an approach to the matter of female imaging of God is Elizabeth A. Johnson, in *She Who Is: The Mystery of God in Feminist Theological Discourse* (New York: Crossroad, 1992).

72. Phil. 2:12.

73. See John 15:15.

74. See Phil. 2.

75. See John 21.

76. Specifically, Grant says that, in the context of slavery, "Black women's affirmation of Jesus as God meant that White people were not God" [Jacqueline Grant, *White Women's Christ, Black Women's Jesus* (Atlanta: Scholars Press, 1989), 213].

CHAPTER 5

1. Donald K. McKim, "Predestination," in *Westminster Dictionary of Theological Terms*, ed. Donald K. McKim (Louisville, KY: Westminster John Knox Press, 1996), 217.

2. Ibid.

3. Dewey D. Wallace Jr., "Predestination," in *Encyclopedia of the Reformed Faith*, ed. Donald K. McKim (Louisville, KY: Westminster/John Knox Press, 1992), 291.

4. Pierre Maury, *Predestination and Other Papers* (Richmond, VA: John Knox Press, 1960), 19.

5. For contemporary Reformed confessions, see Lukas Vischer, ed., *Reformed Witness Today: A Collection of Confessions and Statements of Faith Issued by Reformed Churches* (Bern: Evangelische Arbeitsstelle Oekumene Schweiz, 1982).

6. See chap. 9.

7. Rosemary Radford Ruether, *Sexism and God-Talk: Towards a Feminist Theology* (Boston: Beacon Press, 1993), 235–36.

8. See, for example, the volume *Liberating Eschatology: Essays in Honor of Letty M. Russell*, ed. Margaret A. Farley and Serene Jones (Louisville, KY: Westminster John Knox Press, 1999).

9. Cf. Maura A. Ryan, "Agency," in *Dictionary of Feminist Theologies*, ed. Letty M. Russell and J. Shannon Clarkson (Louisville, KY: Westminster John Knox Press, 1996), 4–5.

10. Ibid., 5.

11. Kathryn Tanner, *The Politics of God: Christian Theologies and Social Justice* (Minneapolis: Fortress Press, 1992), 23.

12. Max Weber, quoted in Karl Barth, *Church Dogmatics* II/2 (Edinburgh: T. & T. Clark, 1958), 13. (Hereafter cited as *CD*.)

13. Letty M. Russell and Lee Palmer Wandel, "Predestination," in *Dictionary of Feminist Theologies*, 226.

14. Letty Russell, *Church in the Round: Feminist Interpretation of the Church* (Louisville, KY: Westminster/John Knox Press, 1993), 170.

15. Judith Plaskow, *Standing Again at Sinai: Judaism from a Feminist Perspective* (San Francisco: Harper & Row, 1990), 97.

16. Ibid., 118.

17. John Calvin, *Institutes of the Christian Religion*, ed. John T. McNeill, trans. Ford Lewis Battles, LCC (Philadelphia: Westminster Press, 1960), 3.23.7. The Latin reads, "Decretum quidem horribile, fateor." It is important to note, though, that Calvin used this term in order to describe the doctrine of reprobation, not election.

18. John H. Leith, *Introduction to the Reformed Tradition: A Way of Being the Christian Community* (Atlanta: John Knox Press, 1981), 103.

19. Otto Weber, *Foundations of Dogmatics*, vol. 2 (Grand Rapids: Wm. B. Eerdmans Publishing Co., 1983), 416.

20. Russell, *Church in the Round*, 169.

21. See Weber, *Foundations of Dogmatics*, 414–15, for a discussion of Augustine's precursors in the debate about predestination and election.

22. Augustine, "The Trinity," in *The Works of Saint Augustine: A Translation for the Twenty-first Century*, vol. I/5, ed. John E. Rotelle, trans. Edmund Hill (Brooklyn: New City Press, 1991), 153. Here and in the following I quote the authors without changing their exclusive language for God and human beings into inclusive lan-

guage. Note, though, that very often the inclusive Latin and German term for "human being" is translated into "man" in English.

23. According to a pilot study conducted by the British theologian Julie Hopkins with Dutch women ministers, feelings of guilt and unworthiness are a particular problem of women in ministry, and this can, and very often does, lead to not only professional but also existential and theological crises. See Hopkins, *Towards a Feminist Christology: Jesus of Nazareth, European Women and the Christological Crisis* (Grand Rapids: Wm. B. Eerdmans Publishing Co., 1994), 14–21.

24. Angela West, *Deadly Innocence: Feminism and the Mythology of Sin* (London: Cassell, 1995), 144.

25. Ibid., 132.

26. Augustine, "The Grace of Christ and Original Sin," in *The Works of Saint Augustine: A Translation for the Twenty-first Century,* vol. I/23, ed. John E. Rotelle, trans. Roland J. Teske (Hyde Park: New City Press, 1997), 410.

27. Augustine, "On Rebuke and Grace," in *Nicene and Post-Nicene Fathers of the Christian Church,* vol. 5, *Saint Augustine: Anti-Pelagian Writings,* ed. Philip Schaff (Grand Rapids: Wm. B. Eerdmans Publishing Co., 1956), 477.

28. Augustine, "On Rebuke and Grace," 490.

29. H. Barnikol, quoted in John T. McNeill's introduction to Calvin, *Institutes,* lviii, footnote 59.

30. Richard Muller, *Christ and the Decree: Christology and Predestination in Reformed Theology from Calvin to Perkins* (Durham, NC: Labyrinth Press, 1986), 22.

31. Cf. Wilhelm Niesel, *The Theology of Calvin* (Philadelphia: Westminster Press, 1956), 159.

32. Weber, *Foundations of Dogmatics,* 424.

33. Calvin, *Concerning the Eternal Predestination of God,* trans. J. K. S. Reid (Louisville, KY: Westminster John Knox Press, 1997), 113, 127.

34. Calvin, *Institutes* 3.22.10.

35. Calvin, *Institutes* 3.24.4–5.

36. Calvin, *Institutes* 3.22.1.

37. Russell, *Church in the Round,* 170.

38. Cf. Karl Barth, *CD* II/2:18.

39. Calvin, *Institutes* 3.21.5.

40. Weber, *Foundations of Dogmatics,* 426.

41. For a discussion of the doctrine of predestination in Reformed theology after Calvin, see Muller's extensive study *Christ and the Decree.*

42. Barth, *CD* II/2:3, 14.

43. Barth, *CD* II/2:10.

44. See, for example, Karl Barth, *CD* II/1:641: "[A]t the core of His being, and therefore in His glory, God is the One who seeks and finds fellowship. . . . He is in Himself, and therefore to everything outside Himself, relationship, the basis and prototype of all relationship."

45. Barth, *CD* II/2:9–10.

46. Cf. Eberhard Busch, *The Great Passion: An Introduction to Karl Barth's Theology,* trans. Geoffrey W. Bromiley (Grand Rapids: Wm. B. Eerdmans Publishing Co., 2004), 47–48.

47. Barth, *CD* II/2:103.

48. Belá Vassady, "Gleanings," in *How Karl Barth Changed My Mind,* ed. Donald K. McKim (Grand Rapids: Wm. B. Eerdmans Publishing Co., 1986), 32.

49. Barth, *CD* II/2:120.

50. William Stacy Johnson, *The Mystery of God: Karl Barth and the Postmodern Foundations of Theology* (Louisville, KY: Westminster John Knox Press, 1997), 63.

51. Cf. Barth, *CD* II/2:353.

52. Barth, *CD* II/2:351.

53. See Barth's discussion "The Vocation of Man," in *CD* IV/3.2:481–680.

54. Cf. Karl Barth, "The Gift of Freedom," in *The Humanity of God* (Atlanta: John Knox Press, 1960), 78.

55. Barth, *CD* IV/3.2:664.

56. See Barth's discussion "The Election of the Community" (§34) in *CD* II/2:195–305.

57. See Johnson, *Mystery of God*, 64.

58. Barth, *CD* II/2:353 [my emphasis].

59. Tanner, *The Politics of God*, 23.

60. See, for example, Letty Russell, *The Future of Partnership* (Philadelphia: Westminster Press, 1979), 67.

61. Rosemary R. Ruether, "Christology and Feminism: Can a Male Savior Help Women?" *An Occasional Paper of the Board of Higher Education and Ministry of the United Methodist Church* I (December 25, 1976).

62. "Nonwhite peoples, it is believed by many white people, were created for the primary purpose of providing service for white people. Likewise, in patriarchal societies, the notions of service and servant were often used to describe the role that women played in relation to men and children. . . . How does one justify teaching a people that they are called to a life of service when they have been imprisoned by the most exploitative forms of service?" Jacquelyn Grant, "The Sin of Servanthood and the Deliverance of Discipleship," in *A Troubling in My Soul: Womanist Perspectives on Evil and Suffering*, ed. Emilie M. Townes (Maryknoll, NY: Orbis Books, 1993), 200, 209.

63. Kathryn Tanner, *Jesus, Humanity and the Trinity: A Brief Systematic Theology* (Minneapolis: Fortress Press, 2001), 4.

64. Ibid., 53. Cf. also 57: "[W]e act in a purified, elevated fashion (to the extent that we do!) only because Christ first acts for us by assuming us to himself, through the power of the Spirit."

65. See Tanner's discussion "The Shape of Human Life," in ibid., 67–95.

66. Serene Jones, *Feminist Theory and Christian Theology: Cartographies of Grace* (Minneapolis: Fortress Press, 2000), 67.

67. This is why Barth's discussion "The Election of God" is followed immediately by a discussion of Christian ethics in "The Command of God"; see *CD* II/2, §§ 36–39.

68. West, *Deadly Innocence*, 132.

69. See Manuela Kalsky, "Vom Verlangen nach Heil: Eine feministische Christologie oder messianische Heilsgeschichten?" in *Vom Verlangen nach Heilwerden: Christologie in feministisch-theologischer Sicht*, ed. Doris Strahm and Regula Strobel (Fribourg/Luzern: Exodus, 1993), 226 (my translation).

70. Russell, *Church in the Round*, 171.

71. G. C. Berkouwer, *Divine Election* (Grand Rapids: Wm. B. Eerdmans Publishing Co., 1960), 208.

72. Amy Plantinga Pauw, "Jesus Christ as Host and Guest," in *Renewing the Vision: Reformed Faith for the Twenty-first Century*, ed. Cynthia M. Campbell (Louisville, KY: Geneva Press, 2000), 20.

73. The confession and its accompanying letter are printed in G. D. Cloete and Dirk J. Smit, eds., *A Moment of Truth. The Confession of the Dutch Reformed Mission Church* (Grand Rapids: Wm. B. Eerdmans Publishing Co., 1984); the citation is quoted from 6 (my emphasis).

74. See Helga Kuhlmann, "Solus Christus? Zur feministisch-theologischen Kritik am christologischen Exklusivitätsanspruch," in *Ihr aber, für wen haltet ihr mich? Auf dem Weg zu einer feministisch-befreiungstheologischen Revision von Christologie*, ed. Renate Jost and Eveline Valtin (Gütersloh: Christian Kaiser/Gütersloher Verlagshaus), 55–56.

75. Clark Pinnock, *A Wideness in God's Mercy* (Grand Rapids: Zondervan Publishing House, 1992), 141.

76. Kathryn Tanner, *The Politics of God*, 23.

CHAPTER 6

1. *Imago Dei* is the Latin phrase for "image of God."

2. Mary Daly, *Beyond God the Father: Toward a Philosophy of Women's Liberation*, with an original reintroduction by the author (Boston: Beacon Press, 1985), 13.

3. See Rosemary Radford Ruether's discussion of the latter in *Sexism and God-Talk: Toward a Feminist Theology* (Boston: Beacon Press, 1983), 116–26.

4. John Calvin, *Institutes of the Christian Religion*, ed. John T. McNeill, trans. Ford Lewis Battles, LCC (Philadelphia: Westminster Press, 1960), 1.1 and 2.3–4.

5. Kristen E. Kvam, "Anthropology, Theological," in *Dictionary of Feminist Theologies*, ed. Letty M. Russell and J. Shannon Clarkson (Louisville, KY: Westminster John Knox Press, 1996), 10–11.

6. Views of women's diminished capacities are legion in the history of Western thought, going far beyond the work of biblical exegetes. Early on there were a host of books by feminists that collected the misogynist sayings of the church fathers. See Elizabeth A. Clark and Herbert Richardson, eds. *Women and Religion: The Original Sourcebook of Women in Christian Thought* (San Francisco: HarperSanFrancisco Press, 1996).

7. For one of many treatments of the racialized female body, see Michael Bennett and Vanessa D. Dickerson, *Recovering the Black Female Body: Self-Representations by African American Women* (New Brunswick, NJ: Rutgers University Press, 2001).

8. R. Douglas Breckenridge and Lois A. Boyd, "United Presbyterian Policy on Women and the Church—An Historical Overview," *Journal of Presbyterian History* 59:3 (Fall 1981): 384. See Jane Dempsey Douglas on Calvin in her *Women, Freedom, and Calvin* (Philadelphia: Westminster Press, 1985).

9. *The Constitution of the Presbyterian Church (U.S.A.)*, Part I, *Book of Confessions* (Louisville, KY: Office of the General Assembly, Presbyterian Church (U.S.A), 1991), 5.032.

10. A number of critiques have been lodged on this subject. See Judith Plaskow, *Sex, Sin, and Grace: Women's Experience and the Theologies of Reinhold Niebuhr and Paul Tillich* (Washington, DC: University Press of America, 1980); Susan Dunfee Nelson, "The Sin of Hiding: A Feminist Critique of Reinhold Niebuhr's Account of the Sin of Pride," *Soundings* 65, no. 3 (Fall, 1982): 316–27; more recently, Serene Jones, *Feminist Theory and Christian Theology: Cartographies of Grace* (Minneapolis: Fortress Press, 2000), 108–55.

11. See Calvin's prefatory letter to King Francis in *Institutes*, 14. I thank Amy Plantinga Pauw for this reference.

12. Modern theology, beginning with Reformed theologian Friedrich Schleiermacher (1768–1834), started filling out the more complex structure of human being as creature of God. However, it took liberation theologies and the galvanizing of marginalized populations to challenge the false universal character of mainstream theology's anthropology.

13. For an excellent example of such expansion, see Mary Potter Engel's essay "Evil, Sin and Violation of the Vulnerable," in *Lift Every Voice: Constructing Christian Theologies from the Underside*, rev. ed., ed. Susan Brooks Thistlethwaite and Mary Potter Engel (Maryknoll, NY: Orbis Books, 1998), 159–72.

14. The Geneva Catechism (1545) says that the highest human good and the chief end of "man" are the same: knowing and glorifying God, who made human being.

15. See Brian A. Gerrish's discussion of this point in *Grace and Gratitude: The Eucharistic Theology of John Calvin* (Minneapolis: Fortress Press, 1993), 42–49.

16. Calvin, *Institutes* 3.7.6.

17. De Gruchy points out that, for Calvin, the *imago Dei* is fundamentally about our human relationships, and he thinks it is key for Calvin's ethics. It is "the doctrine which brings together not only our knowledge of God and of ourselves but also our relationship to others. We are to relate to other people on the basis of our all having been made in the 'image of God'" (*Liberating Reformed Theology: A South African Contribution to an Ecumenical Task* [Grand Rapids: Wm. B. Eerdmans Publishing Co., 1991], 136). Brian Gerrish points out that this image guarantees the sacredness and dignity of human life; thus such social relations as racism and sexism are idolatry. See *The Old Protestantism and the New: Essays on the Reformation Heritage* (Chicago: University of Chicago Press), 152.

18. De Gruchy, *Liberating Reformed Theology*, 110.

19. Ibid.

20. This is the way Rosemary Radford Ruether puts it. My challenge to this is found in "Contesting the Gendered Subject: A Feminist Account of the *Imago Dei*," in *Horizons in Feminist Theology: Identity, Tradition, and Norms*, ed. Rebecca S. Chopp and Sheila Greeve Davaney (Minneapolis: Fortress Press, 1997), 99–115.

21. Valerie Saiving, "The Human Situation: A Feminine View," *Journal of Religion* 40 (April 1960): 100–12.

22. Analogously, Jacquelyn Grant's work has shown that issues of race are always operative in theology as well, including theology written by white feminists focusing on the gendered character of all theological discourse. See Jacquelyn Grant, *White Women's Christ, Black Women's Jesus: Feminist Christology and Womanist Response*, AAR Academy Series, vol. 64, ed. Susan Thistlethwaite (Atlanta: Scholars Press, 1989).

The issues of race and ethnicity are much broader than I cover here and include racially "marked" communities other than African Americans, such as Chicana and Latin American women, to name a few. I will confine myself to gender, race, and sexuality in this discussion, using womanists to represent communities raising race issues. Although it is not completely satisfactory, I do this in the attempt to avoid additive strategies.

23. The inclusive language discussions were and continue to be crucial in the development of these insights.

24. Rosemary Radford Ruether's definition of feminist theology's uniqueness is an example of this method. "The uniqueness of feminist theology lies not in its use of the criterion of experience but rather in its use of women's experience, which has been almost entirely shut out of theological reflection in the past" (*Sexism and God-Talk*, 13). The shift I refer to has only begun to happen in white feminist theology and more in race theorists than in womanist work, at least as far I am aware. See Ellen Armour's *Deconstruction, Feminist Theology, and the Problem of Difference: Subverting the Race/Gender Divide* (Chicago: University of Chicago Press, 1999); Kimberle Crenshaw, "Demarginalizing the Intersection of Race and Sex: A Black Feminist Critique of Antidiscrimination Doctrine, Feminist Theory and Antiracist Politics," *University of Chicago Legal Forum* (1989): 139–67.

25. "Interpellation" is Louis Althusser's term for the social production of a subject by the discourses of power in a society. A variety of discourses have the effect of "hailing" the subject as a citizen, as a minority, or as a woman, to which the self responds.

26. Sheila Briggs, "A History of Our Own: What Would a Feminist History of Theology Look Like?" in *Horizons in Feminist Theology*, ed. Chopp and Davaney, 168–69. She notes the significance of her title: she is not referring to a feminist history of Christianity but to the theological construction of reality. Thus there is a distinction "between a discourse's theoretical constitution and its effects in the social realm."

27. Joan Scott, "Experience," in *Feminists Theorize the Political*, ed. Judith Butler and Joan W. Scott (New York: Routledge, 1992), 27.

28. F. A. Ross, *Slavery Ordained of God* (1857; repr., Miami, FL: Mnemosyne Publishing Co., 1969), 67–68.

29. *All the Women Are White, All the Blacks Are Men, But Some of Us Are Brave: Black Women's Studies*, ed. Gloria T. Hull, Patricia Bell Scott, and Barbara Smith (Old Westbury, NY: Feminist Press, 1982).

30. Ellen Armour coined the term "whitefeminism." See *Deconstruction, Feminist Theology, and the Problem of Difference*.

31. Sample histories of construction of race include Ivan Hannaford, *Race: The History of an Idea* (Baltimore: John Hopkins University Press, 1998); David Theo Goldberg, *Racist Culture: Philosophy and the Politics of Meaning* (Cambridge: Blackwell, 1993).

32. The theorist most noted for this new direction is Judith Butler. See her *Gender Trouble: Feminism and the Subversion of Identity* (New York: Routledge, 1990) and *Bodies That Matter: On the Discursive Limits of Sex* (New York: Routledge, 1993).

33. See, for example, Karl Barth, *Church Dogmatics*, III/4 (Edinburgh: T. & T. Clark, 1958), 118: "No other distinction between man and man goes so deep as that in which the human male and the human female are so utterly different from each other. And no other relationship is so obvious, self-explanatory and universally valid as that whose force resides precisely in the presupposed underlying otherness."

34. See Mary McClintock Fulkerson, "Postmodernism and Feminist Theology," in *The Cambridge Companion to Postmodern Theology*, ed. Kevin J. Vanhoozer (Cambridge: Cambridge University Press, 2003), 109–26. See also Serene Jones, "Bounded Openness: Postmodernism, Feminism, and the Church Today," *Interpretation* 55, no. 1 (January 2001): 49–59.

CHAPTER 7

1. For a much more refined discussion of Calvin's psychological state, see William J. Bouwsma, *John Calvin: A Sixteenth-Century Portrait* (New York: Oxford University Press, 1988).

2. See Ludwig Feuerbach, *The Essence of Christianity*, trans. George Eliot (New York: Harper, 1957).

3. John Calvin, *Institutes of the Christian Religion*, ed. John T. McNeill, trans. Ford Lewis Battles, LCC (Philadelphia: Westminster Press, 1960), 1.16–18.

4. John Calvin, *Treatises Against the Anabaptists and Against the Libertines*, trans. and ed. Benjamin Farley (Grand Rapids: Baker Book House, 1982), 243.

5. Calvin, *Treatises Against the Anabaptists*, 245.

6. Brian Gerrish, *Grace and Gratitude: The Eucharistic Theology of John Calvin* (Minneapolis: Fortress Press, 1993), 28.

7. Jean-François Lyotard, *The Postmodern Condition: A Report on Knowledge*, trans. Geoff Bennington and Brian Massumi (Minneapolis: University of Minnesota Press, 1999).

8. I do, however, find Kathryn Tanner's discussion of divine and human agency to be a helpful explanation of compatibilist arguments. See *God and Creation in Christian Theology: Tyranny or Empowerment?* (Oxford: Basil Blackwell Ltd., 1988).

9. Reinhold Niebuhr, *The Nature and Destiny of Man*, vol. 1, *Human Nature* (New York: Charles Scribner's Sons, 1964).

10. See Judith Plaskow, *Sex, Sin, and Grace: Women's Experience and the Theologies of Reinhold Niebuhr and Paul Tillich* (Washington, D.C.: University Press of America, 1980).

11. Maurice Wiles, *God's Action in the World* (London: SCM Press Ltd., 1986). Because I am giving a broad summary of the content of this work, I will cite page numbers only where I use a direct quotation.

12. Ibid., 28.

13. I am grateful for Amy Plantinga Pauw's caution not to render God's omnipotence and human freedom as a zero-sum game, wherein human freedom decreases as God's exercise of power increases, and vice versa. (See especially Tanner, *God and Creation in Christian Theology*; and William C. Placher, who builds on Tanner's argument, *The Domestication of Transcendence* [Louisville, KY: Westminster John Knox Press, 1996], ch. 7.) However, as I suggest toward the end of the essay, a zero-sum game may indeed be the image presented in popularized versions of Calvin's doctrine; it is likely also the interpretation of providence to which Wiles responds.

14. Delores Williams, *Sisters in the Wilderness: The Challenge of Womanist God-Talk* (Maryknoll, NY: Orbis Books, 1993). See also the treatment of Williams in Joan M. Martin's essay in this volume. As with Wiles, I am giving a broad summary of Williams's book and so will cite specific pages only for direct quotations.

15. Williams, *Sisters in the Wilderness*, 108.

16. Ibid., 203.

17. Marilyn McCord Adams, "Evil and the God Who Does Nothing in Particular," in *Religion and Morality*, ed. D. Z. Phillips (London: Macmillan Press Ltd., and New York: St. Martin's Press, 1996), 107–31.

CHAPTER 8

1. See John Calvin, *Institutes of the Christian Religion*, ed. John T. McNeill, trans. Ford Lewis Battles, LCC (Philadelphia: Westminster Press, 1960), 2.16.13.

2. John McLeod Campbell, *The Nature of the Atonement and Its Relation to Remission of Sins and Eternal Life*, 6th ed. (London: James Clarke & Co., 1959), 151.

3. *The Constitution of the Presbyterian Church (U.S.A.)*, Part I, *Book of Confessions* (Louisville, KY: Office of the General Assembly, Presbyterian Church (U.S.A.) 1991), 9.09 (inclusive language text).

4. *Book of Confessions,* 4.011, 4.011, 4.037, 4.039.

5. Ibid., 4.045

6. Ibid., 4.052.

7. Calvin, *Institutes* 2.12.13; 2.15.6; 2.16.5; 2.17.4.

8. Ibid., 2.16.13.

9. Kathryn Tanner, *Jesus, Humanity, and Trinity: A Brief Systematic Theology* (Minneapolis: Fortress Press, 2001), 76–77.

10. Calvin, *Institutes* 2.16.13.

11. Mary Beaty and Benjamin W. Farley, trans. *Calvin's Ecclesiastical Advice* (Louisville, KY: Westminster/John Knox Press, 1991), 26.

12. Leanne Van Dyk, "Toward a New Typology of Reformed Doctrines of Atonement," in *Toward the Future of Reformed Theology: Tasks, Topics, Traditions,* ed. David Willis and Michael Welker (Grand Rapids: Wm. B. Eerdmans Publishing Co., 1999), 232. See also Leanne Van Dyk, *The Desire of Divine Love: John McLeod Campbell's Doctrine of the Atonement.* vol. 4, *Studies in Church History,* ed. William L. Fox (New York: Peter Lang, 1995), 54.

13. Leanne Van Dyk, *The Desire of Divine Love*, 49.

14. Ibid., 92.

15. Ibid., 50.

16. Delores S. Williams, "Black Women's Surrogacy Experience and the Christian Notion of Redemption," in *After Patriarchy: Feminist Transformations of World the Religions,* ed. Paula M. Cooey, William R. Eakin, and Jay B. Daniel; Faith Meets Faith: An Orbis Series in Interreligious Dialogue, ed. Paul F. Knitter (Maryknoll, NY: Orbis Books, 1991), 10–11.

17. Delores S. Williams, *Sisters in the Wilderness: The Challenge of Womanist God-Talk* (Maryknoll, NY: Orbis Books, 1993), 166.

18. Jacquelyn Grant, *White Women's Christ and Black Women's Jesus,* Feminist Christology and Womanist Response, American Academy of Religion Series, no. 64, ed. Susan Thistlethwaite (Atlanta: Scholars Press, 1989), 102.

19. Ibid., 212.

20. Cynthia L. Rigby, "Are You Saved? Receiving the Full Benefits of Grace," *Insights: The Faculty Journal of Austin Seminary* 115, no. 2 (Spring 2000): 14.

21. See Katie Cannon's essay on the power of grace in this regard (chap. 9, this volume).

22. Karen Baker-Fletcher has made this same point in "The Strength of My Life," in *Embracing the Spirit: Womanist Reflections on Hope, Salvation, and Transformation,* ed. Emilie M. Townes, vol. 13, The Bishop Henry McNeal/Sojourner Truth Series, ed. Dwight N. Hopkins (Maryknoll, NY: Orbis Books, 1997), 134.

CHAPTER 9

1. See Katie G. Cannon, "Out of the Shadows of Death: Representations of Womanist Homiletical Praxis in the Sacred Rhetoric of Dr. Martin Luther King, Jr.," *Princeton Seminary Bulletin*, vol. 21, no. 2 (new series 2000): 196–210.

2. I was a member of the 2001–02 Grace Colloquy in the Institute for Reformed Theology at Union Theological Seminary-PSCE. My colleagues and I wrestled with the meanings of biblical passages along with numerous other texts that address grace's central role in a wide range of settings and debates, both historical and contemporary. Throughout the year I read the texts of black Presbyterians in order to place the moral wisdom of the African American church community within the wider context of these diverse understandings of grace.

3. Frank T. Wilson Sr., "A Continuing Pilgrimage: Black Presbyterians and Black Presbyterianism," in *Periscope*, vol. 2, *Black Presbyterianism: Yesterday, Today and Tomorrow, 175 Years of Ministry* (New York: Office of Black Mission Development Program Agency, United Presbyterian Church in the U.S.A., 1983), 4.

4. Frank T. Wilson Sr., *Black Presbyterians in Ministry* (New York: Vocation Agency United Presbyterian Church in the U.S.A., 1979); reissued in Vera Swann, *Lest We Forget* (Louisville, KY Black Congregational Enhancement Office, Racial Ethnic Ministry Unit, Presbyterian Church (U.S.A.), 1992).

5. Priscilla Massie, ed. *Black Faith and Black Solidarity: Pan-Africanism and Faith in Christ* (New York: Friendship Press, 1973), 11.

6. Gayraud S. Wilmore, *The Nature and Task of Christian Education from an African American Presbyterian Perspective* (Louisville, KY: Witherspoon Press, Presbyterian Church (U.S.A.), 1998), 7.

7. Gerald West and Musa W. Dube, "An Introduction: How We Have Come to 'Read With,'" *Semeia* 73 (1996): 7–17; Muse W. Dube, "Readings of Semoya: *Batswana Women's Interpretations of Matt 15:21–28*," *Semeia* 73 (1996): 111–29.

8. Anna Pauline Murray and Mary Eastwood, "Jane Crow and the Law: Sex Discrimination and Title VII," *George Washington Law Review* 34 (December 1965): 232–56. See also Pauli Murray, "Black Theology and Feminist Theology: A Comparative View," in *Black Theology: A Documentary History, 1966–1979*, ed. Gayraud S. Wilmore and James H. Cone (Maryknoll, NY: Orbis Books, 1979), 398–417; *Song in a Weary Throat: An American Pilgrimage* (New York: Harper & Row, 1987); rpt. *Pauli Murray: The Autobiography of a Black Activist, Feminist, Lawyer, Priest, and Poet* (Knoxville: University of Tennessee Press, 1987); *Proud Shoes: The Story of an American Family* (New York: Harper & Row, 1956).

9. C. Vann Woodward, *Origin of the New South, 1877–1913* (Baton Rouge: Louisiana State University Press, 1951).

10. Farai Chideya, *The Color of Our Future* (New York: William Morrow & Co., 1999), 25.

11. Katie G. Cannon, *Black Womanist Ethics* (Atlanta: Scholars Press, 1988), 50–51; W. Fitzhugh Brundage, ed. *Under the Sentence of Death: Lynching in the South* (Chapel Hill: University of North Carolina Press, 1997); Leon Litwack, *Trouble in Mind: Black Southerners in the Age of Jim Crow* (New York: Alfred A. Knopf, 1998); Sandra Gunning, *Race, Rape, and Lynching: The Red Record of American Literature* (New York: Oxford University Press, 1996); Ida B. Wells-Barnett, *On Lynching: Southern Horrors, A Red Record and Mob Rule in New Orleans* (New York: Arno Press, 1969).

12. Gayraud S. Wilmore, *Black Religion and Black Radicalism: An Interpretation of the Religious History of Afro-American People*, 3rd ed. (Maryknoll, NY: Orbis Books, 1998).

13. Indeed, Valentin Y. Mudimbe insists that despite country specifics and regional differences, the West, as far back as the narrative history of the ancient world by Herodotus (probably 430–420 BCE), not only defined the spatial representation of Africa as a nonresidential habitat, but also created images of African women, men, and children as bestial beings, without history, culture, or religion. V. Y. Mudimbe, *The Invention of Africa: Gnosis, Philosophy, and the Order of Knowledge* (Bloomington: Indiana University Press, 1988), 70.

14. Matthew H. Edney, *Mapping the Empire* (Chicago: University of Chicago Press, 1997), 16.

15. Cornel West, *Race Matters* (Boston: Beacon Press, 1993), 122.

16. Rosetta E. Ross, "Grace" in *The Dictionary of Feminist Theologies*, ed. Letty M. Russell and J. Shannon Clarkson (Louisville, KY: Westminster John Knox Press, 1996), 133–34.

17. William T. Catto, *A Semi-Centenary Discourse, Delivered in the First African Presbyterian Church, Philadelphia, May, 1857* (Philadelphia: Joseph M. Wilson, 1857; rpt. Freeport, NY: Books for Libraries Press, 1971); Andrew E. Murray, *Presbyterians and the Negro* (Philadelphia: Presbyterian Historical Society, 1966); and Inez Moore Parker, *The Rise and Decline of the Program of Education for Black Presbyterians of the United Presbyterian Church U.S.A., 1865–1970* (San Antonio: Trinity University Press, 1977).

18. Gayraud S. Wilmore, *The Nature and Task of Christian Education from an African American Perspective* (Louisville, KY: Witherspoon Press, Presbyterian Church (U.S.A.), 1998), 2.

19. Toni Morrison's 1987 interview with the BBC.

20. Toni Morrison, *Beloved* (New York: Knopf, 1987), 88.

21. Charles H. Long, "Structural Similarities and Dissimilarities in Black and African Theologies," *Journal of Religious Thought* 32 (Fall/Winter 1975): 14.

22. Notes from a lecture delivered by Charles H. Long, April 2, 2002, at Virginia Union School of Theology in Richmond, VA.

23. Gayraud S. Wilmore, "Theological Dimensions of Black Presbyterianism," *Periscope*, vol. 3, *African American Presbyterianism–Preparing for the 21st Century* (Louisville, KY: Racial Ethnic Ministry Unit, Presbyterian Church (U.S.A.), 1992), 11–15.

24. W. E. B. DuBois, *The Souls of Black Folk* (Chicago: McClurg, 1903; rpt. New York: American Library, 1969), xi.

25. For a detailed discussion, Gayraud S. Wilmore, *Black Presbyterians: The Heritage and the Hope* (Philadelphia: Geneva Press, 1983; rpt. 1998).

26. Wilmore, *Periscope* 3, 12.

27. Ibid.

28. Wilmore, *The Nature and Task of Christian Education*, 2.

29. See Earl Ofari, *"Let Your Motto Be Resistance": The Life and Thought of Henry Highland Garnet* (Boston: Beacon Press, 1972); Hollis R. Lynch, *Edward Wilmot Blyden: Pan-Negro Patriot, 1832–1912* (London: Oxford University Press, 1967).

30. Henry Highland Garnet, *An Address to the Slaves of the United States* (Troy, NY: 1848).

31. Hollis R. Lynch, ed. *Black Spokesman: Selected Published Writings of Edward Wilmot Blyden* (New York: Humanities Press, 1971).

32. Delores Williams's comments on the atonement at this 1993 Minneapolis conference were sharply criticized by some Presbyterians and others.

33. David T. Shannon and Gayraud S. Wilmore, eds., *Black Witness to the Apostolic Faith* (Grand Rapids: Wm. B. Eerdmans Publishing Co., 1985), 63.

34. Delores S. Williams, "ReImagining Truth: Traversing the Feminist Christian Backlash," *The Other Side* (May–June 1994): 53–54.

35. As a Presbyterian minister, James Herman Robinson (1907–1972), founded the Church of the Master, Camp Rabbit Hollow, and the Morningside Community Center in Harlem, New York.

36. Established April 12, 1871, by a gift of ten thousand dollars from Henry W. Sage, Esq. in memory of Lyman Beecher (1775–1863), a member of the Yale College Class of 1797, the Beecher lectureship is the longest running lecture series on preaching. Sage was a member of Plymouth Congregational Church of Brooklyn, New York, where Henry Ward Beecher, the son of Lyman Beecher, was the pastor for forty years.

37. James H. Robinson, *Adventurous Preaching: The Lyman Beecher Lectures at Yale—1955* (Great Neck, NY: Channel Press, 1956), 31–32.

38. Ibid., 24.

39. Ibid., 44.

40. Robert T. Newbold Jr., *Black Preaching—Select Sermons in the Presbyterian Tradition* (Philadelphia: Geneva Press, 1977).

41. Ibid., 119.

42. Ibid., 43–44.

43. Stephen B. Haynes, *Noah's Curse: The Biblical Justification of American Slavery* (New York: Oxford University Press, 2002); Forrest Wood, *The Arrogance of Faith: Christianity and Race in America from the Colonial Era to the Twentieth Century* (New York: Knopf, 1990); and Robert E. Hood, *Begrimed and Black: Christian Traditions on Blacks and Blackness* (Minneapolis: Augsburg Fortress, 1994).

44. Newbold, *Black Preaching*, 49.

45. Ibid., 141.

46. Ibid., 24.

47. Ibid., 58.

48. Ibid., 18.

49. Ibid., 106.

CHAPTER 10

1. See Philippe Joutard, Jacques Poujol, and Patrick Cabanel, eds., *Cévennes: Terre de Réfuge 1940–1944*, 3rd ed. (Montpellier, France: Presses du Languedoc/Club Cévenol, 1994), especially 53, 221, and 251. Chamson gave the address "La Résistance d'un peuple (Après la Révocation de l'Edit de Nantes)" [translation: The resistance of a people (after the revocation of the Edict of Nantes)] on the occasion marking the 250th anniversary of the Revocation of the Edict of Nantes and the 150th anniversary of the Edict of Tolerance held at the Musée du Désert, a center of remembrance of martyrs of the faith and the struggle of French Calvinists for

survival and tolerance. The occasion and the place could not have had deeper resonance for the Reformed Church of France. All French translations in this chapter are mine.

2. "Sur les drapeaux de la France, / Pour garder leur liberté / Comme à la Tour de Constance / Ils ont écrit: «Résister», [translation: On the flags of France, / For guarding their liberty / As in the Tower of Constance / They wrote: 'Résister']. The third stanza of the *Complaint du maquis cévenol* by Jacques Poujoul, as cited in Patrick Cabanel, Jacques Poujoul, and Bernard Spiegel, "Quelques Juifs dans les Cévennes," in Joutard, Poujol, and Cabanel, *Cévennes*, 207.

3. On Marie Durand, her brother Pierre's ministry and martyrdom, and the rest of the Durand family see Étienne Gamonnet, ed. and intro., *Lettres de Marie Durand (1711–1776): Prisonnière à la Tour de Constance de 1730 à 1768*, 2nd ed. (Montpellier, France: Les Presses du Languedoc, 1998). See also André Chamson's fictionalized *La tour de Constance* (1970; repr., Paris: Éditions J'ai lu, 1992). In English, but dated, is Charles Tylor, *The Camisards* (London: Simpkin, Marshall, Hamilton, & Kent, 1893), especially part 3, chaps. 13–15 on Pierre Durand, the Tour de Constance, and Marie Durand, respectively.

4. As quoted in Tylor, *The Camisards*, 293.

5. "Cherchons le règne de Dieu et sa justice, et toutes choses nous seront données par-dessus. . . . Il aura pitié de sa désolée Sion et la remettra dans un état renommé sur la terre." Marie Durand to Anne Durand, 25 November 1755, in Gamonnet, *Lettres*, 111.

6. Gamonnet, *Lettres*, 52. He cites chap. 1 of Calvin, *De la connaissance de Dieu*.

7. "Anéantir l'être, c'est la loi de toute tyrannie; écraser toute personnalité intellectuelle et religieuse qui se dresse, briser les coeurs en même temps que les esprits et les volontés. C'est contre cette tentative des autorités, plus que pour la survie ou la sauvegarde du patrimoine, que Marie Durand eut à «résister»." Gamonnet, *Lettres*, 43.

8. John Calvin, *Corpus Reformatorum* 14.638, as quoted in Carlos N. M. Eire, *War Against the Idols: The Reformation of Worship from Erasmus to Calvin* (Cambridge: Cambridge University Press, 1986), 264.

9. John Calvin, *Institutes of the Christian Religion*, ed. John T. McNeill, trans. Ford Lewis Battles, LCC (Philadelphia: Westminster Press, 1960), 11.

10. I have relied on Carlos Eire's account of the affair of the placards, 189–93, and, more generally, on his argument about the central role of "idolatry" in sixteenth-century Calvinist thought.

11. Compare the explicit iconoclasm in *Institutes* 1.11, where Calvin charged "the papists" with putting "monstrosities" like statues of saints and elaborate rituals in place of God, and denounced these seductive "pictures" and counseled Christians to rely on Scripture alone.

12. For example, Calvin writes that "the church is holy, then, in the sense that it is daily advancing and is not yet perfect: it makes progress from day to day but has not yet reached its goal of holiness . . ." (*Institutes* 4.1.17). Calvin's emphasis on the possibility of the sanctification of all life in history—and the correlative possibility of the historical degradation of life—distinguished his thought from Luther's paradoxical construal of salvation and history and from what he saw as Roman triumphalism.

13. Eire, *War Against the Idols*, 310.

14. Calvin, *Institutes* 1.11.8.

15. Ibid., 1.5.12.

16. Ibid., 1.11.8.

17. Let me be clear: I do not mean to suggest that an "idolatry critique" à la Calvin is fully adequate to the complexity of our cultural-political-economic situation and thereby to eschew the use of other critical theories. Rather, I want to suggest the opposite. To receive "Résister" as a call to public confession and engagement necessarily involves a theological diagnosis of the idolatries (and glories) of our situation and also necessitates the deployment of a range of political, cultural, and social theories, using both theology and theory to inform transforming engagement that advances the well-being of life before God.

18. In 1933 a confederation of Lutheran, Reformed, and United Churches had joined together in opposition to Hitler's rising power and the pro-Nazi stance of the Reich Church and convened themselves as the Confessional Synod of the German Evangelical Church, or, more simply, the Confessing Church. They united behind "the inviolable foundation" of "the gospel of Jesus Christ as it is attested for us in Holy Scripture and brought to light again in the Confessions of the Reformation," a statement drafted substantially by Karl Barth.

19. For the text of the 1934 Barmen Declaration, see Arthur C. Cochrane, *The Church's Confession under Hitler* (Philadelphia: Westminster Press, 1962), 237–42.

20. Calvin railed against this third group, referring to them as "Nicodemites." See Eire, *War Against the Idols,* chap. 7.

21. Eire, *War Against the Idols,* 266.

22. Philippe Joutard, "Postface," in Joutard, Poujol, and Cabanel, *Cévennes,* 333.

23. Georges Gillier as recorded in "Table ronde des pasteurs à Valleraugue (août 1984)" in Joutard, Poujol, and Cabanel, *Cévennes,* 240. "Nous en avons pris conscience: la question juive n'était pas simplement une question biblique, mais une réalité."

24. Philip P. Hallie, *Lest Innocent Blood Be Shed* (New York: Harper & Row, 1979; HarperPerennial ed., 1994), 85. Today in the small museum in Le Chambon-sur-Lignon, they insist that the effort to shelter lives was shared by seven villages in the Lignon plateau and ecumenically with various Protestant congregations and a Catholic parish.

25. Cabanel, Poujoul, and Donadille, "Pasteurs en Cévennes," in Joutard, Poujol, and Cabanel, *Cévennes,* 216. They summarize an article by Avril W. Monod, "Deux métaphysiques (à propos de Karl Barth)," *Revue du Christianisme social* (April 1934): 258–61.

26. Mary Daly, *Beyond God the Father: A Philosophy of Women's Liberation* (Boston: Beacon Press, 1973), 19, 13.

27. Sallie McFague, *Models of God: Theology for an Ecological, Nuclear Age* (Philadelphia: Fortress Press, 1983), ix.

28. Implicit in McFague's approach is a point worth making explicitly. We do not have metaphors or discourse, power, knowledge, relations, or institutions untinged by idolatry. Yet they are not in themselves idolatrous. Our economies and polities, our language, power, knowledge, and relations are also the basic means through which we are enabled to respond to the grace of God (that is to say, basic even to Calvin's means of grace). They can be means for both losing and gaining a sense of God's glory, for both denying and being granted some comprehension of truth, and for both tearing down and striving toward "the good repair" of Christ's kingdom.

29. Beverly Wildung Harrison, "Restoring the Tapestry of Life: The Vocation of Feminist Theology," *The Drew Gateway* 54 (Fall 1983): 45. See also her *Making the Connections: Essays in Feminist Social Ethics*, ed. Carol S. Robb (Boston: Beacon Press, 1985), 221, 228.

30. Delores S. Williams, *Sisters in the Wilderness: The Challenge of Womanist God-Talk* (Maryknoll, NY: Orbis Books, 1993), especially chap. 5. See also her "Women's Oppression and Lifeline Politics in Black Women's Religious Narratives," *Journal of Feminist Studies in Religion* 2 (Fall 1985): 59–71.

31. Katie Geneva Cannon, "Surviving the Blight," in *Katie's Canon: Womanism and the Soul of the Black Community* (New York: Continuum, 1996), 28–37.

32. Beverly Wildung Harrison, "Feminist Thea(o)logies at the Millennium: 'Messy' Continued Resistance or Surrender to Post-Modern Academic Culture?" in *Liberating Eschatology: Essays in Honor of Letty M. Russell*, ed. Margaret A. Farley and Serene Jones (Louisville, KY: Westminster John Knox Press, 1999), 163; *Making the Connections*, 8.

33. See Harrison, "Feminist Thea(o)logies," 159. See also Mary McClintock Fulkerson's discussion of the problem of closed theological systems: "[Theology's] truth is ragged, not systematic or complete; its future is literally open." She argues instead that "a more appropriate characterization of the truthfulness of theology" is as passionate commitment and persuasive testimony. Fulkerson, *Changing the Subject: Women's Discourses and Feminist Theology* (Minneapolis: Fortress Press, 1994), 376–77, and chap. 7 passim.

34. Harrison, "Feminist Thea(o)logies," 157.

CHAPTER 11

1. Gerald Jaynes, "Plantation Factories and the Slave Work Ethic," in *The Slave's Narrative*, ed. Charles T. Davis and Henry Louis Gates Jr. (New York: Oxford University Press, 1985), 103.

2. I use the term *blackwomen* as a more accurate social construction of identity than *black* as a racially negative description of a particular group of women. It denotes the interrelationship between and inseparability of the experience of race and gender interwoven as social constructions. In this chapter I will similarly use such language for African American men, boys, and girls.

3. Jürgen Moltmann, *On Human Dignity: Political Theology and Ethics* (Philadelphia: Fortress Press, 1984), 40.

4. See Alan Richardson, *The Biblical Doctrine of Work*, Ecumenical Biblical Studies, no. 1 (London: SCM Press, 1952), 13.

5. Renita J. Weems, "Reading Her Way through the Struggle: African American Women and the Bible," in *Stony the Road We Trod: African American Biblical Interpretation*, ed. Cain Hope Felder (Minneapolis: Fortress Press, 1991), 59.

6. Ibid., 58–59.

7. Early examples include James H. Cone, *God of the Oppressed* (Maryknoll, NY: Orbis Books, 1997); Phyllis Trible, "Depatriarchalizing in Biblical Interpretation," *Journal of the American Academy of Religion* 41 (1973): 30–48; and Dorothee Soelle with Shirley A. Cloyes, *To Love and to Work: A Theology of Creation* (Philadelphia: Fortress Press, 1984).

8. Delores S. Williams, *Sisters in the Wilderness: The Challenge of Womanist God-Talk* (Maryknoll, NY: Orbis Books, 1993), 3. For an in-depth discussion see chap. 1 on the themes of black mothers, surrogacy, and the biblical story of Hagar. See also Kalbryn McLean's treatment of Williams in chap. 7 of this volume.

9. Williams, *Sisters*, 15.

10. Ibid., 20–21.

11. Ibid., 22.

12. Ibid., 23.

13. J. Cheryl Exum, "You Shall Let Every Daughter Live: A Study of Exodus 1:8–2:10," *Semeia* 28 (1983): 72.

14. Soelle, *To Work and to Love*, 12.

15. Exum has twice revisited her thesis in the above-cited essay in "Second Thoughts about Secondary Characters: Women in Exodus 1:8–210," in *A Feminist Companion to Exodus to Deuteronomy*, ed. Athalya Brenner (Sheffield: Sheffield Academic Press, 1994), 75–87, and *Plotted, Shot, and Painted: Cultural Representations of Biblical Women* (Sheffield: Sheffield Academic Press, 1996), chap. 4. Her self-criticism concerns the marginality of women in the full Exodus narrative, even though chaps. 1–2 focus so positively on women, and the role the early focus on women has for a basically androcentric and patriarchal text whose central character is Moses, the male hero. Methodologically, Exum also has shifted to deconstructive and feminist literary critical readings of texts. I note her concern and attempt to address it somewhat through a "blackwoman's" reading. It is, however, a problem for which neither Exum nor I has a solution.

16. Sojourner Truth, *The Narrative of Sojourner Truth* [1850 edition as dictated to Olive Gilbert], ed. and intro. Margaret Washington (New York: Vintage Books, 1993), 31. Harriet Jacobs, *Incidents in the Life of a Slave Girl. Written by Herself*, ed. L. Maria Child [1961], intro. Jean Fagan Yellin (Cambridge, MA: Harvard University Press, 1987).

17. George P. Rawick, *The Arkansas Narrative*, vol. 11, in the series *The American Slave: A Composite Autobiography*, 41 vols. (Westport, CT: Greenwood Publishing Co., 1972), part 7, 21.

18. Deborah Gray White, *Ar'nt I a Woman? Female Slaves in the Plantation South* (New York: W. W. Norton & Co., 1985), 112.

19. Martin Luther, *Luther's Works*, vol. 44, ed. Helmut Lehmann (Philadelphia: Fortress Press, 1966), 129–30.

20. Moltmann, *On Human Dignity*, 47.

21. John Calvin, *Institutes of the Christian Religion*, ed. John T. McNeill, trans. Ford Lewis Battles, LCC (Philadelphia: Westminster Press, 1960), 3.10.6.

22. Ibid., 3.7.5.

23. Jane Dempsey Douglas, *Women, Freedom, and Calvin* (Philadelphia: Westminster Press, 1985), 114–15.

24. Calvin, Sermon 53 on Timothy 6:17–19, as quoted in Lee Hardy, *The Fabric of This World: Inquiries into Calling, Career Choice, and the Design of Human Work* (Grand Rapids: Wm. B. Eerdmans Publishing Co., 1990), 63.

25. John T. McNeill, *The History and Character of Calvinism* (New York: Oxford University Press, 1967), 221.

26. Ibid., 185.

27. Abel Athouguia Alves, "The Christian Social Organism and Social Welfare: The Case of Vives, Calvin and Loyola," *Sixteenth Century Journal* 20, no. 1 (1989): 8.

28. Ibid., 9.

29. For further discussion of this interpretation of Calvin's theology, see Barbara Hilkert Andolsen, *Good Work at the Video Display Terminal—A Feminist Ethical Analysis of Clerical Work* (Knoxville: University of Tennessee Press, 1989), 99–100.

30. Robert Wuthnow, *Poor Richard's Principle: Recovering the American Dream through the Moral Dimension of Work, Business, and Money* (Princeton, NJ: Princeton University Press, 1996), 59.

31. Luther, *Luther's Works*, 189–90.

32. Alves, "Christian Social Organism," 12–13.

33. Ibid., 19.

34. See Hardy, *Fabric of This World*, 65–66, for quote and accompanying footnote comments.

35. Andolsen, *Good Work at the Video Display*, 97, 102.

36. Richard Baxter as quoted in Winthrop S. Hudson, "Puritanism and the Spirit of Capitalism," *Church History* 18, no. 12 (1949). For the contestable scholarly arguments about the relationship of Calvinism to capitalism, see Max Weber, *The Protestant Ethic and the Spirit of Capitalism* (New York: Charles Scribner's Sons, 1958), and R. H. Tawney, *Religion and the Rise of Capitalism* (New York: Harcourt, Brace, and Co., 1926).

37. Mechal Sobel (*The World They Made Together: Black and White Values in Eighteenth-Century Virginia* [Princeton, NJ: Princeton University Press, 1987], 3) asserts that by the eighteenth century, Virginia was the largest, most populous colony, and the "home for a significant number of emigrants to virtually all the later [southern] colonies."

38. Ibid., chap. 1.

39. Daniel T. Rodgers, *The Work Ethic in Industrial America, 1850–1920* (Chicago: University of Chicago Press, 1978), 12.

40. James B. Gilbert, *Work without Salvation: America's Intellectual and Industrial Alienation, 1880–1990* (Baltimore: Johns Hopkins University Press, 1977), ix.

41. Rodgers, *Work Ethic in Industrial America*, chap. 1.

42. Gilbert, *Work without Salvation*, viii–ix.

43. Ibid., ix.

44. See Ernst Troeltsch, "Calvinism and Capitalism," in *The Social Teachings of the Christian Churches*, vol. 2 (Chicago: University of Chicago Press, 1931; reprint 1981), 644–46.

45. Katie G. Cannon, *Black Womanist Ethics* (Atlanta: Scholars Press, 1988), 3.

46. C. Vann Woodward, "The Southern Ethic in a Puritan World," in *Myth and Southern History*, vol. 1, ed. Patrick Gerster and Nicholas Cords (Urbana: University of Illinois Press, 1974; rev. ed. 1989), 51.

47. W. J. Cash, *The Mind of the South* (New York: Alfred A. Knopf, Inc., 1941), quoted by Woodward, "The Southern Ethic in a Puritan World," 43.

48. Eugene D. Genovese, *The Political Economy of Slavery: Studies in the Economy and Society of the Slave South*, 2nd ed. (Middletown, CT: Wesleyan University Press, 1965), 28.

49. Rodgers, *Work Ethic in Industrial America*, 7.

50. I am indebted to Dr. Aminah Beverly McCloud for the notions of enforced dependency and other corollary ideas regarding work. Our conversations in 1994–95 at the Annual Meetings of the American Academy of Religion, and a reading of her unpublished manuscript, "A Response to John C. Raines and Donna C.

Day-Lower," *Modern Work and Human Meaning* (Philadelphia: Westminster Press, 1986), have been invaluable.

51. Jacobs, *Incidents*, 10.

52. William Harris, "Work and the Family in Black Atlanta," in *Black Women in United States History*, vol. 2, ed. Darlene Clark Hine (Brooklyn, NY: Carlson Publishing Co., 1990), 319.

53. *Aunt Sally or the Cross the Way of Freedom: A Narrative of the Life and Purchase of the Mother of Rev. Isaac Williams of Detroit, Michigan* (Cincinnati: American Reform Tract and Book Society, 1858; reprint, Miami: Mnemosyne Publishing Co., 1969), 97–98.

54. Vann Woodward, "The Southern Ethic in a Puritan World," *William and Mary Quarterly* 24 (1968): 343–70.

55. Ibid., 57–58.

56. Harold Courlander, *Negro Folk Music, U.S.A.* (New York: Columbia University Press, 1963), 117, as quoted in Sterling Stuckey, "Through the Prism of Folklore," *The Massachusetts Review* 9 (1968): 417–37.

57. Kleckley, *Behind the Scenes*, 28.

CHAPTER 12

1. John Calvin, *Institutes of the Christian Religion*, ed. John T. McNeill, trans. Ford Lewis Battles, LCC (Philadelphia: Westminster Press, 1960), 4.2.12. In this essay, *church* will refer primarily to the gathered disciples of Jesus Christ in all times and places, of which each particular community is a full expression.

2. Karl Barth, *The Theology of the Reformed Confessions*, trans. Darrell L. Guder and Judith J. Guder (Louisville, KY: Westminster John Knox Press, 2002), 105.

3. *The Constitution of the Presbyterian Church (U.S.A.), Part I, Book of Confessions* (Louisville, KY: Office of the General Assembly, Presbyterian Church (U.S.A.), 1991), 3.20.

4. See Andrew Walls, "Christianity in the Non-Western World: A Study in the Serial Nature of Christian Expansion," *Studies in World Christianity* 1, no. 1 (1995): 1–25.

5. Stephen J. Stein, ed., *Notes on Scripture*, The Works of Jonathan Edwards, vol. 15 (New Haven, CT: Yale University Press, 1998), 271.

6. Calvin, *Institutes* 4.1.2, emphasis in the original text.

7. Ibid., 2.15.6. See 2.15.1–4 for descriptions of our participation in Christ's prophetic and priestly offices.

8. Nicholas M. Healy, *Church, World and the Christian Life: Practical-Prophetic Ecclesiology* (Cambridge: Cambridge University Press, 2000), 12.

9. The Donatists were a schismatic body in the fourth-century African church who held that the church must remain holy and that sacraments conferred by priests who betrayed the faith were invalid.

10. Calvin, *Institutes* 4.3.1.

11. Ibid., 4.8.1.

12. *Book of Confessions*, 5.131.

13. Though see Margo Todd, "Bishops in the Kirk: William Cowper of Galloway and the Puritan Episcopacy of Scotland," *Scottish Journal of Theology* 57, no. 3

(2004): 300–312 for an account of the acceptance of bishops in early Scottish Presbyterianism.

14. Lynn N. Rhodes and Kathleen M. Black, "Church Ministries and Worship," in *Dictionary of Feminist Theologies*, ed. Letty M. Russell and J. Shannon Clarkson (Louisville, KY: Westminster John Knox Press, 1996), 46.

15. Lois A. Boyd and R. Douglas Brackenridge, "Presbyterian Women Ministers: A Historical Overview and Study of the Current Status of Women Pastors," in *The Pluralistic Vision: Presbyterians and Mainstream Protestant Education and Leadership*, ed. Milton J Coalter, John M. Mulder, and Louis B. Weeks (Louisville, KY: Westminster/John Knox Press, 1992), 291.

16. Friedrich Schleiermacher, *Die christliche Sitte nach den Grandsätzen der evangelischen Kirche im Zusammenhange dargestellt*, ed. Ludwig Jonas in *Sämmtliche Werke*, div. 1, vol. 12 (Berlin: G. Reimer, 1843), 158. Quoted in James M. Brandt, *All Things New: Reform of Church and Society in Schleiermacher's Christian Ethics* (Louisville, KY: Westminster John Knox Press, 2001), 94.

17. Kathryn Tanner, "The Care That Does Justice: Recent Writings in Feminist Ethics and Theology," *Journal of Religious Ethics* 24 (Spring 1996): 183.

18. See Miriam Therese Winter, ed., *Defecting in Place: Women Claiming Responsibility for Their Own Spiritual Lives* (New York: Crossroad, 1994).

19. Account drawn from personal conversation and from Sara Lawrence-Lightfoot, *I've Seen Rivers: Lives of Loss and Liberation* (New York: Penguin Books, 1995), 17–107, passim.

20. Diann L. Neu, "Women-Church Transforming Liturgy," in *Women at Worship: Interpretations of North American Diversity*, ed. Marjorie Procter-Smith and Janet R. Walton (Louisville, KY: Westminster/John Knox Press, 1993), 169.

21. Judith Plaskow, *Standing Again at Sinai: Judaism from a Feminist Perspective* (San Francisco: Harper and Row, 1990), 91.

22. Judith Plaskow, "Feminist Anti-Judaism and the Christian God," *Journal of Feminist Studies in Religion* 7 (Fall 1991): 100.

23. Katharina von Kellenbach, *Anti-Judaism in Feminist Religious Writings* (Atlanta: Scholars Press, 1994), 61.

24. Ibid., 43.

25. See Karl Barth, *Church Dogmatics* II/2 (Edinburg: T. & T. Clark, 1958), 197–201.

26. George Lindbeck, "The Gospel's Uniqueness: Election and Untranslatability," *Modern Theology* 13, no. 4 (October 1997): 443.

27. John Calvin, *Commentary on the Book of the Prophet Isaiah*, 4 volumes, trans. William Pringle (Grand Rapids: Wm. B. Eerdmans Publishing Co., 1998), 1:322.

28. Marie Dentière, *The War and Deliverance of the City of Geneva*, cited in Jane Dempsey Douglas, *Reform and Renewal* (Melbourne: Uniting Church Press, 1994), 7.

29. Calvin, *Commentary on Isaiah* 3:142–43.

30. Thomas Hoyt Jr., "Interpreting Biblical Scholarship for the Black Church Tradition," in *Stony the Road We Trod: African American Biblical Interpretation*, ed. Cain Hope Felder (Minneapolis: Fortress Press, 1991), 30.

31. Delores S. Williams, *Sisters in the Wilderness: The Challenge of Womanist Godtalk* (Maryknoll, NY: Orbis Books, 1993), 149.

32. See Kalbryn A. McLean and Joan M. Martin's essays in this volume for more extended accounts of Williams's interpretation of the Hagar stories.

33. B. A. Gerrish, *Grace and Gratitude: The Eucharistic Theology of John Calvin* (Minneapolis: Fortress Press, 1993), 171.

34. See Margit Ernst-Habib's essay (chap. 5 in this volume) for a Reformed view of election that avoids these problems.

35. *Book of Confessions*, 4.054.

36. These images are developed further in Amy Plantinga Pauw, "The Church as Mother and Bride in the Reformed Tradition: Challenge and Promise," in *Many Voices One God: Being Faithful in a Pluralistic World*, ed. Walter Brueggemann and George W. Stroup (Louisville, KY: Westminster John Knox Press, 1998), 122–36.

37. Letty M. Russell, *Church in the Round: Feminist Interpretation of the Church* (Louisville, KY: Westminster/John Knox Press, 1993), 14.

38. These four ministries correspond respectively to the Greek terms *kerygma*, *koinonia*, *diakonia*, and *didache*. See James H. Evans Jr., "Race, Body, Space, and Time: Ecclesiological Reflections," in *Constructive Theology: A Contemporary Approach to Classical Themes*, ed. Serene Jones and Paul Lakeland (Minneapolis: Fortress Press, 2005), 219–30.

39. Wallace M. Alston, *The Church of the Living God: A Reformed Perspective* (Louisville, KY: Westminster John Knox Press, 2002), 97.

40. *Book of Confessions*, 5.133.

41. Russell, *Church in the Round*, 11.

CHAPTER 13

1. This version of Calvin's preface to the Olivétan Bible is from Belden Lane, *Spiritus* 1, no. 1 (Spring 2001): 1–30. A condensed version of this article appears in *Perspectives: A Journal of Reformed Thought* (November 2001): 10. I have changed masculine pronouns, which Calvin used in the original French, to "God" in this citation. This citation practice is used throughout the chapter, including biblical citations.

2. I will use, interchangeably and synonymously, the terms *Lord's Supper*, *communion*, and *eucharist*.

3. John Calvin, *Institutes of the Christian Religion*, ed. John T. McNeill, trans. Ford Lewis Battles, LCC (Philadelphia: Westminster Press, 1960), 4.14.18. Citations from Calvin's writings have been modified slightly; inclusive language is used with respect to human beings and non–gender specific language is used with respect to God.

4. Calvin, *Institutes* 4.14.1.

5. Ibid., 4.14.3.

6. This theme of God's resourceful grace appears in *Institutes* 4.16.19 as well, in Calvin's discussion of infant baptism. To the objection that infants ought not to be baptized because they do not have a full knowledge of God, Calvin asks with some impatience, "[W]hat is the danger if infants be said to receive now some part of that grace which in a little while they shall enjoy to the full?"

7. The ecumenical and theological scope of Calvin's sacramental theology is noted by Calvin scholars such as Brian Gerrish in his book *Grace and Gratitude: The Eucharistic Piety of John Calvin* (Minneapolis: Fortress Press, 1993).

8. The particular diminishments and marginalizations women have endured in Christian traditions, including Reformed traditions, are many, depending on the historical and cultural contexts, as well as general societal attitudes toward women.

Most obviously, these exclusions include a ban from ordination to the ministerial offices of the church. More subtly, they include all the entrenched patterns of sexism, such as trivialization of women's experience, deafness to women's voices, and blindness to women's actual presence. Statistics of the number of women in leadership positions in denominational structures, prominent churches, and theological seminaries is one indicator of continuing marginalization of women. More powerful are the anecdotes of women themselves who have encountered demeaning attitudes within the church and found them highly resistant to change.

9. Information on the efforts of the United Nations to advocate for women's rights and safety can be found on www.un.org/rights.

10. Kathryn Tanner, "Social Theory Concerning the 'New Social Movements' and the Practice of Feminist Theology," in *Horizons in Feminist Theology: Identity, Tradition, and Norms*, ed. Rebecca Chopp and Sheila Greeve Davaney (Minneapolis: Fortress Press, 1997), 188.

11. Serene Jones, *Feminist Theory and Christian Theology: Cartographies of Grace* (Minneapolis: Fortress Press, 2000), 14.

12. Tanner, "Social Theory," 192.

13. Cf., for example, J. J. von Allmen, *Worship: Its Theology and Practice* (New York: Oxford University Press, 1965); Don E. Saliers, *Worship as Theology: Foretaste of Glory Divine* (Nashville: Abingdon Press, 1994); Geoffrey Wainwright, *Doxology: The Praise of God in Worship, Doctrine, and Life: A Systematic Theology* (New York: Oxford University Press, 1980); John D. Witvliet, *Worship Seeking Understanding: Windows into Christian Practice* (Grand Rapids: Baker Academic, 2003).

14. Calvin, *Institutes* 1.2.1.

15. Ibid., 4.14.3.

16. Ibid., 4.14.6.

17. Ibid., 4.14.12.

18. David Willis, *Notes on the Holiness of God* (Grand Rapids: Wm. B. Eerdmans Publishing Co., 2002), 93.

19. Ibid.

20. The word "Calvinian" is used to indicate John Calvin's own thought. The more general term "Calvinist" refers to the complex and diverse traditions that followed in the centuries after Calvin. The distinction is important. A "Calvinian" sacramental theology is quite different from a "Calvinist" sacramental theology, the latter bearing greater similarity to a Zwinglian account. It would take a different chapter to spell this out. Here, I wish only to explain the term.

21. Calvin, *Institutes* 4.17.8.

22. Rita Nakashima Brock, Claudia Camp, Serene Jones, eds. *Setting the Table: Women in Theological Conversation* (St. Louis: Chalice Press, 1995), 264.

23. Theological analyses of slave women's work are found in Delores S. Williams, *Sisters in the Wilderness: The Challenge of Womanist God-Talk* (Maryknoll, NY: Orbis Books, 1993), and Joan M. Martin, *More Than Chains and Toil: A Christian Work Ethic of Enslaved Women* (Louisville, KY: Westminster John Knox Press, 2000).

24. An interesting feature of the Exodus 16 narrative is that the people were able to receive the gift of manna from their own particularity, even preference. The text reports that some people baked the manna and others boiled it for their nourishment (v. 23). Receiving divine gifts is not an act that obliterates difference but invites it.

25. Emilie M. Townes, "The Doctor Ain't Taking No Sticks," in *Embracing the Spirit: Womanist Perspectives on Hope, Salvation, and Transformation*, ed. Emilie M. Townes (Maryknoll, NY: Orbis Books, 1997), 192.

26. Paul Wadell, *Becoming Friends: Worship, Justice, and the Practices of Christian Friendship* (Grand Rapids: Brazos Press, 2002), 19.

27. Calvin, *Institutes* 4.14.17.

28. Susan Ross, *Extravagant Affections: A Feminist Sacramental Theology* (New York: Continuum Publishing Company, 1998), 38.

29. Ibid., 85.

30. Calvin, *Institutes* 4.14.16.

31. Ibid., 4.14.6

32. Ibid., 4.14.17.

33. A long bibliography could be cited in support of this discussion. Cf. especially Charles Partee, "Calvin's Central Dogma Again," *Calvin Studies III*, Papers of the 1986 Davidson Colloquium, ed. John Leith (Richmond, VA: Union Theological Seminary, 1986); Lewis Smedes, *Union with Christ* (Grand Rapids: Wm. B. Eerdmans Publishing Co., 1983); Trevor Hart, "Humankind in Christ and Christ in Humankind: Salvation as Participation in our Substitute in the Theology of John Calvin," *Scottish Journal of Theology* 42 (1989): 67–84; W. Kolfhaus, *Christusgemeinshaft bei Johannes Calvin* (Neukirchen: Buchhandlung des Erziehungvereins, 1939).

34. Calvin, "Ninth Sermon of the Passion," *Corpus Reformatorum* 46, 953, quoted in Francois Wendel, *Calvin: Origins and Development of His Religious Thought* (New York: Harper & Row, 1963), 235.

35. Jean Kilbourne's thorough and scathing critique of media advertising documents messages of sexism, sexual violence against women, dismemberment of women's bodies, silencing of women's voices, the sexualization of children, ageism, and other negative messages to women. Her film series *Killing Us Softly* is now in its third edition (2000), demonstrating that these media messages continue to undermine healthy concepts of self in girls and women, not to mention the impact of these messages on boys and men.

36. Diana L. Hayes, "My Hope is in the Lord," in Townes, ed., *Embracing the Spirit*, 23.

37. John Milbank and Catherine Pickstock, *Truth in Aquinas* (New York: Routledge & Kegan Paul, 2001), 71, 72.

38. Ibid., 83. The authors refer to Thomas Aquinas, *Summa theologiae III*, q53, a.6 resp.

39. Ibid., 71.

40. Ibid., 83.

41. Ibid., 75.

42. Ibid., 83.

43. Michael Welker, *What Happens in Holy Communion?* (Grand Rapids: Wm. B. Eerdmans Publishing Co., 2002), 61.

44. Eating disorders also afflict men and older women, but the primary victims are young women.

CHAPTER 14

1. Women have often been the objects of this demonization. But Catherine Keller also criticizes the white-feminist "proclivity to apocalyptic dualisms of 'good feminists' versus 'evil patriarchs'" and notes how this has alienated women of color.

See "Eschatology," in *Dictionary of Feminist Theologies*, ed. Letty M. Russell and J. Shannon Clarkson (Louisville, KY: Westminster John Knox Press, 1996), 87. See also *Liberating Eschatology: Essays in Honor of Letty M. Russell*, ed. Margaret A. Farley and Serene Jones (Louisville, KY: Westminster John Knox Press, 1999).

2. Emilie M. Townes, "The Doctor Ain't Taking No Sticks," in *Embracing the Spirit: Womanist Perspectives on Hope, Salvation, and Transformation*, ed. Emilie M. Townes (Maryknoll, NY: Orbis Books, 1997), 192.

3. Karl Barth, *Church Dogmatics*, IV/3 (Edinburgh: T. & T. Clark, 1961), 460.

4. Through Christ, God "will wipe every tear from their eyes. Death will be no more; mourning and crying and pain will be no more, for the first things have passed away" (Rev. 21:4).

5. Kathryn Tanner, *Jesus, Humanity, and the Trinity: A Brief Systematic Theology* (Minneapolis: Fortress Press, 2001), 87.

6. Joan Martin, *More Than Chains and Toil: A Christian Work Ethic of Enslaved Women* (Louisville, KY: Westminster John Knox Press, 2000), 75.

7. "Concerning the End for which God Created the World," in Paul Ramsey, ed., *Ethical Writings*, vol. 8, *The Works of Jonathan Edwards* (New Haven, CT: Yale University Press, 1989), 400–536.

8. John McLeod Campbell, *The Nature of the Atonement and Its Relation to Remission of Sins and Eternal Life*, 6th ed. (London: James Clarke & Col., 1959), 151.

9. Joe R. Jones, *A Grammar of Christian Faith: Systematic Explorations in Christian Life and Doctrine*, 2 vols. (Oxford: Rowman & Littlefield Publishers, 2002), 1:259.

10. Townes, "The Doctor Ain't Taking No Sticks," 192.

11. Kristine A. Culp, "The Nature of Christian Community," in *Setting the Table: Women in Theological Conversation*, ed. Rita Nakashima Brock, Claudia Camp, and Serene Jones (St. Louis: Chalice Press, 1995), 170.

12. Beverly Wildung Harrison, *Making the Connections: Essays in Feminist Social Ethics*, ed. Carol S. Robb (Boston: Beacon Press, 1985), 225.

SELECT BIBLIOGRAPHY

Adams, Marilyn McCord. "Evil and the God Who Does Nothing in Particular." In *Religion and Morality*, edited by D. Z. Phillips, 107–131. London: Macmillan Press Ltd; New York: St. Martin's Press, 1996.

Alston, Wallace M. *The Church of the Living God: A Reformed Perspective.* Louisville, KY: Westminster John Knox Press, 2002.

————, and Michael Welker, eds. *Reformed Theology: Identity and Ecumenicity.* Grand Rapids: Wm. B. Eerdmans Publishing Co., 2003.

Alves, Abel Athouguia. "The Christian Social Organism and Social Welfare: The Case of Vives, Calvin and Loyola." *Sixteenth Century Journal* 20, no. 1 (1989): 3–21.

Andolsen, Barbara Hilkert. *Good Work at the Video Display Terminal—A Feminist Ethical Analysis of Clerical Work.* Knoxville: University of Tennessee Press, 1989.

Armour, Ellen. *Deconstruction, Feminist Theology, and the Problem of Difference: Subverting the Race/Gender Divide.* Chicago: University of Chicago Press, 1999.

Baker-Fletcher, Karen. *Sisters of Dust, Sisters of Spirit: Womanist Wordings on God and Creation.* Minneapolis: Fortress Press, 1998.

Barth, Karl. *Church Dogmatics*, edited and translated by G. W. Bromiley and T. F. Torrance. Edinburgh: T. & T. Clark, 1936–77.

————. *Humanity of God.* Atlanta: John Knox Press, 1960.

————. *The Theology of the Reformed Confessions*, translated by Darrell L. Guder and Judith J. Guder. Louisville, KY: Westminster John Knox Press, 2002.

————. *Vorträge und kleinere Arbeiten, 1922–1925*, edited by Holger Finze. Zürich: Theologischer Verlag Zürich, 1990.

Bennett, Michael, and Vanessa D. Dickerson. *Recovering the Black Female Body: Self-Representations by African American Women.* New Brunswick, NJ: Rutgers University Press, 2001.

Bouwsma, William J. *John Calvin: A Sixteenth-Century Portrait.* New York: Oxford University Press, 1988.

Boyd, Lois A., and R. Douglas Brackinridge. *Presbyterian Women in America: Two Centuries of a Quest for Status*, 2nd ed. Westport, CT: Greenwood Press, 1996.

Brackinridge, R. Douglas, and Lois A. Boyd. "United Presbyterian Policy on Women and the Church—An Historical Overview." *Journal of Presbyterian History* 59, no. 3 (Fall 1981): 383–407.

Brenner, Athalya, ed. *A Feminist Companion to Exodus to Deuteronomy.* Sheffield: Sheffield Academic Press, 1994.

Brock, Rita Nakashima. *Journeys by Heart: A Christology of Erotic Power.* New York: Crossroad, 1991.

———, Claudia Camp, and Serene Jones, eds. *Setting the Table: Women in Theological Conversation.* St. Louis: Chalice Press, 1995.

Busby, Margaret, ed. *Daughters of Africa.* New York: Pantheon Books, 1992.

Busch, Eberhard. *The Great Passion: An Introduction to Karl Barth's Theology,* translated by Geoffrey W. Bromiley. Grand Rapids: Wm. B. Eerdmans Publishing Co., 2004.

Butler, Judith. *Bodies That Matter: On the Discursive Limits of Sex.* New York: Routledge & Kegan Paul, 1993.

———. *Gender Trouble: Feminism and the Subversion of Identity.* New York: Routledge & Kegan Paul, 1990.

———, and Joan W. Scott, eds. *Feminists Theorize the Political.* New York: Routledge & Kegan Paul, 1992.

Cannon, Katie Geneva. *Black Womanist Ethics.* Atlanta: Scholars Press, 1988.

———. *Katie's Canon: Womanism and the Soul of the Black Community.* New York: Continuum, 1995.

———. "Out of the Shadows of Death: Representations of Womanist Homiletical Praxis in the Sacred Rhetoric of Dr. Martin Luther King, Jr." *The Princeton Seminary Bulletin* 21, no. 2, new series (2000): 196–210.

Charry, Ellen T. *By the Renewing of Your Minds: The Pastoral Function of Christian Doctrine.* New York: Oxford University Press, 1997.

Chaves, Mark. *Ordaining Women.* Cambridge, MA: Harvard University Press, 1997.

Chideya, Farai. *The Color of Our Future.* New York: William Morrow & Co., 1999.

Chopp, Rebecca S., and Sheila Greeve Davaney, eds. *Horizons in Feminist Theology: Identity, Tradition and Norms.* Minneapolis: Fortress Press, 1997.

Clark, Elizabeth A., and Herbert Richardson, eds. *Women and Religion: The Original Sourcebook of Women in Christian Thought.* San Francisco: HarperSanFrancisco, 1996.

Coalter, Milton J, John M. Mulder, and Louis B. Weeks, eds. *The Diversity of Discipleship: The Presbyterians and Twentieth-Century Christian Witness.* Louisville, KY: Westminster/John Knox Press, 1991.

———. *The Pluralistic Vision: Presbyterians and Mainstream Protestant Education and Leadership.* Louisville, KY: Westminster/John Knox Press, 1992.

Cochrane, Arthur C. *The Church's Confession under Hitler.* Philadelphia: Westminster Press, 1962.

Cone, James H. *God of the Oppressed.* Maryknoll, NY: Orbis Books, 1997.

Cooey, Paula M., William R. Eakin, and Jay B. Daniel. *After Patriarchy: Feminist Transformations of World Religions. Faith Meets Faith: An Orbis Series in Interreligious Dialogue,* edited by Paul F. Knitter. Maryknoll, NY: Orbis Books, 1991.

Crenshaw, Kimberle. "Demarginalizing the Intersection of Race and Sex: A Black Feminist Critique of Antidiscrimination Doctrine, Feminist Theory and Antiracist Politics." *University of Chicago Legal Forum* (1989): 139–67.

Daly, Mary. *Beyond God the Father: Toward a Philosophy of Women's Liberation,* with an original reintroduction by the author. Boston: Beacon Press, 1985.

Davis, Charles T., and Henry Louis Gates Jr., eds. *The Slave's Narrative.* New York: Oxford University Press, 1985.

De Gruchy, John. *Liberating Reformed Theology: A South African Contribution to an Ecumenical Task.* Grand Rapids: Wm. B. Eerdmans Publishing Co., 1991.

DeJong, Gerald F. *The Dutch Reformed Church in the American Colonies.* Grand Rapids: Wm. B. Eerdmans Publishing Co., 1978.

DeVries, Dawn. *Jesus Christ in the Preaching of Calvin and Schleiermacher.* Louisville, KY: Westminster John Knox Press, 1996.

Dillard, Annie. *Pilgrim at Tinker Creek.* New York: Harper's Magazine Press, 1974.

Douglas, Jane Dempsey. *Reform and Renewal.* Melbourne: Uniting Church Press, 1994.

———. *Women, Freedom, and Calvin.* Philadelphia: Westminster Press, 1985.

———, and James F. Kay, eds. *Women, Gender, and Community.* Louisville, KY: Westminster John Knox Press, 1997.

Dube, Muse W. "Readings of *Semoya*: Batswana Women's Interpretations of Matt 15:21–28." *Semeia* 73 (1996): 111–29.

Dubois, W. E. B. *The Souls of Black Folk.* Chicago: McClurg, 1903; reprint New York: American Library, 1969.

Edney, Matthew H. *Mapping the Empire.* Chicago: University of Chicago Press, 1997.

Ehrenreich, Barbara, and Arlie Hochschild, eds. *Global Woman.* New York: Henry Holt, 2004.

Eire, Carlos N. M. *War against the Idols: The Reformation of Worship from Erasmus to Calvin.* Cambridge: Cambridge University Press, 1986.

Evans, James H., Jr. "Race, Body, Space, and Time: Ecclesiological Reflections." In *Constructive Theology: A Contemporary Approach to Classical Themes,* edited by Serene Jones and Paul Lakeland, 219–30. Minneapolis: Fortress Press, 2005.

Exum, Cheryl. *Plotted, Shot, and Painted: Cultural Representations of Biblical Women.* Sheffield: Sheffield Academic Press, 1996.

Felder, Cain Hope, ed. *Stony the Road We Trod: African American Biblical Interpretation.* Minneapolis: Fortress, 1991.

Farley, Margaret A., and Serene Jones, eds. *Liberating Eschatology: Essays in Honor of Letty M. Russell.* Louisville, KY: Westminster John Knox Press, 1999.

France, Nadine, ed. *Hope Deferred.* Cleveland: Pilgrim Press, 2005.

Fulkerson, Mary McClintock. *Changing the Subject: Women's Discourses and Feminist Theology.* Minneapolis: Fortress Press, 1994.

———. "Postmodernism and Feminist Theology." In *The Cambridge Companion to Postmodern Theology,* edited by Keven J. Vanhoozer, 109–26. Cambridge: Cambridge University Press, 2003.

Genovese, Eugene D. *The Political Economy of Slavery: Studies in the Economy and Society of the Slave South.* 2nd ed. Middletown, CT: Wesleyan University Press, 1965.

Gerrish, Brian A. *Grace and Gratitude: The Eucharistic Theology of John Calvin.* Minneapolis: Fortress Press, 1993.

————. *The Old Protestantism and the New: Essay on the Reformation Heritage*. Chicago: University of Chicago Press, 1982.

Gerster, Patrick, and Nicholas Cords, eds. *Myth and Southern History*, 2 vols. Urbana: University of Illinois Press, 1974; rev. ed. 1989.

Gilbert, James B. *Work without Salvation: America's Intellectual and Industrial Alienation, 1880–1990*. Baltimore: Johns Hopkins University Press, 1977.

Grant, Jacquelyn Grant. *White Women's Christ, Black Women's Jesus: Feminist Christology and Womanist Response*. Atlanta: Scholars Press, 1989.

Gunning, Sandra. *Race, Rape, and Lynching: The Red Record of American Literature*. New York: Oxford University Press, 1996.

Guthrie, Shirley. *Always Being Reformed: Faith for a Fragmented World*. Louisville, KY: Westminster John Knox Press, 1996.

Hallie, Philip P. *Lest Innocent Blood Be Shed: The Story of the Village of Le Chambon and How Goodness Happened There*. New York: Harper & Row, 1979; HarperPerennial ed., 1994.

Hampson, Daphne. *After Christianity*. Valley Forge, PA: Trinity Press International, 1996.

Hardy, Lee. *The Fabric of This World: Inquiries into Calling, Career Choice, and the Design of Human Work*. Grand Rapids: Wm. B. Eerdmans Publishing Co., 1990.

Harrison, Beverly Wildung. *Making the Connections: Essays in Feminist Social Ethics*, edited by Carol S. Robb. Boston: Beacon Press, 1985.

————. "Restoring the Tapestry of Life: the Vocation of Feminist Theology." *The Drew Gateway* 54 (Fall 1983): 39–48.

Haynes, Stephen B. *Noah's Curse: The Biblical Justification of American Slavery*. New York: Oxford University Press, 2002.

Healy, Nicholas M. *Church, World and the Christian Life: Practical-Prophetic Ecclesiology*. Cambridge: Cambridge University Press, 2000.

Hick, John. *The Metaphor of God Incarnate: Christology in a Pluralistic Age*. Louisville, KY: Westminster/John Knox Press, 1993.

Hoezee, Scott, and Christopher Meehan. *Flourishing in the Land: A Hundred-Year History of Christian Reformed Missions in North America*. Grand Rapids: Wm. B. Eerdmans Publishing Co., 1996.

Hood, Robert E. *Begrimed and Black: Christian Traditions on Blacks and Blackness*. Minneapolis: Augsburg Fortress, 1994.

Hopkins, Julie. *Towards a Feminist Christology: Jesus of Nazareth, European Women and the Christological Crisis*. Grand Rapids: Wm. B. Eerdmans Publishing Co., 1994.

Hull, Gloria T., Patricia Bell Scott, and Barbara Smith, eds. *All the Women Are White, All the Blacks Are Men, But Some of Us Are Brave: Black Women's Studies*. Old Westbury, NY: Feminist Press, 1982.

Irigaray, Luce. "Divine Women." In *Sexes and Genealogies*, translated by Gillian Gill. New York: Columbia University Press, 1993.

————. *An Ethics of Sexual Difference*, translated by Carolyn Burke and Gillian Gill. Ithaca, NY: Cornell University Press, 1993.

————. *Speculum of the Other Woman*, translated by Gillian C. Gill. Ithaca, NY: Cornell University Press, 1985.

Jacobs, Harriet. *Incidents in the Life of a Slave Girl. Written by Herself,* edited and with an introduction by Jean Fagan Yellin. Cambridge, MA: Harvard University Press, 1987.

Jantzen, Grace. *God's World, God's Body.* Philadelphia: Westminster Press, 1984.

Johnson, Elizabeth A. *She Who Is: The Mystery of God in Feminist Theological Discourse.* New York: Crossroad, 1992.

Johnson, William Stacy. *The Mystery of God: Karl Barth and the Postmodern Foundations of Theology.* Louisville, KY: Westminster John Knox Press, 1997.

Jones, Joe R. *A Grammar of Christian Faith: Systematic Explorations in Christian Life and Doctrine,* 2 vols. Oxford: Rowman & Littlefield Publishers, 2002.

Jones, Serene. "Bounded Openness: Postmodernism, Feminism, and the Church Today." *Interpretation* 55, no. 1 (January 2001): 49–59.

———. *Feminist Theory and Christian Theology: Cartographies of Grace.* Minneapolis: Fortress Press, 2000.

Jost, Renate, and Eveline Valtin, eds. *Ihr aber, für wen haltet ihr mich? Auf dem Weg zu einer feministisch-befreiungstheologischen Revision von Christologie.* Gütersloh: Christian Kaiser/Gütersloher Verlagshaus, 1996.

Joutard, Philippe, Jacques Poujol, and Patrick Cabanel, eds. *Cévennes, Terre de Réfuge 1940–1944.* 3rd ed. Montpellier, France: Les Presses du Languedoc/Club Cévenol, 1994.

Kellenbach, Katharina von. *Anti-Judaism in Feminist Religious Writings.* Atlanta: Scholars Press, 1994.

Kelsey, David H. *The Uses of Scripture in Recent Theology.* Philadelphia: Fortress Press, 1975.

Kilbourne, Jean. *Killing Us Softly,* directed, edited and produced by Sut Jhally. 3rd ed. 2000. Video recording. Distributed by Media Education Foundation.

Kimel, Alvin F., Jr., ed. *Speaking the Christian God: The Holy Trinity and the Challenge of Feminism.* Grand Rapids: Wm. B. Eerdmans Publishing Co., 1992.

Kimmel, Haven. *A Girl Named Zippy.* New York: Doubleday, 2001.

Kristeva, Julia. *The Powers of Horror: An Essay on Abjection,* translated by Leon Roudiez. New York: Columbia University Press, 1982.

———. *Strangers to Ourselves,* translated by Leon S. Roudiez. New York: Columbia University Press, 1991.

Kromminga, John. *In the Mirror: An Appraisal of the Christian Reformed Church.* Hamilton, Ontario: Guardian Publishing Company, 1957.

Lacan, Jacques. *Ecrits: A Selection,* translated by Bruce Fink. New York: W. W. Norton, 2002.

LaCugna, Catherine Mowry, ed. *Freeing Theology: The Essentials of Theology in a Feminist Perspective.* San Franciso: Harper San Francisco, 1993.

———. *God for Us: The Trinity and Christian Life.* San Francisco: HarperSanFrancisco, 1991.

Lancaster, Sarah Heaner. *Women and the Authority of Scripture: A Narrative Approach.* Harrisburg, PA: Trinity Press International, 2002.

Lawrence-Lightfoot, Sara. *I've Seen Rivers: Lives of Loss and Liberation.* New York: Penguin Books, 1995.

Leith, John H. *Introduction to the Reformed Tradition: A Way of Being the Christian Community.* Atlanta: John Knox Press, 1981.

Lindbeck, George. "The Gospel's Uniqueness: Election and Untranslatability." *Modern* Theology 13, no. 4 (October 1997): 423–50.

Lindley, Susan Hill. *You Have Stept Out of Your Place: A History of Women and Religion in America*. Louisville, KY: Westminster John Knox Press, 1996.

Lynch, Hollis R., ed. *Black Spokesman: Selected Published Writings of Edwards Wilmot Blyden*. New York: Humanities Press, 1971.

———. *Edward Wilmot Blyden: Pan-Negro Patriot, 1832–1912*. London: Oxford University Press, 1967.

Lyotard, Jean-François. *The Postmodern Condition: A Report on Knowledge*, translated by Geoff Bennington and Brian Massumi. Minneapolis: University of Minnesota Press, 1999.

Mahony, Rhona. *Kidding Ourselves: Breadwinning, Babies, and Bargaining Power*. New York: Basic Books, 1995.

Martin, Francis. *The Feminist Question: Feminist Theology in Light of Christian Tradition*. Grand Rapids: Wm. B. Eerdmans Publishing Co., 1994.

Martin, Joan M. *More Than Chains and Toil: A Christian Work Ethic of Enslaved Women*. Louisville, KY: Westminster John Knox Press, 2000.

Maury, Pierre. *Predestination and Other Papers*. Richmond, VA: John Knox Press, 1960.

May, Rollo. *The Meaning of Anxiety*. New York: Ronald Press, 1950.

McFague, Sallie. *The Body of God: An Ecological Theology*. Minneapolis: Fortress Press, 1993.

———. *Models of God: Theology for an Ecological, Nuclear Age*. Philadelphia: Fortress Press, 1987.

McLaughlin, Eleanor. "Christology in Dialogue with Feminist Ideology—Bodies and Boundaries." In *Christology in Dialogue*, edited by Robert Berkey and Sarah Edwards, 308–39. Cleveland: The Pilgrim Press, 1993.

McNeill, John T. *The History and Character of Calvinism*. New York: Oxford University Press, 1967.

Migliore, Daniel L. *Faith Seeking Understanding*. Grand Rapids: Wm. B. Eerdmans Publishing Co., 1991.

Milbank, John, and Catherine Pickstock. *Truth in Aquinas*. London and New York: Routledge & Kegan Paul, 2001.

Moltmann, Jürgen. *On Human Dignity: Political Theology and Ethics*. Philadelphia: Fortress Press, 1984.

Monod, Avril W. "Deux métaphysiques (à propos de Karl Barth)." *Revue du Christianisme social* (April 1934): 258–61.

Morrison, Toni. *Beloved*. New York: Knopf, 1987.

Mudimbe, Valentin Y. *The Invention of Africa: Gnosis, Philosophy, and the Order of Knowledge*. Bloomington: Indiana University Press, 1988.

Muller, Richard. *Christ and the Decree: Christology and Predestination in Reformed Theology from Calvin to Perkins*. Durham, NC: Labyrinth Press, 1986.

Murray, Anna Pauline, and Mary Eastwood. "Jane Crow and the Law: Sex Discrimination and Title VII." *George Washington Law Review* 34 (December 1965): 232–56.

Murray, Pauli. "Black Theology and Feminist Theology: A Comparative View." In *Black Theology: A Documentary History, 1966–1979*, edited by

Gayraud S. Wilmore and James H. Cone, 398–417. Maryknoll, NY: Orbis Books, 1979.

Nelson, Susan Dunfee. "The Sin of Hiding: A Feminist Critique of Reinhold Niebuhr's Account of the Sin of Pride." *Soundings* 65, no. 3 (Fall 1982): 316–27.

Newbold, Robert T. Jr. *Black Preaching—Select Sermons in the Presbyterian Tradition.* Philadelphia: Geneva Press, 1977.

Niebuhr, H. Richard. *Christ and Culture.* New York: Harper, 1951.

Noddings, Nel. *Caring: A Feminine Approach to Ethic and Moral Education.* Berkeley: University of California Press, 1984.

Ofari, Earl. *"Let Your Motto Be Resistance": The Life and Thought of Henry Highland Garnet.* Boston: Beacon Press, 1972.

Parker, Inez Moore. *The Rise and Decline of the Program of Education for Black Presbyterians of the United Presbyterian Church (U.S.A.), 1865–1970.* San Antonio: Trinity University Press, 1977.

Pauw, Amy Plantinga. "The Church as Mother and Bride in the Reformed Tradition: Challenge and Promise." In *Many Voices One God: Being Faithful in a Pluralistic World,* edited by Walter Brueggemann and George W. Stroup, 122–36. Louisville, KY: Westminster John Knox Press, 1998.

———. "Jesus Christ as Host and Guest." In *Renewing the Vision: Reformed Faith for the 21st Century,* edited by Cynthia M. Campbell, 12–23. Louisville, KY: Geneva Press, 2000.

Pinnock, Clark. *A Wideness in God's Mercy.* Grand Rapids: Zondervan, 1992.

Placher, William C. *The Domestication of Transcendence.* Louisville, KY: Westminster John Knox Press, 1996.

Plaskow, Judith. "Feminist Anti-Judaism and the Christian God." *Journal of Feminist Studies in Religion* 7 (Fall 1991): 99–108.

———. *Sex, Sin, and Grace: Women's Experience and the Theologies of Reinhold Niebuhr and Paul Tillich.* Washington, DC: University Press of America, 1980.

———. *Standing Again at Sinai: Judaism from a Feminist Perspective.* San Francisco: Harper & Row, 1990.

Procter-Smith, Marjorie, and Janet R. Walton. *Women at Worship: Interpretations of North American Diversity.* Louisville, KY: Westminster/John Knox Press, 1993.

Rawls, John. *A Theory of Justice.* Cambridge, MA: Belknap Press of Harvard University Press, 1971.

Richardson, Alan. *The Biblical Doctrine of Work.* Ecumenical Biblical Studies, no. 1. London: SCM Press, 1952.

Rigby, Cynthia L. "Are You Saved? Receiving the Full Benefits of Grace." *Insights: The Faculty Journal of Austin Seminary* 115, no. 2 (Spring 2000): 3–18.

———. "Free to be Human: Limits, Possibilities, and the Sovereignty of God." *Theology Today* 53, no. 1 (April 1996): 47–62.

Rodgers, Daniel T. *The Work Ethic in Industrial America, 1850–1920.* Chicago: University of Chicago Press, 1978.

Rohls, Jan. *Reformed Confessions: Theology from Zurich to Barmen,* translated by John Hoffmeyer. Louisville, KY: Westminster John Knox Press, 1997.

Ross, Susan. *Extravagant Affections: A Feminist Sacramental Theology*. New York: Continuum, 1998.

Ruether, Rosemary Radford. "Christology and Feminism: Can a Male Savior Help Women?" An occasional paper of the board of higher education and ministry of the United Methodist Church, no. 1 (December 25, 1976).

————. *Sexism and God-Talk: Toward a Feminist Theology*. Boston: Beacon Press, 1983.

Russell, Letty. *Church in the Round: Feminist Interpretation of the Church*. Louisville, KY: Westminster/John Knox Press, 1993.

————. *The Future of Partnership*. Philadelphia: Westminster Press, 1979.

————, and J. Shannon Clarkson, eds. *Dictionary of Feminist Theologies*. Louisville, KY: Westminster John Knox Press, 1996.

Saiving, Valery. "The Human Situation: A Feminine View." *Journal of Religion* (April 1960): 100–112.

Satterthwaite, Philip E., and David F. Wright, eds. *A Pathway into the Holy Scripture*. Grand Rapids: Wm. B. Eerdmans Publishing Co., 1994.

Schüssler-Fiorenza, Elisabeth. *Bread Not Stone: The Challenge of Feminist Biblical Interpretation*. Boston: Beacon Press, 1984.

————. *Jesus: Miriam's Son, Sophia's Prophet*. New York: Continuum, 1994.

Scott, Joan Wallach. "The Problem of Invisibility." In *Retrieving Women's History: Changing Perceptions of the Role of Women in Politics and Society*, edited by S. Jay Kleinberg, 5–29. Providence, RI, and Paris: Berg Publishers/Unesco Press, 1988.

Shannon, David T., and Gayraud S. Wilmore, eds. *Black Witness to the Apostolic Faith*. Grand Rapids: Wm. B. Eerdmans Publishing Co., 1985.

Sobel, Mechal. *The World They Made Together: Black and White Values in Eighteenth-Century Virginia*. Princeton, NJ: Princeton University Press, 1987.

Soelle, Dorothee, with Shirley A. Cloyes. *To Love and to Work: A Theology of Creation*. Philadelphia: Fortress Press, 1984.

Strahm, Doris, and Regula Strobel, eds. *Vom Verlangen nach Heilwerden: Christologie in feministisch-theologischer Sicht*. Fribourg/Luzern: Exodus, 1993.

Stuckey, Sterling. "Through the Prism of Folklore." *Massachusetts Review* 9 (1968): 417–37.

Tanner, Kathryn. "The Care That Does Justice: Recent Writings in Feminist Ethics and Theology." *Journal of Religious Ethics* 24 (Spring 1996): 171–91.

————. *God and Creation in Christian Theology: Tyranny or Empowerment?* Oxford: Basil Blackwell Ltd, 1988.

————. *Jesus, Humanity, and Trinity: A Brief Systematic Theology*. Minneapolis: Fortress Press, 2001.

————. *The Politics of God: Christian Theologies and Social Justice*. Minneapolis: Fortress Press, 1992.

————. "Scripture as Popular Text." *Modern Theology* 14 (1998): 279–98.

Thistlethwaite, Susan Brooks, and Mary Potter Engel, eds. *Lift Every Voice: Constructing Christian Theologies from the Underside*, rev. ed. Maryknoll, NY: Orbis Books, 1998.

Tillich, Paul. *The Shaking of the Foundations*. New York: Charles Scribner, 1976.

Townes, Emilie, ed. *Embracing the Spirit: Womanist Reflections on Hope, Salvation, and Transformation.* The Bishop Henry McNeal Turner/Sojourner Truth Series, vol. 13, edited by Dwight N. Hopkins. Maryknoll, NY: Orbis Books, 1997.

———. *A Troubling in My Soul: Womanist Perspectives on Evil and Suffering.* Maryknoll, NY: Orbis Books, 1993.

Trible, Phyllis. "Depatriarchalizing in Biblical Interpretation." *Journal of the American Academy of Religion* 41 (1973): 30–48.

Truth, Sojourner. *The Narrative of Sojourner Truth,* edited and with an introduction by Margaret Washington. New York: Vintage Books, 1993.

Van Dyk, Leanne. *The Desire of Divine Love: John McLeod Campbell's Doctrine of the Atonement.* Studies in Church History, vol. 4, edited by William L. Fox. New York: Peter Lang, 1995.

Vischer, Lukas, ed. *Reformed Witness Today: A Collection of Confessions and Statements of Faith Issued by Reformed Church.* Bern: Evangelische Arbeitsstelle Oekumene Schweiz, 1982.

Wadell, Paul. *Becoming Friends: Worship, Justice, and the Practices of Christian Friendship.* Grand Rapids: Brazos Press, 2002.

Walls, Andrew. "Christianity in the Non-Western World: A Study in the Serial Nature of Christian Expansion." *Studies in World Christianity* 1, no. 1 (1995): 1–25.

Welch, Sharon. *A Feminist Ethic of Risk.* Minneapolis: Fortress Press, 1990.

Welker, Michael. *What Happens in Holy Communion?* Grand Rapids: Wm. B. Eerdmans Publishing Co., 2002.

Wells-Barnett, Ida B. *On Lynching: Southern Horrors, A Red Record and Mob Rule in New Orleans.* New York: Arno Press, 1969.

West, Angela. *Deadly Innocence: Feminism and the Mythology of Sin.* London: Cassell, 1995.

West, Cornel. *Race Matters.* Boston: Beacon Press, 1993.

West, Gerald, and Musa W. Dube. "An Introduction: How We Have Come to 'Read With.'" *Semeia* 73 (1996): 7–17.

White, Deborah Gray. *Ar'nt I a Woman? Female Slaves in the Plantation South.* New York: W. W. Norton & Co., 1985.

Wiles, Maurice. *God's Action in the World.* London: SCM Press Ltd, 1986.

Williams, Delores S. "ReImagining Truth: Traversing the Feminist Christian Backlash." *The Other Side* (May-June 1994): 53–54.

———. *Sisters in the Wilderness: The Challenge of Womanist God-Talk.* Maryknoll, NY: Orbis Books, 1993.

———. "Women's Oppression and Lifeline Politics in Black Women's Religious Narratives." *Journal of Feminist Studies in Religion* 2 (Fall 1985): 59–71.

Williams, Rowan. *A Ray of Darkness: Sermons and Reflections.* Cambridge, MA: Cowley Publications, 1995.

Willis, David. *Notes on the Holiness of God.* Grand Rapids: Wm. B. Eerdmans Publishing Co., 2002.

Wilmore, Gayraud S. *Black Religion and Black Radicalism: An Interpretation of the Religious History of Afro-American People.* 3rd ed. Maryknoll, NY: Orbis Books, 1998.

————. *Black Presbyterians: The Heritage and the Hope.* Philadelphia: Geneva Press, 1983; reprint ed. 1998.

————. *The Nature and Task of Christian Education from an African American Presbyterian Perspective.* Louisville, KY: Witherspoon Press, Presbyterian Church (U.S.A.), 1998.

————. "Theological Dimensions of Black Presbyterianism." In *Periscope,* vol. 3: *African American Presbyterianism—Preparing for the 21st Century, 185 Years of Ministry,* 11–15. Louisville, KY: Racial Ethnic Ministry Unit, Presbyterian Church (U.S.A.), 1992.

Wilson, Frank T., Sr. *Black Presbyterians in Ministry.* New York: Vocation Agency, United Presbyterian Church in the U.S.A., 1979. Reissued with Vera Swann, *Lest We Forget.* Black Congregational Enhancement Office, Racial Ethnic Ministry Unity, Presbyterian Church (U.S.A.), 1992.

————. "A Continuing Pilgrimage: Black Presbyterians and Black Presbyterianism." In *Periscope,* vol. 2: *Black Presbyterianism: Yesterday, Today and Tomorrow, 175 Years of Ministry,* 4–7. New York: Office of Black Mission Development Program Agency, United Presbyterian Church in the U.S.A., 1983.

Winter, Miriam Therese, ed. *Defecting in Place: Women Claiming Responsibility for Their Own Spiritual Lives.* New York: Crossroad, 1994.

Wood, Forrest. *The Arrogance of Faith: Christianity and Race in America from the Colonial Era to the Twentieth Century.* New York: Knopf, 1990.

Wuthnow, Robert. *Poor Richard's Principle: Recovering the American Dream through the Moral Dimension of Work, Business, and Money.* Princeton, NJ: Princeton University Press, 1996.

Young, Iris Marion. *Justice and the Politics of Difference.* Princeton, NJ: Princeton University Press, 1990.

INDEX OF NAMES

INDEX OF SUBJECTS

CPSIA information can be obtained
at www.ICGtesting.com
Printed in the USA
LVHW081729231218
601537LV00017B/597/P